EVERYONE IS TALKING ABOUT . . .

#1
book for independent entrepreneurs
—*Inc. Magazine*

working SOLO®

Also by Terri Lonier

Books
Working Solo Sourcebook (John Wiley & Sons)
The Frugal Entrepreneur

Audio programs
Working Solo: Getting Started
Working Solo: Getting Customers

working SOLO®

THE REAL GUIDE TO FREEDOM & FINANCIAL SUCCESS WITH YOUR OWN BUSINESS

SECOND EDITION

Terri Lonier

JOHN WILEY & SONS, INC.

New York · Chichester · Weinheim · Brisbane · Singapore · Toronto

Published by John Wiley & Sons, Inc.
Published simultaneously in Canada.

Library of Congress Cataloging-in-Publication Data

Lonier, Terri,
    Working solo / Terri Lonier. — 2nd ed.
        p.   cm.
    Includes index.
    ISBN 0-471-24713-8 (pbk. : alk. paper)
    1. Self-employed—United States—Handbooks, manuals, etc.   2. Small business—United States—Handbooks, manuals, etc.   3. Self-employed—Handbooks, manuals, etc.   4. Small business—Handbooks, manuals, etc.
    5. Entrepreneurship—United States.   I. Title.
    HD8037.U5L66   1998
    658'.041—dc21   98-10660
                                                                               CIP

Printed in the United States of America.
10 9 8 7 6 5 4 3 2 1

Author photo: Arthur L. Cohen

To my parents,
CARL LUSTIC and RUDOLPHIA MEYER LUSTIC,
who taught me at a very young age,
"You can be anything you want to be."

Acknowledgments

A book, like a successful solo business, is a solitary effort enriched by the involvement of others. In putting together *Working Solo,* I have been fortunate to work with many individuals who generously shared their thoughts, time, and energy.

This revised edition reflects the changes in the world of self-employment, as well as a shift in the publisher of the *Working Solo* books. I am pleased to have publisher John Wiley & Sons as a partner, and I extend my appreciation to Mike Hamilton and the entire Wiley team for helping me reach independent entrepreneurs.

Working solo is not working alone, and I am grateful to many colleagues and friends who assisted me in this project. Special thanks to my managing associate, Anne Allen, for her enthusiasm and daily efforts in making the Working Solo vision a reality. Appreciation goes to the many individuals who shared their words of wisdom for this edition, especially Lisa Aldisert, Ilise Benun, Dan Burrus, James Comiskey, Albert J. DeLorenzo, Beth Dempsey, Richard Dempsey, Marylyn Dintenfass, Elaine Floyd, Cynthia Harriman, Barbara Hemphill, Patte Hoffman, Tom Hopkins, Erik Kahn, Mark Kawakami, Batt Johnson, Mark LeBlanc, Donna Morabito, EddieLynn Morgan, Raleigh Pinskey, Barbara Sher, David Tisdale, and June Walker. Thanks to Bradford Veley for his cartoons, and Fred Showker for his illustration. For their help in matters both large and small, I also would like to acknowledge William and Yvonne Allenson, Arthur Cohen, Jr., Christine Goodno, Colleen Kelly, Marge Lovero, Diane Mataraza, Flora Wong, Ken Yancey, and Dr. Thomas Zwart.

Technology has created a digital network of individuals producing books, audiotapes, Web sites, and other entrepreneurial projects, and they are a source of valuable feedback and inspiration. My appreciation goes to Jane Applegate, Jeff Berner, Bill Bonnstetter, Barbara Brabec, Alice Bredin, Judy Byers, Sheila Delson, Jim Donovan, Ed Dudkowski, Jonathan Evetts, David Garfinkel, Greg Godek, Azriela Jaffe, Terri Kabachnick, Jeff Keller, Larrry Kesslin, Peggy Kilburn, Robb Kinnin, Constance Hallinan Lagan, June Langhoff, Jeffrey Lant,

Michael LeBoeuf, Jay Conrad Levinson, Julie Morgenstern, Dan Poynter, Sarah Reeves, Susan RoAne, Mitchell Schlimer, Barrie Selack, Mark S. A. Smith, Barbara J. Winter, David Zach, and other entrepreneurial colleagues who keep my phone, fax, and e-mail lines busy with ideas and inspiration. Thanks also to my agent, Joe Spieler, for sharing late-night phone calls and understated humor, and to Tom Woll, who always asks the thoughtful question that keeps my vision in focus.

The contributions by members of the original editorial team remain a legacy in these pages. For their support of Working Solo since its earliest days, I extend particular recognition to Ellen Leanse, Leslie Newman, and Tim Celeski. Thanks, too, to the thousands of individuals who have participated in my seminars, written letters, and sent e-mails over the last decade. Your ideas and enthusiasm continue to inspire me.

Most of all, a special note of appreciation to my husband, Robert Sedestrom, who has offered humor, encouragement, and companionship as this Working Solo adventure has unfolded during the past few years. I feel fortunate to have him as a partner on this journey.

Contents

PART II: THE DECISION

PART III: THE DETAILS

PART IV: THE DELIGHT

Introduction

Freedom, flexibility, and financial control. Those three ideas sound pretty attractive, don't they? Twenty-seven million Americans think so, and they're joined by millions of others around the globe. All are people who have created independent businesses—individuals who are working solo.

These independent entrepreneurs have chosen to *design a life* as well as make a living. You'll find them working in offices, studios, lofts, homes, garages—even outdoors—from the largest urban centers to remote rural settings. They are bursting with dreams and ideas waiting to be expressed. Passionate about their work, they are committed to creating a better life for themselves, their families, and their communities.

Solo workers embrace the challenges and responsibilities of charting their futures. In exchange, they find their lives filled with excitement and personal satisfaction. They've discovered new meaning in the maxim, "Good things come in small packages," and believe that solo businesses are the best businesses of all.

Since you've picked up this book, it seems you're thinking of joining this group whom I consider our modern-day pioneers. Congratulations! You're in great company, alongside some of the most energetic, imaginative, inspiring, and talented individuals alive today.

Solo businesses come in all shapes and sizes, and they're as varied as the individuals who run them. Some are full-time enterprises, while others are moonlighting ventures, designed to run after regular workday hours or on weekends. Many solo businesses operate on a part-time or seasonal basis—in response to holidays, family demands, or other circumstances. Some are intentionally kept on a small scale; others expand to include freelance associates. Because solo businesses are designed to be flexible, they can adapt rapidly to market needs or to new ideas and interests of their founders.

What do all these businesses have in common? Each has one person at the helm—an individual with an idea and the determination to make things happen, a person who is not content to let others decide. They're individuals with the energy and passion to turn dreams into realities—someone probably like you.

Perhaps you've been thinking about launching a business for some time, and you're ready to make the jump. Or you've been independent for a while, but you're looking for ways to make your business grow and prosper. Even solo businesses that have been running for years can be improved. But where can you turn for information? That's the challenge.

The School for Solo Workers

How do most solo workers learn to run their businesses? Primarily by trial and error—making a lot of mistakes and facing a load of frustration. I know, because I've made those mistakes and faced that frustration as I've developed my own solo business.

While there's been a recent explosion in entrepreneurial education, there are very few courses for one-person businesses. Solo businesses are very personal—extensions of the inspiration, hopes, dreams, and abilities of the individuals who own them. These unique situations represent equally unique challenges—challenges that often aren't discussed in business books and magazines. Yes, there are numerous books and other information sources on small business, and we'll be reviewing many of these important resources in these pages. But most information focuses on "big" small businesses and is woefully neglectful of addressing the needs and concerns of one-person enterprises.

The Book I Always Wanted to Read

During the last 20 years of developing my own business, I kept searching for a book that would help me understand what it takes to succeed at working solo. I discovered books that talked about small business marketing and finances, and others that filled me in on legal issues and taxes. There were seminars on entrepreneurial topics, and I attended them constantly, devouring the information and translating it into principles that would work for solo businesses. But nowhere could I find a single source that fully addressed the special needs and concerns of the individual who wants to work independently.

Working Solo is that source. It pulls together the answers to the thousands of questions I and other solo professionals have asked as we've built businesses of all types over the years. You'll find nuts-and-bolts information to help you get your one-person business off to a successful start. Or if you've been running your solo enterprise for a while, you'll discover on-target information about how to take your business to its next level of success.

This book is divided into four parts, with a total of 14 chapters, and also includes two valuable resource sections at the end. Here's a brief summary of them.

Part I is titled "The Dream." Its two chapters lay out the crucial preliminary steps as well as the exciting future that awaits you on this adventure of working solo. It also pinpoints specific strategies to guarantee your solo success.

Chapter 1 introduces you to the nationwide community of solo workers and the benefits they enjoy by working independently. This chapter asks you to consider carefully if you're ready to commit to this lifestyle and reap its great rewards. A candid self-evaluation is your first important step to success, and I've provided a series of questions to guide you.

Chapter 2 takes you through the steps of how to select the solo business that's best for you. Solo businesses come in many varieties—and the basic question is how to choose the one that suits you. This chapter leads you in matching your personal interests, dreams, and goals with a business destined for success.

Part II is titled "The Decision." In its four chapters you'll discover step-by-step guidelines to put your ideas into action and launch your solo business.

Chapter 3 shows you how to chart your road map to success by writing (and then *using*) a business plan. Most new businesses fail because they don't have a written plan. And most solo business owners don't write a business plan because they don't think they need one—or because they don't know how. This chapter demystifies the writing of a business plan and helps you easily create this crucial tool that serves as the cornerstone of your prosperity.

In **Chapter 4** you'll learn how to create a personal and financial support structure for you and your business. Getting money is a significant challenge for a new business, and this chapter shows you ten innovative ways to get the funds you need. You'll also learn how to create a success team for your new business and how to maximize the advice of individuals who counsel you on legal matters, finances, collections, and marketing—and those who can offer a general reality check from time to time.

In **Chapter 5** you decide what form you want your solo business to take, both in legal terms and in physical choices. You'll discover the pros and cons of structuring your business as a sole proprietorship, a partnership, a limited liability company, or a corporation. You'll also learn about the many options of setting up your physical office and how to design it so that it works as an invisible partner, assisting you in your daily work.

No business exists without customers, and **Chapter 6** takes you through the process of getting those first accounts, letting the world know about your business, and creating a professional image for your new enterprise. With an eye on your bank account, together we'll explore ways to stretch your marketing dollars to generate a big impact from a small investment.

Part III is titled "The Details," and it presents tips on handling the day-to-day workings of your business. Managing daily details is the area where many small businesses get off track. After reading these pages, you'll know how to make all your start-up efforts pay off.

Chapter 7 focuses on one of the most important partners you can have for your solo business—technology. These pages show you how to get the most out of modern office equipment and gets you thinking about other ways to turn your computer into a powerful assistant. You'll also discover how to incorporate technology such as fax machines, voice-mail telephone systems, photocopiers, and the Internet into your business—and at what point it makes sense to invest in them.

Chapter 8 takes up the question of money—and how to keep it. You get simple, straightforward methods of managing your business financial records. You find tips on claiming every tax deduction, so you can hold on to your hard-earned income, while keeping the local, state, and IRS agencies happy. Part of the joy of having a successful solo business is looking ahead to times when you may not want to work quite so hard. These pages empower you to turn today's earnings into future financial freedom.

In **Chapter 9** you'll see how daily guidance comes from a tool already in place—your business plan. Businesses fail because their owners set goals, then don't know how to follow through on them. Never again will you be confused about what crucial next step is needed to make your business prosper. You'll know—and be on your way to success.

Chapter 10 makes you a master over time wasters and paperwork, two of the deadliest enemies of independent businesses. The solo entrepreneur who cannot control time and paperwork is a slave to inefficiency and is doomed to failure. This chapter gives you specific methods to take command of your day, so you can turn your minutes into money.

Independent professionals don't always work alone, and in **Chapter 11** you discover how to have a staff—but only when you need one. Alliances with other solo entrepreneurs can expand your business opportunities, but there are important considerations regarding management, legal, and tax issues. This chapter shows you how to get all the benefits of employees, with none of the hassles.

Contrary to common belief, successful solo business owners are not hermits. **Chapter 12** demonstrates how solo workers stay connected—on personal, regional, national, and even international levels. You'll see how it pays off for their businesses and how it can do the same for yours.

Part IV is titled "The Delight," and these pages present a look at the opportunities available once you have gained a level of success with your business. This section also casts a glance to the future and where this booming business sector is headed.

Chapter 13 takes you beyond the struggles of start-up and shows you how to design your business so it reflects the ever changing you. You'll see how to adapt your business quickly so it remains fresh and inviting to both you and your customers. We'll also review options such as moving on, changing focus, or selling your venture.

In **Chapter 14** you get a look at the future of solo businesses and the expanding opportunities that await you. Three factors—technology advancements, upheavals in traditional corporations, and a renewed spirit of independence in our country—have coalesced to create the astonishing growth in the number of solo ventures in the last few years. This chapter shows you the role your solo business can play in this growing entrepreneurial movement in the years ahead.

At the back of the book are two appendixes that will be of great interest and value to you as a solo entrepreneur. **Appendix A, "Solo Resources,"** features a selected bibliography of the best books, magazines, newsletters, and other publications, so you can continue learning about a specific topic of interest to you. This section also includes detailed information on national associations, government agencies, businesses, and other organizations that can assist you.

The **"Solo Business Directory"** in **Appendix B** features the most comprehensive listing of solo enterprises available. More than 1,000 solo business opportunities await your exploration. The listing is organized by 20 interest areas such as business, sports, children, outdoors, leisure and entertainment, construction and home improvement, visual and performing arts, medicine and health, education, and many others. This section will guide you in choosing the perfect business for you and will inspire you to try new ideas once your solo enterprise is up and running.

Throughout the book you'll discover "Words of Wisdom" from other independent entrepreneurs. These short sections are brimming with insights from others who have tackled—and succeeded at—a specific aspect of the solo workstyle discussed in the chapter. Their comments offer you additional experienced viewpoints and give you a personal glimpse of the variety and vitality of solo businesses around the country.

Your Solo Business Coach

Inside these pages you'll also find a colleague and a coach. As a colleague, my goal is to help you succeed, and I know, firsthand, the challenges you are facing. Unlike other friends, however, who may be too kind to tell you hard-nosed news, I'll lay it on the line for you. Your goal is in sight—success in your solo business. As your colleague, I'll give you unbiased, straightforward information, because I've been down the road you're traveling, and your success is my success.

I'm also here as your coach, to keep you on target toward your goal. I'm *not* here to run your business for you—that's the challenge you have undertaken. But as your coach, I'll point out some areas that may be problematic, and I'll ask you questions that lead you to think about things in fresh, new ways.

How to Get Your Money's Worth from This Book

Successful solo entrepreneurs have a common trait that guarantees their prosperity. They are risk takers—but they are *intelligent* risk takers. They find the information they need, then plan and chart out exactly what they want—and expect—to achieve. Then they go after it. By investing in this book, you've taken an important first step of finding information—a step never achieved by thousands of people who only dream of "one day" having their own solo businesses.

You've already established yourself as a cut above the others. Now make sure that you take advantage of all the benefits this book can bring you. That begins with using this book as a tool.

Working Solo is not meant to be a breezy, take-it-to-the-beach book. Yes, you'll have fun in these pages, but I'm here to take you through the paces and to make sure that you have the solid information you need to succeed. This book is densely packed with information—a detailed road map for your working solo adventure. Keep it nearby as a handy reference, and come back to it often. Read with a marker or pen in hand, and keep a notebook nearby. Make this book an active partner as you make your journey—a place where you can find answers to your questions, record ideas and goals, and return frequently for moving your business to its next growth step.

We're in This Together

As you read *Working Solo,* I think you'll discover that it's unlike most other business books. I'm not here merely to tell you how to do something and send you on your way. Rather, I want to establish a connection with you, an ongoing dialogue, because we're in this together. In developing my solo business over the last 20 years, I've been through many of the experiences, frustrations, and joys you'll encounter.

The greatest lesson (and one of my biggest joys), however, is that there is always more to learn. I invite you to stay in touch with me—to share the news of your success as well as other information that may help solo entrepreneurs around the country. In turn, I will stay in contact with you and keep you up to date on information that will keep your solo business prospering. As a reader of *Working Solo,* you get the bonus of receiving my free monthly e-mail newsletter that's filled with news, tips, and insights about self-employment. All you need to do is send an e-mail to solonews@workingsolo.com, and you'll automatically receive it each month in your e-mail in-box.

Welcome to *Working Solo.* Grab a pen or a marker to make notes, and turn the page. We're on our way together to make your solo business a success.

Your solo business coach,

Terri Lonier
terri@workingsolo.com

PART I

THE DREAM

I nside you is this little spark, this vision that won't go away—the dream of taking charge of an idea that excites you and making it work like no one else can. Millions of others had that vision once—and now they're working solo.

What does it take to make that dream a reality? Where do you begin the task of sketching in and shaping the details of your dream? How do you escape the black hole of insecurity, the quicksand of procrastination—all those things that make you timid and give you a queasy stomach when you think about working on your own and keep you working for someone else, frustrated, because you know there's this independent spirit inside you? How do you make the jump?

These first two chapters can lead you out of the darkness and into the light where you can see clearly, objectively, just what having a solo business is all about—and how it can work for you. You've probably heard your self-employed friends complain about their long hours, their cash-flow problems, the annoying clients who always want too much. In the same breath they tell you that they find the personal rewards unmatched, and even though they have challenges, they're delighted with the choice they've made. So whom do you believe? How can you know if the challenges or the joys will weigh heavier in the balance for you?

The answers to these questions lie in the pages ahead. Let's take a look at what a solo business lifestyle is all about—and what it can mean to you and your future.

Chapter 1

The World of Working Solo— and What It Can Offer You

All our dreams can come true, if we have the courage to pursue them.

—Walt Disney

Meet today's new pioneers—the freelancers, consultants, independent contractors, mobile professionals, and solo business owners of the world. Like their explorer counterparts of long ago, these solo workers have a strong independent spirit. The confines of routine and security are not for them. They have gladly exchanged those limits for the chance to scout new domains and build a better life—for themselves and for the ones they love. Along the way, these modern-day adventurers have built new communities and structures that have redefined contemporary business and created new opportunities for themselves and others.

While the imagery may call to mind days of the American Wild West, the impact of these independent entrepreneurs is most definitely a modern one. In the United States alone, more than 27 million individuals are involved in solo enterprises right now, and the number is growing by more than 2 million every year. That's more than 200 new businesses every hour! It's an exciting time for this new entrepreneurial energy in many countries around the world, and I'm pleased that you've decided to join this journey to explore this new frontier.

What kind of people are these new explorers, the individuals who are starting solo enterprises? And what businesses are they choosing? Let's take a look.

Solo by Choice, Solo by Circumstance

One of the great attractions about working solo is the notion that the business can reflect personal interests and needs. That individuality begins with the reasons someone starts a solo enterprise and the type of business he or she chooses to pursue.

According to the New York City research firm IDC/Link, there were 27 million self-employed at the end of 1997, up from 24.9 million just the year before.

By the end of 2001, researchers estimate that more than 36.5 million individuals will be working on their own. These numbers keep climbing every year, and if we listen to these new solo workers we hear comments such as:

> *"I had this dream that had to get out, and I knew I didn't want to wait any longer. My new business is stretching me in ways I never thought possible, and I'm enjoying every minute."*

> *"With all the downsizing at work, I was looking for something that would bring a little more security. I started my own business on weekends. Now, even if the company downsizes further, I feel I'll be financially OK."*

> *"My spouse just got transferred to another region, and I decided that I'd rather start a solo business than try to find employment with someone else."*

> *"Now that my kids are finally in school, I was ready to do something on my own. I knew I had skills, because I'd been volunteering for years. My business gives me new ways to express myself and my talents."*

> *"I didn't quit my job, my job quit me. I was laid off and knew I had bills to pay. So I started my own business."*

> *"We have two kids who will be starting college in a few years, and I knew that the extra income from a solo business would come in handy to pay those tuition bills."*

> *"I just got fed up playing office politics and knew I could do better. I'd always wanted to start a company, and now I have."*

> *"The early-retirement package they offered me was too good to turn down. I used the money to start my own one-person firm."*

Solo workers start their businesses for many reasons. Some are solo by choice, fulfilling their dreams and desires of being self-employed. Others are solo by circumstance, opting to work solo in order to maintain household income that may have been lost by a job layoff or other unexpected situations.

Of course, it's never as simple as that. The dividing line between choice and circumstance is a fuzzy one, since all solo businesses include both the freedom of choice in deciding what the business should be and the desire for financial success from their efforts. Of the millions of self-employed workers, I wager that most of them will admit to having fun in their businesses—but few would say that they are engaged in the hard work and long hours solely for the pleasure of it, with no care for financial rewards.

The reason people start solo businesses is that they want to use their time and talents in unique ways to make a living. Like you, they value their individuality and know that they can do better—better pay, more interesting work, an increase in responsibility, more freedom—and they are willing to gamble that they can make it succeed.

The Challenge to Succeed

Unfortunately, not all of the millions of new businesses started each year will succeed. Statistics show that eight out of ten new businesses will fail within the first three years. Happily, the odds are better for solo businesses—nearly 75 percent are still operating after five years. This is particularly true for home-based businesses, where overhead costs are more easily managed.

But even home-based businesses are not immune to disaster. Just having a good business idea and hoping it all works out is not enough. It takes commitment: a promise to keep stretching and growing and learning every day, a dedication to study and apply the business methods you will be learning in the pages ahead, a pledge to make your business the best you know it can be.

If you can't make those promises, I strongly encourage you to reconsider working solo. (Remember how I said I would lay it on the line for you?) If you cannot completely dedicate yourself to working solo—to making the sacrifices and taking the risks inherent in the building process—close this book and decide that it was a good idea, but not for you. Better to choose that now than to make a half-hearted commitment. Why put yourself through all the pain and effort of making a semisuccessful business? Maybe it's easier to stay employed, take a weekly paycheck, and enjoy the other benefits working for someone else offers—and there are many.

Only you know the answer to the question of whether working solo is right for you. Of course, I hope you'll join me and the millions of others who have discovered the joys of working independently—and the rewards that come from doing work that is meaningful to all aspects of your life.

The Choice Is Yours

Now, this does not mean you have to drop everything and start working on your own tomorrow. Working solo does not always mean working full-time solo. Many people have established successful solo businesses as part-time, seasonal, or after-hour moonlighting enterprises. Whichever format you choose for your business, the total, focused commitment is necessary—even if it is a part-time enterprise. The hours may be partial, but the understanding and the dedication to make it the best it can be must be total.

If you're willing to make these commitments, I'm glad you're here. You have freely chosen to undergo the hard work, the long hours, the unending search for daily improvement. You know that your freedom and individuality are worth it. You recognize your goal, and you keep it always in sight: to make sure that you're among the business owners who celebrate that famous thrill of victory.

Along the way to solo success, there are many pitfalls to avoid. One of the deadliest traps that ensnare newcomers to the world of working solo is believing in the long list of myths that are attached to this lifestyle. Fall for these myths, and you are sure to fail. Know them, understand them, and conquer them, and you are on your way to mastering the solo workstyle.

These myths are tempting because they are tied to ego—the notion that "Oh, that doesn't apply to me" or "I can overcome that." Let's face it, to succeed as a solo entrepreneur you need a strong can-do attitude. The challenge is to look at these myths for what they are—untrue—and to understand the lessons that are contained within them. Let's review these myths now.

The 12 Biggest Myths about Working Solo

Myth #1: If I Go out on My Own, I Won't Have to Work So Hard or Such Long Hours.

Many people believe not only that independent workers don't work as many hours, but also that they don't work as hard. In actuality, most solo workers will tell you that they've never worked as long and hard before—but they've never been more fulfilled. If you're thinking about starting a solo enterprise because you feel that you're working too hard now, think again. Sixty-hour weeks may be common, particularly for full-time solo businesses just getting up and running.

Why do solo business owners put in these kinds of hours? Because they want to—not for a paycheck or because someone is closely tracking their every move. Remember the last time you were deeply involved in doing something you cared about and how the time just seemed to pass by unnoticed? For many solo business people, working on their own brings the same effect. They're so engrossed in creating a business based on something they care about passionately that 60-hour weeks, which would be a burden if they worked elsewhere, suddenly become tolerable, even enjoyable.

Truth #1

As a solo business owner, you'll probably work longer and harder than you've ever worked before—but you'll enjoy it, because you'll experience the zest and enthusiasm of creating something on your own. Exhaustion fades at the moment you proudly reflect on your business and say, "I did this!"

Myth #2: Solo Workers Have Lots of Free Time to Do All the Things They Want.

Flexibility is a big part of being self-employed, but the myth about free time is one of the biggest illusions attached to working solo. Yes, independent workers do have a certain liberty in designing their workdays. But if a solo worker isn't devoting time to developing a business, he or she is risking inevitable failure. A solo entrepreneur must wear many hats—CEO, marketing maven, financial wizard, customer service rep, secretary, mail clerk—in addition to satisfying the primary functions of his or her business. There's not much extra time.

If you're working solo and have lots of free time on your hands, it usually indicates one of two things: Either you've just won the lottery and you don't need to work at all, or you're not devoting the energy needed to make your solo business a success.

People will tell you many other myths about free time. One says that independent workers get to sleep in every morning. The other is that they can take long vacations if they want. Of course, there is a grain of truth in each of these attitudes, since solo workers dictate their own schedules and working hours.

When, where, and how long you work are your decisions. You can do anything you want—you just need to take responsibility for your choices. For example, if your business is based on offering services generally conducted during the nine-to-five workday, then sleeping late can significantly shorten the number of productive work hours—and income—that the business can generate. Similarly, if a solo business owner disappears for too long, the business will likely evaporate, too. It's an example of the old proverb: "Out of sight, out of mind."

Truth #2

To achieve solo success, you must understand that time is your most valuable commodity. Master the ability to use it wisely. Your days will be long and busy, with little room for rest. But if you are truly committed to your solo success, the days won't feel burdensome, because they'll be filled with activities that are important and meaningful to you.

Myth #3: People Working Solo Can Charge High Prices and Make a Lot of Money Fast.

The allure of making big hourly fees or profits is very attractive to people who are working in a nine-to-five job. When I talk to people about how much they could charge per hour if they decide to go on their own, their eyes light up. Or if they have ideas for products to sell, I can almost hear the calculators clicking in their heads as they smile and say, "Hey, that's not bad. . . ." Mentally, they're already on the way to the bank with their first million.

At first glance, the high fees charged by some independent services lead outsiders to imagine all sorts of get-rich-quick schemes. Others see products that seem simple to produce yet carry higher price tags, and they imagine fast and easy profits.

Outsiders usually don't take into account the many other expenses related to running a business. They mistakenly think that the price you charge for your product or service is profit directly in your pocket. Those who have worked independently know better. They've faced the tax collector, the insurance agent, the office-equipment repair technician, the delivery service. . . .

Truth #3
Solo businesses operate in a competitive environment like any other business and are affected by supply and demand. Their pricing must be high enough so that they can cover expenses, yet low enough to be within customer reach. Income and profits are directly tied to the value of the services or products provided. Solo businesses have the freedom to choose any prices they want to set for their services or products—but the market chooses whether to buy.

Myth #4: Solo Workers Can Deduct Everything, So They Don't Have to Pay Any Taxes.

There is perhaps no ruder awakening to the realities of working solo than the moment it comes time to pay your first self-employment taxes. When you work for someone else, you become accustomed to basing your income on net figures, knowing that the boss has already taken out taxes, Social Security payments, and other deductions. Often, working-solo newcomers look at a big check they've just received and erroneously think they get to keep it all.

On the basis of current tax structures, it is not unusual for some solo workers to lose 50 percent of each earned dollar to taxes—because as a solo worker it is now your responsibility to cover federal, state, and local income taxes, as well as both employee and employer portions of Social Security contributions. A big part of that check can disappear in the blink of an eye. (The savvy solo worker can, however, hold on to more of his or her earnings through good bookkeeping and deductions. We'll get into that in Chapter 8.)

While it's true that self-employed workers pay a significant amount in taxes, they also reap the benefits of that magic phrase, "It's tax deductible." The government realizes that it takes an investment to run a solo business and allows the self-employed to deduct any work-related expense from gross income. This means that legitimate business expenses—from something as small as the paper clips in your office to big-ticket items such as a new computer—possibly can be subtracted from the gross revenue you receive. The result? You pay taxes only on the remaining portion, the net income.

This notion of business costs being tax deductible is why outsiders think that the self-employed never pay any taxes. But if solo workers don't pay any taxes, it means one thing: Their expenses totaled more than their earnings. This also means they didn't have any net income—they paid their expenses, but they didn't make enough money to keep a profit.

To some solo workers, it's a two-edged sword: If you make money, you have to pay taxes on it—but it also means you've created a successful enterprise. And as your income grows, you can also feel pleased that you're able to contribute to the growth of our country, just like other citizens and businesses.

There are strict regulations for allowable deductions, and the IRS says that you must show a profit in three out of five years for your business to be considered more than a hobby. In the pages ahead, you'll see how you can lower your tax bill and build your business at the same time.

Truth #4

Taxes for solo businesses are based on net income. This number can be lowered by subtracting expenses related to the running of the business. As a savvy solo worker, learn how to make the tax system work for you by closely following tax guidelines, keeping good records, and investing in your business.

Myth #5: If I Work Independently, I Won't Have to Report to a Boss.

One of the most frequently listed reasons people begin solo businesses is that they no longer want to have someone else be the boss. They are tired of giving away the power to make decisions, to determine salary levels, to choose what type of work fills their day. So they launch businesses of their own, where they are the bosses. They get to be responsible for their actions, be the highest-level decision makers, and put "President" on their business cards.

They also get customers—people who have ideas of their own, and demands, and restrictions to place on the boss. One day the boss realizes that he or she is not really the one who totally dictates what the business is about—it's the customers who do, since serving them makes the business what it is. Bingo! Reality has arrived. As any seasoned solo professional will tell you, the real bosses are the customers.

If you've started a solo enterprise to avoid being bossed around, you may have to adjust your thinking. As an independent entrepreneur, you'll have as many bosses as you have clients. Each will have his or her own needs, ideas, and demands. Just remember that you need them—they are your business.

Naturally, if any single, bossy client becomes too difficult, the solo business owner can make the ultimate boss statement: The owner can fire the customer by dropping the account. You must be willing to accept the financial consequences of this decision, of course. If you fire too many of your clients, you may not have much of a business left—even if you are the boss.

Truth #5

As an independent professional, you realize that, unlike an employee, you don't have a single boss—you have many. These bosses are the clients or customers of your business, each of whom has specific needs and demands. Your challenge as a solo business owner is to keep all of these bosses happy so the business will prosper.

Myth #6: All I Need Is One or Two Good Customers, Then I'll Be Set.

Many one-person businesses get launched by individuals leaving companies and then enticing those same companies to be their first major clients. In fact, some solo businesses have only a single client—the owner's previous full-time employer.

This can be a positive situation, but also a very risky one. Why? Because businesses are fickle, particularly in changing economic times like ours. Hiring and firing a contractor is much easier than laying off an employee. There are usually few legal restrictions on terminating a contractor's agreement. Also, there is often a greater psychological distance than with a full-time employee. It may be difficult for a business to call you and tell you that the budget can no longer support your contract—but businesses can do it, and they will.

By limiting your customer base, you are giving up the power to control your business. It is easy to do the math: If you have two clients and lose one, you have lost 50 percent of your income sources. Depending on the size of the client, you may have lost more than 50 percent of your income. This places you in a very vulnerable position. It makes your clients much more powerful—and often forces you to tolerate unpleasant circumstances. You lose your freedom. And isn't freedom one of the things that prompted you to become self-employed in the first place?

Focusing on a very narrow market can also be risky. There are solo businesses that deal with dozens, even hundreds, of clients, but they concentrate their business on specific markets. Even though their total numbers of clients may be great, they are vulnerable because they have limited the scope of their potential client bases.

There is safety in numbers and diversity. If any one customer or market segment chooses to leave you, your business will survive—because you have others to fill the income hole the loss created.

Truth #6

In determining the number of clients and markets you serve, there is a fine line between comfort and vulnerability. At first it may seem easier to deal with only one or two clients or markets, but the risk is high that limiting yourself could sink your business. Commit to diversifying your income sources as a way to solo success.

Myth #7: If I Work on My Own, I Can Work without Interruption and Won't Have to Go to Any Annoying Meetings.

Ah, those insidious time wasters: meetings. Many a solo entrepreneur has been born of the frustration of sitting through one more pointless meeting.

CATHY © Cathy Guisewite. Reprinted with permission of UNIVERSAL PRESS SYNDICATE. All rights reserved.

The alluring thought that working independently means you won't have to attend any more meetings is, alas, a myth. There may not be as many, and they may not take the same form, but you will have to exchange ideas with customers in some type of forum. This may be face to face or on the phone. The difference will be that you have a vested interest in each of these interchanges, because they're directly tied to your income.

As for working without interruption, that's another major myth that often explodes during the first few weeks of self-employment. The challenges to focused, uninterrupted work come from both outside and inside the solo worker. Because he or she must fulfill many roles, the one-person entrepreneur is frequently pulled off track by business details—office operations, bills to be paid, phone calls, and so forth. Just as annoying are the inner distractions—the incessant mental voices, the thoughts that race toward no particular end.

Those with home-based businesses are particularly prone to interruptions. Let someone know you are now a home-based worker, and often you become the UPS drop-off point for arriving packages, the emergency baby-sitter, the car-pool driver, the afternoon golf or tennis partner, or the midday coffee break companion. The challenge is to establish a structure and discipline to working solo, so that you maintain control over your inner and outer environments as much as possible. Without this structure, the days can fritter away with no accomplishments, and your business will suffer.

Truth #7

As a solo business owner, you understand that you may not have to attend as many meetings. You also realize that you can face great challenges in creating a productive working environment. Establish a focus and structure to your business—and to each working day—to lay the groundwork for ongoing growth and success.

Myth #8: Independent Workers Get to Do Only the Work They Want to Do and Only the Things They Find Interesting.

Perhaps you've decided to become a solo worker because you are hungry to find that single activity that will bring you joy, fill your days, and make you wealthy along the way. You might be someone who's frustrated at doing paperwork, writing reports, or filling the day with repetitive tasks that hold little meaning for you. You long for some adventure, a chance to do new things—something with which you know you'll never be bored again.

I promise that if you commit to the life of a solo worker, you won't be bored. There is always too much you want to accomplish, and the potential of other opportunities is always in front of you. You'll soon find yourself wishing for longer days—or some way to clone yourself so you can achieve all the goals that mean so much to you.

What I cannot promise you is that you'll be spared from doing mundane tasks. The best solo workers are those who have a bit of the Renaissance person in them—they can tackle many different duties requiring a diverse set of skills. A typical day might have you writing letters, calling people on the phone, licking stamps, packaging a product, hounding an overdue receivable, or driving across town. You may be salesperson, accountant, inventory clerk, secretary, janitor, and CEO all within the space of eight hours. Bored? Probably not, because there's too much to do, and it's all relating to your goal. Will you be required to do boring tasks? Probably yes, if you think of them as boring—because the reality is that someone has to do these tasks, and in a one-person business, that someone is more than likely you.

Truth #8

If you're launching a solo business to escape the boredom of doing work you don't enjoy, think again. A self-employed individual must do jobs of all kinds and skills—some of which are likely to bore you. You must thrive on channeling excitement for every aspect of your work, no matter how annoying or mind-numbing any single activity may be. You understand that every action comes together as a part of your overall success.

Myth #9: I Won't Have to Deal with Any Office Politics If I'm Working Solo.

One of the biggest attractions to working solo can be found in the phrase itself: the word *solo*. Many of us work better independently. After a day of meetings, frustrations, politics, peer counseling, and phone calls, you may think, "If I could just work on my own, I could get it all done."

Some people think that starting an independent business will give them that dream—so they'll never have to put up with distracting coworkers, office politics, or other group work situations where cooperation is required. Work on your own and you never have to deal with the demands of others, right? Well, not quite . . .

Working solo does not mean working in solitude. A self-employed person who wants to be a hermit will enjoy privacy—and poverty. Independent entrepreneurs need to interact with others for many reasons: to generate sales, to learn new ideas, to share work among other freelancers, to conduct day-to-day business operations, and to build social and personal relationships. Instead of being less involved in human interchange, the solo worker will find that success comes from adopting just the opposite approach: using each contact with outsiders as a way to develop the business.

Seasoned solo professionals know that you build a business through others. Remember, those people driving you nuts could turn out to be your future customers.

Truth #9
Solo workers cannot be hermits, and people skills play an important role in growing a successful business. Customers, suppliers, and other freelance associates will all place demands on you. Decide to accept the challenge that every person and every situation can stretch your ability to learn. In the end, you'll be wiser—and wealthier, in both spirit and pocket.

Myth #10: Solo Businesses Get to Pick and Choose the Customers with Whom They Want to Work.

Your solo business is launched and growing, and you know exactly the focus you want it to take. You're ready for something creative, something that will really showcase your talents, and the chance to work with people who will think you're just wonderful.

Then a glitch occurs. Perhaps you lose a key customer, or someone doesn't pay for months and months. A batch of product gets spoiled, or equipment breaks down. Without warning you find yourself in the middle of a credit crunch, and you're scrambling to pay bills.

Suddenly those not-so-glamorous jobs with irritating clients don't look so bad anymore. They offered something you need right now—income. You swallow your pride and discover one of the important realities of working solo: Keeping the business going is more important than ego.

Yes, there will come a time when you can graduate to better customers—when you can draw an imaginary boundary and tell yourself, "I'll never do that type of work again." But almost every seasoned solo professional will tell you that there are times when even the classiest businesses will take on projects they feel are beneath them. Why? To survive. They know that the race is won by those who finish—and sometimes that means digging in and doing work just to keep the cash flowing. The road to success is not an easy, straight-ahead highway.

Fortunately, the twists and turns in the route can be pretty interesting along the way. They also often provide new opportunities.

Truth #10

As a solo business owner, you'll have the freedom to design your own line of work. But you must remain flexible enough to take on jobs that can see you through lean times. Be open to shifting the definition of your business from your needs to those of your customers. Decide that your biggest commitment is to keeping the business going at any cost—even if it means a slightly bruised ego.

Myth #11: If I Choose to Be Self-Employed, I'll Be Limited in What I Can Achieve, Since I'll Be Working Alone.

Self-employment does impose some practical limitations. There are only so many hours in the day during which you can accomplish the things you want to do. But the most important rule of working solo is that there really are no limiting rules. You can choose to work on projects all alone or bring in other associates and contract work to them. When the project is done, they're gone—until the next time you need them, or they call you.

This flexibility is one of the true joys of working solo. Every day can be entirely different—if you want. You can work on big projects that stretch for months or quick ones that take a few hours. Some days you may enjoy the solitude; on others you may delight in the companionship of freelance associates.

While many solo business owners establish firms that exist for years, others turn to working solo for shorter periods or in transition times. You can create your solo business as a weekend enterprise or tie it to a season or holiday. Don't feel that you're locked in to any mandatory structure. Yes, there are definite methods to follow to increase your business success, but the beauty of working solo is that your achievements are dictated by what you are willing to put forth.

Truth #11

Working solo limitations are created in the space between your ears more than anyplace else. If you focus on what cannot be achieved because you are alone, then you immediately set boundaries for your accomplishments. Be realistic in assessing what a single person can attain, but don't trap yourself with self-imposed limitations. Remember: One person can make a difference.

Myth #12: Only Retired Executives Who Are Consultants with High-Powered Clients Make Money Working Solo.

While it's true that there are thousands of people who fit this stereotypical profile, today's solo entrepreneur can no longer be pigeonholed into such a narrow niche.

The millions of new independent businesses springing up each year are remarkable in their imagination and individuality. From bicycle repairers to fitness trainers, tropical fish breeders to Web page designers, the new generation of one-person business owners erases the notion of solo entrepreneurs as being only consultants.

Today's solo pioneers are also redefining the notion of work and how it relates to their lives. Instead of finding a job or building a career, they have chosen to integrate their passions into a business—and *design a life.* Some initiate their businesses slowly, by focusing solo work on weekends and making the transition from full-time employment a gradual one. Others stash savings away while making detailed plans, preparing for the day they can launch a solo effort with full-time focus.

New definitions of business also bring new ideas about success. For some solo workers, success translates easily into quantity of dollars. Others find that earnings are important, but so is the satisfaction they find in their work—and the fact that they now enjoy getting up in the morning to face the day, as well as the feelings of exhilaration they find in growing their businesses.

The hard-line rules are gone. It's an exciting time of exploring new ideas and open-ended possibilities.

Truth #12
Today's one-person businesses go far beyond old notions of independent consultants writing reports for corporate clients (although launching this type of business is still a popular option). To make a solo business work for you, think of it as a fine, handcrafted garment—only this is a special garment that can be altered as you grow and change, giving you maximum comfort and enjoyment at all times. Never forget that you control the pencil and scissors to design this garment. Make sure it is always a perfect fit.

Will Working Solo Work for You?

Each solo business is unique, because it represents the individuality of its owner. There are, however, some common qualities that independent workers share—traits that give them an advantage when struggling to work on their own.

The working solo self-quiz is based on materials published by the U.S. Small Business Administration (SBA) and has been modified to reflect the qualities needed in people launching independent businesses. Its purpose is to provide a self-evaluation of how well you might succeed working solo.

If you score high marks, it doesn't necessarily mean you'll be a whiz-bang success working on your own. But if you score poorly, you may want to seriously reconsider whether a solo business is the best match for you.

WORKING SOLO SELF-QUIZ

Answer yes (if you agree) or no (if you disagree) in response to the following statements:

1. I'm a self-starter. Nobody has to tell me to get things going.
2. I enjoy competition and do not get intimidated easily.
3. I can make decisions if I have plenty of time. If I have to make up my mind quickly, I often think later and regret what I've decided.
4. I have willpower and self-discipline.
5. I feel comfortable knowing that I don't have all the answers and feel comfortable taking advice from others.
6. I get things done on time.
7. I'll take over if I have to, but I'd rather have someone else be responsible.
8. I am adaptable to changing conditions.
9. I can give three clear reasons why I want to go into business for myself.
10. I am good at planning ahead.
11. Once I create a plan, I consider it finalized. I follow it to the letter, no matter what else may come up.
12. I understand that working solo may entail working 12 to 16 hours a day, six days a week. I am willing to devote the energy needed to make my business a success.
13. I have seriously reviewed the financial needs of my solo business. I have enough money set aside, even if my business does not make any income for three to four months.
14. I have a good understanding of my strengths and weaknesses.
15. I feel comfortable asking others for help.
16. I have carefully reviewed whether I could make more money working for someone else.
17. I know I could hire experts to help me, but I'd rather do it myself, since I trust my own judgment more.
18. My family and/or loved ones go along with my plan to start a one-person business.

(Continued) ⟹

19. I find a big thrill in taking risks at any time.
20. I am in good physical health.
21. Once I make up my mind to do something, I am committed to finishing it.
22. I know other self-employed individuals and have seen how their businesses work.
23. I am prepared to lower my standard of living, if necessary, until my business becomes a success.
24. I am willing to devote the time, energy, and money to my new business, even though I understand that many new businesses don't succeed.
25. I have a clear understanding of what success means to me, and I know that money is only one of the measuring factors.

Of the 25 statements, all your responses should be "yes" except numbers 3, 7, 11, 17, and 19. If your responses do not match up with this, it doesn't mean you can't start a solo business or that your efforts won't be successful. But individuals with qualities demonstrated by correct responses are generally better matched for being on their own.

Did you respond to all the statements? Were there some things you hadn't considered before? Keep in mind that these statements are geared only to start you thinking about personal qualities of solo business owners. There are many other aspects you'll need to consider before you start your business, such as how to define your business, who your customers are, and how you'll reach them. But that's jumping ahead. For now, reflect on the statements in the quiz, and think about your answers—and what they reveal to you.

Now that you have a better understanding of the world of working solo and have realistically assessed if it's right for you, it's time to move on to discover the business that makes the most sense for your talents, interests, and needs.

Chapter 2

How to Choose a Solo Business That's Perfect for You

Choose a job you love, and you will never have to work a day in your life.

—Confucius

Now that you have a better understanding of the personal qualities that are needed for working solo, it's time to embark on the next exciting leg of our journey: discovering the business that matches you best. It's important that you find this match, for you must have a passion for what you do in order to succeed. At least in the beginning, you'll be living this business from the time your eyes open in the morning until your head touches the pillow at night—and sometimes longer if you're like most solo entrepreneurs, because your business will become such a central part of your life that it will even sneak into your dreams.

Two kinds of passions inhabit the souls of solo entrepreneurs. The first is a passion for an activity. This is demonstrated in the person, for instance, who lives, breathes, and dreams of antique toys and opens a business that finds and repairs these treasures. It's a natural step for this entrepreneurial type to take a personal passion and design a business—and a life—around it.

The second kind of passion is enthusiasm about business itself. Individuals with this entrepreneurial style are excited foremost about the prospect of having their own enterprise. They choose a business that is of interest to them, but without feeling a focused commitment to any specific activity. Many are drawn to business because they see an opportunity to improve an existing idea in the marketplace.

This latter approach can be puzzling for people who believe that the sole path to success is to have a burning passion for an activity. For example, the idea of translating one's passion for business in general instead of for a specific activity was strange to me until a childhood friend started a venture with a partner several years ago. I remember being surprised when she told me they were choosing between opening a store that sold storage and organizational items or one that carried lingerie. These two ideas seemed at different ends of the spectrum to me.

On closer reflection, I realized they were not that far apart. Both were about small indulgences—items that aren't necessary for survival, but pleasures that improve daily life on a personal level. To the new business owners, each was a business they thought could be successful—which turned out to be true, because the lingerie in their small boutique goes flying out the door, even in tight economic times.

A business grows from a desire to translate an individual interest into something greater. It's best to choose your business based on what you enjoy doing—whether it's a specific activity or the notion of business itself. Make your commitment as if money were not an issue. Of course it is, but in the early days you can't always count on it coming in. What you can count on is that you'll be spending a ton of hours focused on making this business work. You better enjoy it, or you may end up resenting the time and energy and soon give up.

Four Common Reasons for Starting a Solo Business—and Why Each May Be Wrong for You

In my work as a speaker to thousands of solo professionals each year, I continually meet people seeking to make their enterprises work. They tell me that they just aren't getting enjoyment out of the business or that it's taking all their time with no apparent return on investment. When I ask them why they chose the business they're in, I'm not surprised to hear one of the following four reasons:

1. It's a business that seemed like a good idea.
2. I saw other people doing it, so I thought I'd do it, too.
3. I know people who make a lot of money doing this.
4. Doing this type of thing interests me as a hobby.

Now, each of these reasons is legitimate, in its own way, for starting a solo business. What's missing is the *passion* behind the statement—why someone can't possibly resist *not* doing this business. Whether others are making a success of a landscape gardening venture may be inspiring at first, but it's also likely that the reason they've created that success is because they can't imagine life without being surrounded by green, growing things. They probably read bulb catalogs or scout plant stores in their free moments. You, in contrast, see them as making a good living, but you can't tell an elm from a maple, and the thought of dirt under your fingernails gives you the willies. There's slim chance you'll find the same enjoyment—or success—in the same business.

This cannot be overstated. Choosing a business based only on someone else's instincts, or quick-money possibilities, or having a passing fancy for an idea will sink you in the long run. That's not to say there haven't been great successes built out of following the ideas of others. But even someone who chooses to start a business as an outgrowth of hobby activities will need to transform that interest into a stronger emotion. Passion brings dedication and focus, two key ingredients to get you through the early stages of growing a business, when the days are long and the income may be slim.

Passion also brings enthusiasm, which bubbles over and turns you into a natural marketer for your product or services. Energy is attractive. Customers are drawn to this natural enthusiasm, and your passion can give you a valuable competitive advantage in the marketplace.

For example, imagine the reluctant landscape gardener trying to woo a customer into replanting shrubs and bedding plants, when what the gardener really wants to do is stay inside and curl up with a book. It's unlikely you're going to see much enthusiasm there—or a sale. In contrast, the gardener brimming with excitement about new varieties of greenery soon convinces the customer how great his yard will look.

The passion needed for solo success springs from the particular interests and abilities of each person—which makes each business unique, too. Discovering that personal passion, and how it translates into a solo business, is our next stage on this journey.

As a first step, let's take a look at the many options of working solo available to you.

Variations on Working Solo

One of the most attractive aspects of working solo is the flexibility you have to choose the framework for your business. It can be truly unique, and it can adapt and change to your interests and needs. After reviewing thousands of independent enterprises, I've found four general structures that seem to emerge. None is cast in concrete, however, since each individual defines what his or her solo business becomes. Take a look at these four categories and let them spur your imagination about creating *your* solo enterprise.

Part-time self-employed workers constitute nearly half of all solo businesses. These are individuals who may have other, full-time commitments, such as parenting, or another regular part-time job. Part-time solo ventures operate on a regular basis but are scaled back in terms of number of hours or days per week. For example, a housecleaning service may be available only on certain days, or a caterer may work only on weekends. These entrepreneurs promote their businesses as ongoing entities that function usually within specific time frames.

Full-time solo businesses generally replace other full-time employment and serve as the primary income source for an individual. Some may operate within established daytime working hours; others may focus on nontraditional hours of service, such as the late-night security service provider or the daybreak pet walker. Full-time solo workers may take on other freelance associates as need dictates. The determination to make a full-time solo business successful is usually great, since success relates directly to income—and survival.

Moonlighting solo businesses are started by people who have an activity interest they want to pursue in addition to a full-time job. Such an individual may be testing the waters to see if there is enough interest in the product or service to turn it into a full-time enterprise, or learning skills to run the business successfully. Another may be moonlighting as a way to solve a short-term cash crunch or to stash away enough money to one day launch a full-time solo effort. Moonlighting efforts usually focus on evening and weekend hours.

Seasonal solo businesses are tied to events or specific times of year. There are many types of seasons and many variations of seasonal solo businesses. For instance, some enterprises are linked to seasonal weather, such as snow removal or lawn maintenance. Other seasonal businesses are associated with holidays, such as the Christmas wreath maker or the Valentine's Day chocolate, flowers, and cookie delivery service. Ever changing sports seasons also bring business opportunities. Seasonal solo ventures operate on a consistent basis but can differ in their off-season level of activity. Some operate only at specific times of the year, while others spend off-season months preparing materials, developing new products, and expanding their markets.

As you can see, these four categories are generalized structures. Some solo efforts are combinations of two or more of the categories. Some may have started out in one category and transformed into another—and may change again and again as the business grows. Trying to establish a strict definition of a solo business is as elusive as holding water in your cupped hands. Instead of thinking in terms of rigid boundaries, let these categories inspire you to imagine the many possible forms your solo business can take. (Appendix B, "Solo Business Directory," will give you even more ideas. You'll be learning more about that in just a bit.)

Did this discussion get your brain going? Don't stop now. Keep these options in the back of your mind and let's take a look at some other factors about your solo business.

Service or Product?

What a solo business does comes down to two basic things: It either offers a service or offers a product. They are two very distinct approaches and attitudes toward business. Read on to see which seems more attuned to your interests and needs.

Service-based businesses provide assistance to others, whether individuals, groups, or other businesses. Sample service businesses include typists, bookkeepers, auto repair technicians, pet sitters, private investigators, carpet installers, image consultants, public relations professionals, technology consultants, marketing advisors, and reunion planners. As you can see, they range across the entire spectrum of interests and abilities of solo entrepreneurs.

Some service-based firms offer services *away* from their business locations, such as the cleaning service that works at a company or other residential location.

Others offer services that are based *from* their business location, such as the tax preparer who takes your figures and calculates them on computer equipment in his or her own office.

Product-based businesses offer a manufactured item that can be sold to a customer or to another business for resale to customers. The distinction is that the customer is receiving a tangible item in exchange for payment. The products of artists, furniture makers, herb growers, clothing designers, and cake decorators are examples of this approach. Some solo businesses offer products that other businesses have manufactured, such as health products, household supplies, or greeting cards. In this case, the emphasis of the solo business is on sales, rather than split between creating *and* selling.

Products are generally sold either retail or wholesale. *Retail* sales are those made directly to the end user—the maker of the item sells it face to face through fairs, bazaars, home parties, or demonstrations. Retail sales can also be made indirectly through the mail—you are reaching the customer but not face to face. *Wholesale* sales are made to other sales outlets, such as retail stores or distributors, which in turn make the sale to the customer.

Of course, the distinctions between products and services are not always clear-cut. Consider caterers. Do they offer a product or a service? Both, in some ways, since they're cooking *and* providing a marvelous end product—the food. Sometimes the product implies a service, such as that of a tailor or dressmaker.

Which approach to choose? That depends on you—and what you want your business to become. Some people are more comfortable starting a service-based business, since it often doesn't require much capital investment in tools or equipment. Others feel lost without having a tangible item to sell and prefer to focus on a product-based enterprise. The option of selling products created by someone else is often appealing to those attracted to the notion of business and not any particular activity.

These categories, like the ones before, are not hard-edged, because there is no *one* answer. Rather, they are intended to stimulate your thinking about the endless varieties of working solo. Have they? Is your head spinning with possibilities? I hope so—it's a good sign. Hold on to all those thoughts, because we now come to one of the most revealing (and fun) exercises of all in choosing your solo business.

The Ten Easiest Ways to Choose What Your Solo Business Should Be

I firmly believe that those who want to succeed by working solo can do so, if they discover the businesses that match their unique interests and abilities.

How do you make that happen? Most simply, by asking yourself some questions—and answering them honestly.

Isn't it funny how often we are able to see great things in others and not in ourselves? As you plan your solo enterprise, persevere to find those things in yourself that others see. Don't be afraid to make a long list of ideas, some that you think are way too foolish or impractical for a business. You may not end up using that silly idea, but it could be the one that's just a single step away from the one you are searching for.

Brainstorming sessions with others can also yield ideas. Invite others to give you feedback on your ideas. Ask those who know you well—a mentor, colleagues, friends, relatives—about the qualities they value in you and the business activities they see you doing.

This review period is a time of no evaluation or refusals—everything is allowed. You'll have plenty of time later to whittle the list. For now, stay open to the possibilities.

Here's a fun exercise that's helped hundreds of people launch their solo businesses. To maximize its results, allow yourself at least 24 hours for the images to simmer in the back of your mind.

Begin by finding a quiet spot, where you won't be distracted. Pull out a pad of paper and a pen to jot down your ideas, and get comfortable.

Think of yourself as going fishing—you're out on a big boat, surrounded by miles and miles of ocean. With a wide, powerful sweep of your arm, you cast your net across the water's surface, and you watch it slowly disappear. As it sinks, you have confidence that it is going deep into areas that will catch all sorts of ideas and memories for you to use in planning your new solo adventure.

Now, as the net sinks deeper and deeper, let your mind sink deeper into your memories. Let your mind flow as you answer the ten questions that follow:

1. Think back to when you were young. See yourself on the school playground. Who was that person back then? What were you like? What interested you? Did you have a favorite sport or subject in school? A favorite toy? Jot down some memories of those times.

2. What awards or achievements have you received in your life that gave you special pleasure? These don't have to be only major events—they could include that star you got on your second-grade spelling test. Try to remember what it was that brought you that recognition and how you felt receiving it.

3. Come back to the present and consider the things you do as easily as breathing and walking. What are the activities that you don't even have to think about to do well? Don't be hard on yourself here—*everyone* has things to put on this list.

4. Imagine that you have ended up on a desert island. But this is a magic desert island, where you can bring anything or anyone you want. What and/or whom did you bring?

5. What things do you do that draw compliments from others? Try to recall their voices as they told you the compliment and what you were

doing. Also try to remember how you felt when they said those wonderful words.

6. Think back to some of your most recent pleasurable experiences. What common key ingredients were in them?

7. If someone asked you to name some of your favorite group activities, what would they be?

8. You have been given the magic power to design your *perfect* day. What would you do? Take your time to design this day. Would you get up early with the sunrise or sleep in? Would you spend it outdoors or inside? Alone or with friends? A few friends or many? What activities would you do? Now, if this were not a single day but *every* day, how might you design it?

9. What can you talk about for hours and hours, until your friends say, "Enough already!"?

10. If money were no matter, how would you create your life? Or, as one of my seminar participants asked, "If every job paid a dollar, what would you do?"

As you do this exercise, take time to fully answer each question. If nothing comes to you right now, mentally carry the question with you during the next 24 hours. Ideas may come to you right before you go to sleep or just upon waking—or even in your dreams.

It's also important to write your answers down on paper. We all think we remember ideas, but they escape so easily. When you write something down, it takes on a different attitude—more concrete, more *possible*. The process of writing often brings a clarity to your thoughts, because you need to express in words what this fuzzy idea is all about So keep a small notebook or pad nearby as you go through this exercise period.

Don't count anything out when the memories or ideas come to you—they will all come together to give you a sense of who you are and the solo work that will bring you satisfaction. I remember several years ago when I started to focus on remembering my childhood games and toys. Slowly I began to recall how interested I was in connect-the-dots pictures. I enjoyed seeing what the connections made, and I could do them for hours. As I reflected on those memories over the next few days, I realized that my childhood diversion was now my focus on connecting people with others to help them accomplish their entrepreneurial dreams.

What were *your* childhood interests? Are you a budding architect who spent hours stacking blocks or building tree forts? Did you count everything in sight, and now are considering an accounting service? Were you the kid who could name every single model of car on the road, and now dream about restoring antique cars?

The seeds of success are closely tied to childhood memories such as these. In his book, *Timing Is Everything* (Pocket Books, 1996), psychologist and high-level achievement expert Denis Waitley reports on a series of studies conducted by British behavioral scientists on the relationship between youthful dreams and adult success. Fifty individuals were tracked over a period of 28 years, from the age of 7 until the age of 35. The findings were remarkable, as Waitley explains: "Incredibly, nearly all of the subjects eventually ended up engaged in a professional pursuit related to their interests *during the age span of seven through 14.*"

The study revealed that most of the individuals discarded or strayed from the interests after these childhood years. Significantly, Waitley observes, the successful adults were those who "all found their way back to recapture their early childhood dreams by the age of 35, even if only as a hobby or an avocation."

What happened to that childhood self you used to know? What were those childhood passions? Take time to dig for him or her. The child you find will guide you in molding a solo business perfectly matched to you.

Feel free to revisit these exercises and do them often. Each time you will discover something new about yourself and about what you want your solo business to become.

Also, record the date on your notes. It's great fun to reexamine these sheets and see how your ideas have changed and become refined over time—and which ones have stayed with you. In creating this book, for example, I went back to sheets I had created more than six years earlier. I found that the seeds for this book and the title *Working Solo* were all there. It just took those intervening years for the idea to germinate and come to fruition.

Words of Wisdom

On Choosing a Business

Deciding which solo business to launch is often the result of many factors. Here are the thoughts and experiences of one independent entrepreneur.

"Choosing the right business is often a process that contains much self-reflection—and can even be somewhat painful. As we look at different opportunities, we are faced with things we could do, things we feel we should do, things others' feel we should do, things we would like to do, and things we would love to do.

"Too often our choices are influenced by what others think or the articles we read that promote the 'hot' businesses of the future. If you have a tremendous amount of interest in a 'hot' business, then go for it. If not, then re-evaluate before you jump in with both feet, even if it can be a moneymaker.

"For me, it was the result of sitting down and truly answering the question, 'What do you want to do?' After much time and reflection, I came up with: I want to work with people who want to start a business, and small business owners who want to grow their business. Once I had clearly chosen this, it was a turning point in my life and career. Today my business, Small Business Success, is a training and speaking company that works one-on-one with aspiring entrepreneurs and small business owners, and conducts presentations and workshops for the small business marketplace.

"What can you get really excited about? After you can answer that question, the challenge is in working through how you can do that in a way people will pay for your products and services. If you can get excited about it, then the frustrations of owning and operating your own business are worthwhile—and the money will follow.

"Step back, think it through, make a decision, create a plan, be creative, and reach out for help along the way. Remember, no one accomplishes anything great alone!"

—Mark LeBlanc

Mark LeBlanc runs Small Business Success and works with individuals who want to start and grow businesses. His "Growing Your Business" presentations are popular with associations, professional organizations, and franchisors.

Turning What You Love into What You Do

Now that you have this expanding list of memories, ideas, and activities that bring you excitement and satisfaction, what's the next step?

Think of this list as a tool, one that is active and organic. It will keep changing and growing as you and your business ideas change and grow. For now, review it and see if you can find any patterns. Compile your list with two parts: things you enjoy and those you don't. Is there a common thread that runs through this tapestry of your life's memories and desires? Think about themes such as:

- ✓ Organizational skills
- ✓ Physical abilities, such as sports, or skills such as carpentry or plumbing
- ✓ Outdoors/indoors preference
- ✓ Tasks involving a particular focus, such as food, pets, or plants
- ✓ Expressive interests, including language skills and speaking abilities
- ✓ Facility with math or calculations
- ✓ Artistic talent and creative abilities

✓   Social skills or people-oriented interests

✓   Fashion or beauty/personal grooming interests

✓   Repairing/restoring/collecting interests

✓   Listening versus speaking skills

✓   Technology interests or tinkering abilities

Perhaps there are other themes you find running through your list of memories and interests. Jot them down as well. Now, with your sheets in hand, let's go browsing and window-shopping for a solo business.

Browsing and Brainstorming the Solo Business Directory

Ready to go? In hand, you should have your list of answers to the ten questions listed previously. It's also helpful if you've taken the time to find the common threads in these memories, ideas, and activities.

Turn now to Appendix B, "Solo Business Directory," which lists more than 1,000 independent businesses. Within these pages lies an invaluable treasure for you: one of the most complete listings of solo business opportunities available, just waiting to inspire *you,* the solo adventurer.

Take time to browse through this section, and mentally try on some businesses. See how they fit your interests, your abilities, your dreams. The listing is arranged by interest areas so you can review a wide range of business ideas easily.

Peruse the listings with a pen or marker in hand, and highlight those of interest to you. As you browse, brainstorm possibilities of how you might transform a business idea into one uniquely suited to you. Do you like plants *and* baking? Perhaps it becomes a business that uses fresh herbs or offers cakes decorated with real flowers. Enjoy sports *and* woodworking? How about a business that creates games that use handmade wooden equipment or playing pieces? Interested in technology *and* the law? Maybe you'll launch an online legal research firm.

Don't be afraid to include a wide variety of possibilities. For now, give them all equal acceptance. Brainstorming is a time for *generating* ideas, not *evaluating* them. It's a mental free-for-all that encourages your brain to make creative associations.

Also, don't self-edit your choices based on that little voice inside you that says, "Gosh, what would so-and-so think if I said I'd like to do *that?*" Silence that judgmental voice for now. You'll have plenty of opportunities later to whittle this list down for other reasons. For now, let your mind run free, and take the time to mentally picture yourself as the owner of these solo enterprises.

The Solo Business Directory will give you a title of a solo business, which in many cases will summarize what the business is all about. As you consider the listings, think about the pros and cons of each business, too. Each opportunity has its positive and negative aspects, but each person brings individual preferences. Qualities that you may find unappealing—such as working outdoors, or at night, or in solitude—may make someone else's list as the ideal situation.

If you don't find a listing that matches your needs, create your own. You can combine them, tweak them, personalize them—whatever it takes to make a business match *you*. If you discover or create a solo enterprise that's not listed here, I hope you'll put it on a postcard or in an e-mail and send it my way. I'd love to hear about it and include it in an updated listing.

Take time to browse the Solo Business Directory now. Come back with your list of at least three or four possibilities—or as many as 20, if you want.

The Most Important Ingredient for Solo Business Success

Welcome back. Did you have a great time browsing the directory? Isn't it fun to let your imagination run free and think about all the businesses you might create? Did you have a hard time limiting yourself because you found so many that were interesting? That's a good sign. Remember, a big part of business success comes from the enthusiasm to make things happen. Even though you are focusing on starting only one business, ideas from other businesses might tie in—or you may later start another type of business, or several.

Now let's explore how your ideas can translate into a viable business. You've probably heard the statement, "It takes more than a good idea to start a business." But have you ever really thought about what that means?

There are literally millions of people who have good ideas for businesses and who tell themselves (and whoever else will listen) that it could make them a million bucks, if . . . Then the list begins: if only they had the money, if only they had a partner, if only they didn't have other responsibilities, if only they could have some free time. These are all legitimate concerns, *but* . . . what's missing from this list is the most important necessity of all. Without this key ingredient, no business can succeed.

Can you guess what it is? Money? Talent? Sufficient time? Ideas? Experience? Those qualities are all important. But there is still one ingredient that is even *more* important. Without this, *no* business can succeed.

Have you figured it out? The crucial ingredient needed for your business to succeed comes down to one word:

Customers

Yes, that's right. Customers, clients, patrons—whatever you'd like to call them. They are *the* most important factor in your business success.

Were you surprised at the answer? Many people are, particularly solo business owners-to-be who think that their ideas make great sense to them and that therefore they should have great appeal to others—and make them very rich, very quickly.

The reality is that you can have all the money you'd like to start your business, but if it's offering a service or product that people don't want, it won't succeed. Similarly, you might have the snazziest four-color brochures, the most spacious office, all the high-tech equipment your heart desires—but if you don't have customers, what does it matter? Like water and sunshine to a seedling, customers are vital to growing your fledgling business ideas into a thriving enterprise.

An idea that seems irresistible to you doesn't automatically translate into a successful business. The philosophy that says "If you build it, they will come" worked fine for a Hollywood movie. Yet that type of thinking has landed many solo entrepreneurs on their behinds, staring dumbfounded at their rapidly diminishing bank accounts. Where did they go wrong? They thought they could have a business without customers—a fatal assumption.

Customers are the most important factor in your solo business. Getting them, keeping them, growing them in number—these are key tasks for you. So pull out your marker or pen and put a big star next to this key *Working Solo* rule:

> *Solo businesses can operate without employees but not without customers.*

Later on, we'll explore specific actions you can take to establish strong connections with your customers and show how to make them partners on your road to solo success. For now, let's take a look at how you can discover who your customers will be and how many of them are out there, just waiting for your business to arrive.

Is the World Ready for Your Solo Business?

If I told you to spend lots of money, endless hours, and incredible amounts of energy to launch a business that would have no customers, you'd think I was crazy, right? Unfortunately, that's what thousands of people do each year when they start their own businesses. They print up fancy business cards, rent big office space, *then* try to find some customers. All too often they discover that there aren't any. Or if there are a few, they aren't sufficient enough in number or need to sustain the business. End result? Frustration, bitterness, and, often, hard financial losses.

Where did these entrepreneurial enthusiasts go wrong? They assumed that potential customers had the same passion they did for their ideas. Sometimes that's right, and a business can succeed, even if the owner has not completely thought through the plan for customers and marketing. Many times, however, the assumptions are *not* on target, and the businesses fail.

Fortunately, there are simple things you can do to avoid this trap. Before you invest a lot of time, money, or energy in a solo business effort, find out how many potential customers you have and who they are. How to do that? It's called *research*. It doesn't have to cost a lot of money, and it will show you the feasibility of your potential business and the realistic chances for success. It's also a great deal of fun, because along the way you'll discover much more about what your solo goals are and what you want your solo business to become.

Finding Your Future Customers

Armed with your lists of potential businesses and the things you've discovered that they have in common, let's find the necessary ingredient to turn these ideas into real businesses: your future customers.

There are many ways to do research on customers and your potential market. Big companies, of course, call in market research firms to conduct extensive surveys, interviews, and other studies. (Maybe this is a business you'll start!) In contrast, solo business owners can conduct research on a slimmer budget, yet still find answers that are valuable to them.

Your market research goal is to find the answers to two general questions:

1. Are there any potential customers out there for the service or product I want to offer? If so, who are they, and what are they like?

2. Are there any businesses currently serving their needs? If so, how might my idea or approach be different?

These questions may seem deceptively simple at first. Don't short-circuit yourself at this stage and be fooled into thinking you already know the answers. That's what market research is all about—keeping an open mind until you have all the data. Then you can take a reality check and look at what your research shows you, in comparison to what you may *want* to believe. As the saying goes, "A mind is like a parachute—it has to be open to work."

As you use these avenues of exploring who your potential customers are and what your business might become, try to visualize typical customers. What are they like? What age are they? Where do they live? What do they do for a living? What else do they spend their money on? Is it personal discretionary income, or is it for business-related expenses? What service or product do they need that you are perfectly matched to deliver? How can you structure your business to serve those needs now as well as in the years to come?

As you put together the profile of your potential customers, keep your business ideas fluid, and understand that your thoughts may change and adapt as you learn what your customers really want from a business like yours. Some of the most successful solo businesses start out with an inkling of an idea, then go on to become great successes because they listen and respond to what customers want.

Seven Masterful (and Cheap) Ways to Conduct Market Research

There are many ways to obtain answers to your key questions about who your customers are and how your business can serve them. Here are seven that I've found helpful. None costs a lot of money, and each will give you insights into your potential customers and whether there is a need for your business.

1. Yellow Pages and Other Directories

If you're trying to figure out whether there is a need for your business in your area or what the competition might be, pull out the Yellow Pages of your telephone directory and other business directories. As you flip through the pages, don't overlook listings that may be related to your business idea. A desktop publishing company, for example, might be listed under graphic design, business services, computers, word processing, printing, or publishing. See if there are any area networks or professional associations related to your interests. In addition to the Yellow Pages, check out the advertising in regional newspapers or in the free shopping paper, if one exists in your area.

If you find one or more businesses similar to the one you want to launch, it's a good sign. It means your community is large enough to support them. Then your focus shifts to discovering if your region is large enough to support one more—yours. Find out all you can about your potential competition, and consider ways you could improve their idea or tailor it to a slightly different audience.

If you don't find any listings related to your business idea, it's a trickier thing to interpret. It may mean that the market is wide open for your business, and the time is ripe to plant your business seeds. The flip side, of course, is that there isn't a business like yours in the region for a good reason: There aren't the customers to support it.

Keep in mind that competition is not necessarily a bad thing. When two or more businesses operate in the same region, they raise the awareness that the product or service is needed and enjoyed by others. The customer, instead of saying yes or no to the product or service, is saying, "Which one?" Competing for customers' business is often a much easier battle to win than convincing them of the need in the first place.

2. Trend Books

Do you have friends who always seem to know what the next hot thing is going to be? You know the type—they have this uncanny ability to sniff out the next fashion trend or the type of food that turns into the next big rage.

Some people have turned this talent into a business, and they consult with corporations for thousands of dollars, advising them on where they should focus their business in the coming years. Fortunately for us, several of them have written their thoughts down in books, and their ideas are available to us, solo entre-preneurs. Books such as *Clicking* and *The Popcorn Report* by Faith Popcorn, *Megatrends 2000* by John Naisbitt and Patricia Aburdene, and *Technotrends* by Daniel Burrus are excellent resources for the solo business owner. (For details on these and other valuable business books, check out Appendix A, "Solo Resources" and the companion volume to *Working Solo,* the *Working Solo Sourcebook,* which is chock-full of helpful information.)

By paying attention to trend books, you can peek into the future and find out what consumers will be buying and what they will consider to be important in their lives. (You'll probably discover a lot of yourself in these books, too, since the emphasis on the individual and small businesses are two key trends for the future.) Trend books can help you see how viable your small business idea is, or they can give you ideas on how to fine-tune your business so that it is more in sync with sociological changes—and the needs of your customers.

3. Bookstores, Department Stores, and Supermarket Shelves

The items you find on the shelves of your local bookstore, department store, or grocery can reveal a lot about current trends and can be a signpost for you in deciding whether your business idea makes sense. Thinking of starting a sports-related business? Check out the current sports books on your local bookstore shelves. Is there a common trend? Do they seem to be aimed at a particular type of customer? What about sports items in department stores or special food items that have been developed for athletes, both the armchair and professional vari-eties? What do they tell you about your potential customer base?

The items currently targeted to a specific market segment are on those shelves for a reason. Big corporations have spent thousands of dollars doing research to find out exactly what these consumers want to buy. We, as solo entrepreneurs, don't have large corporate research budgets, but we can access the results indi-rectly by paying close attention to new products that are introduced and by ana-lyzing how they are positioned in the market.

For example, if your business is in a food-related enterprise, you'd be wise to stay up to date on trends in cookbooks, new food items, and so on. Service-based businesses can also gather research from store visits. For instance, a pet-sitting service may discover that people want to pamper their pets more these days or that they're concerned about their pet's health.

As you research, be objective. Be careful not to bias your viewing toward things that will confirm your own assumptions. Also stay aware of other items that may be competing for your target market's dollars.

By monitoring bookstores, department stores, and supermarket shelves, you are extracting valuable research and leveraging the work already completed by large corporations. It can point you to specific qualities of your potential customers as well as give you a general feel for what they value and will spend money on.

4. Magazine and Newspaper Articles

Small business is big news these days. Magazine and newspaper articles can give you important information about current trends in small business—or even ideas about specific businesses started in a different part of the country that you may want to duplicate in your area.

As you read your daily newspaper or skim the newsweekly magazines, sensitize your antennae to pick up on subtle changes in your customers' moods and needs. Are you reading about an increasing frustration with a lack of quality? Maybe you'll decide to offer your service with a quality guarantee. You've read that someone has installed a toll-free number to give customers a chance to offer suggestions? Maybe you'll consider the same, on a smaller scale.

As a solo worker, *everything* you encounter in your daily life can influence and improve your business. It's all in the attitude you take and how sensitive you make your antennae. Often the influences and inspirations come from the unlikeliest places. You're reading that a popular restaurant offers a dozen varieties of chocolate dessert, and you decide to offer a dozen variations of your service or product. Or someone reports a growing interest in single-serving products, and you decide to create individualized packages of your new food item.

Solo businesses are always in a state of flux, constantly changing and adapting to new needs and opportunities. This flexibility is part of the joy and excitement of the independent lifestyle. Staying in touch with the daily changes in the lives of your customers brings you insights to understand your customers more fully and ways to serve them better. As a result, you'll know how to address your customer base and expand your success.

5. Research Studies

Often in a magazine or newspaper article, the writer will mention a research study conducted by an organization or individual. If the study has direct relation to your proposed business, contact the organization and ask for a copy of the study. You'd be surprised at how much information is available to you, either directly from the research source or from your local library. Don't be shy—remember that the research assistant you've just reached on the phone might be delighted that someone cared enough to track down the source. It's true that some reports are proprietary and expensive to obtain, but it's worth a call to ask. If the complete report is not available, ask if you can obtain a synopsis of it for free or at a reduced price.

Also, don't overlook the experience and power of your local librarian. These professionals are masters at tracking down information. Many libraries also offer valuable business and career resources, including computerized database searches, volunteer advisors, and professional seminars.

When doing your research, keep your options open as wide as possible in the beginning. For example, let's say you're thinking of starting a custom furniture business. Instead of marching in and saying to the librarian, "I need to find out how many people buy custom furniture," consider an approach that includes wider options, as well as the expertise of the librarian. "I'm thinking of starting a business that makes custom furniture, and I'm trying to get an idea of who my customers might be. Where do you suggest I look?" This second approach engages the librarian, who could have several new ideas you might never discover on your own. Remember that librarians bring a vantage point that business professionals may not have—a perspective that can be very valuable as you define your business.

Your interchange also might inspire some new alternatives—maybe a business focusing on dining room tables? Maybe rocking chairs? Maybe a custom furniture repair firm? Or a business that rents custom furniture? Keep your options open, and don't overlook any professional talent that can assist you in your cause.

Humans have an instinct to help others, which is a wonderful quality and quite valuable to the solo business owner-to-be. Whether you're dealing with someone on the phone or with your local librarian, the first step is to get up the courage to ask—and then show appreciation. You'll be amazed at how much information you can gather, details that can help you understand who your potential customers might be and how best to design a successful business to serve them.

6. The Internet

By linking your computer to the Internet, you have access to a worldwide collection of information that's often more up to date than any books, magazines, or other paper-based research you might use. The advantage of the Internet is that you can tap into vast information resources in seconds, from almost anywhere in the world. The downside is that it's often difficult to distill what might be most valuable to you in this flood of data.

What might the Internet bring you? Details on market segments and demographics, lists of similar businesses, examples of marketing materials and online ordering options, information on relevant associations or agencies, current statistics and research findings, patent and trademark search capabilities, databases of manufacturers, comments from users of similar products or services, free one-on-one business counseling—the list is nearly unlimited. Keep an open mind and explore the possibilities.

To maximize your online research efforts, spend some time learning how to use the leading World Wide Web search engines such as Yahoo!, Infoseek, and Lycos. Each has a unique way of conducting searches and presenting information. By experimenting, you'll discover how to broaden or narrow your searches so you can retrieve the information you seek.

Browsing the World Wide Web can also lead to unexpected ideas for new business opportunities. Sites may inspire you to make unusual combinations or lead to creative brainstorming. Or you may find someone in another part of the world who has established a business similar to yours, and you can build a relationship over the wires.

7. Soliciting Feedback

Last, but certainly not least, is the research you conduct by soliciting feedback from others. When corporations use this approach, they bring together individuals representing their target market into a *focus group* and gather feedback on their interests, needs, and opinions. As an independent entrepreneur, you can conduct your own focus groups in informal settings—chatting with friends or business colleagues over coffee. Or you can gather your research using a more formalized approach, with written forms or questionnaires you compile.

Many solo entrepreneurs are hesitant to talk about their business ideas with others. Usually I hear two key reasons. The first is that they're afraid someone might steal their ideas. The second reason is just as common but often isn't verbalized: They don't want to hear anything negative about their ideas or plans.

If you let either of these reasons stand in the way of obtaining valuable feedback and research on your potential solo enterprise, you've done yourself a great disservice. First, ask yourself if you're *really* keeping an open mind—because if you are, then you know that the feedback you receive, both positive and negative, can help you in the long run. No one says you have to *accept* everything everyone says. Just *consider* it, and do so with an open mind.

Regarding the issue of stealing ideas: Yes, you do have to be cautious about sharing your ideas. There *is* a degree of protection that's needed—you wouldn't want to tell your detailed plans to a potential competitor. But keep in mind that there is a *huge* gap between having an idea and executing it. We'd all be wealthy if we had a dollar for every person who's come up to us and said they had a great business idea. What's different about *you* is that you're taking *action* on your idea. That's the quantum leap between the thought and the realization of a dream. So be cautious, but also remember that only a small percentage of people actually possess the energy you have to make your dream come true. And while they may not have the persistence you have to make a business idea a reality, they might offer some great feedback you can use on your path to success.

Listening to negative comments about new business plans is not most people's idea of a good time. But if you keep your mind open wide enough and try to really listen to the central objection, you can often learn a great deal. Many solo business owners-to-be think that they have open minds about their plans—until they hear a negative remark. Slam! You can almost hear their minds snap shut. They think they're open, but they've spent so much time, energy, and ego in putting together all their plans that they can't stand the thought of someone not agreeing that it's a perfect business.

Seasoned solo workers, by comparison, know that no business is ever perfect. They understand that learning is an ongoing process and that there is always some way to improve their current operations. They also know that negative feedback may come from people who don't fully understand an idea, which may mean you haven't communicated it clearly enough. The tweaking and fine-tuning go on forever—in fact, it's what keeps many solo entrepreneurs actively interested in their work, long after the thrill of launching the business has passed.

So toss your ideas to others and see what comes back. Talk to friends and family, but remember that they often will just parrot back the kind words you want to hear. Try to find people who fit the profile of your potential customers, and listen closely to their ideas and needs. Often it's best to keep the question structure open, such as: "I'm thinking of starting a [whatever] business. Is this something you might patronize? If so, what would you like it to do for you?"

If you don't feel comfortable being so personal, ask the questions in an indirect way: "A friend is thinking of starting this business . . ." You may gather more honest answers if the respondents don't have to worry about your feelings.

Then, once you've asked, *listen*. That's often the hardest thing for solo entrepreneurs to do during this process. They are bursting with their ideas, and they end up doing all the talking. This may make you feel great for the moment, but, unfortunately, it doesn't help you half as much as actively listening to your potential customers. Squash the notion that if you didn't think of an idea, it must not be any good. Keep a small notebook with you to jot down their feedback, and thank them sincerely for their ideas. Then as you refine your business plans, refer to your notes. It's a delight to rediscover a marvelous suggestion from a casual conversation.

Words of Wisdom

On Researching New Business Ideas

Successful solo entrepreneurs know that soliciting feedback from potential customers is an important part of refining new business ideas. Here are some insights from an experienced independent professional on how to conduct your own informal market research.

"My solo business creates fashion accessories and markets them in crowded, competitive retail environments—so I need to be open to customers' ideas and feedback. If I'm promoting my line at an in-store event or 'trunk show,' I actively solicit customers' comments and suggestions on my products.

"Customers who say 'yes' and buy my product give me the best feedback of all. But those who say 'no' are important, too. With a few friendly, tactful questions, I can gain valuable insights into their real resistance. Maybe they're hesitating at the price, or color, or questioning the durability. Or maybe they're just not sure it's right for them.

Understanding the objection often creates selling opportunities—I can point out a lower-priced item in my line, show a different color, demonstrate the product's strength, or suggest they consider buying one as a gift. When they really don't want to buy, their comments can lead me to make changes in my approach, or direct me toward other product categories that could expand my potential market.

"Getting feedback from store buyers is also valuable. They have a pulse on what's selling, what's needed, and what's just starting to emerge. I also turn to my suppliers for input. They sometimes know of new supplies or ideas that can generate innovative products, easy line extensions, or a fresh approach to the products I make."

—Ellen Leanse

Ellen Leanse founded KEEPERS—Jewelry That Works, in Menlo Park, California. Her fashion accessories were carried by a major national retail chain and at select boutiques across the United States until she sold the business, at a profit, to a solo entrepreneur with a similar vision.

The Triangle for Success

You've answered the questions, you've browsed the "Solo Business Directory" (Appendix B) you've done your research on potential customers. Do you feel as if you're creating this stew that is simmering with ideas? You are! And it's filled with wonderful flavors—the spices of suggestions, new ideas, options, and opportunities. Most of all, it's a recipe created uniquely for you.

The process of choosing a solo business that I've outlined in this chapter may take weeks, months, or even years. It all depends on how ready you are to launch your solo enterprise and how quickly you want to begin working solo. That timing is unique to each person. Some ideas spring forth, fully formed. Others simmer for years, waiting for the opportune moment. Whether you're launching your solo effort right now or a year from now, it's important to keep this stewpot of ideas simmering in your head. Every activity you do adds its flavor.

As you complete the selection process put forth in this chapter, it's time to whittle down your ideas to the one solo business you want to pursue. That's not to say you can't change or adapt your ideas as we continue our journey together. You should expect that and even welcome those alterations. But from this point forward, I'll be assuming that you have a fairly good idea of the type of business you want to establish. I'm also counting on you to have some idea, however vague, of who your customers will be—and on your understanding your business idea well enough to know that there are potential customers waiting for you out there.

As we leave this chapter, I want to share with you one last way of discovering if you've found the perfect business for you. I call it the Triangle for Success, because these three points lay the foundation for every successful solo business. When you feel strongly about all three elements, your chances for success are enhanced greatly.

1.   I believe in the work I do.

I would enjoy it, even if I were not paid a cent. I understand that the going may get rough, but I am committed to this work. My work brings me joy, and I will not get easily discouraged along my path to success.

2.   I respect the customers my work brings to me.

I enjoy interacting with the types of people my business brings my way. Through good times and bad, I understand these customers and want to serve them. The type of people who are my customers bring me as much satisfaction as my work, and they are an important part of my life.

3.   I enjoy bringing my work and my customers together.

I am committed to making a bridge between my work and my customers. I firmly believe that the lives of my customers will be improved by the product or service my business offers to them. Because of this belief, I hold no negative feelings about selling my product or service. I know that promoting my business means that my customers' lives will be enhanced.

All three parts of this triangle are important. For you, one segment may be weaker than others. You may not have the burning passion for the work, or may not enjoy interacting with people, or may dislike the notion of selling. But over time, you will need to develop each of these elements to its fullest strength, for each plays an important role in the success of your business.

Engineers will tell you that a triangle is among the most stable structural forms. (Have you ever noticed how a chair or table can rock, but a three-legged stool does not?) This Triangle for Success is also a stable base, for your satisfaction and for the success of your solo business. When all three legs are strong, the union creates both balance and power for your business to grow.

As we move forward on our journey, review the answers and information you've found in this chapter—information about yourself and about the business that now seems a perfect match for you.

Remember: Your passion + the need | customers = opportunity for you.

You've made your choice, and you are ready to embark on the next part of our working solo journey. Congratulations! You have completed the initial "it's only a dream" stage and are on your way to making your success a reality.

PART II

THE DECISION

L ike the adjustments you make with a camera lens before you snap a photo, the exercises we've done up to now should be helping you bring your solo business ideas into focus. As you stretch to think about the many different ways of turning your dreams into a business, are you getting a clearer picture of what makes the right fit for you?

Finding that fit was our goal in Part I. Now that you've achieved a clarity of what you want your solo business to be, you're ready to make something happen. Moving forward with your decision, by firming up plans, is our goal in Part II. The early stages of decision making are important ones to any new business. They create the basis for what a business becomes and what it can achieve in the years ahead. By laying a strong foundation, you'll empower your business to grow to the heights you want and not be toppled by the slightest setback or crisis.

How to use these important business building blocks is our focus in the next four chapters, as we begin to draw up the blueprint for your solo success. Whether it's how to craft a business plan, funding your business, or securing those first accounts, you're on the right track. Remember to keep your notebooks and markers ready—we're on our way to building a solid foundation for your solo business success.

Chapter 3

Charting Your Road Map to Success with a Business Plan

> *As important as your past is, it is not as important as the way you see your future.*
>
> *—Tony Campolo*

When mountain climbers prepare to scale a major peak, they make detailed plans. They know that reaching their goal—the summit—is not done by waking up one morning and deciding it's a good day to take a stroll. Months of preparation are needed for a major climb, because a lot is at stake. They calculate the terrain, the influence of the weather, their crew's abilities, and other important factors. The climbers know that the exhilaration of reaching the summit is the result of many careful hours of planning done thousands of feet below.

Your destination is the mountaintop where your business success lies waiting. Like professional climbers, to reach your desired goal you need a map and a detailed plan of attack for the climb. For the solo entrepreneur, those tools are found in a business plan.

Why Most Business Owners Resist Business Plans

It's a sad fact that many new business owners don't see this obvious relationship between planning and success. They think they can "wing it" and make their plans as they go along. Some feel that a business plan would limit their creativity or spontaneity. Others are in the dark about where to begin.

Of the dozens of reasons that business owners resist using business plans, here are five I hear most frequently when I'm speaking to small business owners. Read on and see if you've been raising these same objections to writing a business plan, and discover how a change in your thinking can lead to fewer headaches, greater peace of mind, and increased chances for success as you grow your business.

Excuse #1: My Business Is Simple. Plans Seem Too Complex.

It's true that some business plans seem complex. More often, it's the idea of a business plan that intimidates solo entrepreneurs.

In essence, a business plan is a guideline, a map for you to follow. It's created when you start your business, and it becomes a reference as you go along. Like a regular map, it keeps you on track to your final destination, points out potential obstacles along the way, and shows you the best route to reach your goal. Whether for a large business or a solo operation, a business plan generally contains common points of information. These include:

- ✓ A statement of purpose
- ✓ A business description
- ✓ An assessment of the market and a marketing plan, including channels of distribution
- ✓ A description of production of the product or service
- ✓ An assessment of management abilities
- ✓ A timetable and projections
- ✓ Projected finances

Large businesses often hire consultants to create extensive business plans for them, particularly if they are seeking venture capital or major funding. But business plans can be very basic documents and still be just as valuable. For a solo business, five to ten typed pages can contain all the information that's needed.

Excuse #2: Business Plans Are Only for the Big Guys. My Business Is Only Me, So I Really Don't Need a Plan.

Actually, *every* business can benefit from a business plan, no matter what size it is. The process of making a plan organizes your thinking and helps you sort out your priorities. Many times solo business owners will *assume* they have clear ideas and know where they are heading. Once an entrepreneur begins to formalize things on paper, he or she often reviews goals, operations, or marketing ideas at a deeper level and discovers that all the areas are not fully thought out. Writing a business plan provides the chance to change ideas or develop them further on paper, without the risk or cost of fully implementing them to see if they'll work.

Excuse #3: I'm Too Busy Trying to Get Everything Else Going in My Business to Write a Business Plan.

Launching your business will take time and energy. But without a plan, you can let emergencies take over, and reacting to them becomes the focus of your business. Seasoned solo professionals know that the hours spent creating a business plan are time invested well. Writing a plan helps you identify problems, correct organizational errors, establish priorities, and maximize your most valuable resource—your time.

A plan will also serve as the basis for your promotional materials. For example, when it comes time for a new brochure, you won't need to rethink your marketing approach and ask yourself, "Now, what am I trying to communicate to my customers?" You'll already know—it's in your plan.

Excuse #4: What If I Change My Mind after I've Written My Plan? I'm Afraid I Won't Be Able to Stay as Flexible.

A business plan is a guiding tool, but it's not cast in concrete. Small business owners who use their plans most effectively view them as organic documents—the plans change as the owners and businesses change. Especially if you've created your business plan on a computer, you'll find that you can easily update it to have it reflect your up-to-the-minute thinking on your business.

Ideas are the most ephemeral things. Haven't you mentally kicked yourself at times because you *know* there were some things that you had all worked out in your head—only now you can't remember all those inspired ideas? I know it's happened to me. In the weeks and months of launching your business, brainstorms will be flying fast and furious through your mind. But unless you capture them, they'll evaporate. The insights may come again—but maybe not. A business plan helps you keep the best of these ideas, but it is intentionally flexible enough to accommodate your changes. By committing your thoughts to paper, you create your personalized road map. That way, you don't have to start your thinking from point zero every time you want to tackle a business issue.

Your business plan will also be important as you solicit feedback from friends and advisors such as lawyers, bankers, or accountants. A written plan gives them an easy way to understand your business goals. If you'll be approaching a bank for funding, your business plan and your tax returns are the two most important documents they'll want to review. (But you may not have to turn to "expensive" bank money to fund your business—something we'll take a look at in Chapter 4.)

Excuse #5: I Don't Know How to Write a Business Plan, and I'm Afraid I Won't Do It the Right Way.

Yes, it's true, most small business owners are in the dark about how to write a business plan. They don't understand that there are two basic truths to remember:

1. There is no single right way to write a business plan.
2. While others may review a business plan, the most important person it serves is you, the business owner.

THE SECRETS OF WRITING A BUSINESS PLAN

The biggest secret about writing a business plan for a solo business is that there is no big secret to it at all. The mystery behind writing a business plan comes from those who don't understand its purpose as a basic road map. By the end of this chapter, no mystery will remain for you, because you'll have the core of your own plan in hand.

While there are no big, dark secrets, I do have a few tips for you as we begin:

1. *Don't fall into the trap of "paralysis of analysis."*
Try to stifle the urge to make each section of your plan perfect as you go along. It will drive you crazy, and it might put a halt to your progress. Just plow on ahead, even if you don't have every single detail right now. Remember, this is an *organic* document, which means it will grow and change over time.

2. *Keep a double vision of your business—of how you see it now and how you see it in three to five years.*
While you'll be writing your plan for your business as you see it now, don't forget that you're also trying to lay the foundation for where you'll be in the years ahead. Don't be afraid to think big—stretching your mind may bring you and your business other opportunities you can't even imagine right now.

3. *Give your plan time to stew—for a specific amount of time.*
A business plan, like a good pot of soup, gets better as you give it time to simmer. While it's possible to sit down and write your complete business plan in a single, intensive day, it's usually better if you can work on it over time. That way, the ideas can develop and be refined. At the same time, it's a good idea to give yourself a deadline—or else you're likely to have some scattered ideas of a business plan but no solid tool to guide you in your business launch.

These two points are particularly important for solo entrepreneurs, and that is why I encourage individuals launching independent businesses to write their own plans, as opposed to hiring someone else to do it for them. No one understands your dreams and goals as well as you do—and in the end, it will come down to you to follow or change your plan. If you feel you're not a great writer, have someone else polish the words later. But it's important that the plan reflect your passion for this new enterprise. And in writing it, you're going to learn a lot about yourself and what you want your business to become.

Unlike most solo entrepreneurs, who don't know how to write business plans, you have help: this book. And in the next section, I'll guide you through writing your very own business plan, step by step. Pull out your notebook and a pen, or prop this book up next to your computer, and get ready. Together we're going to create the document that will serve as your personalized road map to business success.

The Seven Must-Have Components of a Successful Business Plan

There are seven components to include in your business plan. First you need to . . .

1. State Your Purpose

This is a short section, but it may take some thinking (and some stewing time) until you distill the essence of your business purpose to a few sentences. Don't be intimidated—jump right in by brainstorming a list of all the reasons your business exists.

Begin by writing the sentence:

"The purpose of my business is _____ for _____."

The first blank is a brief description of your business activity the second concerns your customers.

Now, put your mind in gear and fill in the blanks. Your statement of purpose combines what a business does as well as reasons that a business exists. For example, if you're starting a catering business, your list might include phrases such as "to provide low-calorie, healthful food for harried working mothers," "to create one-of-a-kind cakes and desserts for upscale party hosts," or "to offer private residential dinners for homebound individuals who miss their favorite restaurant food." Don't pass judgment on your ideas here—just jot down your list.

Can you see that, even though we're beginning here, this section is actually one you'll come back to when you're completely *done* writing your plan? It's as if you'll be making the circle complete: After filling in all the other details, you'll come back to polish the *essence* of your business.

Your goal is to come up with one to three sentences that summarize your business and its customer focus. It's a challenge, but worth the work. Ask any experienced solo entrepreneur—your statement of purpose may be the most frequently spoken phrase out of your mouth during the first few months of your business. During that time, you'll be asked to explain to friends, relatives, business advisors, and potential customers what your new business is all about. If you've completed this exercise, you'll be prepared and come across as the intelligent, on-the-ball new business owner you are.

Sound like a worthwhile exercise? It is. It's startling how many new business owners can't explain in brief terms what their business is about. They mumble a few phrases or else ramble on and on (and on!), like a runaway freight train, hoping that someone will stop them before they derail. Often they don't even realize that their poor presentation has lost them a potential customer or supporter.

This disregard is due, in part, to the fact that, in this age of instant information, rapid-fire commercials, and MTV quick-cut videos, our attention spans are very brief. In fact, TV network news shows reported that during the last U.S. presidential election, the average sound bite lasted a mere *8.5 seconds*. Our fast-paced culture has trained us to tune out anything that lasts longer than those few seconds. That leaves little time for rambling, if you're a solo entrepreneur trying to get your message across.

So, as you write your statement of purpose, remember that you're striving to capture the *essence* of your business. Begin with a big list, then pare it down to those qualities you feel best represent your business goals.

Once you have this statement, of course, it becomes very useful in other ways, too. Can you see how a marketing slogan might come out of your statement of purpose? Or the basis of a marketing campaign?

Take your time to do this step, but don't expect to finish it at this point. Let it sit and simmer, and know that it will become clearer as you fill in the details of the other parts.

Now let's move on to the second part of your business plan, which asks you to answer the question . . .

2. What Business Is This?

In this section, you write a brief description of the business. Answer questions such as:

- ✓ What type of business is it?
- ✓ Where is it located?
- ✓ What are its major products and/or services?
- ✓ What are its unique features?
- ✓ What is the history of the business?
- ✓ What future directions could this business take?

Writing this section is a lot of fun, because you have a chance to really think about the *focus* of your business. How narrow or broad you make the scope of your business is a very personal decision, but it can have a significant impact on the success of your enterprise, both in its early period and in the years ahead. Too narrow, and you may be limiting yourself to a small niche without flexibility. Too broad, and you may have a difficult time convincing customers of the specific qualities that make your business special.

What do I mean by too narrow or too broad? Consider the person who wants to establish a public relations (PR) firm. Is this too narrow or too broad? That depends. If the person lives in a large community, with thousands of businesses needing PR services, he or she might focus the business on a single industry, such as real estate or financial services. If, on the other hand, the demand is not there, this exclusivity might be too narrow a focus for the business to survive. In that case, the business might expand to offer not only PR services but advertising or special events planning. (This is assuming, of course, that the person has the skills necessary to expand into these areas.)

Now, if this business owner decided that he or she really enjoyed the excitement of PR and stretched the business to include not only writing press releases and planning special events but coordinating industry conferences, then the business would have really changed focus. Is this strictly a PR business anymore? No, it's really a conference-planning business.

Choosing the focus of your business helps you focus your energies, too. Don't be tricked into feeling that once you decide, you can never change your mind. It's just the opposite—you can *always* change your focus. But not having one will leave you wattling and unsure of what you want to achieve.

Having a strong idea of your business focus will also help you put on blinders to distractions that will inevitably creep up in the early stages of your business. Say you run a medical transcription service out of your home. Then one day someone tells you that she's heard that people can make a lot of money selling medical home testing kits. Since you're in a medical-related field, she thought you'd be interested. Is this a distraction or a legitimate possibility for expanding your business? Because you have a clear idea of your business focus, you can easily decide that this opportunity is really a distraction from your core business, and it doesn't make sense for you.

Achieving a balance between narrow and broad, and staying flexible in your focus, are ongoing challenges because changes in your customer base, the economy, and other factors will all come into play. A classic example of this is the response of the American railroad industry in the early part of the twentieth century, when trucks started to haul freight. Instead of expanding into the trucking business, the railroads were convinced that traditional ways would continue and therefore made few changes to their business methods. Even as trucking opportunities continued to expand, they stuck to their stubborn ways. In just a few decades, the rail system that once was the pride of the United States was in shambles, and the former upstart trucking companies were now booming industries. The mistake? The railroads had viewed themselves as being in the railroad business instead of the *transportation* business.

Don't let your business focus prevent you from seeing other opportunities. If your business organizes children's birthday parties, are you in the events-organizing business? Could be. If you groom dogs, do you also do cats? If you do computer repairs, do you also fix VCRs? If your business maintains office parks, do you also do residential work?

All these choices are ones that *you* will make, as the owner of your solo business. Writing this section will give you a much clearer picture of the boundaries of your business. You'll know what you *do* and—just as important—what you *don't* do.

This section may be as long as you'd like, but five to eight sentences could be all you need to capture a summary of your business.

The third segment of your business plan goes hand in hand with understanding your business. It's time for you to . . .

3. Define Your Market

When asked why he robbed banks, outlaw Willie Sutton replied, straight-faced, "Because that's where the money is." (Are you chuckling? So did the courtroom. The judge, however, was not amused and sent him to jail.)

Like Sutton, your goal is to go where the money is. For you, the solo business adventurer, that means finding the market for your product or service.

For this section of the business plan, it's time to commit to two key things:

✓ Developing a profile of your customers, including why they will buy your product or service

✓ Determining how you're going to reach this market and convince them to buy

In the previous chapter, we talked about doing market research. After doing a series of exercises, you determined the viability of your business idea. Now it's time to take the process a few steps further. Our goal here is to determine not only *if* your business will succeed but *how well* and with *what customers.*

A word of encouragement here: Don't freeze up and think you don't possibly know these answers. You do. You probably just haven't completely explored all your ideas yet. Also, understand that the answers and figures you put down here are guesstimates. But that's okay, for aren't all plans guesstimates? We all have 20/20 hindsight and can see the past clearly, but no one can perfectly predict the future, no matter how shiny their crystal ball.

Try to make these answers and estimates as accurate as possible, based on information you've gathered. You'll have a much more useful tool if you don't pull figures out of the air or only go with your gut feeling. Base your results on careful thinking. Let's begin.

First, define your target market as precisely as possible. Get a picture in your head of your ideal customers. Are they of a certain age or gender? Specific profession? Income level? Marital status? Education level? Do they live in a particular region? What are their core interests or hobbies? Are your customers other businesses? If so, what are their needs or interests? (You might, of course, have an image of several types of people or businesses—if that's the case, imagine them all in a room somewhere, as if you're getting ready to greet them.)

Second, try to establish the size of your market. Keep in mind that there may be different segments. Be sure to consider which of these segments holds the *real* buying power. For example, if you make children's toys, it's obvious that one market segment is kids. But who has the buying power here? Kids do, but only to a limited extent. Parents are a key market segment—and grandparents may be the largest market segment of all.

Third, identify your competition. Find out who they are, their target market, their pricing, the sales and marketing approach—anything you can. This is where the reconnaissance skills of you and your friends are put to work. Collect business cards, brochures, rate sheets, whatever competitive materials you can. It's not that you have to mimic their style or match every price, but you need to know the environment you're in. Customers will be choosing among you, so you need to know what you're up against and how you can win customers to *your* business.

Fourth, after you've reviewed the competition, it's time to determine some *unique selling points* that set you apart. If you face competitors who offer precisely the service or product you do, can you add something to make it different? A money-back guarantee? Lightning-fast service? Availability during more flexible hours? Higher quality? Lower price? Personalization to their needs? These are tools you can use to your advantage. Make a list of what makes your business truly *different.*

If your service or product is the same as a major competitor's, have you thought about shifting the focus of your business slightly? Is there a hole just waiting to be filled by you?

Fifth, consider all the ways in which you will reach this market—or if you have several markets, the ways you will reach *each* market. In person? By mail? Through stores? By catalog? By phone? Through newspaper articles or advertising? On billboards? Which avenues make sense for you? You may outline some low-cost approaches for the early stages of your business and also include some more expensive ones as planned for the future. Jot down all your brainstorms, and choose the ones that offer the best mix of *cost* and *reach*—that is, how many pennies (or dollars) it will take to inform enough customers so that a certain number will actually *buy* your product or service.

In doing this step, you may want to pull out your calculator or plug some numbers into a computer spreadsheet. Your goal is to find quantifiable figures, so your judgment isn't based on seat-of-the-pants guidance.

Last, it's time to realistically appraise the potential you have to make money with *this* business, in your target market, using the methods you've just outlined. Think about current potential as well as growth trends. And remember, the more data you can gather, the more informed—and accurate—your estimates will be.

Now it's time to turn all these notes into a few paragraphs or formulas, to capture the essentials of your market and marketing plan. Have you discovered that doing these steps has clarified your thinking? Good. Remember, as you let ideas simmer, new ones will come to you, and your focus will become even clearer. That's the role of a strong business plan. An extra bonus: Now that you have it down on paper, you don't have to start from ground zero every time you want to think about a marketing plan.

You now have a better grasp than ever before of who your customers are, what product or service you will offer, and why these customers will buy from *you* rather than from others.

Words of Wisdom

On Defining Your Business

To succeed as an independent professional, it's important to have a clear understanding of the focus and boundaries of your business. Here are some insights from an experienced entrepreneur about defining your business.

"Writing a business plan is one thing; being able to succinctly describe what your business does is another. The best place to start is with the vision for your business. If you are foggy about your vision, it's time to get clear! Take some quiet time and project three years into the future. Envision what the business looks like and what your lifestyle is like as a result of your efforts.

"If you're having trouble visualizing this image from the future, use the following questions as a guide. What do you do? Which markets do you serve? Who are your target customers and clients? Where do you do business? How do your clients benefit from doing business with you? Why do your clients like doing business with you?

"Once you have clear answers to these questions, practice saying what your business does in simple language. If you're using buzz words or sophisticated language, you will not be communicating your message as effectively as you can. Practice describing your business to your 12-year-old niece—if she understands it, then you're on the right track.

"Practice saying your description in a short period of time—ten seconds or less—and test it on different people. You may be surprised how others view what you do. People have a short attention span, so bring the essence of what you do into a few short phrases.

"This exercise is not easy, and as your business grows, your answers to the questions will change. By reviewing the definition of your business every six months, you'll be able to identify what has changed in your three-year vision, and in how you describe your business."

—*Lisa M. Aldisert*

Lisa M. Aldisert is a consultant, professional speaker, and author specializing in business and life transitions. Based in New York City, she coaches entrepreneurs and executives who want to achieve peak performance and profitably grow their companies.

Even if you haven't nailed down every single detail of your plan the first time through these steps, you've already joined the ranks of an elite group of entrepreneurs. Which entrepreneurs, you ask? The ones who know that careful planning for success is the first step in reaching it—people who are enjoying their solo success because they planned for it, solo adventurers like you who understand that planning and success go hand in hand.

It's time now to review the physical operations of your business. In this fourth segment of writing your business plan, you'll . . .

4. Define Your Production Process

This section of your business plan will explain the physical aspects of your business, including how your product or service will be produced. We'll be looking at the answers to questions such as:

✓ What are your facility needs? Will your business need unusual space or physical requirements such as extra electric capacity, fuel, or light?

✓ Will you need any equipment? If so, what kind, and how much will it cost? Do you currently own it, or will you need to obtain it?

✓ Will you be dealing with suppliers? If so, who are they, and what products or services will they provide?

✓ Do you anticipate doing all the work yourself? Will you hire other independents? If so, who are they, what are their responsibilities, and what is their pay scale?

Perhaps the easiest way of thinking through this section is to imagine your business up and running. Picture in your mind what it is like to deal with a range of customers on a daily basis. Make a mental movie of each step of the process.

For example, imagine you will be running a yard maintenance business. On a typical day in this business, someone calls to contract you for work. What is your office setup like? What office equipment do you need? At least a telephone and an answering machine, in case you're not there, right? What else?

Later it is preparation time before leaving to complete the job. Do you use your own equipment? If so, what type? Do you put it into the back of a truck? How big is the truck? Do you own the truck, or is it rented or leased?

Don't forget to put yourself in the picture. What are you wearing? Do you need special protective gear?

Now imagine doing the work. Have you had special training? Are these skills you already know, or will you need to attend classes or other sessions?

If the task is large, do you hire others to assist you? What effect does this have on your equipment needs and overall operations?

After the work is completed (and the customer is smiling and telling you how great the yard looks), it's time to consider the details of payment. How do you handle your invoicing and bookkeeping? Did you sign a contract up front? Do you write the invoice out there on the spot? Is it created back in your office on a computerized system, then mailed out? Is there special equipment needed for any of this? If you aren't paid on time, what process do you have in place for collections?

Finally, imagine doing this job at different times of the year. What changes, if any, are there in equipment or procedures?

Even if your business will have little to do with yard maintenance work, I hope by now that you've been able to make the connection with your own business operations. Can you see how conducting such an imaginary walk-through gives you a chance to discover potential pitfalls in your operations? It also allows you to think through your equipment and training needs.

Unless your business activities are very complex, distillation to one or two paragraphs should be all you'll need for this section of your business plan. After reading them, even a complete stranger should be able to understand the basic operations of your business and the unique flavor you bring to doing your chosen work.

As we move from considering the day-to-day operations of your business, it's time to think about management issues and the people involved in making your business run. The fifth section of your business plan will focus on . . .

5. Managers, Associates, Advisors

As the owner of a solo business, you're the boss. But there are often many other individuals who play a role in the activities of your business. This section of your business plan addresses your abilities as the business owner and the role of others you've assembled to help you along the way.

Begin by summarizing in two to three sentences your particular abilities, training, or experience as they relate to the business. This may be as general as "I've been baking bread since I was 12 years old," if you're starting up a baked-goods business. Or "My degree is in botany and I've worked for the past four years at Evergreen Garden Center," if your business is focused on landscaping.

Next, mention any associates you intend to involve in your business and the role you see them playing. What are their skills and qualifications? What benefits will they bring to your business? Are they also independents? How will they be paid?

Third, list the individuals who will serve as your advisors, such as a lawyer, an accountant, or an insurance agent. In Chapter 4 we'll explore how to pull together such a team. For now, list these people and how their expertise will help you manage your business better.

Finally, describe the procedures that you'll follow to make sure you're running the business instead of having it run you. Will you have regular meetings with your advisors? Will you set aside a certain time each month and each quarter to review your finances and your operations plans?

This section will indicate to others that you understand that your solo business doesn't operate in a vacuum. It will help you identify others to whom you can turn for advice and assistance. And if you're using your business plan to raise money for your enterprise, it will demonstrate that you've carefully thought through your management needs. Your funders will feel more secure knowing that other skilled professionals are standing by to assist you—and making sure their investment is used well.

One or two paragraphs may be all you need to summarize the management section. It will depend on how detailed your plan becomes regarding advisors and associates.

The sixth section of your business plan lays out the time frame of your business launch and its growth plans. Let's now move on and discover how to . . .

6. Chart Your Timetable

Something powerful takes place when you finally pull out a calendar and set specific dates for your business to happen. Dreams and plans make the leap from imagination to reality. You make the shift from "someday" to "Monday, the 15th," and all of a sudden a business becomes more concrete.

In the chapters ahead, you'll learn how to turn a calendar into a powerful tool and become a master of time management. For now, this section of your business plan is designed to give you and those who will read it a better understanding of the timetable of key events for your business.

Here you should chart dates for launching the business and your target growth dates and goals. For example, if you're starting a financial consulting business, you might establish a launch date, then specify that "after six months, my goal is to have ten regular clients." A business centered on a product might project that "the product line will expand to include at least two new items every six months."

As you make your projections, remember that *you* are the one making these projections—and they're primarily to guide you. Ask yourself how these goals feel. How do the weeks and months chart out? Are they realistic? Break down the timeline to weekly milestones and see if the tasks can be achieved in the given time frame.

These projections are not intended to boast or prove to others that you can make your business huge overnight. Actually, you may find that keeping things small has its advantages—chiefly, that your venture is easier to control. If you're seeking outside funding, bankers and financial advisors will be more impressed with the fact that you have charted realistic growth rather than grand schemes that may be risky and too difficult to accomplish. As seasoned entrepreneurs know, it's often better to *under*promise and *over*deliver.

In this section, also include two other general projections: one for three years out, another for five to seven years in the future. These need to be only in the most general sense, but they will give you a long-range target on which to focus. They'll also reveal to you and others what you envision as the big picture for your business and where you intend to be in the future. Isn't it exciting to cast your imagination that far? It's the first step toward getting there.

The seventh, and last, segment of your business plan concerns money. It's here that you'll . . .

7. Calculate Your Finances

Now that you've pulled together many of your thoughts about the details of your business—what it is, who it will serve, how it will operate, where it is headed—it's time to crunch the numbers and calculate the financial aspects.

There are three key reports that form the basis for financial analysis and decision making in small businesses. As small business consultant Gerry Dodd explains, they are:

✓ *Profit and loss statement.* This is also known as a *P&L* or an *income statement.* It is a summary of the financial performance of a company over a given period of time (typically quarterly or yearly). It shows the difference between your income and your expenses for the period. A P&L statement helps you analyze how the business got where it is and gives you an idea of what may be expected in the future. (A sample P&L statement can be found in Figure 3.1.)

✓ *Balance sheet.* The balance sheet presents a complete financial picture of a business on a given date—its *assets* (things you own, such as equipment), *liabilities* (debts you owe), and ownership of the business. It is usually prepared as of the last day of a month and answers the question, "How did we stand financially at that time?" It shows you whether you own the business or your creditors do. Since a balance

SAMPLE PROFIT AND LOSS STATEMENT

Northern Lights Graphic Design
For the quarter ended March 31

REVENUE		**$78,750**
Cost of Goods Sold		
Printing	28,500	
Supplies	5,500	
Subcontracted services	12,000	
Total Cost of Goods Sold		(46,000)
EXPENSES		
Entrepreneur's salary	13,000	
Payroll taxes	995	
Utilities	1,050	
Equipment	375	
Insurance	650	
Postage/courier	750	
Promotional expense	2,400	
Travel/entertainment	425	
Professional development	395	
Professional services	1,500	
Dues and publications	400	
Total Expenses		**(21,940)**
Net Income before Taxes		10,810
Taxes	(3,243)	
NET PROFIT		**$ 7,567**

Figure 3.1 Since solo businesses vary greatly, it is difficult to create a typical profit and loss statement. Use this example as a guide, and adapt it to your own financial picture during your business planning. The business featured here is an established home-based graphic design firm (low overhead, no rent expense). During the quarter, the solo entrepreneur did several projects that required outside independent contractors and payment to vendors such as printers (Cost of Goods Sold).

(Continued) ➡

The entrepreneur is experienced enough to know that a salary is not allocated out of profits, but is a budgeted business expense, along with appropriate payroll taxes that must be paid regularly.

During the quarter, the designer attended a professional conference and created a promotional campaign to generate new business. It also was necessary to travel to meet with a client several hours away.

This hypothetical example demonstrates the myth of measuring business success by gross revenue. Notice the relationship between the final net profit and the original revenue figure. A company's revenue may be impressive, but if expenses are not managed properly, a business can still lose money. By carefully tracking revenue, expenses, and profits over time, solo professionals can assess how well their business is doing.

sheet includes anticipated revenues and expenses, as well as assets, it gives a much truer financial picture of a business than a profit and loss statement.

✓   *Cash-flow statement.* As its name implies, a cash-flow statement shows the flow of cash into and out of a business. It tells how much cash is needed, when it will be needed, and if you need to borrow. One of its most valuable uses is to alert you to potential cash shortages enough in advance so you can budget accordingly. Creating a regular cash-flow statement can dramatically increase your company's chance of success as a profitable operation. It forces you to be more realistic and disciplined in your thinking by always focusing your attention on the bottom line—on the economics of the situation.

In the chapters ahead, we'll explore in greater detail how to use these three tools to guide your business. While they may sound confusingly similar to you right now, you'll soon know how to use them on a regular basis. They're like a financial mirror—they reflect back to you how well (or poorly) your business is doing and alert you to steps you should take to keep your business on track.

For purposes of writing your business plan, you'll want to include a projected profit and loss statement, a simple balance sheet, and a projected cash-flow statement.

Making Your Projections

If your business is up and running, your financial reports will be based on actual numbers and your best guesstimates of future business activity. If you're starting fresh, try to compile realistic estimates based on your research and understanding of your business needs and goals.

Remember, these figures are not set in stone. They can be refined and updated as your information and business ideas change. Take care in compiling them, however, since they will be an important tool in guiding you to solo business success.

Projected P&L Statement

If your business has been going for some time, your business checkbook already provides the basis for a P&L statement. If you're just launching your business, you'll want to create a projected P&L statement for the first year of business.

To begin, estimate the typical income and expenses you anticipate in a given month in your business. The easiest way to do this is to create two sheets of paper, labeled "income" and "expenses." Now go back through your notes and scan through your thoughts on your daily operations. Consider all the expenses you will incur as you do business.

First, consider overhead expenses. These are expenses that you will incur, whether you do a freightload of business or none at all. They include, but are not limited to, the following:

- ✓ Rent (if applicable)
- ✓ Utilities, including telephone
- ✓ Office equipment
- ✓ Office supplies
- ✓ Insurance
- ✓ Taxes
- ✓ Bank charges
- ✓ Professional services
- ✓ Dues and publications

Don't forget to include overhead expenses that may be particular to your business, such as:

- ✓ Special equipment
- ✓ Vehicles
- ✓ Licenses or registrations

Then consider expenses that may vary according to the amount of promotion you do, such as:

- ✓ Marketing materials (brochures, flyers, and so on)
- ✓ Postage
- ✓ Advertising

In some businesses, there will be expenses that vary based on the quantity of work you do, including:

✓ Raw materials or merchandise
✓ Subcontractors
✓ Shipping/freight

If some of these expenses are one-time start-up costs, indicate that on your list with a star or asterisk. Stationery, business cards, and brochures, for example, are expenses that you won't have every month, but you will have to account for them in the first few months of your business.

Next, on the second sheet, tally your projected income. Estimate how many customers you will have in a month and how much income you expect to take in. Yes, this may be difficult to project, but make a guesstimate based on your research. Also, by adding up your expenses, you'll have a pretty good idea of how many customers you *must* have each month to stay afloat.

Your start-up costs, your marketing expenses, and fewer customers may result in your business not showing any profit in the first months. That's why it's important to have a projected P&L for the entire first year of your business—so you can carefully follow if you're on track for the date you expect to break even or make money.

Projected Balance Sheet

If your business is already under way, you can create a simple balance sheet by listing the assets of the business (such as equipment, inventory, accounts receivable) against the liabilities (debts such as bank loans, accounts payable, or income taxes payable). The final figure will indicate if you or your creditors own your business at this time.

If you're just launching your business, your projected balance sheet will be fairly straightforward, since we're assuming that you may have a few assets, such as equipment, but probably few loans or other liabilities.

Projected Cash-Flow Statement

This financial report will vary a lot, based on the type of business you have. Do you need to buy large quantities of materials or supplies in advance of making an income? Will you keep an inventory of items? If so, then cash-flow projections will be crucial to running your business, since your suppliers will want to be paid, and you may not have customers who have paid you at that time.

If, however, your business operates as a service business that bills customers upon completion of the work, your cash-flow situation may be a bit simpler. That's not to say you don't need a projected cash-flow statement, however. You will always have *some* monthly costs to cover, and a project may have expenses you may be required to cover in advance. Unfortunately, you may have customers who don't pay you right on time. A projected cash-flow statement will also help you budget for the four times a year your estimated tax payments are due.

Each of these three reports will be on a single sheet of paper at the end of your business plan. They may take a while to prepare—hang in there!—but they'll be very valuable tools for you as you launch your business and in the months ahead. Also, once you set up your company's finances on a computer, you'll discover that business financial software can generate these reports quickly and easily, so you'll never need to be in the dark about where your finances stand on any single day, at any moment.

Celebrate!

If I were standing next to you now, I'd give you a warm handshake and a pat on the back. Congratulations! You've done it! Yes, it takes a lot of thinking to put together a business plan. (Can you see now why so many people decide just to "wing it"? An unwise choice for them and their businesses, though.)

But *you* have persevered. Sure, your plan may not be in tip-top shape right now. Let it simmer for a few days, then go back and give it that last little bit of polish that it needs. The hardest part—getting started—is behind you.

I want to applaud you for sticking with it. I know it's tough to wade through all these details sometimes—particularly when all you *really* want to do is start your business. But after the first glory of launching your business has passed, you'll have something few other solo businesses have when they begin: a solid plan to take you through the early stages, and a much better chance of long-term success.

As we close out this chapter, I'd like to share with you two other important points about your business plan.

Looks Can Make a Difference

Now that you've put all this effort into *writing* your plan, make sure you spend a few moments more making it look professional. Check spelling and grammar, and print out a clean computer-generated copy. It will give your presentation much more substance—and even if you're using your business plan primarily for your own purposes, your efforts deserve the polish of a finished, professional document.

If you'll be approaching a bank for funding, the physical presentation of your business plan can be just as important as its content. The bank wants assurances that you are serious and professional—and that any money it may lend you will be in good hands.

Even if you won't be asking for a loan, your business plan can play an influential role in other dealings with your bank. When I was establishing my solo business several years ago, I remember the hoops I had to jump through to get credit card merchant status (the ability for customers to buy things from me with their credit cards). I was hitting endless brick walls of bureaucracy until I found one bank manager who took a closer look at my business plan. It was only about six to eight pages, but it was laser printed, and I had included some graphs and charts indicating projected income and sales growth. I remember her flipping through the pages, her eyes getting big, and a smile on her face as she told me, "No problem." That brief moment was worth every single hour I put into creating that business plan—for the later success of my business hinged a great deal on credit card orders.

Your business plan may serve a similar role for you, giving you a needed boost from a bank, advisor, or other outside professional. Make sure the information you convey in your plan *looks* as important as you know it is.

Plan Your Work, Work Your Plan

The final tip of this chapter is: *Use* your plan. I'm always pleasantly surprised when I ask new business owners if they have written a plan and they say yes. But I'm startled when I discover how many of these plans are gathering dust in some desk drawer. "Yeah, I wrote a plan once. It's around here somewhere. . . ."

You've spent the time and energy writing this plan so you could have a *working tool* to guide you in your business. Resist the temptation to toss your plan into some bottom drawer once you've finished writing it or are through with the bank.

Remember, your plan is designed as a personalized road map for your business. Refer to it often, update it as you reach your intermediate destinations, and add to it with new ideas. In a later chapter we'll return to this plan, to check in and see how your business is growing and to discover new ways to get the most from these written goals and projections.

In the meantime, persevere to capture all your energy, ideas, and enthusiasm for your new business on paper. I promise, it *is* worth it. No one will care about this business as much as you do—and only *you* know what special dreams of yours can come true through this business. Commit to making these dreams a reality—bring them to life by first putting them on paper. Let your business plan be your written companion and guide on your solo journey to success.

Now let's move on to explore another side of working solo—a part that makes you realize that you're not in this alone.

Chapter 4

Finding Support:
Money, Advisors, and Friends

No man is an island, entire of itself . . .

—John Donne

When you've heard John Donne's poetic lines in the past, you probably weren't thinking they applied to solo businesses. That's okay—Donne wasn't thinking of spirited entrepreneurs when he wrote those words in the seventeenth century, either. What Donne captured, however, is the understanding that every individual needs to be part of a greater whole—a concept that is a key ingredient to solo success.

In this chapter we look at the many ways to get support—in financial terms, to get money for your business in professional ways, to find qualified advisors for your new enterprise, and, on a personal level, to enrich you as a person while you're growing your business. Since all these levels of support stem from building a solo success team, let's begin there. Then we'll move on to the ten most popular ways to launch a solo business financially.

Working Solo Is Not Working Alone

In contrast to common first impressions, working solo is not about turning your back on the rest of the world and becoming a hermit. There's no burrowing deep into a private office, creating a secret world, and letting no one in. That may be a fun escape for a day or so, but—whew! We'd drive ourselves crazy. More important, our isolation would drive our businesses into failure.

We all need other people in our lives. For a solo worker, a network of friends and advisors becomes a lifeline for success. Friends and colleagues can help you find clients, provide you with funding or point you in the right direction, sort out new business ideas, offer feedback on that brainstorm you have, guide you in legal and financial matters, and keep you balanced between the work and nonwork parts of your life.

In a regular job, these supportive activities happen among coworkers—over lunch, at meetings, during impromptu hallway gatherings, or while chatting informally at the watercooler. As a solo worker, you'll have to put forth the effort to create your own support network. The upside of this is that you'll be able to choose some topflight talent to advise you, instead of relying on whoever stops by the watercooler—who may or may not be able to help you.

I've always enjoyed the image of a network, particularly a network of people. In my mind's eye, I see a meshwork of individuals, linked through the holding of the hand or foot of another, creating a continuous grid pattern. There's variation in the detail of the grid, since one person may be larger or smaller, male or female, young or old. Each brings unique qualities to the framework. I always get a reassuring feeling about this image, because I know that it is an image of strength—if one link becomes weak or breaks, the overall framework will stand.

Such is the network you will build for your solo business. Interconnected with many others, you will share in their unique insights and strengths. Your business will be stronger because of this network, because all those links provide an underlying support grid for you.

Growing this network is one of the joys of working solo. Your "success team" will change and grow, just as your business does the same. You'll meet new people with whom to share ideas, and later you'll be able to connect others to individuals building their own network.

Your success team will enrich your life on many levels, including making your business prosper. Let's explore how to grow one that benefits you and your solo business.

Putting Together Your Solo Success Team

As seasoned solo professionals know, working on your own challenges you to understand the unique abilities that you have—and to fully appreciate your limitations. A solo workstyle brings some practical limitations—after all, you are only one person. Once you've discovered your niche, based on your abilities and your interests, your task is to learn, find, hire, barter, or invent the other skills and things you need.

No one can be an expert in every area. But there is one skill you *must* develop if you're to succeed at working solo.

> *The most valuable skill you can develop to ensure your solo success is the ability to connect with others.*

You need to find experts and advisors so you can tap into their knowledge and experience. Sound obvious? It is. But you'd be surprised at how many new solo workers are afraid to admit they don't know *everything*. Remember, *no one* knows everything, not even the masters of business who have amassed fortunes while building their empires.

What they *do* know is how to overcome their deficiencies by connecting with people who are experts in these areas. You can do the same. Your task is to find advisors who are knowledgeable, experienced, and approachable. They should share your passion for making your business a success. Who will you need, and how can you find them? Let's take a look.

Many Needs, Many Advisors

Just as your solo business requires you to wear a lot of different business hats during a day, you need a variety of advisors on your solo success team. Some may bring skills and experience that are more general; others may specialize in a very precise area. Below are some general categories of advisors. In the section following this one, we'll talk about how and where to find them.

Small Business Advisors

One of the best sources for general information on small business is Uncle Sam. The U.S. Small Business Administration, known as the SBA, is set up to "aid, assist, and protect" the interests of small businesses. To accomplish this goal, the SBA offers a wide variety of information and services, often at little or no cost.

The SBA sponsors Small Business Development Centers (SBDCs) in every state, often at universities. Bringing together the resources of the university, the local private sector, and the government, these centers provide entrepreneurs free one-on-one counseling with professional advisors on all aspects of starting and running a business. Most participants receive approximately ten hours of counseling, and follow-up studies show a remarkable success rate in the businesses that have participated. Some SBDCs also house resource libraries; others organize workshops or seminars on small business topics, often at low cost. To find the SBDC nearest you, contact your area SBA office (details below).

A valuable SBA resource partner is the volunteer advisory program known as SCORE (Service Corps of Retired Executives). All of the nearly 13,000 SCORE members are retired or active businesspeople who have volunteered to share their knowledge and professional experience to help small business owners succeed. When you contact one of the SCORE offices, they'll ask you about your business and what you'd like to learn. Then they'll try to match a SCORE member's experience to your business needs. SCORE has 389 chapters throughout the United States and its territories. Some SCORE offices are located at SBDCs; others are at an independent site. To find the location of the SCORE office near you, call (800) 634-0245, or check out the SCORE Web site at http://www.score.org. Another bonus of the SCORE Web site: You can get one-on-one business counseling by e-mail!

Two other popular SBA programs are:

✓ A *publications program,* which features more than 50 booklets, reports, and videos on small business topics. Most of the publications cost $3 or less; videos are about $30. Call and ask for the free brochure listing available publications (details below and in Appendix B, "Solo Resources").

✓ A *loan program,* which works with local banks to support small businesses through guaranteed loans, seasonal lines of credit, handicapped assistance loans, and international trade loans. These loans, however, are sometimes tough to come by for solo entrepreneurs. Since one of the primary goals of the SBA is job growth, it often directs its financial support to businesses creating new jobs in the area.

There's one thing to keep in mind when working with the SBA. In the government's eyes, a small business is any enterprise with 100 employees or less. To us solo entrepreneurs, a business of 100 employees is *huge.* In its quest to have the greatest impact with increasingly scarce government dollars, the SBA may not give the highest priority to solo entrepreneurs. That said, I'd like to point out that all my dealings with the SBA as a solo business owner have been top-notch. Its representatives have been friendly and helpful. This organization has great information to share, and, after all, it is your tax money.

To receive more information about the SBA and its programs, check the blue (government) pages of your telephone book for the office near you. Or call the SBA's toll-free information hotline at (800) 827-5722. You'll get a voice-mail system that gives you access to recorded topics and tells you how to contact your local SBA office. The SBA also has a Web site at http://www.sba.gov that's filled with helpful information and links to other small business resources.

Legal Advisors

Technically you don't need a lawyer to start a solo business, but it's important to have one on your success team. Your success team lawyer can review contracts, advise you on legal status such as incorporating, keep you up to date on current legal changes and how they might affect your particular business, and generally keep you out of trouble legally.

Whether your legal advisor is a personal friend or a hired professional is a matter of individual choice. That's not to imply that a friend may be any more or less professional, or that a hired advisor is any less a friend. Some solo workers use only one legal person; others turn to a friend for general advice, then seek out a specialized professional for the details.

It's good to remember that law can be very specialized, and the good friend of yours who may know real estate law may not be as up to date on small business legal matters. Just because it's legal advice doesn't necessarily make it good legal advice for your situation. (This applies to all your advisors, and in the section below on interviewing advisors, you'll learn how to ask the important questions so that your advisors become a powerful addition to your team.)

Many solo workers have a concern about lawyers, often due to the fear of high fees for legal services. But I have found many independent lawyers—solo entrepreneurs themselves—who are willing to help fledgling business owners. They view their work with solo newcomers as a professional investment, since they know that a small company today can become a thriving business—and a valuable client—later on.

What's important is that you have a clear understanding of lawyers' fees and how they charge them, right from the beginning. Some offer flat fees and will handle common business procedures for a set price. (Negotiating to a fixed cost has its advantages: You can budget better, and you'll likely make full use of the legal expertise.) Other attorneys offer new business owners the option of working with a junior partner at a lower rate. With a clear mutual understanding, you can avoid awkward situations such as receiving an invoice for a ten-minute phone call that you thought was casual conversation.

Don't overlook the valuable legal information you can obtain on your own from books. Many solo workers do their basic legal research from books, then turn to lawyers for times of necessity. Armed with information as they enter their lawyers' offices, these entrepreneurs find they are better prepared to ask appropriate questions as that expensive legal clock ticks away. As a result, they get better value for the money they've spent.

The legal materials produced by Nolo Press are particularly good. Nolo focuses on self-help books and software that present legal information in a clear, easy-to-use manner. The company was started more than 25 years ago by two legal aid lawyers and has grown into a publishing company with hundreds of titles. A free two-year subscription to its quarterly newsletter, *Nolo News,* is available to anyone who orders a book or software program from the company. You can contact Nolo at (800) 992-6656, or visit the company's Web site at http://www.nolo.com. Many of the Nolo books that are especially helpful for small business also are featured in this book's companion volume, *Working Solo Sourcebook.*

Financial Advisors

Another key part of your solo success team is people who can help you with financial matters. These may include a tax preparer to assist you with IRS dealings, a financial planner to help you with current and retirement planning, or a certified public accountant (CPA) for bookkeeping and financial statements.

As with legal assistance, the groundwork begins with you. Your business will be strengthened if you know the essentials of your financial matters. Yes, you can expect to need help—but make sure you understand what is at the core of your business. Thinking "Oh, I thought so-and-so was taking care of that" is a sure step toward business disaster.

What type of financial advice will you need? That depends on the type and complexity of your business. If you're operating a part-time solo service business, your needs might be fairly straightforward: awareness of tax laws, billing and bookkeeping advice, perhaps an annual review to gauge how you're growing. On the other hand, if you're running a solo sales or manufacturing business, and you're dealing with dozens of small products, your needs could be more extensive, such as tracking inventory for tax purposes, record-keeping advice, collections methods, or calculating invoices and payments in different currencies if you're working internationally.

Financial advisors can also help you weigh the benefits of incorporating. They might help you decide whether you should buy or lease that new piece of equipment. Their suggestions on new ways to shelter your income from taxes may be worth their fees alone. Tax laws and other financial regulations for small business are always in flux. Like other members of your advisory team, financial professionals can fill you in on the information you lack, allowing you to make an informed decision with confidence.

Your bank also plays an important role in the financial planning aspects of your business. Take the time and energy to find a bank that feels right for you and your solo business needs. It may take some shopping, but once you've made the connection, you'll discover that a banker can play a key role on your success team—and for more reasons than just getting that loan when you need it (although that may be handy, too).

Marketing Advisors

Marketing includes tasks such as advertising, publicity, public relations, and packaging—all elements that help you put forward your best solo business image and entice your customers to buy your product or service.

Marketing advisors are as diverse as the tasks they do. You may turn to a graphic designer to create your business stationery or to design the package for a new product. Another marketing advisor may help you with a direct-mail campaign, showing you how to assemble a mailing list and prepare a snazzy brochure to reach potential buyers through the mail. A specialist in public relations may put you in contact with newspapers or magazines to write stories about your business service or product.

Marketing is a crucial step in the success of your solo business (and there's a whole chapter on it later). Unless you have a big bank account, you'll probably be doing most of it yourself—which is okay, since you understand your business the best. But there are times when it's preferable to call in outside professionals—either to refine your idea or to give you basic information on which you can build.

For example, if you have a great new product and are light on artistic skills, turn to a graphic designer to polish your efforts. If you have some ideas of what the package should look like, great. Pass them along to a designer—perhaps another solo professional—and let him or her work the artistic magic. Similarly, if you're trying to get a story about your business printed in the local paper, write up a media release (you'll find out how in Chapter 6). But if English wasn't your favorite subject in school, pass it along to a professional for a quick review and polish.

It's important to know when to call in the outside troops. Pediatricians may be licensed medical doctors, but they wouldn't attempt brain surgery. The parallel: Focus your skills on what you do best, and turn to professionals for advice—in this case, for marketing needs.

Finding and Interviewing Your Advisors

The advisors we've just discussed are what I call the Big Three: legal, financial, marketing. In a perfect world, they are your best friends and offer you advice at no charge. More likely, you'll be paying for these services. How do you find advisors who are worth your time and money and who will give you reliable information? Read on.

The most common way of finding a Big Three advisor is to ask fellow solo professionals. As you'll soon discover, word travels quickly about who has had success with—and who's been burned by—a professional advisor.

Once you've collected a few names and phone numbers, don't be shy about calling and interviewing them. You're trying to see if they would make a good match to you and your business needs. Make it clear that you're "shopping" at this time and that you're gathering information to make an informed decision. You're interested in the following three areas:

Experience

Ask each advisor what experience he or she has with small businesses or with self-employed individuals. What is the percentage of their business with solo business owners? Have they worked with businesses that are similar to yours in the past? If so, what services did they offer?

Also ask if they would be willing to give you the names of some current clients as references. They may want to check with these clients first before releasing their names—that's fine. But when you get the names, call these other business owners and interview them, too. Find out what type of work the advisor has done and how long they've been working together. Ask about the strengths and weaknesses they feel this advisor has.

Fees and Flexibility

Of course, one of your key interview questions will be about fees. Again, don't be shy, and don't hang up until you are very clear about how much the advisor's services would cost. If things are vague, you might say something like, "Now, as I understand it, if I wanted to have you do _____, it would cost me _____. Am I understanding you correctly?" This is a way of getting more specific information, and it often opens up the communication channels. Another approach is to use "for examples." "For example, if I needed to have _____ done, how would you approach doing it, and what would the fees be?"

Seasoned solo professionals advise that you let the person know up front that you're not a business with unlimited financial resources. Setting the correct expectation at the very beginning creates the basis for a clear understanding and a good future relationship, they explain.

Many professional advisors offer initial consultations at no charge, and one specific question to ask when shopping for advisors is whether they offer this option. A preliminary meeting is a good way to get a feel for an advisor's style and the possibility that the relationship would work. Look for professionals who are willing to familiarize you with business practices and who help you understand how to work with them effectively.

Don't forget to ask about payment requirements and what kind of flexibility there may be. Is payment expected immediately or within 30 days? Is the advisor open to nontraditional methods of payment, such as barter? Your service or product may be something the other professional needs—but you'll never know unless you ask.

One of the best questions I've learned to ask at the end, when you think you've covered everything, is: "Now, is there anything else you think I need to know that I haven't asked?" Boy, does *that* question sometimes bring up new information. It's a simple way to say "I think I understand everything, but what else haven't we covered?" It also makes it a shared responsibility that all the information has been exchanged.

Rapport

By the end of the interview, you should have a pretty good sense of your general rapport with the advisor and whether you think there's a personality match between you. Did the advisor show a genuine interest in your business? Did the advisor ask you questions about your business, or spend most of the time bragging and making a sales pitch.

Close the conversation by thanking the person for the time and restating that you're currently researching your needs and options. If the advisor has spent a lot of time with you, it might be appropriate to follow up with a quick note, even if you won't be using the person's services anytime soon.

Local or Long Distance?

In this day of computers, fax machines, and the Internet, your advisors can be literally anywhere in the world. I know solo business owners who use legal, financial, and marketing advisors who live across the country. They stay in touch by phone and online, and if business travel permits, they meet once or twice a year. That's as often as many New York City professionals see their advisors, too—even if they're just across town from each other.

Don't let distance deter you from finding and using the best advisors you can. If you've found a specialist who knows your business like no other and can help you succeed, you can make it happen at a distance. It might take a little more effort to exchange information and share ideas if you're not face to face, but the results may be worth it to you.

Whether near or far, choose your business advisors—especially those in the Big Three category—with care. Cost may be an important factor, but don't choose on that basis alone. The right advice may save or make you more money than their fees.

Whether you're paying with cash or with services in kind, remember that your relationship with your business advisors is a professional one. You may end up becoming friends, but you always want to be able to remain objective about the work they do for you. The focus should be on results, not the relationship. So choose them with care, and use them wisely.

Words of Wisdom

On Working with Advisors

Maximizing the effectiveness of professional advisors begins with understanding the nature of your relationship with them. Here are some thoughts from a seasoned entrepreneur to guide you.

"Success in working solo depends in part on playing to your strengths and finding others to help you minimize your weaknesses. Often that means turning to professionals for advice.

"It's important to have a rudimentary understanding of everything associated with your business. Then you can rely on specialists to fill in the gaps and to recommend certain courses of action. After you've received their guidance, it's up to you to factor in your own knowledge and experience before you make a decision.

"No matter how skilled your advisors, don't be tempted to abdicate responsibility for any decision affecting your business. Remember, no one knows, cares about, or has a greater stake in your business than you.

"Also, don't confuse advisors with clean-up workers. If you walk into your CPA's office and dump a bag of receipts on her desk and say, 'Thanks. I'll be back in a few weeks,' she's not an advisor, she's a tax preparer. If you work in partnership with your advisors, you can develop specific strategies and techniques that will benefit your business year-round, making it stronger over time."

—Mark Kawakami

A longtime solo entrepreneur, Mark Kawakami is head of After Hours Communications Corporation, an advertising and design firm in Los Angeles, California. He is also the Executive VP/Marketing of Aportis Technologies Corp., a start-up personal computing software concern.

Just as valuable as the advice you get from paid professionals is the support you find from your peers, friends, and family. Each brings to your solo success team an understanding of you and your business. With an open mind, you can learn a lot from their input.

Peer Support

As the saying goes, "Birds of a feather flock together." Experienced solo workers know that some of the best advice and support they receive comes from other independent workers. As solo workers, we all admit we can't stay up to date on everything. In exchange, each of us keeps others informed of news, legal or tax developments, the latest technology, the best place to buy office supplies, or that great new restaurant in town.

Fellow solo workers and advisors are found in many places. Some you may meet at a regional or national conference, or a trade show of your specialty. Others may be neighbors or members of the local PTA. As the network expands, your colleagues will introduce you to others they think share a common interest with you.

This network of professional colleagues can include individuals both near and far. Telephones, modems, and fax machines allow long-distance relationships to flourish. I feel lucky to have many colleagues scattered around the country. Fortunately, many of them are connected to the Internet. Even though I may see these colleagues face to face only once or twice a year, I stay in touch with them every few weeks. We exchange hellos, news, questions, information, contacts, and support across the miles. Without this network, my decisions would be made in isolation and my business opportunities wouldn't be as plentiful.

I encourage you to seek out these contacts, for both professional and personal development. Find out about professional organizations in your field and join. Attend meetings if you can, and get involved. You have much to learn—and to share.

Other solo entrepreneurs know better than anyone else exactly what we're going through as independent professionals. As I see it, we're all on different rungs of the solo success ladder. You may have a question about something you've never tried, so you turn to someone a few rungs higher on the ladder for help. In exchange, you turn around to help someone below who's facing what you've just been through. That person is able to climb the next rung, and turn around and help someone else.

Remember that the next day, you may be back on that ladder, only the person below you yesterday is now ahead of you—because he or she previously solved a problem you're now facing. It feels just as great to receive the help as it does to give it. Together, everyone makes progress up the ladder. Since the ladder goes on until you sell your business or die, there are plenty of rungs to climb—and lots of interesting people to meet along the way.

"Reality Check" Friends

Some colleagues belong to a special class of solo advisors. These are people you know well, and who may or may not be independent entrepreneurs themselves. Based on your close relationship, you trust them enough to bounce even the craziest ideas off of them, confident they won't laugh or shoot you down.

I call these advisors my "reality check" friends. I can call them up and say things like: "I'm thinking of telling this client to go jump in the lake because she's driving me nuts. Only she wants me to do a really big job for her. Give me a reality check." Or "I just saw this great, new, expensive _____. I'd have to borrow the money to get it. But I *really* want it. Give me a reality check." Or "I'm thinking of expanding the business to do _____. It sounds like fun, but I'm not sure. What do you think? Give me a reality check."

Reality check friends can help you sort out all types of business ideas, problems, and opportunities. For me, they are among my most valuable allies. Your mind can do some pretty convoluted twists and turns when you're working alone. All of a sudden, something you wouldn't have even *considered* a week ago now looks terrifically appealing. Or you think you may be overreacting to a situation, but you're not sure. You're wondering, "Has anyone else ever faced this crisis?" (Probably yes.) For these times and many more, a reality check call can really help.

When you verbalize your ideas to someone else, another thing happens: You often see the issue in a new light yourself, since you're forced to think about how to explain it to someone else.

Another approach is to ask your friends, "How would *you* handle this?" (Just be prepared to accept an honest answer.)

Begin now to put together your team of reality check friends. They may change as your business changes and depending on your specific need at the time you make the call. It's another level of valuable information exchange you'll need on your way to solo success.

Personal Support Services

There's another collection of advisors and success team members that solo entre-preneurs value. These are professionals who often become an extended part of our business because of the important role they play in keeping our lives running smoothly. They vary with each solo business and have many different titles—hair stylist, chiropractor, massage therapist, caterer, wardrobe consultant, media coach, day care provider, personal trainer, or professional organizer. Seasoned solo professionals know that these providers of personal support services are often just as valuable as more traditional business colleagues such as a printer, a photographer, or a computer consultant.

As you put together your team, don't overlook the seemingly minor elements that must come together for your success. Choose your personal support services team with care, and be sure to share your successes with them. They can be some of your biggest cheerleaders as you build your business.

Families

Often we overlook the important role our families—particularly spouses and chil-dren—play on our support teams. They provide financial assistance, lend a help-ing hand, or bring small comforts such as back rubs and smiles after a long day's efforts. They also offer moral support, frequently believing in our abilities and chances for success more than we do ourselves.

It's tricky sometimes to balance the deep emotional ties we have with our families against the demands of a solo business. Particularly in the early years, a solo enterprise can be like a black hole that absorbs every available part of you.

As you pull together your support team, leave a special space for your family members. Think about how they might become involved in your business. Maybe it's physical assistance you'll need or advice they can give from their own past work experience. As with other advisors, the final decision on how to use them will be yours. But you may gain some valuable insights from asking those close to you.

One of the reasons you're working solo is to integrate your life and your work. What better place to start than with your family?

Advisory Meetings Can Happen Anywhere

It's likely that the meetings you have with your Big Three advisors, particularly if you're paying for their services, will take place at their office or yours or at a mutually chosen site such as a restaurant. If you're dealing with advisors at a dis-tance, the meetings may take place on the phone, with support from fax machines.

In contrast to these structured meetings, the majority of your information sharing will be done on a casual basis, among friends and colleagues who are informal members of your solo success team. When thinking about connecting with others, consider these creative solutions contributed by solo workers around the country.

Meetings over Meals

It's a natural part of business culture to meet over meals, and "Let's do lunch" has become a humorous cliché. But having an excuse to get away from your usual surroundings can open your mind to new ideas or give you a new perspective on your business. Another lunch option is for a group of people to get together on a regular basis, rotating the site among different offices. Home-based office or not, there's always pizza or Chinese carryout.

If you hate the idea of breaking up your day with a lunch get-together that may drag on, consider getting up a little earlier and sharing breakfast with a colleague. The ideas you generate could keep you buzzing all day long. Or plan a dinner meeting with fellow solo professionals to share ideas after your workday ends.

Phone Dates

This is an option discovered several years ago and used regularly with success. Instead of sharing a lunch, share a phone call. It's especially popular if you have friends who live thousands of miles away. Consider the money you would have spent in the restaurant the same as what you're sending the phone company. It's a good way to stay close to important colleagues—and it's much less fattening.

Online

If you have an Internet connection, you can exchange electronic mail with other soloists around the world. Have an idea you want some feedback on, or looking for some information about a specific subject? Search the online database, or send a message to a dozen colleagues. You'll have the answer in no time.

Faxes

When it's time to share graphics as well as words, nothing beats a fax. I work with graphic designers and illustrators who live thousands of miles away. Why? I think they're among the top in their field, they're fun to work with—and a fax machine makes it all possible. Sharing ideas by fax gives a sense of instant communication, and it allows you to get hard-copy feedback and information from colleagues who may be several time zones away.

Conferences

Have you ever noticed that much of the information that's shared at conferences happens *between* the panels—in the hallways, lounges, or coffee shops? When you're planning to attend a conference, check to see if distant members of your support team may be there, too. Set aside specific times to share information with them. If you leave it to chance, the days may zip by and you won't connect. Be sure you also use the conference to expand your network. Make an effort to meet new friends, and stay in touch to offer mutual support after the conference has ended.

Wishcraft Success Teams

For those who prefer a more formal means of sharing information, look into Barbara Sher's books, *Wishcraft* (Ballantine, 1986) and *I Could Do Anything If I Only Knew What It Was* (Bantam Doubleday Dell, 1995). This dynamo has been helping people make their dreams come true for more than 20 years. Her books provide a step-by-step system on how to create a support group to help you achieve your goal. Thousands of these Success Teams are now operating around the country, and Sher has included in her books hundreds of comments from people who have achieved remarkable things using this approach. And if you ever have a chance to attend one of Sher's workshops, go. The room becomes electric with the energy of participants helping each other make connections to achieve their goals.

Words of Wisdom

On Creating Success Teams

Individuals around the world have used Barbara Sher's approach to Success Teams to make their dreams come true. Here are her thoughts on what they are and why they work so well.

"A Success Team is a group of people, of any size, called together for the express purpose of helping you get what you want—and who get what they want in the process, too. A team can be as small as one friend on the other end of the phone, or as large as an auditorium packed with 150 people or an open-ended national network.

"Because teammates have no negativity about your dreams, they look at your problems with unfettered imagination. They can brainstorm to help you clarify or set a personally tailored goal. They can figure out how to get your dream for the least possible money or help you schedule time to make it happen. They can give you other support, too—the name of someone who knows all the singing teach-

ers in town, the title of a book on starting your own small business, or a practice session before you make a client presentation. With a team behind you, doubts and negativity lose their power in keeping you from getting what you want.

"Trusting your own judgment, fighting your own fights, and being allowed to do the very best work that's in you is powerfully creative and satisfying. You're your own boss, and that's the way it should be. But stay connected. It's the warm way to the top."

—Barbara Sher

Barbara Sher has been working solo for 25 years and admits that she has "never regretted it for a moment." The author of five books (see Appendix A, "Solo Resources") and a popular workshop speaker, she lives in New York City.

Advisory Etiquette

Regardless of whether your advisors and supporters are paid, there's a certain level of etiquette that goes along with tapping into their information. Here are five guidelines to keep in mind.

1. Respect their time.

Be prepared with a concise question when you call, not a ramble. Ask them if they have a few moments to talk—and use only those moments, not more. If you've set up a meeting, make sure you're on time. All these things show that you value them and their support of you and your business.

2. Your request, your nickel.

If you're asking someone at a distance for advice by phone, you should be paying for the call, not them. Likewise if you invite them to lunch, you pick up the tab. What they're giving you is valuable information. Don't insult them by making them pay to give it to you.

3. Show your appreciation.

Let the other person know you are grateful for the time and information they've shared. Even if you don't end up following their advice this time, you may want to go back to them later with more questions. I've also discovered that a handwritten thank-you note has a powerful effect these days, since so much correspondence is done by fax or e-mail.

During the holidays, consider sending a small gift and a note of thanks for their continuing support. It doesn't take much time, and the business gift may be tax deductible. The cost of the gift isn't as important as the care you take in choosing it and the thought you've placed behind it.

4.   Share the news of your success.

Once you've achieved a goal that your advisors have helped you obtain, let them know. In the excitement of accomplishment, we often forget this important step. They'll be happy for your success and proud that they were able to be part of it.

5.   Pass it on.

Your obligation as an advisee, or support receiver, is to turn around and help others on their journey to solo success. As someone who knows a lot about computers, I've spent endless hours fielding phone calls and giving demonstrations to friends (and strangers) who called to say, "I'm thinking of getting a computer and I don't know what kind to get. Can you help?" After they've been shown my system and given detailed advice on things they should consider before buying their own, I tell them they must promise me one thing.

"What?" they often ask, a little apprehensively. "My payment for this is simple," I explain. "Once you're set up and computer literate, you have to do the same thing for someone who calls you. It's a learning chain, and you can't break it." They always agree, and I feel good about getting them started and continuing the chain.

It's up to you to continue the solo business support chain, too. Once you've received advice from your solo success team advisors, it's time to pass along what you know. This is how the strength of our community of independent workers grows—one link at a time.

Now let's turn our focus to another type of support most solo businesses need: money.

Finding Money to Launch Your Solo Business

A major hurdle for many budding solo entrepreneurs is how to find the money to launch their one-person businesses. At first review, most would-be business owners think a bank loan is their only option—and they're discouraged, because they've heard horror stories about the frustrating bureaucracy of banks.

It's true that banks are *one* option for obtaining funds for your new solo business. Fortunately, they're not the only option—or many small businesses would still be only ideas, instead of the thriving enterprises they are today.

The amount of money needed to launch a solo venture is as varied as the businesses themselves. Don't let the notion of needing a big bankroll stand in the way of your business dreams. First, determine how much you'll need by doing your business plan and speaking with your financial advisors. Prepared with this information, you can then make an informed choice: Either raise the funds or scale back your plans to match your current financial situation.

Surveys show that many self-employed businesspeople start their businesses with $5,000 or less—sometimes *much* less. For many small service businesses, this amount is enough to establish the business, create some marketing materials, and invest in inventory or materials (if it's a product-based business). In contrast, if you're planning a business that requires expensive equipment, $5,000 might seem on the low side. But there are always options of leasing equipment for monthly payments, until you become established.

What the $5,000 start-up figure does *not* include are your daily living expenses, if you're leaving a full-time business. According to financial advisors, if you're launching a business that will be your only income source, you should have a financial cushion equal to six to nine months of income. This serves as your security blanket and allows you freedom from financial worries. With this in the bank, you can focus exclusively on launching your business and building a new income stream.

A new business does not happen overnight, and success comes from laying a good foundation and making a smooth transition from former to new income sources. No matter how much you may be tempted to pack up your desk and quit your job tomorrow, resist the urge. There are safer—and saner—ways to launch your business. Let's take a look at them now.

The Top Ten Ways to Finance Your Solo Business

1. Moonlighting

Moonlighting, or conducting your business during the off-time hours from your regular job, is a popular approach to launching a solo business. Many businesses start as hobbies or sideline interests, then develop full-time focus once the owners realize the joy and financial potential their efforts contain. Moonlighting is a great way to ease into a solo business. It gives you a chance to try on the business and to discover if the activity is as fun when it's a real business instead of a secondary activity.

Moonlighting also gives would-be entrepreneurs a chance to develop their skills without the pressure of generating a lot of income right away. If you need particular training or information, this is the time to take classes and learn from others who are successfully self-employed in the field of your interest.

2. Part-time

If you're confident that your new business can generate at least half your income, consider cutting back your full-time job to part-time, and dedicate the remaining time to focusing on your new business. These days, more employers are willing to consider this option, since it can save them money. If you're currently in a part-time job, think about using your other hours to launch your business.

Many new solo entrepreneurs use part-time jobs to cover their basic living expenses so they can enjoy a little more freedom from financial worries while they get their businesses up and running. A classic example is the artist working in a restaurant or store so he or she has money and free time for creative endeavors. The challenge is to find part-time work that pays more than minimum wage, so you have enough hours and energy left for your new business. Also, if you're leaving a full-time position with benefits—particularly health insurance—make sure you have carefully considered alternative coverage.

3. Jump-start

An increasingly popular approach to jump-starting a solo business is to work independently for your former company, which becomes your first key client. I've seen this happen successfully many times, particularly if the work is something the company doesn't necessarily need to have done in-house. If you enjoy your work but long for a little more independence and a chance to be your own boss, look carefully at your current situation. Could part of your work be done just as well by an independent contractor—such as *you?* No matter what your current occupation, you might be able to change your full-time employer into a client. It often becomes a win/win situation: The company saves money on benefits and other full-time employee costs, while you have the option to expand your financial base by serving other customers, too.

Another variation on the jump-start theme is to entice clients or customers away from your former employer to your new service or product. As an independent, you may be able to offer greater flexibility and a more competitive price than the current supplier (your employer) can provide. Beware the ill will that may result from this situation, however. Some new businesses are launched with the blessing of their owners' former employers, and they thrive. Others are founded on spite and resentment, and they're quickly sent to ruin by the powerful influence of the larger, more established company.

If you choose to compete with a former employer, be aware that you may face legal complications, particularly if you signed a contract that prohibits employees from engaging in conflict-of-interest matters. These stipulations generally cover a specific period of time after you leave the employer, or any information the employer considers confidential. If you anticipate this situation, a check with your legal advisor is an important business planning step.

As you can see, it's best not to burn your bridges behind you. They can often give you a shortcut on your route to solo success. Remember, solo doesn't mean "so long."

4. Twofer or Piggyback

Some solo businesses are launched with the support of an employed spouse or partner. With one full-time salary to cover basic needs, the would-be entrepreneur can focus on the new business. Single business owners sometimes move in with families or roommates to cut costs until the venture is profitable. The goal is to channel money usually spent on other living expenses toward the new business.

If you choose this approach, don't overlook the potential psychological stresses this can put on a relationship. It's crucial to have a spouse or partner who understands that you're piggybacking until your new business can make its own contribution. Just as important, you must accept that it's okay to freeload for a while and have confidence that the sacrifices you and your loved ones are making for your business are worthwhile.

Some spouses mutually establish a set length of time or a cutoff date for funding the business effort. This arrangement often serves as a strong motivator and a realistic boundary for the commitment.

5. Squirrel Approach

This method takes its inspiration from the autumn activity of squirrels, who scurry around and build up a supply of acorns and other nuts to carry them through the long, cold winter. Like those quick-footed creatures, you can create your own stockpile of money while you're working at another job. As you're planning your business, this financial reserve can be growing, ready to take you through the potentially harsh first months of your new venture.

This is a conservative approach, but one that gives you freedom when you're ready to launch, since you'll have enough saved to fund the necessary start-up costs. The time spent saving and preparing becomes more than waiting for the money pot to build. It can be a valuable period to test ideas and put together your plans. When the launch moment arrives, you'll be off like a rocket.

6. "Found" Money

Sometimes money comes into our lives in unexpected ways, such as a lottery, a stock windfall, an inheritance, or that garage-sale painting that Sotheby's says is worth thousands of dollars. While the found money approach to launching a business is not very common, I include it here to make you aware that if and when a chunk of money comes into your life, consider how you might use it.

Now, I'm *not* advocating that you spend your Wednesday nights at the bingo parlor or in a poker game trying to raise funds for your business—although if it brings you success, who's to knock it? My point here is to increase your awareness that found money could be just the amount you need to start you on your solo business adventure. The next time it comes into your life, think twice about how to spend it.

7. Money Pool

If you know you'll need a larger amount of start-up money, and you're looking for outside funding other than a bank, consider creating a money pool with contributions from family, friends, or colleagues. A colleague I know was looking for $50,000 as seed money to start a publishing venture. The bank turned him down, and he didn't know anyone who could make a personal loan for such a hefty amount. Instead, he tried a creative method of contacting his circle of family, friends, and colleagues and asking each of them for a $5,000 loan. He quickly found ten participants, and his financial needs were met—without going to a bank.

Since this is a business loan, each of the participants is paid interest equivalent to what the money would have been earning in a savings account. As a loan, the investment gives no official involvement or ownership in the business (in contrast to a limited partnership, in which an investor receives part ownership).

The bookkeeping for ten contributors is a bit more complex than for a single investor, but the financial goal has been realized. An added benefit for the investors is that each feels a part of the adventure. Using this approach, you can gain valuable success team advisors and goodwill ambassadors for your business—as well as the money you need.

8. Credit

Gather a group of solo entrepreneurs together, and the stories will begin about how many of them have financed their businesses with their credit cards. In addition to purchasing computers, office equipment, furniture, and other supplies, I've heard of individuals charging rent and food by credit card, so they could keep their businesses going. High credit card interest rates make this a very expensive way to finance your business—and the reason it's toward the bottom of this list of funding options. It can also create heavy psychological burdens. You feel yourself in a deep financial hole when your statement arrives each month.

Another choice that offers more reasonable rates is a credit-line extension to your bank checking account. Based on your current financial status, the bank allows you to extend your checking account beyond the money you have in the account, up to an established limit. The amount you exceed your own money is considered a loan, and interest charges begin the moment the check is cashed.

Banks offer credit extensions to personal accounts more frequently than to business (commercial) accounts. A line of credit is an appealing alternative for many solo business owners, since the money is available when you need it, but the interest fees don't begin until the check clears.

If you own your own home and have paid off a sizable part of the mortgage, you might consider a home equity loan to fund your new business venture. Originally intended for home improvements, home equity loans have grown in popularity in recent years to pay for expenses such as college education, medical costs, or other emergencies. Once the papers are approved, the bank often looks the other way at how you spend the money—although they expect full payback, with interest.

Many solo entrepreneurs use a home equity loan as a security blanket. They get approval while they are still employed full-time, then quit their jobs, knowing that they have a financial cushion, should they need it. The money borrowed must be paid back with interest, of course. But the option of having a source of money to draw on gives many new business owners valuable psychological comfort and a sense of security.

All solo businesses use credit to survive, whether it's purchases made by credit card or bills that are paid on a 30-day basis. The challenge is to learn to use credit power wisely, so it becomes your tool and not a burden.

9. Bank Loan

Here, nearly at the end of the list, is the bank loan. Banks are in the business of lending money, but the cliché about banks being more willing to lend money to people who don't need it still rings true to many solo entrepreneurs who have been to their local banks lately. As one bank manager explained, "It takes just as much paperwork for a $5,000 loan as a $150,000 loan, and we'd rather spend the time on the larger, more profitable transactions. You may have more success asking for the larger amount, if you can justify your need for it."

There are four key questions that loan officers will ask you when you approach them for money:

1. How long have you been in business?
2. Can you provide us with the last two to three years' tax returns and a business plan?
3. Why do you want the money?
4. How are you going to pay us back?

Of all these questions, bank officers explain that number 4 is the most important. It's their key factor in deciding if they should make a loan—so be prepared to answer it during your discussions.

If you're just starting your business and don't have two years of business tax returns, you'll be asked to present personal financial information instead. As a new business owner, it's likely that you'll be asked to sign a personal guarantee for a business loan. If you're operating as a sole proprietor, this is the case anyway, since your business debts automatically become your personal responsibility, too.

Another loan option is a 90-day note, which is a short-term loan payable at the end of three months. These notes are often renewed and extended at the end of the term, sometimes for up to three cycles, or nine months—although you can't automatically count on this option. Interest payments are due monthly, and the principal is due at the end of the term.

Words of Wisdom

On Working with Your Banker

Most solo entrepreneurs consider only what it's like on *our* side of the desk when dealing with a banker. Here are some insights from an experienced bank loan officer about the *bank's* viewpoint on dealing with new small business owners.

"What's the most important thing I'd tell new solo workers about working with their banker? Be honest. We're not interested in every nitty-gritty detail of your life and business. But we do expect you to tell us your ideas, your abilities, your concerns. Don't put the lending officer in a bad spot by hiding something that will come up later and embarrass both of you.

"If you do run into financial problems—for example, not being able to make a loan payment—don't hide your head in the sand. We want to work things out. We react the same way anyone else would when ignored.

"Many small business owners seem to think that the bank is just waiting for them to mess up so we can take their house or car. We don't want your property! We'd rather have you as a successful customer who'll be using our services for a long time."

—*Patte B. Hoffman*

Patte Hoffman is branch manager of First Hudson Valley Bank in Fishkill, New York. Prior to joining the banking industry 17 years ago, she managed her own small business, a clothing store.

10. Venture Capitalists

Statistics show that less than 1 percent of all small businesses rely on venture capitalists for start-up funds. Yet these investors seem to attract the most attention. Perhaps it's the risk and the high-profile clients involved. I've always thought it a little odd that this tiny segment of funding generates so much attention.

If you have an innovative, sizzling business idea that needs heavy capitalization—to the tune of hundreds of thousands (or even millions) of dollars in initial financing—then venture capital fund-raising may be the route for you. In exchange for their investment, venture capitalists acquire partial ownership in the business, generally through shares of stock. To budding entrepreneurs, this can often seem painless—but it can come back to haunt them later, as they realize that all their efforts to build the company now amount to a small percentage of ownership.

It's important to remember that most venture capitalists are professional money investors, and they'll probably not share your passion for your business. Their primary goal with a business is to increase their investment, whether the company involves software or soybean farming.

Of course, there are substantial benefits to obtaining venture capital—it can turn your big plans into reality. If you're leaning toward seeking venture capital, you'll need extensive business plans—and professional advice. Use the lessons you learn in these pages, and make the choice of how big you want your business to grow. It's probably far beyond a one-person business, but that's not to say it won't be terrific fun. Good luck!

There you have it, the ten most popular ways of funding your new solo business. Many business owners have used combinations of them. Don't be afraid to add a creative interpretation to your own funding needs.

In this chapter you've discovered the importance of building support for your new venture, on both personal and financial levels. Now it's time to determine the best legal and physical structure for your solo business.

Chapter 5

Choosing Your Business Structure: Legal Matters and Physical Setup

Good order is the foundation of all things.

—Edmund Burke

Up to now, we've focused on the direction, foundation, and planning of a new business, and we've seen how important these elements are in launching a solo enterprise. Now it's time to move forward and transform the ideas for your business into a more solid form. Two tasks await us in this chapter: determining which legal structure is best for your business, including naming your new enterprise, and choosing the best location and layout for your office.

One of the best parts about working solo is that you have the chance to choose *every* detail of your business and to design the business to be a strong match for you. But before you can choose wisely, you need to discover the effects each particular choice may have on your business. Making an *informed* choice is always the goal. Understanding your options and deciding the legal structure and physical setup that work best for you is our next step together.

Establishing the Best Legal Structure for Your Business

There are positive and negative aspects to almost every choice in life. It's that way with choosing the legal structure of your business, too. You'll be faced with many alternatives, and each option has advantages and disadvantages attached to it. Based on the nature of your business, your own needs and style, and the details you'll learn from reading this chapter, you'll be able to make an informed decision about the best choice for your business.

Three main areas of concern come into play when you're choosing your business structure, advises New York City attorney Erik Kahn. "Tax considerations, liability issues, and organizational structure matters—such as ownership, control, or the ability to sell parts of your new entity—are all important factors in deciding

COMPARING LEGAL STRUCTURES FOR YOUR BUSINESS

Sole Proprietorship

+ Controlled by owner
+ All profits to owner
+ Little regulation
+ Easy to start and maintain
+ Earnings taxed at personal level

− Personal liability for business debts
− Limited resources
− Likelihood of no continuity at retirement or death
− Potential increased risk of IRS audit

General Partnership

+ Joint ownership and responsibility
+ Access to more money and skills
+ Earnings taxed at personal level
+ Limited regulation and easy to start

− Conflict of authority
− Partners liable for actions of others
− Profits divided
− Possible end of business at retirement or death of one partner

Limited Partnership

+ General partner(s) runs business
+ Limited (silent) partners have no liability beyond invested money
+ Earnings taxed at personal level

− Limited partners have no say in the business
− General partners have personal liability for business debts
− More regulations than for general partnerships

Limited Liability Company

+ Limited personal liability
+ Unlimited number of shareholders
+ Profits and losses taxed at personal level

− Relatively new entity with untested legal issues
− Costly to form and maintain
− Closely regulated by state and IRS

(Continued) ➧

S Corporation

+ Limited personal liability
+ Legal entity with transferable ownership
+ Earnings taxed at personal level

- Closely regulated by state and IRS
- Costly to form and maintain
- Restricted to 75 or fewer stockholders
- Not recognized by all states

C Corporation

+ Limited personal liability
+ Legal entity with transferable ownership
+ Employee benefits deductible

- Closely regulated by state and IRS
- Costly to form and maintain
- Potential double taxation on personal and corporate income

Figure 5.1   This chart presents the advantages (+) and the drawbacks (–) of each of the six legal structures discussed in this chapter.

which legal structure to adopt," he says. "It's important to choose wisely so the legal structure supports what you want to do with your company."

There are four main types of legal business structures: sole proprietorships, partnerships, limited liability companies, and corporations. Partnerships come in two varieties: general partnerships and limited partnerships. There are also two kinds of corporations: regular, or C, corporations and S corporations. In all, that makes six options. Let's take a look at each of them and what they mean to the solo professional.

Sole Proprietorships

A sole proprietorship is a business owned and operated by one person, although there can be employees.

Most small businesses are sole proprietorships because this is the easiest form to establish and maintain. In a sole proprietorship, you and your business are one and the same—you are the business. If you move to another location, in most cases your business will move, too. If you die, the business generally also dies. (Upon death, the business becomes part of your estate, and it may or may not be continued by your survivors.) Even if you hire employees, as a sole proprietor you have final responsibility for the services or products of the business.

Financially, a sole proprietor receives all the profits from the business, but incurs all the liabilities of the business, too. Since you and the business are one, if you are sued, the court can demand personal property—such as your home, car, or equipment—to pay off your business debts, if necessary.

Sole proprietorship profits (or losses) are tied to personal finances and are reported on your personal tax return by filing IRS Schedule C (Form 1040), Profit or Loss From Business (described below). This potentially can bring significant tax benefits to you. For example, if you're launching your solo business while holding down a full- or part-time job, any loss from your business can be deducted from your regular job earnings, which will lower your taxable income. Also, if you have more than one business, a loss in one business can offset profits in another business or other income. (Before your eyes light up, remember that a loss is a loss—it may save you money on your taxes, but you've still lost the money.)

All sole proprietorship profits (or losses) are calculated on net income, after you have deducted all business-related expenses such as office equipment depreciation, professional travel, automobile mileage, supplies, and many others that we'll cover in Chapter 8. Your business income or loss is submitted on Schedule C of your IRS tax return, and you pay taxes calculated at your personal rate, instead of at a corporate rate. Of course, good record keeping is a must, since the IRS is very strict about the distinctions between personal and business income and between multiple businesses.

As a sole proprietor, you cannot hire yourself to your business as an employee. If your business makes a $5,000 profit, you owe taxes on that $5,000 (less deductible expenses), even if you used some of that money to pay yourself a salary. Though you technically aren't an employee, you can establish a tax-deductible retirement plan for yourself, known as a SEP-IRA. The contribution is based on a percentage of your net business profits and generally is allowed even if you already have an established retirement plan with another employer. You'll see more about this in Chapter 9.

One of the drawbacks to a sole proprietorship is that your tax return can be subject to more scrutiny, and a possible audit, by the IRS. Solo business owners who know they will have a significant number of large deductions on Schedule C of their tax return often decide to incorporate as a way to reduce their risk of an IRS audit and the time and expense involved with that process. Tax professionals advise that, while this is one tactic, it should not be the only reason to incorporate. It's important to carefully review *all* the implications—with taxes as one part—in making your decision.

While the tax issues, the glamour of being incorporated, and having "Inc." after your business name can be appealing, most solo business owners decide it's not worth the expense, the complexity, or the regulations. They choose sole proprietorship because it is the simplest option for their businesses, particularly if they are offering services with little associated risk.

In contrast, individuals who own businesses with potential liability concerns—such as a boat rental company, a dance or aerobics studio, or a tree removal service—often decide to incorporate as a way to protect their personal income and property from business-related lawsuits and from creditors, should the businesses fail. Yet even incorporating is no guarantee that your personal property remains protected, since in some cases you can be sued in your own name as well as in the name of the corporation. Many states, however, favor protecting individuals through a corporate structure, unless there is fraud, significant undercapitalization, failure to follow corporate rules, and tax and payroll obligations (which can pass directly to officers and shareholders).

As you're launching your business, you'll be faced with many trade-offs about where to invest your money—and incorporation can be costly for many solo professionals. If your primary reason to incorporate is for legal protection, many small business advisors suggest that you choose sole proprietorship and invest in additional liability insurance instead. This approach allows you to save the money from incorporation legal and filing fees and to purchase more comprehensive liability coverage. (If you have significant assets, however, this may not be the most cost-effective approach.) It's worth asking your legal and tax advisors their opinion of how well this approach works for you and your business.

Partnerships

> A partnership is an association of two or more persons who serve as co-owners of a business.

It may seem odd to include a section on partnerships in a book titled *Working Solo*. Yet it's been my experience that many solo adventurers turn to partners to help them launch their businesses. Later, they may continue on their own. But a partner often can be a valuable counterpart to a new business dream. Another person may bring energy to share the workload, skills or talents to expand the business, or money for financial stability.

Partnerships share the risks and rewards in a business. In the best partnerships, the abilities of one person offset the needs of the other. Together the partners are stronger than either would be alone—a classic example of 1 + 1 becoming greater than 2.

Partnerships can also offer individuals who have part-time freedom but full-time dreams the option of pooling resources. With several people involved in a business, each can work part-time, and the business can operate full-time. The key to a successful partnership, observes attorney Erik Kahn, is clearly thinking through future events and contingencies. "It may not be pleasant, but it pays to consider issues such as termination, bankruptcy, death of one of the partners, or a future buy-out," he says.

There are two kinds of partnerships: general partnerships and limited partnerships. Let's take a look at each of them.

General Partnerships

In a general partnership, all co-owners play an active role in the business.

When two or more individuals come together to own a business, a partnership is created. As with a sole proprietorship, the business is inseparable from these individuals—it is jointly owned by them. This has important legal implications, since the actions of one partner on behalf of the business affect the others, too. For example, if your partner gets into legal or financial trouble related to the business, you share in the responsibility, even though you may not have known or agreed to the actions.

In a partnership, taxes are paid individually, based on a split of the profit or loss of the business. The split, based on the percentage of ownership, can be 50/50 (equal ownership), 49/51 (showing one person's slight dominance), or some other agreed-upon division. Partnerships file tax returns by completing IRS Form 1065, which indicates how much money each partner earned or lost during the year. Each partner then files Schedule E (Form 1040) with his or her personal tax return, showing the income earned (or lost) from the business.

When one partner dies, the partnership legally is terminated. The business might continue, however, if the right provisions were made in the partnership agreement—it all depends on how forward-thinking the partners were when they drew up their original agreement.

Limited Partnerships

Limited partners (sometimes known as "silent" partners) have no say in the management or control of a business and no risk of liability beyond their invested money.

A limited partnership may have several silent partners, but there must be at least one general partner who assumes full legal and financial responsibility. For solo entrepreneurs whose business dreams require substantial investment, this option may offer an ideal solution—the individual runs the business alone, and the silent partners provide the funding. Profits and losses are shared proportionately, in accordance with the percentage established in the partnership agreement. Of course, it's up to the solo entrepreneur to find those wealthy and adventuresome limited partners.

Limited partnerships are closely governed by state and federal regulations. Special income tax rules apply to limited partnerships, since the government wants to ensure that they're used for the right reason and not as a questionable write-off for wealthy tax dodgers.

In whatever legal form it takes, a successful partnership requires a special understanding. In fact, many business advisors suggest that would-be partners consider their union like a marriage, since you may be spending more hours in this relationship than with a spouse. If you decide to partner with a friend, be sure you have clear mutual expectations about the business. Taking the time to create detailed written agreements will protect each person, the business—and your relationship. Nolo Press's *The Partnership Book* by attorneys Denis Clifford and Ralph Warner (details in Appendix A, "Solo Resources") offers practical advice and sample partnership agreements.

Just as you have an opinion of a favorite sports team, musician, or book, you probably have a strong idea of whether a partnership will work for you. If it does, go for it! Just make sure you put your agreement in writing.

Limited Liability Companies

A limited liability company (LLC) is a hybrid; it provides liability protection similar to that of a corporation, but taxes are paid like in a partnership.

A limited liability company (LLC) is a relatively new legal entity that brings together several valuable benefits for some types of businesses. An LLC combines the characteristics of a corporation and a partnership, giving liability protection to its owners (generally reserved for corporations) and simplifying taxes by passing through the profits and losses to the owners (like a partnership).

The "limited liability" aspect found in the name of this form of business is one of its main attractions. For instance, if an LLC is sued or has debts it can't pay, the opposing party can go after only the assets of the business, not the individual owners. When business owners can get this powerful protection coupled with the straightforward handling of taxes like a sole proprietor or partnership, the appeal of an LLC becomes clear.

There are some drawbacks to LLCs, however. LLCs are still somewhat untested as a business entity, and many tax and legal issues remain to be resolved. For example, while the IRS has ruled that a solo entrepreneur can establish an LLC, some states require at least two parties to be involved. In addition, the expense of starting an LLC can frequently be two to five times higher than that of starting a corporation, depending on the state in which you set it up. If you're thinking of a partnership and would like the liability protection, ask your legal advisor if this is the best choice for your business.

If you're too independent to consider legal and financial ties with others, that's understandable—it's probably one of the things that made you pick up a book titled *Working Solo* in the first place. Consider a sole proprietorship, or read on to see how a corporate structure might work for you.

Corporations

> *A corporation is a business established as a distinct legal entity, separate from the individuals who own it.*

Mention the word *corporation,* and an image of a big, powerful, stable company generally comes to mind. But as we approach the twenty-first century, the status of the corporation is changing rapidly, as some of our most respected corporations have shown that size and power may not automatically lead to success.

What does incorporation have to offer a solo entrepreneur? Is it worth the paperwork and expense—often several hundred dollars—to become a corporation? The answers to those questions depend on your business and your plans for its growth.

There are two basic types of corporations: regular, or C, corporations, and S corporations. Both offer similar advantages of corporate structure; S corporations handle taxes a little differently.

Corporations require a more formalized structure than do sole proprietorships—there are shareholders, regular meetings, and officers. Both types of corporate structures, whether C or S, offer potential benefits for solo entrepreneurs. Let's take a look at both of them now.

Regular, or C, Corporations

> *A regular corporation gives owners liability protection, and taxes are paid by the business itself, at a corporate rate.*

Since a corporation is a legal business structure that exists separately from its owners, it offers several benefits. A corporation has a life of its own, and it doesn't end at the death or retirement of a shareholder. It can also be sold or transferred, without many of the legal complications of other forms.

Another advantage a corporation offers is limited liability. For example, if the corporation incurs heavy debts, in most cases the creditors cannot come after the owner's personal property. Be aware, however, that while a corporation can protect you from acts of the corporation, you remain liable for your own acts. (One tip: Make sure, when you're signing contracts, that you do so in the name of the corporation and not your own name.)

While limited liability is one of the classic reasons to incorporate, many new business owners are finding an even greater incentive: soaring health care costs. Since a corporation can hire the owner as an employee, this means that salary and other benefits, such as medical insurance, can be deductible expenses.

Being able to deduct health care expenses for the employee and his or her family—including insurance premiums, deductibles, and copayments—is an increasingly popular motive to start a C corporation, particularly for individuals who have left large employers to start their own businesses. (A C corporation allows you to deduct all medical expenses, while an S does not.) For solo entrepreneurs with high medical costs, this choice could result in a potential (but not guaranteed) tax savings. As with all tax matters, this may change, so it's important to stay in touch with your legal and financial advisors.

A corporate structure can also be beneficial if you're trying to raise money for your solo business. Incorporating can lend you more status, and investors sometimes feel more comfortable lending to a corporation than to an individual. Of course, this leverage is often primarily psychological—the business usually depends on the savvy, intelligence, and determination of the individual anyway.

A disadvantage to a C corporation is that both the corporation and your salary are taxed. There are also expenses and regulations in setting up and maintaining a corporation, which can be considerable. Some states have minimum taxation levels, so even if you aren't making a lot of profit, you still must pay a certain amount of corporate tax. In the end, you may end up paying a higher tax rate overall. On top of that, you'll likely need to pay accountants to file the complex quarterly and annual reports required from corporations.

As you can see, small businesses need to think through the benefits of incorporating. If you consistently incur significant medical expenses, then a C corporation may offer financial benefits. If the other corporate advantages, such as limited liability and survivorship, are important to you, and you don't want to be taxed at the corporate rate, consider the other corporate structure, the S corporation.

S Corporations

An S corporation provides the liability protection of a corporation, but taxes are paid on a personal level (as in a sole proprietorship or a partnership).

Most solo entrepreneurs who want the benefits of a corporation without the headaches of complicated taxes choose the S corporation form. Think of this option as a blend between a corporation and a sole proprietorship. You receive all the benefits of a corporation's liability protection, but taxes are assessed to you at a personal level. As in a sole proprietorship, any business losses can be offset against income from another job. (A C corporation must accrue the losses.)

As with a C corporation, operating as an S corporation involves expenses of setting up your corporation and the ongoing costs of filing regular returns. Another potential drawback: While the IRS recognizes S corporations, not all states do, and your tax advantages may be negligible. Your decision is whether the advantages—liability protection, ability of the business to be sold, taxation at a personal level, and the survivorship of the corporation in spite of a shareholder's death—outweigh these costs and make it a worthwhile choice.

A final note: Changing from a sole proprietorship to a single-shareholder corporation is a relatively easy thing to do, and there are services that can expedite the process and reduce your legal fees. The process is best done with an attorney who understands your desire to economize, rather than attempted alone, however. For details, see Appendix A, "Solo Resources."

Should I Incorporate?

If, after reading all these options, you're still puzzled, don't worry. Determining the best legal structure for your business will take some time. It's also a decision you should make after consulting with your legal and financial advisors.

To help you in your thinking and in your discussions with your advisors, here are some questions to ask yourself.

1. Do I intend to keep my business on a part-time basis or at a small level?

If so, incorporation for you may be like using a sledgehammer to kill a mosquito—sure, you can do it, but there are more efficient ways that aren't so cumbersome. Think about a sole proprietorship instead.

2. Will I be working with one or more people and sharing the profits?

Then consider a partnership, but make sure you put it in writing. A corporation or limited liability company might also be an option, if you want the liability protection and the ease of selling or transferring the business.

3. Is it important to me that my business have a life longer than mine and that it have value in its own right?

The main distinction of a corporation is that it can live beyond its owners. A sole proprietorship or partnership can be sold or transferred, but not without setting up new bookkeeping, licenses, and so on. If this is important to you, consider a corporate structure—but don't use it as the only reason to incorporate.

4. Will I be seeking substantial outside funding?

Most solo businesses are launched with personal or family funds, although there are many ways to find financing for your enterprise. If your dreams are on a grand scale, and you'll be seeking substantial amounts of money from banks or venture capitalists, then incorporation may give you more credibility with your potential investors.

5. Do I have large health care expenses?

In a C corporation, you can be an employee, and the health care expenses of you and your family are deductible. If you have a spouse and young children and must pay all your own medical costs, incorporating may bring you some tax advantages.

6. Will I have significant deductions?

Major deductions on a Schedule C tax return may raise a red flag with the IRS, leaving you vulnerable to a possible audit, and the time and expense that entails. There are no general rules as to types or quantities of deductions that will provoke an audit, so it is best to run several scenarios with your financial and tax advisors to see if this should be a factor to consider.

7. Do I have significant assets to protect?

The cost of incorporating is a relatively small price to pay if your business activities would expose your assets to risk. Again, consider the full implications and consult your legal and financial advisors.

If you answered no to questions 2 through 7, then you are like most solo business owners, and a sole proprietorship is probably the best option for you. If you answered yes to these questions, investigate with your professional advisors the potential benefits of incorporation.

If you decide on a sole proprietorship, it doesn't rule out a corporate structure later—you can always graduate to become a corporation. But it's much more difficult, and expensive, to dissolve a corporation.

Most experts agree that a sole proprietorship is the easiest and most efficient legal structure for the majority of small businesses, and I agree. If you're worried about liability, buy more liability insurance—it may give you better protection in the long run. As for taxes, unless you have large medical costs, or until your business is making about $100,000 a year, incorporating may not be worth the unending paperwork and procedures.

Of course, rules and regulations change, which is the reason this decision must be made after you've received some feedback from advisors who are up to date on current laws and tax regulations and who know you and your business plans.

Assuming you're among the majority of independent professionals who will decide on a sole proprietorship, let's discover how to establish one. We'll start with how to choose a name for your business.

Naming Your Business

If you're like most solo business owners, your business means a lot to you—in some ways, you consider it your baby. You've planned for it since its conception, nurtured it from birth, given it tender loving care, and have great hope for its future.

It makes sense, then, to consider naming your business with the same intelligence and care that you would exercise in naming a child. Here are five guidelines to help you name your business.

1.   Make the name meaningful.

Since the name is often the first thing someone knows about your business, consider it an important marketing tool. Avoid vague names by thinking about the key focus of your business. "Pat's Carpentry Services" is more descriptive than "ABC Industries." Some people, especially artists and designers, like to include their first or last names in their business names. This can help personalize your product or service, and it is easier to avoid conflicts with a business name that includes your personal name.

2.   Make sure the name is easy to understand and pronounce.

Often your business name will be shared in conversation, so make sure it is one that can be easily understood—and repeated. Those of us with unusual first or last names know the challenge that this can present. (I like my last name, but I have spent a good part of the last 24 years pronouncing and spelling it for people. At times I even offer a phonetic spelling—lone-YAY—so that it doesn't get mangled.)

Of course, the flip side of this is that an unusual name can be memorable, once people have it in their minds. It's up to you to decide if you want to put your potential customers (and yourself) through that work.

Also, keep your business name short enough so that it doesn't get a nickname you didn't choose. "Jerry's Roofing, Siding, and Home Improvement Services" may end up being "that guy who puts on shingles"—not quite what you had in mind, right?

3.   Choose a name that you can live and grow with.

Be forward-thinking in your choice of a business name, so that it can expand as you do. For example, what happens if you name your business "Anytown VCR Repair," and you decide later also to fix laser disc players, camcorders, or other electronics equipment? Yes, you might have to change your name. A better choice might have been "Anytown Electronics Repair," assuming you felt comfortable with this business focus when you first named your company.

The point is to give your business name enough growing room to accommodate the changes it undoubtedly will face. Too narrow a name, and you limit your options; too broad a meaning, and you lose the power to communicate.

Also try to choose a name that you think will outlast current fads or trends. You're searching for a name that you will feel proud to say for a long, long time—

and one that will retain your original meaning. Imagine "Jan's Radical Clothing Design" in five to ten years. It's likely that *radical* will either have changed meanings or sound hopelessly dated.

4.   *Make it unique.*

Your name must also be unique, since two businesses in the same geographic area cannot legally operate under the same name. As a sole proprietor, you'll be required to file some legal forms indicating your business intent and the fictitious name you have chosen. (We'll be talking about the details in the next section.) When you file, the county clerk will make sure that no one else is currently using your proposed name. It's a good idea to prepare a list of three or four other business names you could use (possibly by adding your own name), in case your first choice is taken. By thinking this through in advance, you can avoid confusion and possible embarrassment.

5.   *Try it on for size.*

In choosing your business name, jot down a list of possibilities, and try them out on friends and family. Don't rush the process. Live with each possibility for a while. Remember, you'll probably be using this name for quite some time.

As you can see, choosing a business name is not an easy task, but it is a fun one. By selecting wisely, you'll make your business name a valuable company asset and a phrase you'll say with pride for many years to come.

Words of Wisdom

On Trademarking Your Business Name or Product

The name of your business or product can become an important and valuable asset, and one that you want to protect. Here are some insights from an experienced trademark attorney on how to do so.

"Business owners can benefit from carefully choosing and protecting their company's name or product. These are the questions I'm asked most frequently.

"When are trademarks protected? Unlike copyrights, which are protected upon creation, trademarks are protected upon adoption and use. First legitimate and continuous use wins, even if the secondary user files for and obtains a federal trademark registration.

"Why register a trademark? Federal registration of trademarks gives trademark owners numerous rights and advantages, including nationwide notice to others, and the exclusive rights to the mark *nationwide, under certain circumstances. A registered trademark is also a significant advantage when litigating or advising others to stop using the mark. Additionally, the U.S. Customs Service, when put on notice, will impound infringing goods that are imported into the United States—but only if you have a valid federal trademark registration. Business owners should also remember that registered trademarks are a corporate asset which may be licensed, assigned, or in some cases held as a security and borrowed against.*

"When can I use a ™ or ®? How much does it cost? Anyone can use ™ in connection with their name, without even filing an application to register the mark. The ®, however, is reserved for registered marks only. The cost for a trademark registration is $245 for the filing fee, plus attorney costs, which generally range from $200–500, depending on the lawyer. A lawyer is recommended, but not required.

"Can any mark be protected? It is important that business owners avoid 'descriptive' marks that call to mind an aspect of the goods or services. The trouble with distinctive marks is that they aren't distinctive or memorable, and are legally difficult to protect from infringement. For example, courts have held that the following marks were descriptive: 'Car-Freshener' for auto air deodorizer, '5 Minutes,' for glue that sets in 5 minutes, and 'Beef & Brew' for restaurants."

—Erik Kahn

Trademark attorney Erik Kahn is a principal with Kahn & Block, LLP, based in New York City.

Once you have chosen your business name, it's time to register it with the appropriate county agency and to find out about other licenses or permits you may need.

Licenses and Permits

When you decide to start a business, you enter the world of rules and regulations—and they bring with them licenses, permits, and forms. Once you've completed and paid for one, it often leads to the proverbial Pandora's box of many more.

As a personal business philosophy, I've divided these bureaucratic requirements into two categories: the ones you must have to do business and the ones that might be optional. It's your job as a savvy entrepreneur to discover which are which.

Now, don't get me wrong. Ignoring requests to file forms or to pay fees can get you into hot water—and big fines—in a hurry. You don't want to be foolish with legal or tax matters. But there are some licenses, forms, and permits that may not be applicable to your business. Will the county or state object to your getting dozens of permits? Not a chance! Your mission is to research the ones that are needed for your business—and the ones that aren't.

You can conduct this research in the same way you've done the other research we've talked about in *Working Solo*. Begin with your phone book, and make some calls to local government agencies. Tell them you're considering starting a business, and ask if they have any information to send you. In some areas, the chamber of commerce puts together business start-up kits that provide all the necessary regulations and forms in one place—sometimes even on their own Web site on the Internet.

Don't forget about your (by now) good friend, the librarian. He or she can direct you to the information you need. Also, check out local professional organizations, including the Better Business Bureau and the chamber of commerce. As you discovered in the last chapter, the Small Business Administration is another great resource for start-up information.

You can also talk to other business owners in the area and find out from them how strict or lenient your local, regional, and state governments are. Don't be shy about asking. Learn from the wisdom and mistakes of others—heaven knows, you'll have your own to share after a few years in business.

Since every solo business is unique, and laws are constantly in flux, it would be impossible to try to present details on every regulation and permit. Instead, here's an overview of the ones you'll most likely encounter as a sole proprietor.

Fictitious Name Filing

Since you will be conducting business with the public, the law requires sole proprietorships to file a fictitious name statement, known as a d/b/a (doing business as) form, with the county clerk's office. This form states to the public the name of the individual behind the company name. For example, "Software Concepts" may be the name of the computer consulting firm owned by Chris Smith. If there were ever any legal dealings with the company, it would be officially on record that Chris Smith is the person responsible for the company's actions.

Filing a d/b/a takes place at the county clerk's office. It is a straightforward procedure. You purchase a blank certificate at a stationery store or at the office where you do the filing. Complete the form, have your signature notarized, and return it to the office. Filing fees generally range from $15 to $35, although New York City raised the fee to $100 (!) a few years ago. Most offices request payment in either cash or money order.

You will need two additional certified copies of your d/b/a, which will run about $5 each. One is to be posted in your place of business; the other is for your bank, when you set up your business checking account. Some counties also require you to publish a small ad in the local paper stating that your business has filed a d/b/a form. Check to see if your county requires this added step.

State and City Business Permits

The government loves to get involved in regulating businesses. In New York state, there are more than 42 regulating agencies and 1,100 business permits—enough to fill a five-volume set of 1,500 pages! In addition, many cities have instituted required permits for small businesses.

Permit requirements for businesses dealing with the public—for example, selling food or running a day care service—are generally much more rigidly enforced than are those for small service businesses such as freelance writing or consulting. Since the regulations and permits vary from region to region and are changing all the time, check with fellow business owners and your local and state government offices to see which ones might pertain to you. The phone number(s) can be found in the blue, or government, section of your phone book.

Professional or Occupational Licenses

Some occupations are regulated by the state, and businesses may need a specific professional or occupational license to operate. These include businesses that require educational training and certification, such as medical professionals, CPAs, engineers, auto repairers, and beauticians. Many are issued for one or two years and must be renewed—of course, for a fee.

In some states, professional or occupational licenses are administered by the state education department; in others, they are part of general business licenses and permits. Again, check your telephone directory's blue pages, or check with your librarian, to find out details for your state.

Employee Identification Number

You will be required to identify your business on government forms by one of two numbers: your Social Security Number or an Employee Identification Number (EIN). An EIN is assigned by the federal government to track the contributions an employer has made to independent contractors or to employee accounts such as federal withholding or Social Security.

If you are a sole proprietorship, you will most often use your Social Security Number. Even if you do not intend on hiring employees, however, you can obtain an EIN for your business. Why would you want to do so? Because some forms, such as tax resale certificates (coming up next) and other business forms, ask for it.

To obtain an EIN, file an IRS Form SS-4, which you can get by calling the IRS and requesting one, or pick up one at your local IRS office. (It's likely your accountant may have a copy of the form, too.) If you do not have employees, make sure you write in big letters "FOR IDENTIFICATION PURPOSES ONLY" on the form—or else the IRS will assume you have employees and will automatically start sending you quarterly reports to file. Don't be alarmed if this happens to you, even if you have stated this clearly on the form. Simply return the forms, stating that you have no employees and that the number is for identification only. It may take several attempts before the IRS finally stops sending the forms.

State Sales Tax and Resale Certificates

If you will be selling anything to the public and you live in a state that collects sales tax, you have the obligation to collect and submit state sales tax on each item you sell. If you run a small business, you probably will need to file this only once a year—but make sure you keep good records, because sales tax forms can be among the most confusing to file. Why? Because each county may charge a different sales tax rate, and if you sell statewide, many states require you to calculate sales tax according to the rate *at the point of delivery.*

If you conduct a mail-order business and your state operates this way, this is an important detail, since the point of delivery may be in another county. Also check with your state to learn its regulations on taxing shipping and handling charges—some states say these are taxable, others say they are not.

Along with sales tax come resale considerations. The responsibility to collect sales tax lies with the person (or organization) who ultimately sells the product to the customer—in other words, the person who conducts the retail sale. Therefore, if your business sells wholesale goods to retail shops or outlets, it becomes the retail shop's responsibility to collect the tax from the buying public.

Similarly, if you are buying raw materials to turn into finished goods that you will sell to the public, you don't pay sales tax when you buy them. For example, let's say your business sells silk-screened T-shirts. When you buy the T-shirts from your supplier, you give them your resale certificate number, and they don't charge you sales tax on them, since they will be taxed when they become finished goods and are bought by consumers.

If you sell your finished T-shirts to a boutique, no sales tax is charged, because it is the boutique's responsibility to collect the tax from the final customers. (When you complete a wholesale transaction, be sure to keep good records, including the buyer's EIN, so you have proof that the sales tax responsibility was not yours.) In contrast, if you sell a T-shirt directly to a customer, you must collect the sales tax. Do you see how the tax is charged only once—when the final sale is made?

A common misunderstanding about resale certificates is that businesses pay no sales tax on any purchases—no such luck! For example, the T-shirts you bought from your supplier were tax exempt because they were for resale. The desk you bought on which you do your bookkeeping is not exempt, however, and you'll pay sales tax on it.

The point to remember is that your business is exempt from paying sales tax on resale items—elements that are part of the raw materials in your product for sale. Equipment used in making the item or brochures and business cards used in promoting the item are not exempt from sales tax.

To obtain a resale certificate, call your state office of taxation. (This often has a name such as the Franchise Tax Board or the Taxation and Finance Department.) They'll send you information and forms to complete and return. Some states require you to refile the certificate every two to three years.

If you operate a service-based business, your activities may or may not be subject to sales tax, depending on your state regulations. Businesses such as telephone answering services and ad agencies, for example, are subject to sales tax in some states but not in others. Check with your state taxation office to obtain the latest rulings regarding sales taxes on service businesses in your state.

As you can see, keeping up with the government rules and regulations can be a challenge, particularly for the small business owner. That's why it's important to remember that, even though you're a solo business, you're not alone. Don't be afraid to ask questions or call on other small business owners in your area for advice. Sharing information about business laws and taxes is a key part of that survival network. If you have a question, reach out and ask.

Zoning Regulations: Being in the Know

If you decide to run your business out of your home, be sure to look into zoning ordinances in your area. Nearly every state has zoning against home-based businesses. Many date back to the turn of the century and were designed to protect against sweatshop conditions for work-at-home textile employees. Later they gained strength as a way to protect neighborhoods from becoming industrial centers.

With the advances of computers and other technology, hundreds of thousands of home offices are springing up each year. Some are an extension of offices at a regular work site, while others form the central operations center for many solo businesses.

It's important to find out what *is* and what is *not* allowed in your community regarding home-based businesses. A call (anonymously if you choose) to your municipal clerk's office may get you started.

After that, a big part of staying out of trouble with zoning problems is common sense and common courtesy. Here are some guidelines to follow.

1. Be a good neighbor.
    Depending on your locale, many neighbors don't mind if you're running a small business out of your home, as long as they can't tell it exists or aren't dis-

turbed by it. In fact, some will envy your entrepreneurial spirit. Others will like the idea of having someone home all day to keep an eye on the neighborhood.

2. *Be sensitive to the traffic you create.*

If you have trucks regularly rumbling down your street to deliver materials to your business, you can bet that you're going to attract some attention. Be aware of the traffic your business might generate and do all you can to schedule it so it won't bother your neighbors. Fortunately, delivery vans of all kinds are frequent sightings these days, since more and more people are turning to catalog shopping. Who knows? Instead of a home-based business, your neighbors may think you just have a penchant for buying a lot of L.L. Bean merchandise.

3. *Keep parking accessible for neighbors.*

If you live in a rural area, parking may be plentiful. In residential areas, however, parking is often a major concern. Be aware of the impact your business has on your neighborhood. For example, if you have employees or operate a business that requires customers to visit your home, make sure that you plan for adequate parking. If all the cars can fit within your driveway, that's ideal. If, however, they end up blocking the street, you can stir up some complaints—either directly from your neighbors or as a report to your local zoning board. Do all you can to avoid this unpleasant situation by keeping business-related parking under control. If you don't, you may be forced to locate your office elsewhere.

4. *Consider obtaining a post office box for your business mail.*

You can obtain a P.O. box at your local post office by paying an annual rental fee. Or you might consider using one of the numerous mail service centers that have sprung up around the country—they offer P.O. box rentals, shipping, photocopying, and other valuable support services for small businesses.

A P.O. box can provide four important benefits:

> *First,* it can shield you from revealing that you obviously have a home-based business and guarantee your privacy to some extent. Of course, the flip side to this reasoning is that many people think that a business with a "real" address seems more substantial than one operating out of a P.O. box. In some industries, an office address carries a cachet that a P.O. box just can't acquire.

> *Second,* a P.O. box address can provide insurance against theft, since the location of your business is not immediately apparent. This may be a benefit for you, particularly if you have expensive equipment.

> *Third,* if you move your business, a P.O. box will give you a stable business address. For example, if you start your business at home, then move to another location, your business address will remain the

same. You'll avoid the costly and confusing details of getting checks and stationery reprinted and having mail forwarded.

Fourth, mail delivery and parcel pickup is often more convenient with a P.O. box. The mail usually gets put out early in the day, and if you have any packages, you can pick them up immediately. It also saves the mail carrier from toting all that extra mail to your home, which he or she will appreciate.

In spite of your best efforts at maintaining a discreet home-based business, you may one day be cited with a zoning violation and receive a notice from the authorities ordering you to stop. Do not ignore it! If you do, you can be charged for violations for each additional day that you operate illegally. You generally have two options: One is to apply for a use permit, which allows you to use your home for your business; the other is to apply for a zoning variance, which can take much longer and requires a public hearing.

If you are involved in a zoning dispute, it's a good idea to have legal assistance at hand, even if you don't involve these advisors. Knowing your rights and the limits of what is allowed in your home is important and may keep you from trouble or from expensive fines.

Your Solo Office: Home or Away?

Choosing *where* to set up your solo office is another important decision. Before you think, "Oh, of course I'll have it at home" or "Jim has space at his place he'll let me use," take some time to consider the pros and cons of having an office inside or outside your home. In the end, you may come to the same conclusion, but you'll know that you've made a deliberate decision, rather than just *assuming* it was the only way to go.

The needs of each solo business—and the personality of each entrepreneur—will dictate to some extent the location of the business. Some businesses are naturals for home-based locations—if the work itself is performed at another location, the business may require only a telephone and an answering machine. Other businesses may involve heavy-duty equipment that is not appropriate for home or extensive involvement with the public—and if you live in an out-of-the-way location, your business may not survive.

Let's take a look at the pros and cons of offices inside and outside the home. Then you can choose the one that matches you and your business needs best.

Staking Out Your Space at Home

Home-based offices are the fastest-growing segment of small businesses, and it's easy to see why. It's simple to set up a home office, and the overhead costs can be controlled more easily.

The benefits to home-based working are many: flexible working hours, a commute measured in steps rather than miles, freedom to structure your own day to accommodate other responsibilities, and the choice to wear whatever clothes you'd like. The flip side is that a home office requires a lot of discipline, since distractions are everywhere—from refrigerators to neighbors who thought they would drop by. Also, it's often difficult to separate work and family concerns, and work can spill over into evening hours and become all-consuming.

This sense of always being at work is particularly relevant if you have customers or clients nationwide and you live on one of the coasts. For example, if you live in the east, you may be just sitting down to dinner with a friend when a phone call comes in from Arizona with that big order. It's at times like this that the solo professional really appreciates a microwave.

I've seen home offices carved out of closets, spare bedrooms, kitchens, under-the-stairs niches, basement corners, and garages. (In fact, some of America's most famous businesses got their start in kitchens and garages, including Mrs. Fields Cookies, Mary Kay Cosmetics, and Apple Computer.) If you're thinking of setting up a space in your home dedicated to your business office, try to assess realistically how much physical space you'll need. If you can establish a space that is dedicated *exclusively* to your office, that's ideal. That way you don't have to waste time setting up and breaking down your office space, and you can potentially write off the space as an office in-the-home deduction. As we'll see in Chapter 8 on taxes, the IRS regulations for home office deductions are fairly strict—so if you have the room, clearly delineate a space that is used only for business.

When an Office Away from Home Makes Sense

Some solo business owners choose to have offices outside their homes. Sometimes this is a matter of preference—they want a dividing line between their work and their personal lives. Other times it's a matter of necessity—their businesses involve heavy or large equipment, or their work requires more space than their homes can offer—for example, a photographer who shoots large installations or products. There are also thousands of individuals involved in solo professions, including lawyers, doctors, dentists, and other medical professionals, who operate independently in solo or shared offices, away from home.

The benefits of an office space outside the home are appealing to some solo entrepreneurs. An away-from-home office sometimes lends a more professional image to the business. It can also bring a sharper focus to work, since there may be fewer distractions, and the structure of the day is tighter. Of course, the commute is probably a bit longer—although many business owners say they actually look forward to this time as a period to gear up for or to unwind from the workday.

While all business expenses related to your office—rent, utilities, phone, and so forth—are deductible, they still must be paid for. Let's look at ways to keep your budget in line.

Finding Solo Office Space
(Away from Home) on a Budget

Before you rule out the possibility of an office away from home as too expensive, investigate ways you can get the space without paying big money. Sound impossible? Maybe not—put on your creative thinking cap and consider these options:

1.   Seek out small business incubator sites.

   Incubators are small business complexes—often warehouse-type space that has been renovated—that are divided up into offices for small businesses. Sometimes these sites are underwritten by the SBA; at other times they are funded by regional economic development organizations. There is a range of options, from small offices to larger manufacturing facilities. To find out about incubators in your area, call your local chamber of commerce or SBA office.

2.   Find some partners to share a space.

   You may know some other independent spirits who are launching small businesses, too. Consider pooling your resources and renting a shared office space—and sharing equipment such as photocopiers and fax machines. Another option is to establish one central reception area and split the salary of a secretary/receptionist among all the businesses.

   If you don't know fellow entrepreneurs, explore the possibility of renting a single office from another business that is still in the growing stages. For a slightly higher rent, you may be able to use the other business's office equipment or receptionist. Of course, make sure you put your agreement in writing. That way you'll know how future changes—theirs or yours—may affect the arrangement.

3.   Inquire about professional office suites.

   If you live in a city, see if your neighborhood has any professional office suites. Renting an office in one of these complexes can be like ordering à la carte from a menu. In some facilities, a package of basic services includes the office and utilities. Then you can choose a desk or other office furniture, access to use office equipment such as a photocopier, the option of sharing a receptionist—you can even rent art for the walls! Offices generally can be rented on a month-to-month basis or on an annual or long-term lease. The small businesses that choose this option enjoy the flexibility and the fact that one rent check covers it all.

4.   Offer to swap services for space.

   Don't automatically assume that you pay for your office rent in dollars. Many solo businesses "rent" space in the office of a larger business and pay with services. Think about what you or your business has to offer, and pull together some creative ways to pay your rent—then approach a business that might be open to the swap. For example, if you run a catering service, you might offer to host the company's Christmas party and summer picnic. Are you a photographer? Consider swapping your services. Snow removal? Public relations? Computer consulting or training? Bookkeeping?

Keep your thinking open-ended, and don't be timid in approaching potential businesses. After all, their space may be sitting vacant right now. While they might prefer to have cash income for rent, your offer might solve other problems for them.

The best way to work the swap is to calculate the value of rent against the retail value of your services. Avoid the temptation to discount your services because it's a barter arrangement—the other party isn't discounting the rent value, right? For instance, if the rent would normally be $450 a month, come up with a proposal for the equivalent amount in services, either each month, each quarter, or over the period of a year. Last, put the agreement in writing—everything you will deliver and everything you expect to receive in exchange.

I've heard of some very creative office space/service swaps from solo businesses of all kinds. A one woman PR firm has a financial consulting agency as one of its clients. In exchange for PR work, she has a space in the agency's office and use of its fax machine and other office equipment. An artist cleans the office of an ad agency two evenings a week in exchange for using the photocopier and word processor to do his correspondence and the other high-tech art equipment to put together a stunning portfolio. A real estate firm has its own computer consultant always on call, because the company has traded his support for office space in the building.

If you really want your office to be outside your home, make it happen. Don't let the price of rent keep you away from your dream.

Now that you've decided whether your office is at home or away from home, it's time to think about setting it up. In Chapter 7 we'll talk in detail about the benefits that computers and technology can bring, and in Chapter 10 we'll explore how to design your office so that it works as an invisible partner for you. For now, let's focus on a few key items of office furniture that have a major impact on your work—and why they must be chosen wisely.

The Three Most Important Ingredients in Your Solo Office

No matter where you locate your solo office, there are three elements that demand your attention: your desk, your chair, and your office lighting. These basics have a great influence on the overall environment of your office operations and, in their own way, on your success.

Desk

Office desks range from the kitchen table to custom-made designs costing thousands of dollars. Even if your desk is a plywood plank stretched across filing cabinets, there are two important design elements you should keep in mind: the desk's height and its shape.

Running a solo business takes a lot of energy, and the ideal office setting will offer you support in your efforts rather than tire you out even more. Your desk height should fit you—your body, your personality, and the tasks you do most frequently.

Ergonomics is the study of human engineering—how to design objects so they are efficient and safe when humans interact with them. Ergonomics has become a very hot topic in recent years, particularly in the area of new product design for consumer items and technology.

In ergonomic terms, your office desk should provide comfort and support to your arms when you are seated. Too high, and you will be straining to reach it; too low, and you will be scrunched over it. Engineers have stated that 29 inches is the

"Our engineers have designed the most ergonometrically-correct work station in the world. The only problem is, nobody can stay awake in it for more than 5 minutes!"

average measurement from the floor to the top of a desk; your desk, of course, may vary with your own body measurements and needs.

If you will be using a computer on your desk, consider having a multiple-level desk, since keyboards are more comfortable and efficient at a level about 2 inches lower than desktop height. The chances of repetitive injuries to the hands and wrists—such as the painful carpal tunnel syndrome, which results from typing in one position for long periods of time—can be reduced if your keyboard and work-surface height can be adjusted.

In addition to the height of your desk, consider its shape. An L-shaped or U-shaped desk allows you to have access to multiple surfaces while remaining seated. In Chapter 10, you'll learn more about designing your desk so that it serves you as your central operations base.

Chair

Back problems are a major cause of work-disabling injuries, and an office chair can contribute to or help alleviate these problems. According to a Yale University study, people who sit more than half the time on the job risk a 60 to 70 percent greater chance of herniating a disk than those who move about. In addition, it is estimated that nearly half a million people suffer from vascular ailments each year as a result of sitting too much. The message here? Invest in a good chair, and intersperse your work periods with breaks to move and stretch.

My office chair is the most important piece of furniture to me. I didn't feel this way in the early days of my solo business, but then I realized that I was spending more time in my office chair than I was in my bed. I decided to buy a very good chair and started right away to save some money for it—and I've never regretted it. Not only does it bring me enjoyable comfort every day and help me in my work, it was tax deductible.

If your business is the type that will keep you in an office chair for long periods each day, I urge you to start saving for a good chair, too. Think about how much a good mattress costs, and estimate the same. Look at features such as adjustable controls for seat height, back height, back tilt, and arm rests. There have been huge ergonomic advances in chair design in the last decade, and designers are much more attuned to merging good looks and full functionality.

There are a large number of office suppliers who sell quality office furniture and seating, and a little research will enable you to find one that matches your needs and budget. Chairs by Herman Miller, Inc. (particularly the company's Ergon 2 series and the new Aeron Chair), Knoll International, and Steelcase are among the best around. Herman Miller has been researching office furniture ergonomics since 1976, and the company's attention to detail in seating adjustments and contours shows it. If you want to invest in a chair like this and save a few dollars in doing so, find an interior designer friend to work with you—he or she can buy the chair for you and might pass along the designer discount savings to you.

Office Lighting

Lighting is an element of office design that is too often overlooked. Poor lighting can cause stress and tire you out, and you may not even be aware of it.

In setting up your office, make sure that you have enough lighting and that it is working as your aid, not against you. Avoid bright overhead lights that cast harsh shadows—your eyes will strain to adjust, even if you don't notice it. Balanced light, coming over your left shoulder (if you are right-handed), is considered the ideal lighting environment for writing and general paperwork. If you cannot achieve this setting in your office, try to come as close as possible.

If you work on a computer, make sure that there are no harsh reflections or glare on your screen and that you're seated about an arm's length away. Also, avoid setting up your computer in front of an outside window—the sharp contrast between your screen and outdoor lighting can cause eyestrain. If you're working long hours in front of a computer screen, be sure to take regular breaks. Frequently shifting your focus from near to far—doing paperwork, then gazing out a window—can also help you avoid eyestrain.

Creating a good lighting environment doesn't require costly fixtures. Even inexpensive clamp-on lights can be positioned to provide correct lighting—just turn them upward and bounce the light off office walls for indirect illumination.

Experiment with different amounts of light and its placement. Discover the arrangement that serves you best, both in functionality and in overall feeling. Throughout the ages, theatrical stage designers have known the power of creating mood and setting with lighting. Do the same for your home office—personalize it, and make it work for you.

Whether you'll be spending only a few minutes a day or endless hours in your solo office, it's worth investing the time and money to make your physical space efficient and comfortable. In essence, your solo office is you—and you're the only one who knows the setup that serves you best.

As we've continued to craft your solo business, we've shaped its legal structure and physical space. In future chapters we'll discuss how you can tweak your physical space to be an even more productive tool.

For now, let's move on to introducing your business to the world and securing those first important clients.

Chapter 6

Getting (and Keeping!) Clients and Customers

The market is as much a part of your company as you are.
—Paul Hawken

B y now you've thought through your decisions and chosen a business idea to pursue. You've also assembled a team of professionals and informal advisors to help you focus your plans. Now it's time to make the final transition from idea to reality, by finding customers who will pay for your product or service.

The link you create between your business and your customers is an important element influencing your business success. You can have the freshest idea, the brightest advisors, the most sought-after product or service, but if you don't connect with your customers, it won't matter. Remember, without customers you don't have a business. In this chapter, you'll see how the selling and marketing of your product or service—making that connection between you and your buyer—is the key to creating business prosperity.

This chapter clarifies the mysteries of sales and marketing. You'll discover how to create high-impact sales and marketing messages (on a small-scale budget), how to get those important first accounts, and how to grow your business to the size you desire.

The World of Marketing and Sales

Though linked, marketing and sales are very separate tasks. I've always thought of marketing as an invitation to the customer—something that entices a customer to buy a product or service. Sales, on the other hand, involves the customer actually signing on the dotted line, paying, and taking ownership of the product or service.

Another way of thinking about marketing is selling *in,* whether into a potential buyer's mind or into another store, if you're creating wholesale products for resale. Sales is selling *through,* with the buyer completing the transaction with his or her cash, check, or credit card, and you realizing the profit.

Both elements are necessary—as when two people shake hands. If a hand is extended but not grasped by the other party, no handshake takes place. We've all experienced an incomplete handshake. Remember how silly it felt to have your hand dangling out there in midair? It will feel even worse if you have terrific products in your basement that remain unsold or if you offer a great service and your phone never rings. You need both the marketing invitation *and* the sale.

We'll first take a look at marketing tools and how you can personalize them for your solo business. A bit later, you'll see how to leverage your marketing efforts so they turn into sales—and dollars in your pocket.

Solo Marketing Possibilities

When most new business owners think of marketing, they usually think only about one limited tool—advertising. Some might include three other additional marketing methods such as promotion, publicity, and PR, but they aren't quite sure what they are or how to use them.

These Big Four—advertising, promotion, publicity, and PR—are the most commonly used marketing tools. How are they different, and how can you use them? Let's take a look.

The best way I've heard to explain the Big Four comes from an example shared by Raleigh Pinskey, a creative dynamo who's head of a Los Angeles–based PR firm and author of *101 Ways to Promote Yourself* (Avon, 1997). As she says: When your circus comes to town, and you put up a sign, that's *advertising*. If you put the sign on the back of an elephant and march the elephant through town, that's *promotion*. If the elephant, with the sign still on its back, tramples through the mayor's flower bed and the paper reports it, that's *publicity*. If you can get the mayor to laugh about it and forgive the elephant and ride in the circus with no hard feelings, then you've mastered the art of *public relations*.

Let's take a quick look at these elements in a little more detail.

Advertising

Advertising generally includes any paid printed, audio, or video announcement that builds awareness of your business. This can range from printed ads in newspapers or the Yellow Pages to commercials on radio or TV.

Promotion

Promotion is anything that establishes or positions your business in the marketplace or develops new business contacts for you. Popular promotions include special coupons or offers, bundling additional services at no extra cost, or freebies that accompany your product or service. Special packaging, merchandising, or point-of-purchase displays are other promotional tools.

Publicity

If your business generates interest or a special event, local media may cover the event, and your business can generate some free publicity. Most publicity is great, but sometimes it can work against you. For example, we've all heard stories of medicine being tampered with, or food poisoning from bad meat at a hamburger chain. That's when you turn to . . .

Public Relations

Public relations is the process of creating a positive public image for your business. It generally involves establishing an ongoing relationship with media professionals, such as writers, photographers, editors, or producers, so they will present your business to the public in a favorable light. It also means maintaining a positive image with the public in general and your customers in particular. The basic tool of forging a relationship with the media is the news release. Later in this chapter, you'll learn how to create one that will gain your business free press.

These four marketing tools, as well as other innovative approaches, are scattered throughout this chapter. As you explore them, keep your own situation in mind. Some methods may seem better matched to your goals than others, but all of them will get you thinking in new ways.

Your Unique Selling Proposition

Before you begin any marketing or sales activity for your solo business, you must first decide what qualities make your business unique. The positioning that set you apart from your competition is often referred to as your *unique selling proposition* (USP). You began this assessment when you made your business plan and defined your market. Now it's time to refine your thoughts and create your marketing and sales messages.

The USP for your product or service might be based on one or more of the following factors:

✓ *Price*—lower, higher, better value for the money
✓ *Availability*—seasons, hours, immediate, ongoing
✓ *Selection*—variety, quality, sizes, colors
✓ *Location*—storefront, urban, rural, convenient
✓ *Service*—personalized, delivery, money-back guarantee

Think about these qualities and how they can be applied to your product or service. What sets *your* business apart? Commit your list to paper and live with it for a while, adding to and updating it as new ideas come to you. This positioning is the keystone for your subsequent marketing efforts.

What marketing options should you explore? Before we answer that question, it's important to understand how most people learn about and decide to buy a product or service.

The Most Powerful Marketing Method

Statistics show that people are influenced by many different factors when they are ready to buy a product or service. These include need, price, quality, availability, and overall trustworthiness of the vendor. How do most people decide?

Think back to the last time you had to make a buying decision, whether it involved a special dinner at a restaurant, a movie for Saturday night, a new dry cleaner, a doctor or dentist—or any new product or service. You checked around and maybe took notice of some signs or reviews. But when it came down to making the decision, you probably did what more than 70 percent of consumers do—you asked your friends.

> *Personal recommendation is the most powerful marketing method for any solo business.*

When someone refers another person to your business, this referral comes with an implied level of endorsement and credibility. People want to believe in you and your business.

Of course, when you're just starting out, there may not be that many people who know of you and your business. Before word-of-mouth referrals can build, you must spread the news about your product or service. Fortunately, there is a way to reach your customers without spending a fortune in the process. What's required is creative inspiration. You need to become a guerrilla.

Becoming a Guerrilla Can Be Fun

Upon first hearing it, some independent entrepreneurs think guerrilla marketing is somehow related to caged primates at the zoo. But this isn't *gorilla* marketing—it's *guerrilla* marketing. Guerrillas are fiercely independent fighters who are committed to a cause and use every possible method and tool to win. If you think that sounds a lot like a solo entrepreneur, you've captured the idea of guerrilla marketing.

Guerrilla marketers go beyond the tried-and-true marketing Big Four of advertising, promotion, publicity, and PR. That doesn't mean they must spend a lot of money. Jay Conrad Levinson, the undisputed guru of guerrilla marketing and author of the best-selling Guerrilla Marketing book series, explains that smallness can be a strength.

"Your size is an ally when it comes to guerrilla marketing," Levinson states. "If you're a small company, a new venture, or a single individual, you can utilize the tactics of guerrilla marketing to their fullest." Levinson points out that guerrillas have the ability to be fast on their feet and that they can change much more quickly than their larger competitors—two qualities that offer significant competitive advantages.

Guerrillas don't mimic the stodgy techniques of large corporations. Instead of being the large, brute-force army, they're the swift-footed commandos, dodging in the forest. Their strength is not huge machinery—they live by their wits and their imaginations. This is precisely your approach as a solo entrepreneur, and it is why guerrilla marketing can be so effective for you.

Guerrilla marketers climb into the customer's head and focus all their marketing from the buyer's perspective. In his book *Guerrilla Marketing Excellence* (Houghton-Mifflin, 1993), Levinson points out that successful entrepreneurs—and guerrilla marketers—must understand what customers really are buying. He lists dozens of reasons, including these:

✓ Customers buy *benefits,* not features.

✓ They buy *promises* you make—so make them with care.

✓ They buy your *credibility,* or they don't buy if you lack it.

✓ They buy *solutions* to their problems.

✓ They buy your *guarantee, reputation,* and *good name.*

✓ They buy *value,* which is not the same as price.

✓ They buy *selection,* and often the best of your selection.

✓ They buy *convenience* in buying, paying, and lots more.

✓ They buy *success*—your success, which can lead to theirs.

Can you see how Levinson's points take you a step beyond your unique selling proposition? As an independent professional, you're not selling a product or service—you're selling the qualities listed above, as well as *yourself.* As you pull together your solo marketing campaign, keep Levinson's thoughts in mind. In addition to the characteristics that define your unique selling proposition, what *other* qualities make up your business? What are your customers *really* seeking in your product or service?

Levinson has published a full collection of books on various aspects of waging and winning this marketing battle. They're among my favorite small business books, and I recommend them to every solo entrepreneur (see Appendix A, "Solo Resources").

Using Creativity Instead of Cash

What guerrilla marketers know is that creativity can be more valuable than cash. A big budget does not guarantee spectacular results—or profits—a fact obvious in the thousands of dollars spent each year by big businesses on marketing mis-fires. Coca-Cola obviously thought we wanted a new Coke—but they were wrong. Years ago the Edsel was touted as the car everyone would love to buy—but they didn't. These are just two of the many examples of expensive marketing campaigns that fizzled trying to launch products to a market that really didn't want them.

Instead of risking marketing dollars this way, look at methods that use your imagination instead of your wallet. Brainstorm ways you can create a distinctive impression on your clients or customers—without a big expense.

I've seen some wonderfully creative promotions done on a shoestring. For example, a child care business uses crayons and brightly colored paper to publicize its services. Materials cost: practically zero. Exposure and memorability: phenomenally high, resulting in lots of new clients.

The opportunities for creative, low-cost marketing are as varied as the businesses they promote. Here's a list to start you thinking about your own marketing:

✓ Create customer appreciation events or coupons, to let your customers know how much you value their continued support.

✓ Include a small gift or bonus with the purchase of your product or service.

✓ Create inexpensive, yet useful, printed items that have your company name on them, such as pens, pencils, bookmarks, or scratch pads.

✓ Offer gift certificates so customers can give their friends your product or service.

✓ Start a club that offers repeat customers a bonus, such as a free item or service, or a discount. After they purchase x number of times, customers receive the bonus.

✓ Offer free samples of your product—a scaled-down version, if appropriate. Sometimes the hardest leap is to get someone to try your product or service.

✓ Volunteer to give a seminar or demonstration on a topic related to your business.

✓ Send thank-you, birthday, or holiday cards to key customers.

✓ Offer your product or service as a prize at a community auction.

✓ Publish a newsletter or flyer about your business to let customers feel they are linked to you personally.

✓ Give discounts to customers who refer others to your business.

✓ Put up colorful flyers about your business on local bulletin boards, if appropriate.

Each of these suggestions captures the essence of effective guerrilla marketing: None needs to be expensive, the approach is flexible, and each can be targeted to specific markets. Many can be adopted for nearly any business. What guerrilla tactics would work for marketing your solo business?

What about Advertising?

Printed display advertising, which generally features graphics or your logo in a newspaper or magazine, is a more traditional marketing option. When it's effective, advertising can bring visibility and create a demand for your product or service. Sales might be easier, since customers have a chance to know something about your business before they meet you.

At first glance, advertising appears to be an inevitable part of a solo business budget. Advertising may not, however, be the best choice for *your* solo business. For instance, if your customers aren't the type who review ads in newspapers or magazines before deciding to buy a product or service, your marketing dollars might be better invested elsewhere.

Each advertising vehicle—newspapers, telephone directories, business directories, magazines, newsletters, radio, TV, and the Internet—has both advantages and disadvantages associated with it. Weigh both sides carefully, and calculate the cost per potential buyer for each advertising choice you make. Also keep in mind that just because your ad appears, there are no guarantees that it will result in income for your business.

As you're determining whether to advertise, be sure to check out Michael Phillips and Salli Rasberry's book, *Marketing Without Advertising*. The authors explain effective alternative options to advertising and present ways small business owners can stretch their marketing budgets (details in Appendix A, "Solo Resources").

It Takes Multiple Contacts

No matter what techniques you use, your marketing must be consistent and repeated. Marketing veterans know that once is not enough.

Marketing takes hard work, dedication, and an understanding that *offering* a product will not automatically translate into sales. You must invite, entice, cajole, urge, tempt, and persuade your customers to buy from you—repeatedly.

Studies have shown that it takes a consumer an average of *seven to nine* exposures to your message before he or she will buy. Seven to nine times! Were you going to give up after only one or two? As you create your marketing strategy, commit your time, energy, and money to a long-term vision.

What does hearing about your product or service seven times feel like? Here's one way a potential customer might hear about your business. First, the person learns about it from a flyer hanging in a store. Then he or she reads about it in a small newspaper article. Over lunch, the person discusses the article with a friend. A few days later, it comes up in a casual phone call. Later, someone knows of a friend who has tried it and was pleased. Driving around town, the person comes across another sign or mention of your product or service and thinks, "Hmmm . . . maybe I'll give that a try." A few days later, when the person gets a special offer from you in the mail, he or she is ready to buy.

Now, it may take several days or a few months for all this to happen, and you have to find your own seven ways that are effective for you. That's the challenge—you really can't predict which message will be the one that finally gets through. Wouldn't it be a shame if you *almost* made it to the consciousness of those customers, but then they stopped hearing about you? That's why marketing has to be an ongoing process in your business—not only to get new customers but to keep existing ones.

Reap the Benefits of Repeat Customers

You've seen how much work it can take to dig into the consciousness of your potential customers. Once you've succeeded and they've decided to buy from you, make sure you keep them! You've done the hardest work—getting the customers. Now don't let them slip away.

Two business rules sum up the importance of cultivating repeat customers:

Rule #1: *80 percent of your business will come from 20 percent of your customers.*

Rule #2: *Getting a new customer can cost up to eight times as much as selling to an existing one.*

Take a close look at both those rules. They are startling in their power. To better understand the importance of developing repeat customers, consider an image that author Zig Ziglar uses to illustrate the value of persistence: priming a pump.

Imagine an old-fashioned water pump, the kind that the pioneers dealt with daily on their farms. If you've had experience with these pumps, you know that it can take a l-o-n-g time for water to rise to the surface. Your arm can get quite a workout getting that water out of the ground. But if you stop, that water goes all the way back down, and you have to start over from scratch.

As a solo pioneer, you'll be putting forth a lot of energy as you launch your new business. Your pumping arm may get pretty tired, as you pump and pump with no water coming out. When the water—your new customers—appears, rejoice, but don't stop pumping!

Once the water has started to flow, it takes a different touch on the pump handle to keep it going. Similarly, once you've won your customers' confidence and they've tried your product, your marketing strategy shifts. You must thank your customers, reward them for their loyalty, and invite them to come back—again and again.

Plan It!

Effective marketing campaigns, no matter how much you spend or what they entail, require planning. You must constantly entice customers to buy, and once they do, you must not let them slip away. All of this takes planning and a commitment to consistently contact your market.

Your marketing plan begins by jumping into the minds of your potential customers and seeing things from their perspective. Review what is special, unique, appealing, or impossible to resist about your product or service. Then consider how your typical customer might discover your product or service. Billboards, free samples, classified ads, flyers in the local grocery store, articles in the area newspaper, helium balloons—skywriting?

Put all of these ideas down on paper, and give your thoughts some structure, including a time frame and a dollar commitment. Many small business advisors suggest investing 8 to 10 percent of projected gross revenues in marketing. While this figure is a good place to start, I've found that each business is different and may require more—or less—financial commitment to make the marketing truly effective. Sketch out your ideas and see what they will cost. If they're too big for your budget right now, don't abandon them. Try to see how you can create a similar result, substituting creativity for cash.

What's most important is that your marketing is *consistent* and *persistent*. Don't give up. Remember, you may almost have that water at the top of the pump. Connecting with your customers through marketing can be great fun and can lead to great profits for your business, too. Let it be a creative outlet for you. Don't be afraid to experiment, and when you find something that works, get every bit of mileage out of it that you can.

Your Business Image Is a Powerful Marketing Tool

The way you present your business face to the public can have a dramatic effect on how potential customers perceive you and your product or service. Particularly in solo ventures, there is often little distinction between *who* the business is and *what* is offered for sale.

A key benefit of this is that you can control your public presentation and fine-tune it so that it communicates your true message to potential customers. It's all related to presenting a professional business image.

Over the past 20 years, I've helped thousands of small business owners become more aware of the personal power they can create through a professional image. Some are skeptical at first. In my seminars I hear them say, "But, Terri, I don't want an *image*—that sounds so fake." While the word *image* does carry some connotations of being false, what we're focusing on is presenting the *true* message you want to communicate to your customers. Your business is going to have an image, regardless of whether you like it. Wouldn't you rather it be a good one?

There are three key areas that form the basis of your professional business image: how you appear in person, on the phone, and in print. Let's take a look at each area.

Your Business Image in Person

As a solo entrepreneur, you'll encounter many situations where you must present your business in person. Before you even open your mouth, your image is already expressed—in the way you dress, your posture, your walk, and so forth.

Volumes have been written on how to dress for success, and I'm not advocating any one style of business attire over another. After all, one of the reasons you started your own business was the freedom to decide the details—and maybe for you, one of those important details is how to dress. My point, instead, is that your attire can be a powerful communication tool. Be aware that your potential customers are relating to you from *their* personal style. If you dress more formally or casually than your customers, it can be awkward or uncomfortable for both of you. Think about the message your clothing conveys. Make it a conscious choice, a valuable tool that works for you.

First impressions are made on looks. This is quickly followed by the first words out of your mouth. I'm continually amazed at how many solo entrepreneurs apologize for what they do or who they are. "Well, I'm running this jewelry repair business, but it's only part-time, and it's not making a lot of money yet." Or, "Yeah, I do tax preparation, but this is only my second year, and I'm just getting started." Or, "I have this catering business, but I'm still testing some of my recipes."

Here are three people who have shown they have incredible guts and the courage to launch their own businesses—and they're apologizing. Imagine what their customers think when they hear those comments. Would you trust your good jewelry to that repair person? Or your tax return to someone with such a lack of confidence? Or hire a caterer for your next dinner party, who admits the food quality is questionable? Probably not. Yet countless solo entrepreneurs undermine themselves in this way—not only once in a while, but all the time. And they wonder why business never comes their way.

Promise yourself that you'll shake this habit. It can be the downfall of even the best-run business, with the finest product or service.

How do you overcome this impulse to belittle or to apologize? You develop something I call . . .

The Five-Minute Brag

This technique is often misunderstood, because its name implies that you become a long-winded, egotistical bore. In reality, if used skillfully, this conversational technique is neither lengthy nor boring.

A Five-Minute Brag is a well-prepared series of phrases about yourself that become a spontaneous and natural part of your conversation. Sound false? It's actually something we do all the time, only we're not aware of it.

For example, most independent professionals are frequently in situations where they are asked, "What do you do?" As we've already seen, many individuals unconsciously give negative or unflattering replies. For unprepared solo entrepreneurs, this awkward moment can be a lost opportunity to gain new customers or to learn something that can benefit their businesses.

With a Five-Minute Brag, you have a prepared response for that question. I call it a Five-Minute Brag, not because it has to last that long—it's not intended to turn you into a resounding bore. Rather, it prepares you to be confident and able to speak comfortably about yourself and your business for *up to* five minutes, if need be.

Think about a situation in which you have only five minutes to connect with someone who could be incredibly valuable to your business. Perhaps you're sharing a cab ride somewhere, or an elevator, or a brief conversation at a party. Chances are, if you're not prepared, you'll spend that time chatting about safe topics, such as the weather, sports, your children, current events, or your pets.

Armed with a Five-Minute Brag, you can turn that brief encounter into a big win for you and your business. Because you're prepared, you feel comfortable speaking about your business, what it does, how it's unique, and the many benefits it brings your customers. You'll also be able to chat about how successful your business already is and your plans for the future.

A Five-Minute Brag is a powerful verbal tool you can use to present yourself and your business in a positive light. To prepare one, write down a list of everything you would like someone to know about you and/or your business. Then review this list, and practice saying some of these things in a conversational tone, *out loud.* It's very important that you verbalize these thoughts—just thinking them isn't enough. Some solo professionals have told me that they like to practice in the shower or in their cars, where they are the only ones who can hear. Others pace around their offices, holding imaginary conversations and refining their responses. It doesn't matter where you practice—only that you do.

When your mouth speaks the words, and your ears hear them, powerful things begin to happen. You begin to say and hear these terrific things about yourself and your business—and you begin to believe them. Your confidence grows, and your business will, too.

The Express Elevator Version

After you've developed your Five-Minute Brag, spend some time creating its cousin, the Express Elevator version. This is a condensed brag that lasts for only a few seconds—about the time it would take to ride from a hotel's 27th floor to the lobby. Most encounters begin with these brief exchanges, and it's often a challenge to present yourself professionally, but concisely. The best Express Elevator self-introductions are crafted so that they'll elicit a response such as, "Oh, how interesting. Tell me more." This is the time to forget the flowery language—your goal is clear communication of who you are and what your business does.

With practice, you'll be able to adapt your Five-Minute Brag and Express Elevator self-introduction to any situation, highlighting things you feel are important in one encounter and emphasizing different points at other times. You'll discover, as most solo entrepreneurs have, that they can be your company's most powerful marketing tools.

Words of Wisdom

On Presenting Yourself with Power

The fine line between your personal and business identities can create challenges for many solo entrepreneurs when they present themselves and their work. Here are some insights from an award-winning actor, media coach, and broadcaster.

"There are many elements that contribute to a sense of perceived power and confidence, whether addressing a client, a live group, a radio microphone, a telephone, or a television camera. In training thousands of professionals, here are some helpful techniques I've discovered.

"Be aware of your non-verbal signals. The body speaks volumes—and can telegraph messages we do not intend. Want to gain power, authority, and trust? Smile. To lose that power, cross your arms and legs and don't employ eye contact. If you use gestures, make them natural, organic, and real. If you're planning gestures, don't. Allow them to happen on their own.

"If you're being interviewed on camera, look directly into the camera when addressing the audience to create confidence and trust in what you say. In contrast, if you look into the camera when being asked questions, you'll appear aloof.

"When speaking into a microphone, never speak too closely or directly into the front of it. Instead, place it at an angle and speak across it—you'll avoid those breathy blasts. Here's where practice

pays off: Remember diction, pitch, tone, pacing, rate, grouping, inflection, volume, coloring, and breath control.

"If you get nervous before a making a call or presentation, here's a simple cure. Simply extend your abdomen—out, way out. This has an overall calming effect on the body. It also gives you a much larger pocket of air from which to speak, which means you can speak for a longer period of time without taking a breath."

—*Batt Johnson*

Batt Johnson is the creator of The Visual and Verbal Image-Personal Training Program™, which helps individuals increase their self-confidence and decrease their self-consciousness when making presentations. Based in New York City, Batt teaches advanced commercial acting courses and coaches entrepreneurs and corporate clients on speech and presentation skills. (See Appendix A, "Solo Resources," for details.)

Your Business Image on the Phone

The second component of your professional business image stems from your ability to present yourself on the telephone. To savvy solo entrepreneurs, the phone is more than a convenient means of communication—it's a powerful marketing tool for their businesses. By maximizing your effectiveness on the telephone, you can boost your business to greater profits and success. Here are some tips to guide you.

1. Be aware.

Most of us take the phone for granted, and doing so causes us to become complacent or to overlook the messages that we are sending out—intentionally or not—over the wires. A casual attitude toward the telephone can undermine your best marketing efforts. Try to be fully "present" when you use the phone—not with your mind rambling to other matters.

2. Project a professional and upbeat tone.

Answer your phone on the second or third ring, with a professional greeting and a smile in your voice. If you're not there, do you have an answering machine or voice mail? Does it contain a professional and clear, concise, and current outgoing message? Can callers leave a message of any length they want? Give options for callers to get information they need or to reach you in other ways, such as by fax or online. Call the number yourself from time to time to see how the quality of the message sounds and if it represents you well.

3. Get organized.

Establish a part of your office (or desk) as the phone center. Keep information and supplies you need at your fingertips, so you can answer questions, take orders, or refer to files quickly and easily. Consider buying a headset to save time and cramped neck muscles if you're on the phone for more than a couple of hours a day.

4.   Be prepared.

If you're making the call, don't count on being able to remember everything you want to discuss. If necessary, write a script. This may be as simple as a list of bulleted items that you want to make sure you cover, or it may be as detailed as the exact phrasing you want to use in a situation. A script can help you overcome nervousness or mental distractions. It can also prevent those embarrassing moments when you finish a phone call and realize—often as the receiver hits the hook—that there was one more detail you wanted to clear up, so you have to call back.

5.   Be considerate.

Your goal is to capture the other person's attention, and this can't happen if he or she is in the middle of a meeting, has a call on another line, or is otherwise occupied. When calling, state your request succinctly and present an option: "Do you have two minutes to talk about the materials I sent you last week? Or what time would be good for me to call?" If the person can't talk at that moment, try to get a specific time when you should call back. You then have a phone date that the other party is much more likely to keep with you.

6.   Review and confirm your agreements.

At the end of a conversation, particularly when a verbal negotiation has been completed, it's often valuable to repeat to the other party your interpretation of the agreement, using a summation such as, "Now, as I understand it, here are my responsibilities . . . and here are yours. . . ." This approach frequently clarifies details that were overlooked during the original discussion. It also communicates to your clients or customers that you really want to meet their needs, down to the smallest detail.

Some solo entrepreneurs have found that faxing a summary of their notes of the conversation and agreement is an effective way of following up with a client. It paves the way for a clear understanding of the agreement and it provides prompt confirmation of each party's responsibilities.

Your Business Image in Print

The third element of your professional business image is presenting yourself in print. Sometimes clients and customers don't get to see your smiling face or hear your cheery voice when they first come in contact with your business. Instead, they see a printed message, such as an ad or a brochure, that communicates your business identity. The effect of your image—whether positive or negative, haphazard or planned—can influence the manner in which you and your business are perceived.

Studies indicate that the average person receives more than 3,000 visual messages each day. Your printed materials must be able to break through this visual clutter and deliver your message to potential customers. Whether it's a brochure, a flyer, a business card, or the design of your packaging, your image in print is recalled every time someone thinks of you or makes a decision to buy.

Design plays a strong psychological role in creating a business identity. Consider the difference in the logos for Coca-Cola and Pepsi, for example. You get a very different feel from each of them. The same holds true for nearly every major product brand you buy. The shape, the color, the style of type—each lends an element to the overall image of the company.

As a solo business, you may not need—or want—to invest in creating a logo or expensive packaging. But you will need *some* type of identity for your business. If art was never your strong suit, don't despair. There are literally millions of graphic design professionals around the country, and you'll be able to find one to help you. Many, in fact, are solo businesses, too.

One of the best ways to work with a graphic designer is to start a clipping file. In it, put samples of printed material—business cards, flyers, direct-mail pieces, announcements, ads—that you find appealing. Jot down a note or two about why you liked a particular sample and how something similar might work for your business. When it comes time to meet with the designer, take your file along. Have some clear ideas of what you like, what you're trying to accomplish, and an estimated budget. With this feedback, the designer then can give you an idea of cost, and you can decide whether it fits your needs and budget.

Then let the professional take over. This is sometimes very difficult for solo entrepreneurs to do, since this graphic represents *your* business, *your* life. There's some inexplicable me-too attraction about graphic design. Few professions seem to attract as many people who think they, too, can do it. Of course, professional quality always shines through. Among all the hats that you might wear in your solo business, this is one you should almost always pass off to another professional.

There are ways to work with designers, though, so that you can do things on your own once they've established the basic designs. For example, an increasing number of graphic designers offer services to design the logo and underlying structure, or templates, for a business. Using this approach, the solo entrepreneur can make minor changes to an ad or update a brochure on his or her own while still retaining the overall professional look of the original design. This is particularly easy when the design is done on a computer, since templates become electronic files.

Not all designers work this way, however, and you need to be careful not to destroy the strength of their work by tweaking things on your own. Discuss the template option with the designers you interview—it's one way of getting great design and a consistent look, without having to run to the designer for every small change. You save time and money, and the designer likes it, too, since he or she can concentrate on bigger projects than changing a line of type for you.

Designing Backward

Most of all, make sure every printed piece *works* for you. I know of so many small businesses that have printed fancy brochures and expensive presentation packages—and they don't know why. When I ask them what these are used for, they reply, "Oh, I thought they looked great, and it seems everyone has them." It's true, they often do look very impressive, but they are also very expensive. I always wonder if that money might not have been better spent in other ways, getting customers to add profits to their pockets instead.

To avoid this expensive mistake, begin by closely analyzing the *function* of every piece you want to create. Keep your end result always in mind. What are you trying to achieve? To introduce people to your business? To give them a card to send in for more information? To get them to put your name in their Rolodexes? To entice them to stop by for a sample?

Also keep in mind how your piece will reach intended buyers. By mail? In an envelope or not? Inside another package? Hand-delivered?

If you are very specific about your objective and other requirements, you'll discover that your design will come together much more quickly—and it will deliver the results you want. It's backward-thinking of the best kind.

A last note on graphics: Don't feel you must keep your graphic image forever. The world changes, and so will your business. When it's time for a new look, carefully consider the customer recognition value of your current visual image and whether it makes sense to change it. A slight update to freshen the look may be all that's needed to stay contemporary. On the other hand, there are businesses that have kept the same image for more than a century with great success. See what works for you.

In the meantime, use your graphic image consistently and professionally on everything you present as part of your business. It's true that a picture is worth a thousand words. The graphic identity you present for your business carries a valuable message to your customers. Take time to invest in it. Then use it wisely, consistently, and with care.

Up to now, we've explored many low-cost, creative ways you can promote your product or service and how your professional image can be a powerful marketing tool. Let's move on to explore the remaining two marketing elements—publicity and public relations—and the benefits they offer.

Getting Free Press

Does the chance to get newspaper articles, TV coverage, radio interviews, or other media coverage promoting your business sound like it's beyond your reach as a solo entrepreneur? It's not at all. Keep in mind that the media have an unending appetite for news. Stories about your business can fill that need.

Studies show that more than 75 percent of the material you see in newspapers or on TV is placed by individuals or organizations intent on promoting themselves, their cause, or their business. Their primary tool is a *news release,* a one- or two-page written statement that tells a story with a unique, catchy slant.

To capture an editor's interest, news releases must have *news value.* "Your news release must contain information that an editor believes will excite the reader," explains former newspaper editor Kay Borden, author of *Bulletproof News Releases.* "It may be funny, heartwarming, or sad. It may make you angry or fearful, or attract you because of some interest you have in the subject. News value may be found in a new law, a tragic mishap, higher prices, or a medical breakthrough. Editors know what makes readers laugh, cry, love, and learn, and constantly look for news that works at sparking these reactions," Borden adds.

In a world with more than 27 million self-employed individuals, sending a news release that says you're a new solo business will cause most editors to say, "So what?" Instead, share information that will position you as an expert, and a valuable resource for readers—your potential customers.

To demonstrate how to construct an effective news release, I asked publicity consultant Kay Borden to share a before-and-after example of a news release from one of her clients. The original news release can be found in Figure 6.1. In the revised release in Figure 6.2, however, you'll see how Kay has increased its attractiveness to editors and improved its chances of getting printed. Study Kay Borden's changes carefully and you'll find ways you can improve your own news releases.

WANT YOUR NEWS RELEASE PRINTED?
AVOID THESE NINE FATAL ERRORS

1. Reads like advertising
2. Unsuitable subject matter
3. Poor writing
4. Not enough information
5. Too technical
6. Unsuitable writing style
7. Poor timing
8. Useless, uninteresting information
9. Poor graphics or photos

—Kay Borden, author of *Bulletproof News Releases*

Contact: Jean Heine (804) 498-4060
             J-Mart Press
             P.O. Box 8884
             Virginia Beach, VA 23450-8884

News Release

AUTHORS AND PUBLISHERS SELL MORE BOOKS

Everyone has a story. Many of these, though written, go unpublished. Not because the stories are poorly written or uninteresting, but because their authors don't know what to do next. There are thousands of other stories published every year that do not sell out of their first printing. Again, not because of a lack of quality or even an uninterested public, but because the public, the customers, don't know they're available. Perhaps you know of or even have one of these stories crying to be read.

Art and Jean Heine have been publishers and in the business of marketing books for over five years. Drawing on their frustrations, sleepless nights, failures and successes, they coauthored *Book $elling 101, A Marketing Primer for Authors and Publishers*. This unique book begins where the other books on writing and publishing don't,

Figure 6.1 This is an example of a press release drafted by small business owners to announce the publication of a new book. Compare it to the revised version in Figure 6.2.

at the beginning. Each chapter is packed with advice for authors, would-be authors, publishers and would-be publishers. Jean even shares her secret for booking Art as a guest on nine TV shows, in 12 days, in five states, for a total of 90 minutes of free air time. More than a regular how-to book, each chapter in *Book $elling 101* ends with an assignment, practical exercise or quiz to further reinforce the topic discussed.

Readers not only learn the secrets of getting their stories published, they also discover how to assist in marketing so their books don't end up on shelves gathering dust.

```
┌─────────────────────────────────────────────┐
│  ①                                          │
│  NEWS RELEASE          For Immediate Release │
│                                         ④    │
│  ② June 1, 1995                              │
│                                              │
│     Contact:  Jean Heine (804) 498-4060      │
│           ③  J-MART PRESS                    │
│               P.O. Box 8884                  │
│               Virginia Beach, VA 23450-8884  │
│                                              │
│       ⑤                                      │
│         NEW BOOK REVEALS HARD FACTS          │
│          TO AUTHORS AND PUBLISHERS           │
│   ⑥                                          │
│     VIRGINIA BEACH, VA — So you've written a │
│     book—or want to—do you know how to sell it? A │
│     new book, Book $elling 101 by Art and Jean Heine, │
│   ⑦ supplies plenty of hard-fact answers for both │
│     the author looking for a publisher and would-be │
│     self-publishers.                         │
│                                              │
│     The 15-chapter marketing primer for authors │
│     and publishers retails for $9.95 and uses actual │
│   ⑧ elements of the book to reinforce the material. For │
│     instance, Chapter 3 shows publishers how to │
│     figure a book's retail price. The samples and data │
│     are real, not fictitious.                │
│                                              │
│     "To make the information more realistic, we use │
│     the book as its own example. We used the actual │
│     costs and expenses for Book $elling 101 as an │
│     example to reinforce the formula for computing │
│     retail price," Art Heine explains.   ⑨   │
│                                     More...  │
└─────────────────────────────────────────────┘
```

Figure 6.2 Here is the improved news release, revised by publicity consultant Kay Borden. Notice how it has a much more engaging tone and draws the reader in. The numbers refer to important elements found in all news releases, explained in detail elsewhere in this chapter.

The Heines stress writing for the customer to produce quality material that sells, and packaging for eye appeal. The book also covers promotional topics such as maximizing positive book reviews, producing winning media kits, and increasing exposure through co-oping opportunities. Each chapter concludes with an exercise or assignment for the reader, either author or publisher.

"The book is based on hard-to-find answers to the questions we faced when starting our own ⑩ publishing company," explains Heine. He and his wife, Jean, own and operate J-Mart Press in Virginia Beach, Va.

Art Heine is the author of *Surviving After High School*, winner of the 1991 National Association of Independent Publishers' AWARD FOR CONTENT, and its Teacher's Guide, also a J-Mart Press Publication.

For more, contact J-Mart Press at (804) 498-4060 or P.O. Box 8884, Virginia Beach, VA 23450-8884. ⑪

###
⑫

Figure 6.2 shows numbers alongside the parts of the news release that relate to these important elements:

1. *Label.* Obvious, but necessary. So much mail comes into media desks each day that it helps to note that this is a news release.

2. *Date of information.* In case this release gets lost on an editor's desk and is discovered six months later. (You think I'm kidding?)

3. *Contact person.* If the editor wants to expand on the release or do a full story, he or she knows whom to call for more details.

4. *Release date.* Either undated, or if the material is held for release on a special date, this line then reads: "Hold for release until _____" or "Release on _____."

5. *Headline.* Make it accurate, short, and snappy. Avoid weak verbs and prepositions. This is your one chance to grab the editor's (and, subsequently, the reader's) attention.

6. *Dateline.* This identifies the origin of the news. For national releases, the city and state would be listed. It is always typed in all capital letters.

7. *First (or lead) paragraph.* Try to cover the who, what, when, where, why, and how in the first paragraph. The editor may have room to run only a few sentences of your release. If you save your key information for the last few paragraphs, it may end up on the layout room floor.

8. *Secondary paragraph.* Expand on the main topic, giving some background.

9. *The best news releases are no longer than 250 to 300 words.* If the release goes on for more than one page, type "More . . ." at the bottom of the page. In the event that any pages get lost, the editor will know—and not run half your story.

10. *Additional paragraphs.* These sentences give further details and may spark interest for related stories. Biographical material sometimes is featured here. Quotes break up the text and create a bond with the reader.

11. *Wrap-up paragraphs.* These sentences usually give telephone numbers and other information. They offer the reader the chance to act on the information given in the release.

12. *End.* Type "end" or "###" marks so the editor understands the release is finished.

News releases are often part of a larger package called a *media kit,* which may include a sample of your product, photos, reprints of articles on your solo business, or other information. By customizing each of your kits for a particular media outlet, you can adapt your pitch to most closely match the editor's (and audience's) interests.

The methods for getting free press are literally endless. It all depends on your energy and your gumption. The bonus is widespread free publicity for your product or service. Another benefit: Since it comes as a third-party endorsement, an article carries more credibility than a paid ad or announcement. You can get extra mileage from your efforts by reprinting the articles or by using the best quotes and their sources in your next flyer or brochure.

Words of Wisdom

On Self-Promotion

One of the greatest challenges for solo entrepreneurs is the high-wire balancing act of promoting yourself and your business. You don't want to seem too egotistical, yet you must market your business effectively. Here are some insights from a self-promotion strategist on how to maximize your visibility when your company is "me, myself, and I."

"Publicity is by far one of the most effective marketing tools for garnering visibility. But how do you promote yourself to the media so that they will give your growing business the spotlight it needs?

"Storytelling That's right, because ultimately, business stories are human interest stories, and every reporter is looking for a good story. You don't need any special literary skills; storytelling is completely natural. Just listen to yourself—you're probably doing it every day.

"To use storytelling as a marketing tool, talk about what you do in terms of real-life anecdotes and examples of how you've solved your client's problems. Bring your story to life by infusing it with your own personality and a few facts and figures. A little drama doesn't hurt either.

"It's the personal connection between you and your press contacts that matters, so nurture these relationships the same way you do those with your most important clients. Sharing personal details builds rapport, so be open in an interview and show them how who you are affects your vision of the business.

"Once you get that invaluable exposure, be appreciative and grateful. Send a thank-you note and let the reporter know what kind of response their story elicited. Then, keep in touch, because you never know when they might need you as a resource again in the future.

"If you focus on giving instead of getting, and if you devote your energy to offering a reporter a story their readers can learn from, you'll get all the publicity you want."

—*Ilise Benun*

Self-promotion specialist Ilise Benun is the author of *Making Marketing Manageable: A Practical and Painless Guide to Self-Promotion* and *Toot Your Own Horn: 133 Ways to Promote Yourself and Your Business.* She is also the editor and publisher of the quarterly newsletter, *The Art of Self-Promotion* (details in Appendix A, "Solo Resources").

Let's now leave the world of marketing and move on to the other important half of getting your product or service into customers' hands, the world of sales.

A Few Words about Sales

When it comes to understanding sales, many small business owners are either puzzled or put off by the idea. Ask a roomful of hopeful entrepreneurs how many of them want to be business owners, and hands shoot up. Then ask how many see themselves as salespersons, and only a few hands rise, slowly.

Now, be honest. Would you have raised your hand to the second question? If so, you've got a head start on business success. If not—and I suspect that many of you are like my seminar participants who don't raise their hands either—it's time for you to take a new look at sales.

By now, you know that, without customers, your business can't exist. But how do your potential customers take that last step and trade their dollars for your product or service? Someone makes a sale and completes that crucial final link between your product or service and the customer.

If your marketing materials are strong, they may be your silent sales force out there. In most cases, however, it takes a personal connection. This may be a phone call from you offering more information. It may be a personalized demonstration of your product or service. Your product may be sold in a retail store, where informed salespeople tell customers of its value. Or your business may be selling products of other companies, and your income is based on the many person-to-person encounters you have each day.

Whatever your business may be, its growth and success will be directly tied to the quality of the salespeople. Since you've chosen to work solo, it's likely that the sales force will be you. Your goal is to develop a successful selling style that matches both your personality and your solo business.

Sell Is Not a Four-Letter Word

Well, actually *sell* is a word with four letters, but I think you get the idea. To many people, selling is distasteful. It often has bad connotations, calling to mind over-hyped pitches, sleazy deals, or slippery promises. But if you stop and think about it, this stereotype really doesn't reflect the reality of selling and salespeople.

Remember that everything in your life that you've bought—from the most recent suit to a new toothbrush—had a salesperson behind it. Salespeople are the important link between the product or service and the ultimate customer.

Nevertheless, many people cringe when they think of selling. Maybe it's the thought of rejection. Or the idea that they wouldn't feel comfortable about selling something to a person they hardly know. Many solo entrepreneurs find it hard to sell their products or services because they're really selling themselves, and they don't want to seem boastful or arrogant.

If you find yourself in one of these categories, it's time to open your mind to new ideas about selling.

Solutions, Not Sales

What you're offering to customers is a product or service you believe will improve the quality of their lives. (This is particularly true if you've chosen a business you're passionate about, one that has a deep level of meaning to you.) With this belief—that your work can make someone else happier, healthier, or wealthier in pocket or in spirit—your attitude toward selling shifts. It no longer becomes a burden to sell. Rather, it is a pleasure, since you are bringing satisfaction to others. Taken a step further, it's almost as if you have a moral obligation to sell your product, for you know, deep inside, that it will benefit others.

It's true that not everyone operates with this attitude toward sales and their business. But if you have chosen a personally fulfilling line of work, then your enthusiasm will spill over to others. Selling will be easy, because you see it as the natural last step in the process of bringing your product or service to its logical end: the customer.

There's a maxim that master motivator and salesman Zig Ziglar uses to sum up his approach to life: "You can get everything in life you want, if you help enough other people get what they want." This is an inspiring attitude that puts the customer at the center, which is a surefire route to success.

By adopting this new approach to selling, you replace the notion of the four-letter word *sell* with 2 five-letter words: *share* and *teach. Share* means you are an understanding counselor and friend, ready to help customers find the answers to their needs. *Teach* means you are able to provide information that will enable them to move a step closer to achieving their goals.

These are two powerful concepts. They involve your customers as partners with you. Embracing this new attitude, you're not looking just for a sale, you're looking for a solution to your customers' problem. You're sincerely interested in helping them get what they want in life—and you're confident that, in doing so, you'll get what you want, too.

As you launch your new solo venture, mentally jump into your customers' shoes. What are they looking for? How does what you offer provide a solution to their problem? How can you share with them your ideas and teach them about the benefits your business can offer? Become their partner in finding an answer to their needs. In turn, they will answer your needs by becoming satisfied, recurring customers—and your business will grow.

Armed with this new attitude toward selling, let's look at getting your first clients and customers.

Getting Your First Accounts

The groundwork for securing your first accounts must be laid long before your first day of business. All during the time you are planning your venture, you need to be cultivating potential clients and customers.

If you're launching your business as an outgrowth of work you're currently doing for an employer, consider planting some seeds that the work could be completed effectively by an outside provider. (That outside provider, of course, will later be you.) Solo entrepreneurs who'll be offering a product or service to their communities need to nurture a local network. Once the business is ready to launch, these supporters will spread the word that your business is an exciting addition to the area.

First accounts are fragile entities. Handle them with great care. They can quickly build or ruin your reputation. To gain experience and to create confidence in potential customers, you may need to convince them of your value. Some solo professionals offer samples or other attractive offers to encourage new customers.

As you build your first accounts, remember that you are facing two opposing psychological forces. First, people are generally very hesitant to change or to take risks. Whether you are offering something they have never tried before or are in competition with an existing business, chances are they'll be hesitant to try it. It's your challenge to make the offer so enticing and of such a great value that they overcome their inertia and make the leap.

The other psychological factor—that people genuinely like to help other people—works in your favor. Positioning yourself as a new business owner (that's *new*—not inexperienced or unprofessional) starting out on this adventure can engender many positive feelings. There will be people who envy you or who can relate to what you're trying to do (in many ways, you're living their dream). Your challenge is to capitalize on their goodwill, offer them premium service, entice them to become repeat customers, and encourage them to spread the news about your venture.

Words of Wisdom

On Getting First Accounts through Volunteering

One of the easiest ways to spread the word about your new solo business is to donate your product or service. Here are some thoughts from a seasoned solo professional about leveraging volunteer efforts to promote your business.

"Solo entrepreneurs can establish credibility and achieve some great visibility for their new businesses through volunteering. When I wanted to break in as a computer consultant several years ago, I used to show up at the public library one day a week to give free advice. The library even let me hang up a sign saying 'Cynthia Harriman will be here Monday nights at 7:00 to answer your computer questions.'

"As I was building my business, I also wrote a newspaper column for a weekly supermarket giveaway. So what if they paid only $43 plus one free ad every week? It was great publicity, and it beat paying for weekly ads. In the end, the writing experience I gained led to an invitation to join the review board of a national weekly computer magazine. This position further increased my credibility and perceived value in my field.

"Actively volunteering in trade organizations can also bring new business. Once people know you and understand the quality of the product or services you provide, they're more likely to hire you, buy from you, or send referrals your way. Whether you're just starting out or you're ready to break into a new arena, volunteering can give you both credibility and a visibility boost."

—Cynthia Harriman

An independent computer and marketing consultant, Cynthia Harriman is also the author of *Take Your Kids to Europe*. She lives in Portsmouth, New Hampshire.

How Many Accounts?

While you may be sending out your message to dozens, hundreds, or even thousands of prospective customers, keep in mind that you actually may need only a few quality relationships to sustain your business. Of course, the quantity of customers depends on the type of business you choose. Some consulting firms may rely on only two or three major clients, while product-based enterprises target thousands of customers.

Trying to find this balance can be challenging in the early days of your business. You must ensure that you have enough business to stay afloat while focusing energy at the same time on the true income-producing segments. The answer to this dilemma for many independent entrepreneurs is to continually monitor and weed their customer bases. As better-paying or more reliable customers appear, clients at the lower end of the scale are not pursued.

Sound callous? It's actually a normal business phenomenon. Working solo, you must face the fact that you have a limited number of income-producing hours in each day. To succeed, you need to focus on the 20 percent segment that accounts for 80 percent of your income. Realistically, you can't be all things to all people. If you try, you'll sink your business—and probably drive yourself to exhaustion in the process.

As you're weeding, make sure you retain enough diversity in your customer base so that no single client's actions can mortally ruin your business. Having one top-dollar client can be a heady experience—until that client decides you're not needed anymore. We're all working solo because we value the control we have over our businesses. Make sure you don't relinquish yours to a lucrative, powerful client.

Having more than one client is also important in retaining your status as an independent contractor in the IRS's eyes—something we'll cover in more detail in Chapter 11.

Expanding Your Business

Many solo businesses are fluid. As they begin to grow, they often branch off into related areas or focus on one specific market segment. After a few years, a business may be very different from the one launched initially.

If this is the route your solo business takes, don't be alarmed. Because independent businesses reflect their owners, they are often very organic, changing as needs and interests change.

If you ask seasoned entrepreneurs what caused the shift in their solo businesses, most will mention a project they fell in love with, a market that was soft or booming, or a new direction that offered an appealing combination of satisfaction *and* money. Their businesses grew as a natural pattern of refinement—a progression they accept with confidence and enthusiasm, knowing that it leads to further adventure.

Central to this growth, however, is the focus on serving customer needs. As you've heard so many times before, your business doesn't exist without customers. Keeping them happy is your #1 job—no matter what business you've chosen.

The dividend of customer satisfaction is that you can grow your business without investing in expensive marketing campaigns. A satisfied customer is going to be a bigger billboard and a louder commercial than your solo business could ever afford.

This philosophy is summed up in a sign I saw several years ago:

THE TWO GOLDEN RULES OF BUSINESS SUCCESS

Rule #1: The customer is always right.
Rule #2: When in doubt, refer to Rule #1.

I chuckled when I saw it, thinking it was cute. Years later, I still think it's cute, but, more important, it's true.

There's been a lot of talk about customer-centered principles in business lately. Many solo business owners think it's expensive to provide customers with what they want. Actually, it's just the opposite—it costs you even more if you don't give customers what they need or desire, because they won't return, and you've lost all future business with them.

This is one area where it definitely pays to adopt long-term thinking. Your goal is to have customers for life, so that your business growth will gain momentum as each satisfied customer tells another potential customer.

Many solo entrepreneurs tend to shrug off these ideas of customer service, or they become indifferent. "Yeah, yeah, I know all about this customer satisfaction stuff. But my product (or service) is so good, they'll be dying to buy it." If this attitude creeps into your thinking, it won't be the customers who will be dying—it will be your business. Read on to see just how great an impact your attitude can have.

The Consequences of Customer Satisfaction

The pie chart in Figure 6.3 paints a remarkably clear picture of the effect of courteous, professional service on customer loyalty. It presents the findings from a study on customer satisfaction conducted by the Research Institute of America and shows that more than two-thirds of all customers leave because they feel a business doesn't care about them. Two-thirds! Imagine the impact this could have on *your* business. Imagine the growth in your business if your superior customer service can lure the dissatisfied two-thirds from all your competitors.

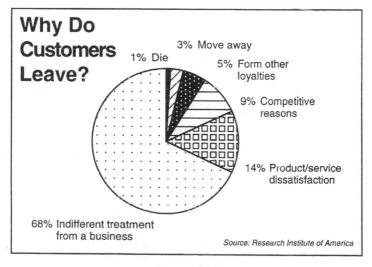

Why Do Customers Leave?

1% Die
3% Move away
5% Form other loyalties
9% Competitive reasons
14% Product/service dissatisfaction
68% Indifferent treatment from a business

Source: Research Institute of America

Figure 6.3

Think back to the last time you experienced exceptional customer service. Didn't it make an impact on you? It's refreshing (and memorable) when you're treated like the important customer you are.

Research shows that modern shoppers, buying all types of products and services, will make decisions based on quality and price, but if customer service is strong, they'll pay more for the same item. The lesson: It may not take much additional effort to offer quality customer service, but it can result in significant revenue for your business.

In contrast, what happens when customers aren't satisfied? They tell their friends—lots of them. The Research Institute of America survey also revealed the following:

✓ Of all unhappy customers, 96 percent will never complain directly about rude or discourteous treatment, but

✓ 90 percent who are dissatisfied with the service won't come back or buy again, and

✓ Each of the unhappy customers will share his or her dissatisfaction with at least nine other individuals, and

✓ 13 percent of those former customers will tell more than 20 individuals about their unhappy experience.

As you can see, this situation can be a word-of-mouth nightmare for your business. It points out how fragile customer loyalty can be and how crucial it is to take customer service seriously. Commit yourself and your business to offering courteous and professional service. It's much more effective than waging a battle to win back customers once you've lost them.

If people are so eager to share bad experiences, are they just as likely to repeat positive ones they've had with your business? Unfortunately, no. Research shows that it's human nature to find some odd pleasure in sharing bad news. While word-of-mouth recommendations will be an important vehicle to fuel your business growth, don't count on customers being as willing to share good news as they are bad news.

The Most Effective Way to Grow Your Business, in One Word

There are many ways to take your business from ground zero to the starry heights of success. Over the years, I've discovered a single word that holds the power to solo business growth and ultimate success. The magic word? *ASK.*

Overcome your hesitations and connect with others. Whether you are just starting out or are a seasoned solo veteran, learn to appreciate the power of asking.

✓ Ask your customers what they think of your business.

✓ Ask them if there are any other products or services they wish you'd offer.

✓ Ask your colleagues for their feedback on new ideas.

✓ Ask your former customers for more work or to recommend you to others.

✓ Ask about your competition and how they're doing.

✓ Ask potential customers what it would take to do business with you.

✓ Ask, ask, ask . . .

✓ Then, be sure to listen.

Too often, solo entrepreneurs are shy or hesitant to tell others that they're looking for work. Yes, it's a fine line between appearing to be starving for work and appearing available. One popular approach adopted by many independent professionals is to contact former clients and say something like, "I'm currently lining up my calendar for the next six months, and I wanted to make sure that if you had any projects for me I could accommodate them." Others call former clients and say, "Hi, I haven't heard from you in a while." Then they pause and listen, and let the other person take it from there.

It's amazing how effective these methods can be. They give you the option of gently reminding clients that you're available and interested, without a hard sell. If they don't have a project for you right away, you've at least moved toward the front of their consciousness again—and you've improved the chances that they'll think of you when the next opportunity comes along.

Your goal is to mine repeat customers. Remember, it costs *eight times* as much to get a new buyer as to retain an existing one. Make your time, energy, and money pay off.

As you've discovered in this chapter, marketing and sales are ongoing processes that require continual refinements as you try to reach potential buyers in new ways. While some entrepreneurs find it a chore, many feel that it's one of the most creative parts of their solo ventures. Each message you present about your business—whether in person, in print, or on the telephone—reflects your unique style and vision. It's an outlet for personal creative expression that never ends.

The amount and quality of your marketing and sales efforts have a direct relation to the growth and success of your solo business. If you're wondering how you can manage these time-consuming tasks, take heart. With the help of a personal computer and other modern technology, your solo business can operate on par with operations many times your size.

Never before has so much power and flexibility been available to businesses on every level—even those with the smallest budgets. Whether you're a seasoned pro or a computer novice, the next chapter shows you how these machines can boost your solo business to new heights of productivity—and profits.

PART III

THE DETAILS

C ongratulations! You've cleared some of the biggest hurdles in creating a successful solo business: You've chosen a business that's right for you, given it a great launch, and lined up some solid first customers.

In its first months of operation, your solo business is like a sapling. It holds the potential to grow big and strong, yet in its early growth stages it remains fragile and easily buffeted by stormy weather. It needs care and guidance at this important period of development. Nothing can be left to chance.

Attention to the daily details of running your business is the water and sunshine your budding venture needs to turn into a powerful, towering oak. Success comes from mastering the daily operations, so that over time you have a solid root system that stabilizes your tree—your business—even in the fiercest weather.

This third section of *Working Solo* guides you in the details of growing your business and sustaining it in changing economic times. While you'll find excitement, glory, and a certain adrenaline rush in launching your new business, the long-term strength and viability of your enterprise come from the daily tasks many businesses take for granted.

Remember, of the thousands of new businesses launched each year, only a percentage survive. Those that do have mastered the details. In the next six chapters, you will, too.

Chapter 7

Solo Office Power:
Computers and Technology

A single idea, if it is right, saves us the labor of an infinity of experiments.

—*Jacques Maritain*

Computers and other modern-day office technology have made a remarkable impact on the lives of solo professionals. In fact, many people feel that computers are the key factor influencing the soaring growth of independent entrepreneurs. Never before has it been so easy for one person to accomplish the work of so many.

Armed with a personal computer, a fax machine, and an Internet connection, independent workers can gain access to information and make connections with colleagues and customers around the world. Mail or other documents can travel thousands of miles in split seconds by telephone wires, giving solo entrepreneurs the freedom to live and work wherever they please. New developments in mobile computing promise to extend the boundaries even farther. Office walls, as we know them, will dissolve. It is truly an exciting time for those of us who are working solo.

Yet many solo workers shy away from using computers and other technology, mostly because they're overwhelmed by the seeming complexity and expense. If you count yourself among those intimidated or confused by technology, take heart. In this chapter, you'll see that computers, fax machines, and other high-tech gear can empower you in your business and alleviate the monotony of many routine office tasks. You may even find, as so many others have, that the high-tech world can be a lot of fun.

If you're an old hand with computers, this chapter will offer a different experience for you. In it, you'll find a review of some fundamentals and perhaps discover new ways to introduce technology matters to your less technically inclined colleagues.

We begin with computers, then explore other digital equipment, such as modems and fax machines, that extends your communication reach. We'll also review office machines that offer basic—but important—services, such as phone systems and photocopiers.

Putting a Computer to Work for You

For many solo workers, computers take on the tasks of a valued employee. Unlike hired help, however, a computer won't call in late, ask for sick days, have to leave early for family crises, or complain about working extra hours. It's no wonder computers are viewed as ideal assistants for solo entrepreneurs.

When buying a computer, the first question you need to address is what you want to use it for. Initially, the answer may seem obvious: "To make my life easier, and my business more productive and profitable." But it's generally not quite as simple as that.

Begin by listing all the activities and tasks you think a computer would help you accomplish. You don't have to figure out every single task, but you should have a pretty good idea of the types of things you want to do. Consider tasks such as:

✓　Keeping a list of all your clients by name, address, or phone

✓　Creating and keeping track of invoices

✓　Keeping your financial records in order

✓　Maintaining inventory

✓　Creating individualized correspondence

✓　Conducting complex numerical calculations

✓　Personalizing letters to groups of people, using mail merge capabilities (which automatically insert names and addresses from your client list into a basic format letter)

✓　Creating presentation materials such as charts, graphs, and slides

✓　Designing and producing brochures or ads

✓　Sharing information with colleagues and customers far away

✓　Connecting you with the Internet for e-mail and research

✓　Creating a Web site to promote your business and take online orders

Next, do some research into the types of software programs that are available to accomplish these tasks. (We'll be reviewing some in just a moment.) Then start taking some opinion polls among other solo colleagues. Don't be overwhelmed by the jargon or the choices—focus instead on the end results you want to accomplish.

Do be prepared, however, for a wide variety of opinions, particularly on the subjects of PC versus Macintosh, price versus speed, and laptops versus desktop machines. For some reason, the choice about a computer involves more than a mere decision about office equipment. In fact, for many entrepreneurs, it can take on the fervor of a religious conviction! This is a result, in part, of computers transcending the role of machine, since they accomplish so much and their owners interact with them on a daily—and often personal—level.

What's more important than the kind you buy is that you *use* a computer. These machines have the potential to expand your abilities—and your profits—more than any other piece of office equipment can. That power comes not only from the computer but also from the software. Let's take a look at both elements.

Hardware Choices

Three main factors will contribute to the speed, performance, and cost of your computer: microprocessor speed, RAM (random-access memory), and disk-drive space. An easy way to understand the relationship of these three elements is to use the analogy of a car.

In your computer (car), the *microprocessor* is the engine, the central power source to get you where you're going. As with a car, there's a price/performance relationship: Faster is usually more expensive. Today, microprocessors are made by companies such as Intel and Motorola, and the competition to develop faster and more powerful chips is ongoing.

Random Access Memory is your computer's temporary memory and is like the interior seating space in your car. It determines how many passengers your car can transport at any one time. Translated to computer terms, the amount of RAM you have determines how much information can be in use at one time. Some of your computer programs may be like sumo wrestlers and require a lot of RAM. Others may be slimmer in size, but you'd like to carry (be able to work with) more of them at the same time. RAM chips generally come in thin, candy-bar-sized strips that are snapped into a slot inside your computer.

The third element, *disk-drive space,* is analogous to your trunk space. It determines how much storage space you have. In computer terms, the bigger the trunk (or hard drive), the more information you can store, and the greater the expense of your machine. Most computers today come with both internal hard drives and floppy drives; many also have CD-ROM drives for reading computer CD-ROM disks. A new popular option is an internal or external secondary floppy drive for high-density disks such as Iomega's Zip and Jaz cartridges that hold many megabytes of data, making extra storage and backup of your data a breeze.

There are also other factors to consider when buying a computer:

- ✓ Expansions and upgrades—can they take place easily?
- ✓ Ports—will your computer be able to connect easily to other devices such as printers and scanners?
- ✓ Modem—internal or external?
- ✓ Fax capabilities—combined with the modem or a separate card?
- ✓ Desktop "real estate"—how much space does it take up on your desk?

✓ Monitor—a dot pitch range of .28 or better (smaller number) is preferred

✓ Keyboard—comfortable to use, with a responsive feel?

✓ Training—is there technical support available, and is it a toll-free call?

✓ Warranty—how long and can you buy extended warranty coverage?

✓ Service options—if something goes wrong, where do you turn for repair?

Like deciding which car to buy, choosing a computer involves a mix of personal needs and preferences. A sports car with a fast engine, a small interior, and little trunk space may suit you just fine. Then again, you may be the station-wagon type. Keep in mind that your goal is what you can *do* with your computer, and that's determined primarily by software.

Software Choices

Software programs, or applications, are the prewritten instructions that you use to tell a computer what to do. There are thousands of software packages to fill every business need, and many more that tackle problems you might not have even considered. While each program has its own set of features, here are some general categories to help you understand the power that awaits you.

Word Processing Software

A word processor program enables you to write, edit, cut, paste, and manipulate words in a document. Most word processors include spelling checkers and will automatically number your pages, create a footnote or an index, and change the style and size of your type. With mail merge capabilities, your word processor can link to your database (see below) and create a list of names and addresses, allowing you to create personalized letters for everyone on your list.

Spreadsheet Software

A spreadsheet program creates an electronic version of the paper grid of rows and columns generally used for financial purposes. The magic of an electronic spreadsheet is that you can put numbers into the cells (the individual boxes) and perform mathematical calculations in the blink of an eye. Formulas can be assigned so that changing one number causes a ripple effect in all other numbers. For example, by setting up a formula to figure profits based on different prices for your product or service, you can change one number and easily see the effect of different prices on your overall profits.

Database Software

Database programs give you the computerized equivalent of a filing cabinet, but with many times more power and flexibility. Instead of keeping information in only one place, a database program allows you to manipulate, gather, and sort information in endless ways. For example, you could find a list of all your contacts who live in California who were your best customers in the last year. The next minute you could find out who had ordered from you the year before but not in the last six months. Or you could sort your list by zip code, telephone area code, or alphabetically. The possibilities are truly endless. And the control over the information can lead you to run your business better and more profitably.

Graphics Software

Graphics software includes painting, drawing, and illustration programs. Artists create the image with a computer mouse or a graphics tablet, a device that looks like a notepad with an electronic stylus attached. The stylus movement on the notepad is translated into lines and shapes on the computer screen; newer models even have touch-sensitive capabilities, allowing control of subtle variations such as the thickness or texture of a line.

Page Layout Software

Page layout or desktop publishing (DTP) software allows you to mix text and graphics on the same page. With these programs, you can create flyers, brochures, books, newsletters, or other printed materials. The more advanced programs have complex color capabilities, and they have replaced publishing systems costing hundreds of thousands of dollars.

Presentation Software

Presentation software allows you to create professional-looking images on your computer screen that mimic slide presentations. The images can be used to create standard color slides or overhead transparencies. Even better, you can link your computer to an electronic device that projects your images onto TV monitors or large-scale screens. Standing at your computer, you control the presentation with a click of the mouse and can easily update or adapt the presentation for new audiences.

Telecommunications Software

Telecommunications programs allow you to connect your computer to other computers and the Internet via your telephone line. Using a modem, you can send anything stored in your computer—letters, files, graphics, music, video, speech—across town or around the world. It makes working with colleagues not only possible but easy.

For example, when my company's product brochure was being created, I asked the designer to send me a sample for review. Sound unusual? Not really—until you realize that my designer lives in Seattle, and she sent it to me in New

York over the phone wires. I was able to see it in full color on my computer less than ten minutes after she sent it to me.

Telecommunication advances are expanding the boundaries for solo workers in exciting ways, bringing increasing opportunities. We'll talk more about the Internet in just a few pages and further explore online ways of doing business in Chapter 12.

Integrated Software

Integrated packages—also known as *suites* or containing the word *office* in their titles—are software's equivalent of music boom boxes. These programs offer an all-in-one solution by bringing together popular components of other packages. Integrated software usually includes a word processor, a database, graphics and presentation capabilities, a spreadsheet, and telecommunications capabilities; some also include page layout or Web page design features. Just as boom boxes generally don't offer the best musical components, each software component in an integrated package is usually not as powerful as its standalone cousin. For many small business users, however, integrated packages from companies such as Microsoft and Claris are an excellent choice and a good value. If you need features beyond those included in the integrated package, you can always purchase a more powerful software program of a specific component.

Financial Software

Financial software ranges from simple checkbook-type programs to sophisticated accounting systems. These programs can give you instant feedback about the financial status of your business and guide you in making informed decisions. Another form of financial software, tax preparation software, guides you through completing your IRS and state tax returns.

CAD/CAM

Computer-aided design and computer-aided manufacturing (CAD/CAM) programs enable mechanical engineers and other design professionals to create complex drawings, renderings, blueprints, and specification sheets electronically. Some of the more advanced programs are linked to machine tools that can generate prototypes—or even finished goods. These programs have changed the notion of the drawing board forever.

Multimedia

Multimedia is a general category that encompasses software using words, music, animation, sound, and video. As computers have become more powerful, their abilities to handle the large amounts of data required for sound and video have increased. Today a desktop computer has the power to be a video-editing or animation center, replacing complex and expensive equipment.

Web Page Design Software

With the growth of the Internet, software companies have designed programs that allow even novice users to create Web pages in minutes. The more sophisticated programs allow greater control over type, graphics, and animation, and instantly convert your existing paper-based documents into HyperText Markup Language (HTML) so they can be viewed on the Web. As Internet commerce becomes more widespread, there are a growing number of software programs that include tools to help you set up an Internet storefront to sell your products or services online, worldwide.

Personal Organization Software

Personal Information Manager (PIM) is a category of software that includes programs to organize your life, such as calendars, schedulers, address books, To-Do list managers, and contact managers. This is a rapidly growing software market, as people struggle to control the huge amounts of information made available to them through computer technology. Some PIMs allow you to print your files to a personal organizer such as a Day-Timer or Day Runner, a handy way to stay organized when you're away from your office.

Utilities

Utilities are software programs that are useful in the daily operations of your computer, such as those that save copies of your files as a backup or that diagnose problems with your computer. Other utilities help you organize your hard drive, which can become as cluttered as your hall closet if you're not careful. Some utilities combine an element of fun, as demonstrated with screen savers that feature fireworks, bouncing balls, geometric patterns, flying toasters, or sound clips from popular television shows or movies.

What about Printers?

Once your information is inside your computer, you need a way to get it onto paper. Most small business owners today choose between two types of printers: ink-jet and laser. Here are the advantages and drawbacks to each.

Ink-jet printers

Ink-jet printers are devices that create characters by spraying tiny droplets of ink into patterns on a page. More precise printhead mechanisms and finer inks have improved the performance of ink-jet printers over the last few years. These devices are a popular choice for value-conscious shoppers looking for near-laser-quality output. Their two primary drawbacks are slower speeds and potential smearing (since the printing medium is soluble ink). Improvements are happening in both these areas, however.

With color ink-jet printers, the print process of spraying a fine mist of ink on paper is the same, only four different colors of ink are used: cyan, magenta, yellow, and black, the same as in offset printing. The computer decides how much of each color should be sprayed, and the ink mixes on paper to create colors similar to those you see on your monitor. Advances in color ink-jet technology mean that you can now print photographic-quality images from your computer.

Laser Printers

Laser printers are today's most popular solution for small businesses seeking professional-looking printed output. As with other technology, the quality has improved and the price has dropped over the last few years, making laser printers an affordable solution for businesses of every size and kind.

Laser printers are similar to photocopiers in that their characters are formed in a xerographic process. Instead of getting the image from an original under glass, however, the laser printer gets imaging information in the form of digital signals from the computer. As a result, your sheet emerges from the printer looking just like the image on your screen.

This effect of having an exact correlation between what's on your computer screen and what emerges from your printer is known as WYSIWYG (pronounced "wizzy-wig"), or "What You See Is What You Get." It's a funny way of saying you want no surprises—and it's your ideal when transferring your computer information from screen to paper.

Prices of laser printers are determined by two primary factors: the speed with which each sheet can be printed and the resolution quality of the image. As you might imagine, faster speed and higher resolution cost more.

Printer resolution is measured in dots per inch, known as *dpi*. The resolution of most laser printers is 600 dpi, although higher resolutions are becoming more common. Unless your business has specific printed-output needs, a laser printer with resolution of 600 dpi is quite satisfactory. The number of printed pages you generate each day will determine if it's a worthwhile investment for you to buy a faster model.

Color laser printers are becoming more popular as their prices continue to drop. The basic mechanism is the same as for black-and-white printers, except four layers of toner are applied—cyan, magenta, yellow, and black—instead of one.

One other category of printers deserves mention before we move on: label printers. These small devices sit next to your computer and can produce labels one at a time. For large quantities of mailing labels, you probably would generate labels with your laser printer or photocopier, using sheets of peel-off labels. For simple jobs, however, it's nice to be able to generate a single, professional-looking label, without resorting to a typewriter. Some printer models accommodate various-size labels, including those for audio- or videotapes, computer disks, and file folders.

Printer Paper

A quick note about printer paper: Once you've invested thousands of dollars in a computer system, do some experimenting to find the paper that will provide the best printed output. The difference in cost is only pennies per sheet, but the difference in the quality and perception of your final printed product can be significant.

For making master copies for reproduction from a laser printer, you want a bright, smooth white sheet. For daily correspondence, you may want a sheet with more texture and some cotton content, so it doesn't look so slick. But experiment, because those microscopic bumps in a textured sheet can cause your laser toner to break up, resulting in a degradation of clarity in your type or graphics. Ink-jet printers work better with a semiabsorbent sheet; the tiny ink drops bond better to the paper, resulting in crisp lines.

Check your local office-supply store for a selection of computer printer paper. It's usually sold by the ream (500 sheets) or by the carton (10 reams/5,000 sheets). Several companies sell printer paper by mail order, including Paper Direct (800-A-PAPERS) and Paper Access (800-PAPER-01). Their free catalogs can give you dozens of ideas for using paper in innovative ways (details in Appendix A, "Solo Resources").

The Three Questions Asked Most Frequently When Buying a Computer

From my experience with hundreds of individuals setting up their solo offices, I've discovered that three common questions arise when discussions turn to buying a computer.

Buying Question #1: Laptop or Desktop?

Whether you choose a computer you can carry with you or one that's permanently parked on your desk is a matter of balancing your preferences, needs, space, and budget. Desktop machines can be less expensive, give you bigger keyboards, allow for larger monitors, and accommodate external disk drives and other devices, but they can take up a substantial amount of real estate on your desk. Laptops and other portable computers condense their power into the approximate size of a notebook, so their keyboards and monitors are smaller, but they enable you to take computing power with you, whether you're traveling or operating at multiple sites.

An interesting compromise can be found in newer models of notebook computers that let you hook up larger monitors, giving you the capabilities of desktop machines with the portability of smaller units. Another option is a notebook computer that docks into a desktop unit. Like a VCR tape sliding into a player, this small computer docks into a desktop station. The notebook unit links to a larger monitor until it's time to hit the road again—at which time you pull out the notebook computer and off you go.

In choosing between a laptop or desktop model, your decision will center on questions such as:

- ✓ Where will I use the computer?
- ✓ How much desk space do I have?
- ✓ Is it important to have a large monitor?
- ✓ Do I feel comfortable typing on a smaller keyboard?
- ✓ Will it be important for me to take the computer on the road?
- ✓ Will I need portability so I can take information to customers, do calculations on the spot, or gather data?

Depending on the nature and focus of your business, you might end up buying two computers—one for desktop and one for the road. If you haven't bought one computer yet, the idea of two probably seems an outrageous luxury. Remember, all these decisions must be based on the value you can derive from them and the profits they can help bring your business.

For example, when I was considering buying a second computer (a notebook model) a few years ago, I hesitated at first. Then I pulled out my calculator. After figuring the cost of the machine and the amount of work I could do while away from my office, I decided it was a worthwhile investment. In fact, the computer quickly paid for itself from the work I was able to do on a few coast-to-coast flights. My office expanded beyond four walls, opening up new income possibilities from time that would have been spent in other ways. If your business has this potential, I encourage you to think about the benefits of taking the technology with you.

Buying Question #2: Should I Buy a Used Computer?

As computers increase in speed and capabilities, more businesses and individuals are upgrading to better machines and selling their secondhand models. Is it worth it to buy one of these older models that carry a lower price tag? The answer is two-part: It depends, and you've got to know what you're doing. Some older machines may be a great bargain, since computers more frequently become outdated than wear out. If you know what you want to do with your machine and the software you want to run, and if the model will serve you, then give it serious consideration. Make sure it has all the parts and manuals you'll need. Have it checked out by a computer pro, and make arrangements with the seller for a return policy if it doesn't suit your purposes in the first 24 to 48 hours.

One warning about buying used equipment: Computer theft is a growing crime, and the machine that's a hot deal may in fact be so hot it's illegal. Carefully consider your buying source, and be suspicious if the source is eager to unload equipment fast or at very low prices. Beware, too, of individuals selling "used" software along with their computers—it's a federal crime. Most software is copyrighted and legally licensed for use on only one computer. It can be transferred to another person only if the original owner signs over the entire package, including master disks and manuals.

What's a good price for a used computer? The Boston Computer Exchange (617-542-4414) keeps an active listing of the buying and selling prices of used computers and printers. A call to the exchange can give you a good idea about the true value of your potential purchase.

For most people, it's a better deal to buy new. As prices drop and capabilities expand, the power you can buy today in a new machine probably equals—or surpasses—that of a used one with a similar price tag. New machines include a manufacturer's warranty, and some also offer free technical support for a period of time—both valuable benefits not found with a used machine. A newer machine can also offer you a better growth path to upgrading your system later on, since it uses current technology.

Buying Question #3: Should I Buy Now or Wait?

If you're preparing to buy your first computer or upgrade to a better one, this question is probably the one that gives you the greatest anxiety. You keep hearing that machines are getting cheaper, and you wonder if you should wait just a little longer.

Until recently, the developmental trend in the microcomputer industry was that computers usually doubled in speed and power every 18 months and that prices dropped as new models were introduced. (A new trend shows that the increase in capabilities and price is happening at an even *faster* rate.) Does this mean your machine will be worthless after that time? How do you know when to buy?

A computer you buy today will be able to perform all the tasks you want it to do—at today's speed and capabilities—for as long as you want. Remember, computers rarely wear out, since they have relatively few mechanical parts. What's more likely is that new features will entice you to buy another or to upgrade your current machine with new additions and enhancements.

An analogy can be found in music technology. Do you still have LP records in your house? Do you still use them, or have you switched to cassettes or CDs? If you've switched, it doesn't mean that you can't play your records anymore. You just chose to move on to a different format that gives better sound (although "better" is another hot topic for debate).

It's the same with computers. Once you have one, you'll see how much it can do for you and your business, and you'll be willing to invest in improvements that pay off.

When does it make sense to buy and when to wait? You want to invest wisely, yet it's easy to fall into the trap of waiting forever, since the industry is always changing.

From advising hundreds of new and solo entrepreneurs about computerizing, I've devised the Six-Month Rule: If you can put the equipment to good use in the coming six months, buy it now. The investment will probably make up for the price devaluation that will undoubtedly occur as the industry matures.

When in doubt, see if the Six-Month Rule works for you. Sometimes it makes sense to wait; other times, the investment in computerization is your best, and quickest, avenue to greater business profits.

Words of Wisdom

On Keeping Pace with Technology

Technology changes at a dizzying speed, and keeping a solo business up to date can be a challenge. Here are some strategies for maximizing your technology investment from an entrepreneur whose business is closely tied to high-tech advances.

"As technology keeps moving forward, solo entrepreneurs must keep abreast of new developments while maintaining a solid watch on what it takes to make a business run. Much new technology adds productivity only after many unpredictable hours spent on integrating the new hardware or software with currently installed machines.

"My approach is to wait for a big influx of several updates—for example, installing or upgrading a computer, printer, and scanner all at once. I plan for it and make a constructive effort to overhaul many things at one time rather than add small items over a longer time frame. Somehow the upheaval seems easier if it happens in one short, intense period.

"As for balancing the ever-present advancements in technology with when to buy a new piece of equipment, I've found that the most important time is when you really need it, and you know the new technology can have a positive impact in your business. Often I'll wait for a major trade show where new models are usually announced, and I'll invest in the new model or get a better deal on the old. Technology is essentially a moving train where you get to decide at which station you want to jump on.

"Computers are constantly improving incrementally, but the use of the World Wide Web is an explosion. Access to information and the ability for small companies to reach enormous markets is just at the forming stage. On the Web, technology is relatively simple. But the innovative way to market a company, product, or service on the Internet is a creative and fascinating arena in which to explore—and one that holds incredible potential for solo entrepreneurs."

—*Marylyn Dintenfass*

Marylyn Dintenfass is president of HandsOn Interactive, a multimedia development company based in New York City.

Let's now take a look at other technology that can boost your business.

Putting Fax Machines to Work for You

A decade ago, fax machines were an expensive rarity in most small businesses. (I recently came across the 1989 receipt for my first fax machine: $1,200!) Today, having a fax machine (and a dedicated phone line to service it) is a baseline standard for most professional-level solo offices. With a fax, your office boundaries expand, additional opportunities become available, and you can easily stay in touch with new and regular customers.

Fax machines work by changing information into digital data, then to sound, and back again. With standalone fax machines, the image begins with a piece of paper, and it spits out moments later from the other fax machine miles away. With fax devices inside of computers, the image doesn't need to go to paper first—it transfers directly from the computer to the other fax machine (or other receiving computer).

What does this mean to your business? Quite a lot, if staying in touch with clients at a distance is important. Fax machines offer instant communication and are cheaper and quicker than even the speediest courier services. After a computer, a fax machine is probably the most powerful piece of technology that can expand your business reach, bring you closer to faraway customers or associates, and increase your income potential.

What to Look for in a Fax Machine

If you're looking to buy a fax machine, check out the following features before making your decision:

- ✓ *Plain-paper versus thermal.* Plain-paper faxes use standard paper and ink-jet or laser-printing technology; thermal fax machines use slippery thermal paper, which tends to fade. Plain-paper fax machines are preferable these days. If you choose a thermal fax machine, be sure to get one with a paper-cutter option.

- ✓ *An integrated telephone,* with voice/data switching, can recognize the type of call and automatically route it to the phone or fax.

- ✓ *Autodial and speed dialing* let you program frequently called numbers into memory.

- ✓ *Auto redial* will retry the last number called.

- ✓ *Broadcasting* allows you to send the same faxed message to multiple parties without having to call each independently.

- ✓ *Wide feed options* can be very convenient if you need to send oversize documents.

- ✓ *Automatic document feeders* allow you to send multiple-page documents (usually 10 to 12 sheets) unattended.

- ✓ *Resolution mode options* allow you to choose print quality, depending on whether you are sending plain documents, detailed drawings, or photographs; a lower print quality transmits faster, saving you money.

✓ *Activity reports* help your bookkeeping by printing out a list of all fax calls made and received, including telephone number, quantity of pages, and duration.

✓ *Memory* saves your fax message in the unit until you can print it out, in case the machine is out of paper when the fax arrives.

Multifunction Devices

A new category of computer equipment has become popular in the last few years: multifunction peripherals. These machines combine a printer, fax machine, copier, and scanner all in one unit. Since all of these devices contain many common elements—print drum, technology to turn printed information into digital data, links between computer and phone transmission—it makes great sense to bring them together in one machine.

But does it make sense for you to invest in one of these devices? It depends. The primary benefit of a multifunction peripheral is that one machine takes the place of several, freeing up valuable space in your office. The main drawback, however, is that if the machine breaks down, you've lost a significant part of your office technology—and your operations can quickly grind to a halt.

One approach adopted by some solo entrepreneurs is to invest in a multifunction device for one of its primary functions—say, as a fax machine. They look at the other features as backup options if their main printer or copier goes down. It's one way of balancing risk and retaining flexibility in your office operations. Since every solo office has different equipment demands, it is wise to carefully think through all the "what if" scenarios before you buy.

Tapping Into the Internet

No aspect of technology has changed more in the past few years than the emergence of the Internet. Once used primarily as a way for researchers and scientists in government agencies and universities to share information, the Internet has transformed into a major global communications medium—and solo entrepreneurs are among those who are reaping the benefits.

The Internet is a worldwide computer network that features a collection of services. The main systems include e-mail, FTP (File Transfer Protocol), newsgroups, information search and retrieval systems such as Gopher and Telnet, IRC (Internet Relay Chat), and the World Wide Web (also known as WWW or the Web). Of these services, e-mail is the most widely used, but the Web is the fastest growing.

It is difficult to write about the Internet without appearing hopelessly dated, because the very nature of the medium—one of instant updates and fluid, ever changing information—goes far beyond static words in print. Not only is this pioneering medium bringing us innovative methods of communicating and doing business, it is creating entire new industries as well.

Even in its relative infancy, the Internet offers remarkable value for anyone who connects to it. Here are a just a few of the resources and capabilities a typical solo entrepreneur can access online.

- ✓ Send e-mail, graphics, sound, video, or other information to anyone in the world within seconds.
- ✓ Conduct research on topics general to arcane, often tapping into data from leading researchers of the world.
- ✓ Make travel reservations and updates instantly.
- ✓ Purchase books from online stores with more than 2.5 million titles.
- ✓ Hear audio clips from leading figures in politics, from a specific industry, or even from a relative a continent away.
- ✓ Get free one-on-one business counseling.
- ✓ Participate in global discussion groups via real-time audio and video capabilities.
- ✓ Post questions and receive answers from a community of fellow solo entrepreneurs.
- ✓ Stay in touch with your clients and customers on an ongoing, inexpensive, and immediate basis.
- ✓ Establish an online storefront to sell your products or services worldwide, 24 hours a day, 7 days a week.

The World Wide Web holds remarkable potential for solo entrepreneurs. The Web gives anyone connected to the Internet access to pages of information that can contain text, pictures, animation, and real-time sound and video. A common analogy is to think of the Web as a digital magazine—only this magazine lets you connect to literally millions of other pages containing related information by simply clicking on underlined text. This hypertext linking concept allows you to browse the Web at your will, collecting information at your own pace and interest level.

Web browsing is intuitive and simple to do—unlike using many software programs—and even novices quickly feel at home clicking from site to site, exploring personal and professional interests. For readers of this book, for example, I have set up a *Working Solo* Web site at http://www.workingsolo.com that contains a broad collection of information and resources specifically designed for solo entrepreneurs. At this site, you'll also find links to dozens of other helpful Web sites for small business owners and entrepreneurs.

To access the Web, you need a computer with Web browser software (the current most popular programs are Netscape's Navigator and Microsoft's Internet Explorer) and a modem, a device that converts computer signals to sound and back again and allows the computer to connect to the network via common phone lines, like a fax machine does.

You'll also need a connection to the Internet. As this book goes to press, the two most common ways of making the Internet connection are through a commercial online service—such as America Online (AOL), CompuServe, Prodigy, or the Microsoft Network (MSN)—or a direct connection with a local *Internet Service Provider* (ISP). In the United States, both options are currently offering an "all-you-can-eat" approach to Internet access, for about $20 a month. As more people come online and the crowding leads to busy signals and delays in service, it is likely that a differentiation will emerge. One scenario is that some services will charge a higher fee in exchange for guaranteed quick and clear connections.

As we enter the transition stage of millions of people joining the online world, here are two tips. First, don't sign any long-term contracts with an Internet service provider. Second, keep in mind that this is a service you're investing in for your company and, as with other business services, you get what you pay for. Choosing an Internet provider that may cost a little more, but will save you time and give you faster connection speeds, can be worth it in the long run.

If you're not online yet, I encourage you to put this at the top of your To-Do list. It's one of the most powerful tools you can add to your solo business resource kit. In Chapter 12, you'll discover specific ways to boost your business productivity and profits by using the remarkable wired network of the Internet. For now, let's return to reviewing some more basic office equipment.

Telephones and Answering Machines

These two basic pieces of office equipment are at the heart of your solo business. They have an impact on every facet of your business, including the image you project, the quality of your daily operations, and your abilities to expand and grow. When all is right, they let the world know you are a professional, in control of your business, and able to deliver a quality product or service. When wrong, they give the impression that your business is in disarray or may not be serious or trustworthy. And as any seasoned solo entrepreneur will tell you, unreliable and troublesome phones or answering machines are more than annoying—they're potential disasters for your business.

With this in mind, choose these important tools with care. Make them work for you as powerful allies for your business success.

Let's take a look at the many features available in today's telephones and answering machines. You may not need all of them, but being aware of what's available can help you consider how to put these tools to best use.

What to Look for in a Telephone

Today's telephones are a far cry from those of just a decade ago. From palm-size wonders to those shaped like tennis shoes or Mickey Mouse, telephones are available to suit your personality, needs, and budget.

Your solo business will have its own set of requirements. Here are a few popular features to keep in mind when you're buying.

✓ *Multiple lines* allow you to handle more calls, and if you're a home-based professional, they help keep your personal and professional lives separate. Some solo workers make outgoing calls on their home lines, leaving the business lines free for important incoming calls. Plan for the future. If you think you'll be expanding phone service sometime soon, buy a two- or three-line unit. The extra-line capability will provide flexibility for future expansion, yet most models will work with a single phone line.

✓ *Speed dialing* enables you to program frequently dialed numbers into your phone's memory. The call is made automatically by pushing one button.

✓ *Redial* lets you punch one button and retry the last number called when you get a busy signal—a handy function that can save time.

✓ A *hold button* is a standard feature on multiple-line phones. On a single-line phone, it can be a professional way of having a caller wait without hearing background noise or your private conversations.

✓ A *conference option* gives you the ability on multiple-line phones to tie together several independent callers for a conference call.

✓ A *speakerphone* option allows you to answer the phone without picking up the handset. Take care, however, since transmission quality is often poor on many models—you may risk sounding like you're talking in a tunnel and alienating those on the other end.

✓ *Cordless phones* offer the convenience of mobility—you can roam your office in search of that file or other item just beyond the reach of a traditional telephone. New digital models enable you to travel even farther while maintaining voice clarity.

✓ *Integrated answering machines* give you the convenience of two devices in one unit, a space-saving approach. One drawback: If the answering machine goes in for repair, you've lost your phone, too.

✓ *Cellular phones* operate on radio waves and offer the greatest mobility options. Usually installed in a car or carried with you, a cellular phone can be a valuable investment, particularly if your solo business requires extensive travel. In addition to purchasing the phone, you're charged per-minute fees for both incoming and outgoing calls. Cellular phone use has exploded in the past few years, and a growing number of mobile solo professionals are finding it to be their communication lifeline.

What to Look for in an Answering Machine

When clients or customers can't reach you, they'll usually end up interacting with your telephone answering machine, so choose this stand-in for you with care. In addition to a machine's reliability and clarity on the outgoing message, you may want to look at the following features:

- ✓ *VOX, or voice-activated,* machines allow callers to leave a message for as long as they'd like instead of being limited to 30 seconds or a minute. VOX outgoing messages let you leave a prerecorded message of any length for callers.

- ✓ *Remote retrieval of messages* lets you check who's called when you're away from the office from any phone, anywhere. Some machines let you play back only messages you haven't heard previously, a feature that can save you time and money.

- ✓ *Automatic interrupt* immediately stops the machine when the phone is picked up, saving you the awkwardness and delay of waiting through your outgoing message to begin your conversation.

- ✓ *Remote turn on/off* lets you activate your answering machine from a remote location with a Touch-Tone phone.

- ✓ *OGM* skip lets callers bypass your outgoing message (OGM) and leave their messages promptly.

- ✓ *Call recording* enables you to record a phone call as you talk, for later review.

Voice Mail and Other Helpful Telephone Services

Voice mail is the next step up on the technology evolution ladder from an answering machine. Instead of recording messages to tape, a computer at your phone company's headquarters acts as a switchboard and message center.

One benefit of a voice-mail system is that it can give the impression that you have a larger, more established business. If your business relies on frequently giving out the same information, a voice-mail system can route callers to multiple mailboxes at any time of the day or night to leave messages or to listen to your prerecorded information. Another benefit: With voice mail, your callers will never get a busy signal. Most telephone companies offer voice mail and the following other options for a monthly fee.

Distinctive ringing is an option that allows you to piggyback an additional telephone number on an existing line and have it ring in a different pattern. This can be a good option for start-up home-based businesses that want to establish some professionalism on a budget. As your business grows, however, you will want to invest in *additional lines* for fax/modem use or for outgoing calls. (One bonus for home-based soloists: Those additional lines can be cheaper residential lines instead of expensive business-rate lines.)

Call waiting gives you a beep to let you know that another caller is trying to get through while you're on the line. While this service was viewed as a great convenience when it was introduced, today most solo professionals opt for voice mail as a more professional approach to managing multiple calls.

Follow-me service, as its name implies, routes your calls to a series of predetermined numbers so your callers can track you down. For example, if a colleague calls your office and you don't answer, it will try your home line. No answer there? It will try your cell phone. Still no response? It will leave a message on your beeper. Think of it as a digital bloodhound—when you really want those callers to find you.

800 and 888 numbers enable your callers to reach you toll-free. Many solo entrepreneurs use these numbers as part of their marketing efforts, setting up order lines or information centers to give their businesses a national presence. Some mobile professionals set up toll-free numbers as an efficient way to call their offices or homes while on the road. Once an expensive option, 800/888 numbers now can be as cheap as other types of long-distance calls. Since they can piggyback on an existing phone line, there are no additional wiring costs.

Photocopiers

Of all the office machines that employees take for granted, I think photocopiers rank at the top of the list. When you're working for someone else, it's easy to walk a few steps down the hall and make a copy of a letter, contract, or page from a book.

On your own, you must find another alternative. Perhaps your office has a copy shop nearby, and you can get a few minutes of exercise as you make the trip. If you're sharing space with another business, you might pay for copies you make on their machine, or consider buying or leasing a machine jointly.

If your copy needs are great, it may be more worthwhile to invest in your own machine, particularly after you factor in time and convenience. Today's desktop models offer a remarkable amount of power for a few hundred dollars. If your business has specialized needs, check out the possibility of renting or leasing more advanced models.

What to Look for in a Photocopier

Here are some features to keep in mind when considering photocopiers.

✓ *Document size options* are important if you'll frequently be dealing with documents larger than letter- or legal-size sheets; make sure the model can accommodate them.

✓ *Reduction/enlargement options* vary according to model. Most desktop copiers offer two or three preset percentages of enlargement and reduction. More expensive models offer controls in single percentage points, an important feature for engineers and other design professionals.

✓ *Automatic paper feed features* let you feed a stack of sheets for automatic copying and are available in higher-priced models; desktop copiers generally accept pages one at a time.

✓ *Automatic collating capabilities* work with a copier's sorting bins and enable multiple sets of documents to be duplicated easily. Some models also include automatic stapling.

✓ *Multiple paper trays* enable you to use standard copy paper, legal- or odd-size sheets, or letterhead. Desktop models have smaller paper trays that generally hold 250 sheets; more expensive machines have larger trays, eliminating the need for frequent refilling.

✓ *All-in-one toner cartridges,* generally found in desktop models, incorporate toner and drum in one cartridge; this makes changing toner simple and repairs minimal. Advanced models often have different toner replacement options, and repairs can be more costly.

✓ *Duplexing features* allow you to automatically copy on two sides of the paper.

✓ *Power savers,* available on some models, will automatically shut off the copier if it is not used for a specific period of time.

As with other technology, choosing a photocopier is a balance between price and performance. If you think you'll need more advanced features only occasionally, get a less expensive machine. You can always rely on your local copy shop's high-performance equipment when necessary.

Getting the Most from Your Technology Investment

Once you've invested in your solo office equipment, make sure you take the next few steps to get the most out of it. Here are five ways to maximize your investment.

1. Learn about your machines.

Yes, this may mean cracking those user manuals and spending a few hours reading. Or buying some training time—either in person or using a video or disk/cassette package. The hours you spend learning will pay off in many more work hours saved, but you have to commit to finding out exactly what your equipment can do.

2.   Register your purchases.

When you get your equipment or computer software, send in those postcards that come with your purchase. They ensure that your warranty is in effect and enable the manufacturer to alert you to possible upgrades or send you special notices.

3.   Buy and use surge protectors.

These power-cord strips have built-in fuses that protect delicate electronic circuitry from electrical power fluctuations or surges during storms and can save you from costly repairs. In the next chapter, we'll also talk about insuring your equipment.

4.   Back up your files.

Computer malfunctions can cripple your business if you haven't kept duplicates of your files. For particularly valuable information, create disk copies to be stored in a safe deposit box or another site away from your office. The rule of thumb is that you should have backup copies current enough so that if you lost everything on your computer today, your business could still function. As one solo professional quips, "He who laughs last is he who has a backup."

5.   Join a user group.

One of the most worthwhile investments you can make is to join a computer user group. These organizations of computer enthusiasts range in size from a dozen people who gather once a month in someone's living room to megagroups of 10,000+ members that sponsor weekly meetings. While each organization differs in personality and interests, all share the goal of increasing members' understanding and enjoyment of using computers. (Sharing information does not mean sharing software, however, and user groups prohibit the copying of commercial software.)

User groups enable you to connect with solo entrepreneurs who have encountered similar challenges in their businesses (computer-related or otherwise). They're also a great source for colleagues to help you sort out buying decisions or software glitches.

There are user groups for nearly every brand of computer and computing interest area. If you're using a PC, you can call (914) 876-6678 and access the user group locator hot line run by the Association of Personal Computer User Groups. If you're a Macintosh user, call (800) 538-9696, extension 500. In each case, you'll be connected to an automated system that responds to the numbers you punch into a Touch-Tone phone (either your telephone area code or zip code) to locate the group nearest you. You'll hear a short recording about the group, its meeting times, and contact information.

You can also ask your local computer dealer or other computer professionals in your area for the names of nearby groups. Or check the pages of *Computer Shopper* magazine in your library or area bookstore; detailed user group listings are in the back. For all these benefits (and more) that user groups can bring, it's worth making the connection.

Tomorrow's Technology?

Technology's progress never stops and, as this book goes to press, new developments linking cellular phone capabilities, miniaturized computers, and handheld communicators are being introduced. These new devices will undoubtedly have a profound effect on workers everywhere—but particularly on solo entrepreneurs. Tomorrow's "office" will be anywhere the individual chooses to be, since communication and information access will be mobile. In Chapter 14, you'll discover more about the impact and benefits that these pocket-size portable wonders will bring to independent entrepreneurs and the exciting opportunities that will accompany this new technology.

There you have it—everything you wanted to know about computers and technology to help you in your solo adventure. Even if you're the type whose eyes glaze over at the prospect of changing flashlight batteries, I hope this chapter has shown you the power and potential these machines can bring to your solo enterprise.

To compete with larger businesses, you must be able to perform like larger firms, and technology can bring you that power. Whether you perform the tasks yourself or hire others is your personal choice. What's important is that you're aware of what is possible to achieve with this equipment. Understanding your options, you can make wiser decisions about appropriate technology for your business and how to maximize it to lead you to success.

Investing in office equipment requires that you have a good sense of your company's financial state. With that in mind, let's now move on to financial matters—bookkeeping, taxes, and insurance—and what they mean for you and your solo business.

Chapter 8

Money Matters: Bookkeeping, Taxes, and Insurance

A million dollars is not what it used to be.
—Howard Hughes (in 1937)

The next step in your solo adventure is an area that's at the heart of your business success: finances. The title of this chapter, "Money Matters," can be interpreted in two ways. In one sense, it reflects the importance of keeping track of the financial details—the money matters—of your solo business. Taken another way, "money matters" is a statement that money does matter to the overall continuance and growth of your enterprise, even if wealth is not the primary reason you're working solo. As an independent entrepreneur, you need to adopt both meanings: a system for charting your progress and an understanding that controlling your financial situation is key to achieving your business goals.

In the coming pages you'll find information, suggestions, and tips based on advice from financial professionals, along with real-world experiences from solo entrepreneurs. You'll discover painless approaches to keeping financial records, tax tips that can save you money, ways to protect you and your business with insurance, and other valuable hints to keep your solo venture running profitably.

As we begin, it's important to state that financial matters are complex and need to be managed with care. This is one area in which most solo professionals depend on the advice of others. These pages will give you a solid understanding of the basics. You should continually add to your knowledge, whether through publications, associations, professional advisors, or other sources. You'll find the listings in Appendix A, "Solo Resources," in this book, as well as the companion *Working Solo Sourcebook,* a valuable reference.

Bookkeeping: A Mirror of Your Business

Some of the biggest groans I hear from solo entrepreneurs come from discussions about bookkeeping. "I'm an artist, not an accountant," the creative types say. "I didn't start this business to spend all this time indoors, crunching numbers," protest the independents who'd rather be out talking to customers. And nearly every solo worker can relate to the complaint, "How am I supposed to find any time to do my business if I'm always shuffling papers?"

Bookkeeping—and its cousin, record keeping—is a fact of life for all businesses, not only solo ventures. It's an essential element in tracking, summarizing, and analyzing business activities.

You can either make bookkeeping work for you or against you—accepting it as a necessary part of doing business or fighting it as a nuisance that you deal with as seldom as possible. Since you have to keep a certain number of records anyway, why not adopt the attitude that record keeping tasks are a guidance tool, helping you navigate the solo business path?

That's not to say you must fall in love with bookkeeping (although some may enjoy it enough to launch solo businesses offering this service). Bookkeeping gets a bad reputation because the focus is on how dull or time-consuming it can be. Hardly anyone highlights the benefits your business derives from keeping good records—advantages that can make a significant difference in the viability and profitability of your efforts.

One of the most valuable ways bookkeeping can serve you is by acting as a mirror, reflecting a true financial picture of your business. You may have an intuitive understanding of how your business is going or instincts about where you should focus money and effort, but there's nothing like a set of numbers to paint an objective picture of your business's current financial status.

Good records show you where you've been and point you in the direction in which you should be heading. Final decisions about the specific route to take—for example, whether to spend money in one area or emphasize another aspect of your business—are still yours. With solid records as a mirror, you can review your options and make *informed* decisions, the hallmark of successful entrepreneurs.

Different Businesses, Different Approaches

Since each solo business is as unique as its owner, bookkeeping preferences, needs, and systems will also be individualized. The basics, however, remain: You're seeking a way to track income and expenses. Depending on your business, you may also want to record time, materials, inventory, or sales history.

There are three popular ways of maintaining records: by hand, on a computer, or by using an outside service. In choosing your approach, be sure to check with your accountant and tax advisor to see if the method you have chosen will provide them with adequate records at year-end. Tailoring your record keeping to their preference will likely save you both time and money.

Let's take a look at the three most common ways of keeping financial records and their benefits and drawbacks.

By Hand

Long before computers, bookkeeping was done by hand, using a pencil and paper—generally wide, ruled ledger sheets. After recording the deposits and checks written in the check register, the business owner would then record the transactions on ledger sheets and categorize all expenses by type, in columns. Hand entry remains an option for some small and start-up solo businesses, and a variety of styles of ledger books can be found in office supply stores. If you're not computerized yet, a time-saving, low-tech option is a one-write check system, such as those offered by financial suppliers Safeguard or Bee. As you write checks, a strip of carbon on the back of each one automatically creates a copy of the important information (such as date, amount, category, or payee) on a ledger sheet. This eliminates the need to transfer numbers from the check register to ledger paper, cutting down on bookkeeping time and potential math errors.

On a Computer

A computer can take the boredom out of bookkeeping tasks and turn figures into valuable financial data for your business planning. A computer's calculation abilities, enhanced by the appropriate software, give it the power to generate numerous financial reports, such as income by client, expenses by category, a balance sheet, or a profit and loss statement.

Financial software packages range from simple checkbook-type programs such as Quicken by Intuit to more advanced accounting programs by companies

---

BANKING ANYTIME, ANYWHERE

With a link to the Internet, your bank can be as close as your personal computer. Many of the country's leading banks now offer services to let you conduct banking business online—anytime, anywhere. You can pay bills, check your account balances, review recent transactions (including ATM activities), transfer funds between accounts, reorder checks, or track budgets to help you achieve your goals. Access is through the bank's own Web site or via services such as America Online. Some also offer links with popular software programs such as Quicken or Microsoft Money to let you pay bills quickly, easily—and with no stamps. Check to see if your bank has joined these digital ranks.

such as BestWare and Peachtree. Checkbook-type programs are very popular with solo entrepreneurs because they offer many report-generating capabilities as well as check-writing features—all in an easy-to-learn program that retails for less than $50. As your business grows, you may want to move up to a more robust accounting program, such as M.Y.O.B. by BestWare, QuickBooks Pro by Intuit, or Peachtree Complete Accounting by Peachtree, that includes options such as inventory, time and job tracking, payroll, and more extensive reports. These small business accounting programs are a little more complex to learn, but the payoff comes from the increased quality of the financial information you'll have to guide your business.

Using an Outside Service

Having another person or outside service maintain the financial books is a dream come true for many solo businesspeople. Before you jump to adopt this solution, however, I encourage you to keep your own records for at least the first 9 to 12 months of your business. There's nothing that keeps a solo entrepreneur more focused than charting business income and expenses on a regular basis. Once you turn bookkeeping responsibilities over to someone else, it's easy to lose touch with the financial reality your bookkeeping mirror presents to you. Reading figures on a prepared sheet has a different impact than charting those numbers yourself.

If and when you decide to delegate the bookkeeping function, be sure to request timely prepared reports to be given to you on a regular basis and set aside periodic meetings to review the reports and projections with your accountant. Use the time previously devoted to record-keeping tasks to analyze and plan your business growth.

Setting Up Your Chart of Accounts

No matter who does your bookkeeping or which method you choose, you'll have to set up a chart of accounts. This is an organized listing, by category, for all sources of cash, as well as all cash disbursements you may have in your business. A chart of accounts is divided into five main categories: assets, liabilities, equity, income, and expenses.

Organizing this list takes a little bit of thought, since the structure you give it will determine, to some extent, the information you're able to extract from your records. For example, many of your income and expense accounts will be taken from the IRS Schedule C (Form 1040), Profit or Loss From Business (which we'll be covering in a little while). You'll have expense accounts such as advertising, rent, and utilities. For the utilities category, you may want to create subcategories in your chart of accounts for electric, water, and telephone. That way, during the year you can easily see how much these items individually contribute to your

THE TOP FIVE TIPS FOR PAINLESS RECORD KEEPING

Ask a group of seasoned solo entrepreneurs for their hottest tips on the easiest way to keep financial records, and these are the five that come up most often:

1. Keep personal and business finances separate.
Make a sharp dividing line between personal and business finances. Set up a separate bank account for your business, and dedicate one general credit card for business purposes only.

2. Use the business checking account whenever possible.
Centralizing your business activity in one checking account can be an enormous help in staying organized, since you'll have a clean paper trail of your finances. For example, deposit all income to your business checking account, even if you will transfer it to savings later. Try to pay expenses with a check whenever possible, noting invoice number and category on the check.

3. Stay current.
Try to set aside regular times to do bookkeeping tasks. Once they pile up, you'll be even less inclined to tackle them. Don't lose control of your business by not staying informed of your financial status.

4. Keep systems simple, and leave a paper trail.
It's better to have a simple system that you'll use faithfully than a sophisticated method that you never touch. Determine the information that is important to run your business, and set up a system that feels comfortable and delivers what you need. If you're using a computer, be sure to regularly back up your files, as well as maintain printed reports for a complete paper trail. Find an easy way to store receipts—such as an accordion pocket folder—and use it consistently.

5. Refine, but have continuity.
As your business grows and changes, it's likely you'll also refine your bookkeeping system. Try to avoid abrupt changes or the temptation to start a new system each year—both can waste valuable time and cause confusion when analyzing past financial performance. Focus instead on tweaking your current methods and incorporating new approaches slowly, until you find the best system for your unique business.

overall expenses—instead of relying on a single utility category that doesn't give much information or help you plan.

Similarly, set up your chart of accounts so that it gives you good feedback on where you're generating income. Consider setting up categories based on key customers or on certain types of work. You'll have an easy way of seeing where it makes sense to focus your energies (remember that 80/20 rule?).

If you're using a software program, the basic chart of accounts structure should already be set up in the program; all you need to do is create the account titles particular to your business. Once an account is established, you can generate a report—for instance, income from a specific client or expenses related to a certain project—and the figures pop up on your computer screen instantly. It's a powerful information and planning tool—one that can quickly confirm or deny those seat-of-the-pants hunches you have about income or expenses.

Keep Other Records of Your Success

Before we leave this section on record keeping, I want to encourage you to keep another category of records: a collection reflecting your business developments. Start a scrapbook or file and fill it with newspaper clippings on your business, brochures, letters of appreciation from customers, a copy of your first invoice— all those items that reflect the spirit of you and your solo venture. Items you may take for granted today can be valuable references in later years, as well as fond memories.

Solo entrepreneurs are often too harried in the early months of launching a business to remember to set aside these clippings, notes, or other memoranda. Try to do so, even if it's only in a simple manila folder stuffed in a back filing drawer until you can create a nicer setting for it. A memory file is a great resource to review as your business grows. It can also provide much-needed cheer and encouragement when you face inevitable solo business struggles, since it will be vivid proof of how far you've come and how much you've achieved.

Tackling the Tax Demon

Successful businesses pay taxes. (As we discussed in Chapter 1, if you're not paying taxes, it means your business didn't make a profit—not exactly a reason to celebrate, even though there's no tax bill.) Your challenge as a solo entrepreneur is to claim as many deductions as you legally can, to reduce the amount of tax you owe.

Tax professionals make it very clear that there's a big difference between tax *evasion* and tax *avoidance*. Willingly evading your tax obligations is a crime that can bring big penalties and possibly land you in jail. Avoiding taxes, and claiming every deduction due you, is your right as a business owner and citizen.

The difference often hinges on details in the law and on the quality of the business records you've kept. Remember, the burden of proof lies with you to convince the IRS and other tax agencies that you have a right to your deduction. Sloppy record keeping or ignorance of the law won't hold up as a defense if you're audited.

Words of Wisdom

On Keeping Your Solo Business Books in Order

Financial record keeping for a solo business doesn't need to be complicated. Here are some insights from a professional tax advisor who has been working with independent entrepreneurs for more than 18 years.

"It's true that some of the paperwork demanded by the government is cumbersome, complicated, often illogical or downright silly. But don't ever let the fear of record keeping, paperwork, or red tape deter you from pursuing your solo business. What's important is that you establish a method to track your income and expenses—one that you'll use.

"Pay absolutely everything you can by check or charge. A single checking account for both personal and business purposes is fine— you just need a good system to track business income and expenses. For those few things you pay for in cash, make sure you get a receipt or keep a record of the amount, the date, and the business reason for the expense.

"Mark your calendar so you'll know when your business taxes are due. Beware of the friend who knows somebody who has tried the same business and knows exactly how to complete a specific tax form. Chances are, they're wrong, and it will cost you more in the end.

"If you work with financial professionals, make sure you understand everything they tell you. If you don't, have them explain it again. Don't be afraid to question your financial advisors. Remember, in the end, you are the person who bears responsibility for your business finances."

—June Walker

June Walker is a professional tax advisor who counsels solo entrepreneurs worldwide through her own practice as well as writing and public speaking. She is based in Santa Fe, New Mexico.

What Taxes and to Whom?

The taxes your business must pay are based on the legal structure of your company and the type of service or product you offer. If you're a solo business operating as a sole proprietor with no employees, you'll pay two kinds of federal taxes: *income tax* and *self-employment tax* (a combination of Social Security and Medicare for self-employed workers).

In addition to federal taxes, you may be subject to state income taxes and, in some areas, local or city taxes may also be due. If you sell products, your business may also have to collect state sales taxes. Sound overwhelming? It can be at first—and it points out how important a good tax advisor can be.

You can also get help directly from the IRS, which puts out an extensive series of free booklets available by calling (800) TAX-FORM. A good place to start is Publication 334, *Tax Guide for Small Business.* Publication 910, *Guide to Free Tax Services,* is a catalog of all IRS publications and tax assistance programs, updated annually. Check Appendix A, "Solo Resources" for a detailed listing of other helpful, no-cost IRS publications.

Another useful IRS service is Tele-Tax, a series of prerecorded information segments on common tax topics available toll-free, 24 hours a day, by calling (800) 829-4477. About 140 topics are available, and a directory can be found in Publication 910 or by selecting recording number 323 when you call.

The IRS has also set up two systems to provide easy access to frequently requested tax forms. IRS forms are available from a fax-back service (see Appendix A, "Solo Resources" for details) and via the Internet at the IRS Web site, http://www.irs.ustreas.gov.

Be cautious about relying on verbal advice from the IRS; it has been known to give out misleading or inaccurate information. You should always maintain a phone log when speaking with the IRS, including the name of the person you spoke with. As with any important matter, it's better to get advice in writing. If you're assessed penalties based on faulty IRS information, you can usually avoid the penalties if you supply a copy of the written information provided you by the agency.

Federal Income Tax

Income taxes on solo businesses operating as sole proprietorships are calculated by taking the business's gross revenues and subtracting all applicable deductions. The profit or loss is the *net income* and this figure is used to determine income subject to federal income tax as well as self-employment tax.

As you can see, whittling away your gross revenue with deductible business expenses has a significant effect on your net income, resulting in reduced taxes. Savvy solo workers can make tax law work in their favor.

Remember, it's considered evasion, not avoidance, if you try to reduce your gross revenue by not claiming income or by underreporting the amount you earned. The IRS cross-checks income sources, and this red flag will greatly increase your chances for an audit.

A sole proprietor's business income and deductions are filed on IRS Schedule C (Form 1040), Profit or Loss From Business. In recent years, the IRS has introduced Schedule C-EZ, a streamlined approach that can be used if your return meets certain criteria.

If you are a sole proprietor, the net profit from your business is treated as earned income. The dollar figure you arrive at after finishing Schedule C is reported on the front of Form 1040, where it is entered as earned income and taxed accordingly—or as a net loss, which reduces your taxable income.

As a savvy solo entrepreneur, your goal is to make that taxable-dollar figure as small as legally possible, so that you will owe less to the IRS. With that in mind, let's take a look at business deductions and how you can use them to chip away at your gross revenue, thereby reducing your taxes.

Maximizing Your Deductions, Minimizing Your Taxes

The IRS says that expenses may be deducted from your gross revenue if they are an "ordinary and necessary" part of your work. What is ordinary for a computer programmer, of course, may be quite unusual for a tropical fish breeder. The burden of proof is on you, the taxpayer, to defend your reasoning and substantiate your expense with records and receipts.

Below is a list of business deductions often overlooked by small business owners. I've included brief details on what to keep in mind if you're thinking of claiming them on your business tax return.

✓ *Advertising*
Include the cost of preparing the ad as well as the cost for running it.

✓ *Automobile expenses*
Can be calculated on a rate per mile or on actual costs of operation, such as gas, oil, and repairs. Keep a small logbook in your car to note date, miles, and business reason for the trip. Fees for rental cars used for business are also deductible. Request toll and parking receipts for all business trips, if applicable.

✓ *Bank fees*
Include setup costs, check printing charges, monthly fees, credit card merchant fees, and safe deposit box rental for your business account(s).

✓ *Books and publications*
Expenses for books, magazines, and journals related to your specific business are tax deductible.

✓ *Business gifts*
You may deduct the cost of gifts to business associates, up to a maximum of $25 per person, per year.

✓ *Dues*
Dues and membership fees for professional organizations related to your business can be deducted.

✓ *Education*
You can write off classes, conferences, workshops, and other educational costs to improve or to maintain business-related skills.

✓ *Entertainment*
Business meals with advisors, parties you give for business associates, tickets for sporting or theater events—these and other entertainment expenses are deductible up to 50 percent if they are directly related to your business. It's important to keep good records and document the reason for the expense, who was there, what took place, and so on.

✓ *Equipment*
Costs of computers and other business equipment are deductible generally in two ways: either through depreciation (by writing off a percentage each year over the anticipated life of the equipment as defined in IRS tables) or as a one-time write-off under IRS tax code Section 179. You can write off up to $18,500 in equipment in 1998, and higher limits (up to $25,000) will be phased in between now and 2003. Remember, however, you cannot expense equipment for any tax year in excess of the total amount of taxable income from any trade or business. You also cannot exceed the maximum dollar limits for total equipment purchases during the tax year. There may be other limitations or tax advantages to calculating depreciation in one way or the other, which your tax advisor can point out.

✓ *Insurance*
The cost of all business-related insurance (which we'll cover at the end of this chapter) is deductible. Health insurance premiums for the self-employed are deductible up to 45 percent in 1998. The 1997 tax code revision mandated this health care deduction to increase to 100 percent in 2007, phased in over the coming years. Check with your tax professional to find the current maximum.

✓ *Interest on business debts*

Interest payments on bank loans, credit purchases, or other business-related debts are deductible.

✓ *Licenses and permits*

You may be appalled at all the required licenses and permits your business may need, but at least these expenses are tax deductible.

✓ *Moving*

If you're moving your office to another location, related expenses are deductible. If you're moving your home, certain expenses are deductible, but not on your Schedule C. For details on moving deductions, check out IRS Publication 521, *Moving Expenses,* and Publication 523, *Selling Your Home.*

✓ *Office furniture*

The cost of desks, chairs, bookcases, tables, even art on the walls is deductible *if* it's for business use only. That means you can't buy a new living room coffee table and deduct the price as a business expense. Think the IRS will never know? Perhaps—but agents have been known to make office visits to check.

✓ *Office supplies*

Expenses for all office supplies, from paper clips to paper to floppy disks, are deductible. As always, keep good receipts, and separate business supplies from personal ones.

✓ *Online services*

Fees for connecting your computer via the telephone to online information services and the Internet are deductible if used for business.

✓ *Postage*

The cost of stamps and mailing permit fees, and rental costs for post office boxes can be deducted.

✓ *Printing*

Expenses for anything you have printed for your business—announcements, invitations, flyers, brochures, and the like—are deductible, as are the design fees associated with its production.

✓ *Professional fees*

Fees paid to lawyers, accountants, bookkeepers, designers, marketing consultants, and other advisors for business assistance are all deductible. If you pay any unincorporated independent contractor more than $600 in a calendar year, you must file IRS Form 1099 to report the contractor's income (details in Chapter

11 when we discuss hiring associates.) A tip: Request the name, address, and Social Security or Federal ID number of any unincorporated independent contractor at the time of service, since this information is often difficult to obtain at year-end.

✓ *Rent*
Office rent and expenses for equipment or tool rental are deductible. If the rented site or item is used for both business and personal use, you must prorate the business part and can claim only that portion as deductible.

✓ *Repairs and maintenance*
It's frustrating when office equipment breaks down, but at least the repair costs are deductible.

✓ *Shipping and freight*
Charges for UPS, FedEx, and other courier services used for your business can be deducted.

✓ *Stationery*
Costs of letterhead, business cards, envelopes, mailing labels, and other business stationery items are deductible.

✓ *Subcontractors*
Fees paid to associates who assist you in your enterprise are deductible. As with professional fees, if the amount exceeds $600 in a calendar year, you must file IRS Form 1099 to report the subcontractor's income.

A word of caution: It is important for small businesses to understand the employee versus independent contractor matter. The IRS has developed new "categories of evidence" to determine if a worker is an employee or an independent contractor. Misclassifying workers can lead to confusion and, even worse, possible fines. More details, including the categories of evidence, can be found in Chapter 11.

✓ *Supplies*
The cost of consumable supplies used in your particular solo business is deductible.

✓ *Taxes*
Business taxes are generally deductible on your Schedule C. States vary in their regulations about deducting other state, local, and sales taxes. Check with your tax advisor regarding your situation.

✓ *Telephone*

If you have a solo office outside the home, all telephone fees, including installation, are deductible. If you're home-based, the IRS says you cannot deduct charges for basic telephone service of the first line into the home. Costs for additional lines and business-related long-distance calls are deductible.

✓ *Trademarks and patents*

If you obtain trademarks or patents for your solo enterprise, the fees associated with filing, obtaining, and renewing them can be deducted. Costs associated with the development of trademarks and patents are written off over a period of 15 years under Section 197 of the Internal Revenue Code.

✓ *Travel*

You can write off business-related travel costs, but be sure to keep good records of why you went, when, where, what you accomplished, and how it helped your business.

✓ *Utilities*

The cost of heat, electric, gas, and other utilities used for your business can be deducted. If the bill includes both personal and business use together, prorate the charges for the business part, and be prepared to defend your calculations.

Office Use of the Home

If you're one of the millions of individuals who operate solo businesses out of their homes, you may be entitled to claim a portion of your home costs such as rent or mortgage interest payments, utilities, property taxes, and homeowner's insurance as a tax deduction.

To claim the home office deduction, you must meet several important criteria:

1. The office is exclusively used to conduct substantial and essential administrative or management activities on a regular systematic basis.
2. The taxpayer has no other location to conduct these essential administrative or management activities.
3. It must be the taxpayer's principal place of business.

For example, if you use a spare bedroom for an office and also let house guests sleep there, you can't deduct it. Ditto for that basement space that doubles as the kids' playroom—not eligible. On the other hand, if you live in a loft space, you can partition off a certain area, dedicate it solely to business functions, and claim the deduction for that portion of your home.

The regulations surrounding the home office deduction have been a battleground for lawmakers for nearly a decade. Previous IRS rulings stated that small business owners who conducted their work away from home—such as tradespeople, sales professionals, repair technicians, and computer consultants—did not warrant the deduction for a home office, since it was not their "principal" place of business.

In 1997, after heavy lobbying by small business advocates, Congress expanded the deduction to include business owners who conduct essential administrative or management tasks on a regular basis from their home offices. The new ruling extended legitimate deductions to thousands of additional home-based workers.

If your home-based office meets the criteria for claiming a deduction and you have good records to prove it, take this deduction that is rightfully yours. If you're cautious about raising a red flag with the IRS, talk to your tax advisor and see how much money the deduction would save you, then decide if it's worth the risk to you.

To claim the deduction, you'll need to complete IRS Form 8829, which asks for related expenses and the percentage of your residence claimed as exclusively business use. You can calculate the business use percentage in one of two ways:

1. *Square foot method.* Determine the number of square feet of office space compared with total square footage in your home.
2. *Number of rooms method.* Calculate the number of rooms used by your business compared with total rooms in the house.

In either case, the resulting percentage is the portion of your total house expenses you can claim as business-related deductions on Form 8829. The deductions cannot be more than the net business income you claim, although you can carry over to future years that portion of the deduction you didn't use.

As the number of home-based workers expands, this tax area will receive increased attention, and additional changes in the regulations are likely. Keep your eyes and ears open for further developments—they could mean money in your pocket.

The Tax Advantages of Retirement Contributions

Another way to decrease your tax bill is to make contributions to an individual retirement account (IRA) or other retirement savings plan for independent professionals. While not technically a business deduction, a contribution to this plan can save you money by allowing you to put "expensive" taxable money into a fund that grows tax-free until you withdraw it after the age of 59½ (when you'll probably be in a lower tax bracket). Retirement funds provide a double bonus—tax savings and future income—and you'll be hearing about them in more detail in the next chapter.

"Creative" Tax Deductions

Even though tax laws are precise, they still contain a fair amount of latitude in their interpretation. For some solo entrepreneurs, these gray areas in tax law are not only a way to save on their tax bills, they also become a creative challenge for the entrepreneurs and their accountants. For instance, instead of making a cash contribution to your local charitable organization (deductible only as a personal itemized deduction, not a tax-deductible business expense), see if you can purchase space in the organization's directory or fund-raising program to place your business card. This will result in an advertising expense—which is a tax-deductible business expense—and you have still helped the charitable organization.

How aggressive you choose to be in claiming these types of business-related deductions is often a matter of your own personality and risk comfort level. Remember, the burden of proof is on you. You'll need accurate and detailed records to support what the IRS calls the "facts and circumstances" that make these costs legitimate business deductions. If the IRS thinks you're stretching the rules a bit too far, your entire tax return might be audited, and you risk paying interest and penalties (nondeductible!) on the tax due.

Hobby or Business?

The IRS keeps a careful eye out for individuals who consistently run businesses at a loss just to amass valuable deductions. Its guidelines state that a business must make a profit three years out of five, or else the enterprise is considered a hobby. This distinction can affect your taxes significantly, since deductions for hobby activities are limited, and no losses can be allowed to offset other income.

Individuals who have fought this ruling and won had strong business records showing that they had consistently operated their businesses in a professional manner and attempted to make a profit. Keep this in mind as your solo venture enters its third year: Either show a profit (no matter how small) or be willing to defend your professional attempts at doing so.

You Are Not a Tax Deduction

One final note about tax deductions: If you're operating as a sole proprietor, money that you pay yourself is not considered wages and is not tax deductible. That money is your profit and, however you spend it—even if it is paying yourself to run your business, cannot be claimed as a business deduction. To deduct wages paid to you as a solo business, you'd have to be incorporated. Turn to your financial advisor for help in determining if the tax savings would be worth the time and expense of establishing a corporation and which type of corporation would best suit your business.

What Kind of Records and How Long Must You Keep Them?

To substantiate your business deductions, you should keep copies of invoices, canceled checks, stubs, and other receipts—particularly if you paid cash for an item. Many solo entrepreneurs have found that the easiest approach to keeping these scraps of paper corralled is to pop them into an accordion folder, with a pocket dedicated for each month or category. At the end of the year, sort through the folder and tally cash expenses. (We'll talk about other ways to tame the paperwork beast in Chapter 10.)

The IRS also accepts "contemporaneous records," meaning a diary or an appointment book. Travel and entertainment expenses under $25—such as that cab ride or business lunch—don't require receipts as long as you've jotted details in your calendar/diary about the who, what, why, when, and where of the business deduction. As expected, a calendar brimming with details will offer more support than a single cryptic line that says, "Tom, lunch, noon." The key is to find a system that works for you—one that feels comfortable and that you'll use.

How long do you have to keep those records stashed away in a basement, closet, or attic? It depends on the records:

✓ *Tax returns*
You should keep these indefinitely, either in a filing drawer or in a three-ring binder. Should you need a copy of a past return, check with your tax preparer—he or she is required to keep returns for at least three years after filing. To request a copy from the IRS, use IRS Form 4506 (Request for Copy of Tax Form), available from your local IRS office or by calling (800) TAX-FORM.

✓ *Supporting documents for income/expenses*
Keeping records such as canceled checks, invoices, or other receipts for five years should be long enough—unless you've filed a fraudulent tax return, which the IRS states can be audited at any time.

✓ *Real estate records*
You should keep records for costs and improvements to any real estate—particularly if you've claimed a home-office deduction—for as long as you own the property, plus five years.

✓ *Retirement fund records*

Advisors suggest that you retain all records documenting your contributions to retirement funds, even after you've withdrawn all the money from them.

Self-Employment Taxes

The other major federal tax that solo entrepreneurs face is self-employment tax, a combination of Social Security and Medicare taxes. When you work for someone else, the employer pays one half of this tax, and the employee pays the other half. When you're self-employed, you're playing *both* roles, and—you guessed it— you are liable for *both* parts of this tax.

Rates for self-employment tax remained the same for 1996 and 1997, although future increases would not be surprising. The 1997 rate is 15.3 percent, which comprises two items: 12.4 percent for Social Security and 2.9 percent for Medicare tax. The Social Security rate is applied to a maximum base rate per person; in 1997, the base rate was $65,400. There is no base amount for the Medicare tax; all self-employment earnings are subject to this rate.

A 15 percent tax on earnings is substantial, and solo newcomers are often in shock when they see the impact on their business profits. Fortunately, self-employment tax is calculated on net income—once again you can see the impact that business deductions can have on your overall tax picture. If your business has less than $400 in profits, no self-employment taxes are due. Self-employment taxes are paid quarterly to the IRS along with estimated federal income taxes, something we'll cover in just a moment.

Taxes for Moonlighters or Part-Time Solo Workers

If you're working solo while holding another job—either full-time or part-time— you've probably already contributed both income taxes and Social Security taxes. In this situation, your "regular" income would be reported on the 1040 Form, and you'd include a Schedule C to report your business income and expenses. By keeping good records, you'll be able to tell when your business income surpasses your business deductions and when you'll need to pay taxes to supplement those already taken out from your regular paycheck.

Paying Your Quarterly Estimated Taxes

If you're self-employed, the government expects you to keep track of how much money you owe in income taxes and self-employment taxes and to send it in four times a year: April 15, June 15, September 15, and January 15 of the following year. To do this, you fill out a payment voucher, Form 1040-ES. If you're just starting your business, call (800) TAX-FORM or stop by your area IRS office to get the forms. Once you've filed estimated taxes, you will automatically receive preprinted vouchers the following years, or you can obtain them from your accountant or tax advisor.

A four-page instruction worksheet included with the forms walks you through the necessary steps in calculating your estimated taxes. In most cases, you must make estimated tax payments if you expect to owe at least $500 in taxes.

Once you get the hang of it, estimated payments become one more "pay this bill" day on your calendar. (The January 15 payment date always makes solo workers groan, since it comes right after the holidays, when money can be tight.) In some circumstances, it's also possible to calculate current tax liabilities based on how much tax you paid the previous year, an approach that can make the arithmetic easier. The IRS 1040-ES instruction sheet has details.

As a solo entrepreneur, you're expected to pay at least 90 percent of your current tax bill (or 100 percent of last year's bill) in quarterly installments during the current tax year. If you underpay or are late with your quarterly payments, you may be liable for penalties.

State and Local Taxes

Most state income taxes are collected in ways similar to the IRS methods—tax liabilities are based on net income, and payments are due quarterly. Check the government (blue) pages of your telephone directory for the number to call to get state income tax information in your area.

Local taxes for regions, counties, or cities vary so much that it's difficult to make any general statements about them. Your network of professional advisors and colleagues can help you navigate the local regulations.

Sales taxes are due from goods sold to individual customers. The hitch about sales taxes is that they can be cumbersome to calculate. For example, in New York State, the law says that sales tax is based on *the point of delivery* of the product. That means a New York State solo business could have six mail-order customers in different parts of the state and each would have a different sales tax rate. In contrast, a retail store in one area of the state would have only one sales tax rate, since the point of delivery is one site.

Another complication for sales tax calculations is that state tax calendars often don't coincide with the standard calendar, since state budget years don't begin January 1. (For example, in New York State the state sales tax year is June 1 to May 31.)

You can see where a computer and good record keeping are necessities if you're selling products to the public. Within moments, a computer can pull out the total dollar figure of sales, amount of sales tax due at a specific rate, and the dates or months involved. This would be incredibly time-consuming if your business was to rely only on records kept by hand.

Contact your state sales tax office to find out if you need to collect sales tax and, if so, how to obtain a certificate of authorization to collect it. The state sales tax office will provide you with the filing and payment requirements, as well as guidance on items subject to sales and use tax.

Preparing Your Return

The options for preparing your tax return range from walking into an accountant's office with a shopping bag stuffed with receipts to calculating every penny yourself and doing the return on your personal computer. Most solo entrepreneurs opt for a solution somewhere in between.

Hiring a tax professional to sort through your individual slips of paper, receipts, and stubs is an incredibly expensive way of preparing your tax return—yet experienced tax professionals admit that a handful of their clients resort to this method each year. With a little bit of organization you can save yourself a lot of money, and I encourage all solo newcomers to tackle the grunt work of organizing and tallying receipts into business deduction categories. This mundane task will help you in two ways: (1) It will give you a better understanding of your income and expenses, and (2) it will encourage you to be better organized next year.

At the other end of the spectrum, a number of solo professionals enjoy figuring out the details of their tax returns by using multifeatured tax software that leads you through each step of the process. When you've finished, the software tells you exactly how much you owe and prints forms identical to official tax forms—only your figures are already filled in. Some solo techno-wizards even go one step further and use their computers to send their tax returns electronically to the IRS.

The majority of independent workers compile the basics of their tax returns, then turn them over to tax professionals for completion or review. This approach gives you the best of both worlds: You save money by doing the paperwork tasks yourself, and you gain from professional advisors guiding you in correcting any mistakes you've made or deductions you've overlooked. With ever changing tax laws becoming more complex, most solo entrepreneurs prefer to focus on areas they know best. Unless your solo business is tax preparation, it's often a wiser financial decision to turn to outside professional help.

A note of caution: Even if you hire outside professionals to help you with your taxes, the final burden of proof during an audit is on you, the solo business owner. It pays to choose a qualified tax preparer carefully and to review the work done for you.

To understand the range in abilities of even experienced professionals, consider a test conducted by *Money* magazine, which sends out an identical set of tax records to 50 tax preparers and asks each of them to compile a return based on the data. Recently, of the 50 responses, only *one* was deemed correct by the IRS—an improvement over past years, when *none* was accurate. The moral: Choose your preparer with care, and double-check to make sure your return represents your business accurately.

Whether you do your own return or turn to outside help, rest assured that over the years you'll refine your methods. Seasoned solo workers know that many ideas arise from the frustrations of saying each spring, "I'll never do it *this* way again!" As each year passes, you'll discover new tricks to make tax time easier. On a subtler level, you'll find yourself thinking throughout the year about each chunk of income and each expense in a new light: "Hmmm . . . Now, how will this affect my tax picture this year?" When that day comes, you'll know that you've arrived as a savvy solo business taxpayer.

Audits and How to Survive Them

If there's anything that can strike terror in the hearts of most solo entrepreneurs, it's the thought of a tax audit. In actuality, less than 1 percent of the total number of tax returns filed each year are audited—and the number won't likely increase anytime soon because the IRS is facing governmental budget cuts like the rest of Washington.

The IRS has up to three years after you file your return to audit it. For example, an audit of your return filed in April 1999 (for 1998 taxes) must begin by April 2002.

If you're facing an audit, suppress the queasy stomach and shaky knees and keep these tips in mind:

1.   Don't ignore it.
Whatever you do, don't ignore the IRS letter informing you of your upcoming audit. If the IRS doesn't hear from you, it assumes you are in the wrong, and things can quickly escalate to become even worse.

2.   Be prepared.
The office audit is the most common form of IRS review. You'll be asked to bring records documenting specific areas of your return—office-at-home deductions or charitable contributions, for example—to the area IRS office to meet with a revenue agent. Before your appointment, review your records and be prepared to answer and defend your reasoning.

3.   Stay cool.
The meeting with an IRS representative is an adversarial interaction, but it doesn't help your position if you're hostile. Stay cool, calm, and collected.

4.   Keep quiet.
On the other hand, it does you no good to be chummy with the IRS agent. Answer the questions posed to you, but don't offer any additional information.

This is not the time for casual conversation—one slip could open up a Pandora's box leading to investigations of other areas of your return.

5. Call in the troops if you need them.

Whether you'll need professional help at an audit depends on the areas up for review. If you're asked to provide substantiation for records and you have them, you probably can handle it on your own. If it's in a more complex area, don't be shy about having your tax advisor assist you—either by preparing you before you go, accompanying you to the meeting, or attending in your place.

With luck, you'll never have to face an IRS audit. If you do, however, your solid record keeping will enable you to sail right through and survive even the closest scrutiny.

Now let's move on to protecting you and your business, and the many levels of financial security that insurance can bring.

Protecting Your Solo Business with Insurance

As your independent venture grows, there will soon come a time when you can't imagine living or working any other way. If someone threatened to make you stop, you'd probably put up quite a fight.

Unfortunately, there *is* a big bully with power to shut down your working solo venture. It's known by many names: fire, lightning, windstorms, floods, accidents, illness, disability, theft, earthquakes, lawsuits, or other calamities. When these disasters strike, your business can be rocked to its core—and may not recover if you're not prepared.

Because they are inherently linked to one person, solo businesses can be very flexible, but they're also very vulnerable. Solo entrepreneurs must be smart enough to launch and grow a business but also wise enough to protect it from harm. The challenge is to invest in enough insurance so that your business can survive if disaster strikes, while not spending a fortune and strapping your operating funds.

Choosing the Right Policy

Insurance comes in many shapes and sizes, but most policies fit into two general categories: protecting people or protecting property. The type and coverage for your solo business will depend on your specific needs, risk tolerance, and budget. Insurance that seems appropriate for someone else may be too conservative, too expensive, or unnecessary for your enterprise. As the CEO of your business, it's up to you to call the shots.

Your choice begins with knowing what type of insurance is available, then deciding how much coverage and at what price. Let's begin by taking a brief look at the different types of insurance for your solo business.

HOMEOWNER'S COVERAGE MAY NOT BE ENOUGH

If you own a home-based business, don't assume that your basic homeowner's policy provides adequate insurance coverage for your business. As insurance consultant Beth Dempsey, president of Educational Insurance Services in Essex, Connecticut, explains, "Numerous home-based entrepreneurs have faced the tragic reality that their enterprises had little or no protection once they had to file a claim." As home-based enterprises grow in number, insurance companies are responding with new options. Ask your agent for details.

Small Business Insurance

As the number of small businesses has grown, so has the variety in small business insurance. Many companies offer business owners package policies that include a combination of property, liability, business interruption, and sometimes errors and omission coverage. As with any all-in-one option, this general policy may be ideal for your business, or you may have special needs it does not address. Consider it a beginning step in your discussions with your insurance agent.

Health Insurance

Probably no other insurance can have as great an impact on you as a solo worker than health insurance. Statistics show that nearly 40 percent of our country's employees would like to quit and start their own businesses—but they can't match their company-provided health insurance benefits.

If you've been shopping for health insurance lately, you know it can be a complex task to compare policies, coverage, and premiums. In response to this, companies are springing up that offer computerized database searches based on your preferences, needs, and budget. For example, Quotesmith Corporation in Darien, Illinois, will generate a free price-comparison report reviewing approximately 400 leading insurance companies. You can also get instant quotes from Quotesmith's Web site at http://www.quotesmith.com. Additional details are included in Appendix A, "Solo Resources."

Group insurance policies offered by professional associations, networks, clubs, and other organizations are another option. These policies often offer premiums at a lower cost than you could obtain individually. As insurance costs have skyrocketed, many solo entrepreneurs have banded together to create their own affiliations to qualify. Group rates often apply to as few as ten members.

If you're currently employed, investigate whether you can continue coverage under your company's group health insurance program if you decide to cut back to part-time work or leave to work on your own. Some firms allow this option for part-time workers or for a length of time after you leave employment.

Don't underestimate the need for health insurance. Unfortunately, it doesn't take a very long hospital stay to rack up a sizable bill. The debt load could create long-term havoc for your business.

Workers' Compensation and Disability Insurance

When a solo worker gets sick, there aren't any employer-paid sick days to help out. Workers' compensation is one answer. It provides financial support to offset the lost income (and to cover medical bills and rehabilitation benefits). Workers' compensation laws vary from state to state, and some states will not cover sole proprietors. Check with an insurance agent or your state compensation bureau for a guide to compensation laws in your area.

Individual disability income policies cover you for sickness or accidents on a 24-hour basis. The disability does not have to be work-related.

Fire (and Other Perils) Insurance

According to the National Fire Association, 30 percent of all businesses that have a major fire go out of business within a year, and 70 percent fail within five years. Those scary statistics point out why fire protection ranks high on the list of insurance essentials for small business owners.

Depending on your business location—both geographically and whether you're home-based—you may want to check out insurance coverage for other perils such as floods, windstorms, or earthquakes. Another option is *all-risk coverage* (sometimes also known as *special coverage*), which includes coverage for a broad range of potential disasters. Obviously, the devil is in the details in this type of insurance. Ask your agent what is not covered.

Business Interruption Insurance

If a fire or other calamity shuts down your venture, business interruption insurance would cover fixed expenses that would continue, such as taxes, interest, depreciation, or utilities—as well as the profits you would lose. There are also related policies that will cover you if a disaster hits one of your suppliers and your business operations are disrupted.

Most business interruption policies include extra expense coverage, which provides funds to keep the business running when it's not advantageous to have a shutdown. It's important to make contingency plans *before* a loss so that you'll have an idea of the emergency steps you'll have to take. For example, your catastrophe may generate expenses over and above what you are now spending to run your business, since you may have to lease other quarters, rent machinery, hire temporary help, and so forth.

Liability Insurance

Liability insurance covers you for bodily injury and property damage you *negligently* cause others in the course of your business operation. An important aspect of liability insurance is the legal defense costs. Remember, if you're operating as a sole proprietor or in a partnership, any lawsuits raised against your business automatically involve your personal finances, exposing them to risk. Claims are so common these days that a million dollars of liability insurance is no longer considered high or unreasonable for small business owners. To protect themselves, many solo entrepreneurs are investing in umbrella policies that add additional insurance above your general liability policies. This includes extra limits of insurance. In addition to *bodily* injuries, many policies also cover *personal* injuries such as libel or slander.

If you sell or design products for public use, be sure to check out *product* liability coverage, which is designed to protect you from legal liability arising from injuries or accidents related to your products.

Property Insurance

As a solo business owner, you may own or be responsible under a lease for a wide variety of property. General business furnishings and equipment may be covered under a basic contents policy. These policies cover normal perils such as fire, windstorm, and vandalism. Theft, water damage, and earthquake coverage usually requires additional premiums.

Special items, such as cars and computers, often have their own specifically tailored policies. If you're using your car for business, be sure to check with your insurance advisor to see if your auto policy covers you—and possible freelance associates or employees—for use of your car for business. Other questions arise with leased cars and with rental cars you pick up on business trips.

Computer insurance is available from several national companies and is an inexpensive way of protecting your valuable investment in hardware and software. For example, coverage up to $5,000 is available for only $69 a year from Safeware in Columbus, Ohio (details in Appendix A, "Solo Resources"). Home-based independents can often obtain partial coverage from a homeowner's policy, but many business computer systems exceed the limits, and specific perils may not be covered. In addition to the hardware, computer policies are also available to cover the data and restoration expense.

One last note on your policies: As more solo entrepreneurs operate within the global economy, their businesses are faced with exposures that arise and are created outside their home territories. Be sure you check the territory limitations for transportation, property and liability insurance, health, disability, fidelity (dishonest acts of an employee), and workers' compensation policies. As with any insurance matter, protection begins *before* a calamity occurs.

Risk versus Recovery

How do you choose what insurance to get and how much coverage to buy? It comes down to a balance between risk and recovery. Think of it as a seesaw, with the degree of risk on one end and how much it would cost you to replace, reconstruct, or recommence your business balancing the other end.

For example, if your office is located in an area that hasn't flooded in 150 years, then flood insurance would be low on your risk priorities. But imagine if a fire hit and took with it a year's worth of inventory—that could seriously damage your business, or even end it completely.

Premiums (the amount you pay for insurance coverage) are determined by many factors, including the likelihood of the disaster striking your business. Premiums are also based on whether you are seeking *reimbursement* for the purchase price of your items or the *replacement* cost to buy them now. Also, if you choose a higher deductible—the amount you must pay before insurance benefits kick in—your annual costs will be lower.

Figuring out all these options can be puzzling. Fortunately, help is close at hand, from a professional who's probably a small business person like yourself: an insurance agent.

Working with an Insurance Agent

Insurance agents, or brokers, serve as matchmakers between your business and the insurance companies whose policies they sell on commission. Some represent a number of insurance firms, while others offer policies from a single company.

An insurance agent is an important member of your solo success team, so take the time to find someone who understands you and your business. Talk to fellow independents and get feedback on their experiences. Ask your financial or legal advisors for their suggestions, too.

Don't be shy about interviewing insurance brokers to find out if the chemistry is right between you and to compare the benefits they have to offer with those of other firms. Evaluate your potential agent on what he or she provides from a ser-

---

CHECKLIST FOR INTERVIEWING
YOUR INSURANCE AGENT

Puzzled about where to begin when interviewing a potential insurance agent? To help you in the process, we've put together a full list of questions and topics on the Working Solo Web site. Check it out at http://www.workingsolo.com.

vice point of view. You're seeking a person who will be able to explain insurance coverages to you as well as analyze your business from a risk-management standpoint and identify where you need coverage. Remember, this relationship will be a long-standing one—it makes sense to put in a little more time to make sure it's the best choice for your business needs.

New Insurance Options

As this chapter has shown, shopping for insurance as a solo business owner can be a frustrating and confusing experience. Fortunately, it seems the insurance world is waking up to the growing number of individuals who are choosing this workstyle—and the buying power we bring.

As this book goes to press, a major insurance organization has announced a new subsidiary specifically devoted to serving small business entrepreneurs. Aon Group, Inc., based in Chicago, has formed Aon Enterprise Insurance Services to offer workers' compensation, multiperil, general liability, excess liability, directors and officers, fidelity, crime, and property insurance packages. Aon is working with a consortium of major insurance companies to offer specific product lines that fit the needs of solo and home-based business owners. They also will provide customer support options such as evening and Saturday service, in keeping with the nontraditional hours that many SOHO (small office/home office) workers follow. Aon has established a toll-free Technical Center hotline at (888) 781-3272. It will be interesting to see what changes Aon's efforts create in the insurance industry as it responds to the growth of the small business entrepreneurial market.

To close this segment on insurance, here are a few tips to keep in mind when reviewing insurance coverage.

Savvy Shopping Tips for Buying Insurance

Determining the right insurance for your solo business can overwhelm you, if you let it. Keep the image of the seesaw in your head—balancing risk and recovery—and follow these suggestions for finding the best coverage for your solo venture.

1. *Know your needs.*
    While you won't know exactly what insurance you'll need (that's why you're shopping), be prepared to answer questions about your business, both current and planned. Mentally prioritize your risks and your comfort level in facing them.

2. *Consider higher deductibles.*
    Insurance premiums can be lowered through increasing your deductibles, the amount you pay before insurance benefits begin. Most insurance offices are computerized these days and agents can quickly calculate "what if" scenarios to give you money-saving options.

3.   *Piggyback on other plans.*

Centralizing all your insurance with one company can sometimes bring you discounts—but it's worthwhile only if you end up with the coverage you want and need. Be sure to ask about these potential cost-saving benefits with your agent.

4.   *Comparison-shop.*

Policies can differ widely in coverage and price. Don't be timid about comparison shopping to find the best match of agent and policies for your solo business. Just be sure that all prices are based on similar criteria, such as amount of coverage or of deductible.

5.   *Don't buy on cost alone.*

When buying insurance, you're investing in peace of mind and a sense of security for your business. You're also establishing a relationship with an agent who can become a valuable business partner as your business grows. If the personal chemistry with an agent seems right, but prices are a bit higher than somewhere else, mention it to the agent—sometimes these brokers have the latitude to match competitive prices. In the long run, it may be a wiser choice to spend a few extra dollars on insurance premiums to work with an agent who understands and cares about your business.

I'll never forget the day I received an unexpected phone call from my insurance agent telling me that she thought I really didn't need a certain type of coverage any longer, because my business circumstances had changed. I was delighted to save some money, but even more pleased that I had this person as a member of my solo success team.

Good insurance agents are out there. Find one who will be an asset to your solo success team.

6.   *Keep good records.*

Once you have chosen appropriate insurance coverage, take the important next step to guarantee that you'll receive compensation if you need to file a claim: Keep accurate records. One of the easiest ways to document the contents of your office is with a video or snapshot camera. Make a mini-documentary of your office and other off-site valuables, and store the tape or photos in your bank safe deposit box. Paper records of major equipment expenses, with serial numbers and so forth, are also valuable.

It is also important to keep accurate financial records concerning your business's operations. Having these figures available for the insurance company's claims person is essential in the event of a business interruption loss.

Remember that children's game in which you stared at a tray filled with a collection of objects, then tried to remember them all when it was taken away? Chances are, you could remember some, but not all, of the objects. Unfortunately, the same is true with our businesses. If a disaster struck tomorrow (heaven forbid), would you be able to make a list of all you had lost? Pull out that camera today. When you do, store the pictures or videotape off-site, such as in your safe deposit box.

7.   *Keep your agent up to date on your business as it changes.*

As your solo business grows, stay in touch with your agent so he or she can better serve you. Tap into the expertise that your agent can bring you, and share your triumphs along the way. As one agent pointed out to me, they like to hear about the joys, too, since so much of their work centers on unfortunate circumstances. In addition to an advisor, you'll have one more dedicated promoter of your business in your community, which is always a welcome addition to any solo business.

Having triumphed over bookkeeping, taxes, and insurance, you're well on your way to mastering your solo business. As years pass, you'll refine many of the methods you discovered in this chapter.

Like a mountain climber making an ascent, you've reached a point where you can look back and see how far you've come—and celebrate!—while maintaining keen anticipation for the path that lies ahead. That dual focus of perfecting daily business details while continually expanding your long-range vision is at the core of successfully navigating the intermediate stages of growing your solo business. Next you'll discover how the best is yet to come on your solo adventure.

Chapter 9

Using Goals to Maximize Your Success

Dreams and goals are previews of coming attractions in your life.

—Denis Waitley

If you've known how to drive a car for many years, you probably take for granted many of the skills it requires. You instinctively speed up or slow down to change lanes, or signal when approaching a corner where you'll turn. Traveling the highway, you intuitively keep a dual focus. You concentrate on things close at hand, yet remain aware of hazards or shifts in the road ahead, always prepared to react if something happens.

As your solo enterprise grows, the business skills you develop also will become second nature. You'll instinctively know how much to charge or when a potential client needs a little more convincing to become a customer.

Of all the skills you'll develop, however, the one that's key to your continued success is your ability to retain a dual focus as you go speeding down the business highway. You must keep your sights on what's at the end of the road, all the while dealing with the traffic of day-to-day details right in front of you.

In this chapter we'll look at how to balance long-range business goals with the daily demands of business operations. Focusing on only one component— either the concerns at hand or long-term dreams—is often a temptation for entrepreneurs, but it's sure to bring problems.

In the pages ahead you'll discover how to chart long-range goals and how to turn them into reality through daily actions. You'll also find how the momentum you've achieved in the early stages of your business can become the basis for an ongoing cycle of growth.

Most of all, this chapter will help guarantee your solo success because it helps you define what success really means to you. A solo business carries with it the hopes and dreams of its founder. When it comes time to celebrate success, will you be able to tell if you've made it? After reading this chapter, you'll have the resources to evaluate your achievements.

Let's continue our solo adventure by looking at the power of goals and how successful entrepreneurs use them as guideposts, incentives, and mile markers on their journey. After looking out at far horizons, we'll come back to daily details and discover how to transform our newly hatched outlooks into reality—by returning to that success tool we developed earlier, our business plan.

The Power of Goals

Goals are amazingly powerful tools. They capture our thoughts of "what might be" and turn them into "what will be." They also clarify our thinking, and clarity is power. When we know where we want to go, we can plan how to get there.

Without goals, a solo entrepreneur is a wandering free spirit, dependent on the winds to carry him or her to some destination, which may or may not be the most desired one. With goals, this same entrepreneur sets off on a path with specific plans and ideas. The trip is much shorter, and the destination is always kept in sight.

Why are goals so powerful? Because *thoughts* are powerful, particularly when committed to paper. Haven't you ever been amazed at how much you can get done on a day before you leave for a trip? List in hand, you scurry from place to place, running errands, making phone calls, finishing up all sorts of work you had been putting off. At the end of the day, your list is complete, and you've probably accomplished much more than you would have on a normal working day. Why? You were motivated by your list—and a goal of completing all the tasks before your trip.

Successful solo professionals know how to transfer this power and make it work for them in every part of their lives. In one sense, they pretend they are going out of town the next day . . . every day! Instead of setting the completion of a single day's To-Do list as their aim, they establish grander targets that will stretch their abilities and bring them long-term success. They commit their goals to writing and follow through on them with daily, short-term, and long-range strategies. At the foreseen time, they reach their destination—and success.

Goals Are Not Wishes

A common misunderstanding is that wishing for something is a goal. "I wish I could spend my summers in France," or "I wish I could quit this job and just work on my own," or "I wish I could win the lottery," or "I wish _____" (you fill in the blank).

The trouble with wishes is that on closer examination you find out that, deep inside, the person probably doesn't *believe* that the wish can or will come true. The wish always remains just beyond reach, ever in the realm of what might have been.

In contrast, a goal is more tangible, more concrete. It may be just as lofty in spirit, but it is grounded in the belief that it is attainable. The shift comes when the wisher decides that the wish *can* happen, and commits to *making* it happen. Just ask any seasoned solo entrepreneur about his or her first thought of working solo. It probably started out as a hope, or a dream, or a wish. But along the way that thought became a *goal,* with plans and strategies. After some time, the goal became a reality, and it gave way to other, larger goals.

Why do some people make the jump from wish to goal while others always seem stuck in the hoping and dreaming mode? Let's take a look.

Why People Don't Set Goals

Psychologists and motivational specialists tell us that there are numerous reasons why people don't set goals, but here are the three most common.

Reason #1: Fear of Embarrassment at Not Reaching Your Goals

Many people never set goals because they're afraid that they'll look silly, or stupid, or feel incompetent if they don't reach their goals. This can be a paralyzing attitude if you let it dominate your thinking.

Achieving goals is a process of human learning. Unfortunately, by the time we reach adulthood, most of us have forgotten how we learn things. Have you ever watched a baby learn to walk? It starts by crawling, then trying to stand on wobbly legs. Then it progresses to "furniture surfing," moving from the edge of a couch to a coffee table to a chair, navigating around a room. Finally, after several months, the baby is able to walk alone. In a short while, he or she is out on the playground, running around with all the other kids.

In the process of learning to walk, babies fall down a lot. Since they're too young to care what other people think, they just get up and try again. Now, imagine if we had to learn to walk as adults. Most of us would probably try it a few times, fall down, get embarrassed, and swear we'd never make fools of ourselves like that again.

We have a lot to learn from the example of infants. They set a goal and let nothing stop them from achieving it. In their world, failure is not an option.

Best-selling author and motivational speaker Tony Robbins has a way of mixing humor with his message about the value of failure. Robbins notes, "Success comes from good judgment, which comes from experience. But where does experience come from? Bad judgment." The only failure is if you stop, Robbins goes on to explain. If you quit, you're sure not to succeed.

Everyone who has achieved greatness has experienced failure. Once you're really committed to a goal, you understand that mistakes are some of the most important indications that you're on the right track. Sound far-fetched? It isn't when you realize that if you're making mistakes, it means that you're *trying*—a much more powerful state than doing nothing and wishing your goal to come true.

Reason #2: Fear of Never Being Able to Change Your Goals Once You've Set Them

The thought of being trapped with a set of goals causes many people to delay or refuse to set them. "The goals seem so *permanent,*" I hear new entrepreneurs say. "What if I change my mind?" they ask.

In another situation, what would you do if you *could* change something you didn't like? You'd change it, right? It's the same with goals. You made them, you set the priorities—therefore, you have the power and authority to change them.

This reasoning seems so logical at a distance, but it often brings great anxiety to individuals embarking on a major goal-setting session. They view goals as laws instead of tools.

Your goals are a reflection of you, your interests, and your dreams. It's expected that you'll change, and your goals will change, too. Yes, you want to have goals that are a bit more permanent than a daily To-Do list. But to feel locked into them without future change is a false tyranny that you create.

Don't let this misunderstanding about goals inhibit you from making them. Everyone who has set goals has changed them. You set a goal, travel down the road a bit, then learn something new, and your goal changes a little to accommodate the new understanding. Without that initial goal, however, it's likely you wouldn't have made it down the road that far.

Reason #3: Fear of Not Having the Ability or Not Being Worthy to Reach Your Goals

Some people don't set goals because they have poor self-images or because they underestimate the power that lies within themselves. They're afraid to push themselves and test the limits of what they're able to accomplish. Why? On a psychological level, they might be afraid to find out just how much they *can* accomplish. Just think what *that* realization might open up. You might be expected to do a lot more *all the time.* To some people, that possibility is just too overwhelming to consider.

Others fear the rejection of outsiders who (they feel) might say, "Just who do you think you are?" When you listen to this question another way, however, it strikes at the very heart of setting goals. It's exactly what you're trying to discover: Who *do* you think you are? What can you do? What makes you special? What unique contribution can your talents and abilities bring to the world?

The trouble most people have with goals is that they don't understand exactly what kind of goals to set. Most solo entrepreneurs, when asked about goals, will speak about finances or business growth. These are valuable objectives to have, but they are only one part of your life and should be only part of your overall goals.

To understand how to make goal setting work for you, it's important to first understand the various types of goals and their time frames.

Many Shapes, Sizes, and Cycles

The most obvious goals for solo entrepreneurs relate to business and career: financial income, scale of your business, retirement options, future plans, and so forth. Yet we as solo professionals too often neglect other aspects of our lives and find ourselves consumed by a work-only existence.

Setting goals for other parts of your life can bring a sense of balance—and probably some smiles from your loved ones. It's also a way to keep your business in perspective, so you stay fresh and don't burn out.

Consider integrating some nonbusiness commitments into your life, but don't let guilt be the motivating force in setting these goals. Rather, be aware that your business efforts are a reflection of the total you. Paying attention to other areas of your life can bring you benefits both subtle and profound.

Here are some goals that can bring a broader perspective to your life. Use them as a jumping-off point for your own thinking. Few people can do them all— kudos to those who can!

- ✓ *Family goals.* Set aside a specific amount of time with your loved ones; improve some area of family relationships; dedicate one day or night a week for family-only activities; schedule regular phone calls to stay in touch with loved ones at a distance.

- ✓ *Social goals.* Are you becoming a hermit? Make a point of interacting more; meet new friends, host a party, or take part in other social activities.

- ✓ *Spiritual goals.* Dedicate some quiet time on a daily or weekly basis to your own spiritual development; attend services and support a church or synagogue of your choice; find inspirational books and read a section or chapter regularly. Even if you are not religious, a system of values can help you focus your life in healthy ways.

- ✓ *Physical goals.* Commit yourself to an exercise program; take control of your diet so your health can offer positive support to all your activities; seek out professional medical/health services when you need them.

- ✓ *Community goals.* Pledge to give back to your community, through volunteering, financial contributions, or other donations; implement recycling in your home and business; be an active citizen by voting and by sending political leaders your feedback.

Did these get your mind going? As you continue this chapter, jot down your own ideas that could become meaningful personal goals.

Goals also relate to specific time frames. *Short-term goals* give you a boost to accomplish things right away, from tomorrow to the next six months. *Midrange goals* are a bridge between upcoming plans and targets three to five years down the road. They serve as important building blocks for major accomplishments, allowing you to accumulate experience and confidence. *Long-term goals* include achievements that must develop over many years, perhaps even a lifetime. Like the brightest stars of the night sky, major goals are always visible on your horizon, keeping you pointed in the right direction as you make life's journey.

Each goal has its own time frame, becoming part of the overall growth of your solo enterprise—and of yourself. Goals reflect what was important to you in the past and what you value and strive for in the months and years ahead.

Goals also serve as a record of your achievements, changes, and development. Viewed from a distance, they reveal patterns of strengths and abilities that you often can't see while engrossed in the activity.

Perhaps the greatest value of goals is that they serve as markers of success. Once achieved, goals let you enjoy the satisfaction that comes from a job well done.

Success Always Out of Reach

Unfortunately, many solo entrepreneurs never feel truly successful. It's not because they haven't reached financial wealth—many are richer than they ever imagined. Others have grown their businesses to grand sizes or enjoy lifestyles that onlookers envy. Yet the feeling of success eludes them. Why? Because they never decided what success was to them.

To celebrate victory in any game, you need to establish the rules of what constitutes a win. For solo entrepreneurs, the feeling of accomplishment comes from meeting requirements you set up for yourself—an understanding that "when I get here, I'll know I've arrived."

If you never take the time to create those standards, victory is always elusive. When the moment comes to celebrate, you'll probably be so engrossed in the *next* problem that you'll be thinking, "Yeah, that's okay, but look at what I have yet to do. . . ." It's a common trap for solo entrepreneurs, and it can demoralize you and sap your energy in many ways.

Instead, commit yourself to celebrating all sizes of wins, from daily achievements to major accomplishments. To do that, of course, you have to decide what's important to you and establish your own rules of success.

Defining Success on Your Own Terms

Ask a group of independent entrepreneurs what success means, and you'll get as many different answers as there are people asked. For some, it's measured in monetary terms. Others value the time they're able to spend with a spouse or children. Some rate the ability to survive outside corporate life a major achievement, while others consider their skills in bringing together diverse associates a key accomplishment. For many, it's a mixture from all these categories.

The definition of success to someone working solo is a very personal statement. It incorporates many of the reasons you start your businesses and the values you hold about working and life. There are no right or wrong answers—it's up to you to write your own entry in this imaginary dictionary.

Don't be tempted to adopt others' notions of success. Abundance to you may be measured in free time spent outdoors, not in monetary value. It's an easy temptation to attach a price tag to success and establish an arbitrary financial figure as the baseline for achievement. Most seasoned solo workers will tell you that while money is necessary to keep a business going, it's not always the primary motivating force.

It's true, creating this personal definition of success is not an easy task. It requires some thoughtful reflection about what you value in your life and in your work. It is, however, a worthwhile activity. Once you've set up priorities, you know what is needed to achieve them. The celebrations are much sweeter when you reach a carefully considered goal, because the victory is infused with deeper levels of meaning.

Two Terrific Ways to Set Goals

There are no rigid formulas for how to set goals, although there are many helpful techniques available to assist you. Here are two creative goal-setting methods that have brought powerful results to many of my workshop participants over the years. Use them with a sense of fun, and see what new ideas you discover about yourself and your solo business.

Before you begin these sessions, find a quiet spot where you can concentrate and mentally focus, undisturbed by your daily work. Then choose one of these two exercises.

Method #1: Meeting Yourself in the Future

Pick a date a few years in the future, and imagine walking into a room and shaking hands with yourself. What is that "future you" like? What are you wearing, what do you look like? Are you happy, smiling, content?

Now have an imaginary conversation with that future self. Find out what you're like, what work you're doing, where you live, what plans you have. What's your personal life like? With whom do you share it? What do you like about your house, your car, your leisure time and vacations? What activity, outside of work, brings you the greatest satisfaction? Interview your future self with a sense of engaged curiosity, as if you've just met a very intriguing new friend (which is true).

Now probe a little deeper and find out what your business is like. Are you still working solo? If so, what type of work are you doing? What are your clients like? What is your office like?

Ask your future self what lessons you have learned about working solo over the past few years. Don't make any judgments—just listen with an open heart and mind to what your future self tells you.

At the end of your conversation, ask your future self if it has any other insights to share with you at this time. Then offer thanks for the interview, and end the scene.

The first time you do this reflection, you may feel silly—or you may be emotionally overwhelmed; I've seen both reactions, and each is okay. What this session often provokes is an inward contemplation that many of us never experience because we are too busy attending to the daily details of our personal and professional lives.

Use this exercise to chart your goals, and come back to it often to check up on the advice that future self has for you. Consider meeting with several selves who represent the you-to-be at different stages of your future development.

Be sure to jot down your thoughts, and formulate them into appropriate short- or long-term goals. Record them in a journal or some other special place where you can refer to them often.

It is a classic spiritual teaching that the answers to all life's questions can be found within us. This method of meeting your future self lets you tap into that inner wisdom.

Method #2: Designing Your Perfect Day

This technique is similar to one we encountered earlier, in the discussion on how to choose your perfect solo business. It centers on creative daydreaming about how you would spend your perfect day, as if there were no boundaries to say, "You can't do that."

Spending time contemplating this open-ended world of options has a very liberating effect. I've known seminar participants who scribbled down ideas that at first seemed outrageous to them but later became core parts of a new or expanded business.

This method also reveals three important things to you: your interests, values, and workstyle preferences. Do you spend your ideal day alone or with others? Inside or out? Physically involved with activities or mentally engaged? Each person constructs a unique, personalized day. What would yours be like? The answer can give you powerful support in setting and keeping your goals.

Now that you've experienced these two approaches to goal setting, experiment with other creative daydreaming techniques. Ideas that zip through our minds as outlandish, zany, or seemingly unrelated to current efforts can grow into wonderful new projects. You'll find other references on goal setting that can help you develop and fulfill your goals in Appendix A, "Solo Resources," in this book and in the companion *Working Solo Sourcebook*.

Mental Movies

What the previous two creative exercises have in common is an approach called *visualization,* or the making of mental movies. Kids do this naturally, imagining themselves as superheroes, doctors, or ballerinas. On a more sophisticated level, world-class athletes have used this mental training technique for years in their quest for Olympic gold.

Recently, visualization has gained a much wider audience as individuals have discovered its power to turn ideas into reality. EddieLynn Morgan, a business consultant with a background in the fields of visualization and motivation, understands the power of this mental training from her days as a competitive figure skater. "Visualization is based on the understanding that the mind is a powerful engine that can trigger mental pictures that can affect us intensely," she explains. "Because our subconscious does not differentiate between real and unreal, we can 'program' our desired outcomes. Once the seed of an image is planted, our imaginations provide abundant watering, and the idea grows on its own," she adds.

All human activities, from deciding what to have for dinner to designing a spaceship, begin as a vision in someone's mind. Artists use visualization every day in their studios, transforming mental images into works of expressive beauty. Engineers visualize new bridges, architects imagine new buildings, musicians visualize or hear music in their minds. Thoughts become reality.

As a solo entrepreneur, visualization can be one of your most valuable business tools. How we control the thoughts and images in our minds determines in large measure what we choose to achieve—and our success along the way. Visualization can help you channel your thoughts into a constructive force. This valuable energy is best summed up by saying . . .

You Are What You Think

Most people would agree with the philosophy that what you eat to a great extent determines your overall health—in essence, you are what you eat. Filling your body with caffeine and food high in calories and fat will take its toll. You won't be as healthy, fit, or productive.

What many people don't realize is that, just as we need to monitor what goes into our physical bodies, we also need to be aware of what we are feeding our minds. Letting your mind run uncontrollably can sap you of energy and derail even the most well-crafted plans.

The key to mental focus and ultimate success comes from controlling the voice I call the Babbler. This is the persistent little voice that gives you nonstop feedback on everything you do. Everyone has a Babbler inside, only some of us are more aware of it than others.

Now, if you think you're the rare creature who doesn't have a Babbler, listen more closely. It's the voice that's whispering right now, "Babbler, what Babbler? I don't have a Babbler. I don't have that voice inside me."

Like many things that are an intimate part of our lives, your Babbler can bring you great joy or unending grief. Unfortunately, most people let the Babbler bring them gloom and doom. Much of this is ingrained from childhood, when we listened to authority figures who tried to protect us by giving us repeated warnings filled with fear. Can you recall those childhood warnings in your mind? They were the Babbler's early teachers.

As a result, the Babbler has been trained to continue that voice of hesitation, fear, timidity, insecurity, and negativity. When we encounter a new experience, the Babbler is right there with a comment. "Oooh, sounds risky. What would other people think? You might look stupid or lose some money. It might hurt in other ways, too." On and on the Babbler runs, until another thought takes over.

As a solo entrepreneur, you must recognize that your Babbler will be your intimate companion and that controlling it is fundamental to your success. You'll be relying on your own judgment when making daily decisions about a wide range of business-related activities. Your Babbler will either give you support or continually challenge your confidence. One thing's for certain: It's not going away.

Training Your Babbler

Now that you understand the influence of this inner guide, you can see how important it is to train it. Awareness is the first important step toward control. I remember when I first discovered my Babbler and the power it had in my thinking. I was both amazed and appalled, and I immediately began a program to make sure that this nonstop voice worked for me instead of against me. You can do the same.

Begin by monitoring this inner voice over a period of two to three days. Discover what you really think about something. When negative thoughts intervene, stop for a moment and ask yourself, "Do I really believe that, or is that a thought left over from an earlier time?" Don't get discouraged that so much negativity may be popping up in your mind—that will only add more to the pile. Instead, be encouraged that you're taking action toward change.

The next step is to acknowledge that the Babbler works from fear. Review your Babbler comments and ferret out the real fear that may be hiding behind the chatter. See if it reflects your true feelings—many times it does not. A great resource during this stage is Susan Jeffers's book, *Feel the Fear and Do It Anyway* (Fawcett, 1992). Jeffers offers a lighthearted, humorous approach to these inhibitions and provides practical advice and inspiring techniques to change fear into freedom.

The third stage is to reeducate your mind to accept, even welcome, new challenges. You've created goals because you want to achieve them, and you think you can. Emblazon these goals on your mind, and let them fill your inner voice. Then, instead of some negative comment pervading your mind, you'll hear, "Wow! I'm one step closer to achieving my goal!"

Remember, the Babbler is a nonstop engine, endlessly spewing out comments. Since it's going to be your constant companion, it's worthwhile to change this inner voice of negativity into your biggest cheerleader, urging you on to your best.

One more note about self-talk: In addition to the inner voice, we reveal a lot about our thinking by the way we express our goals out loud. When someone asks you how your business is going, do you respond with negative comments or tentative answers? Are your phrases filled with words like "I hope" or "If I'm lucky"? Monitor your verbal responses, and check to see that you're not undermining yourself and your business. Casual comments often reveal inner thoughts. Make sure all of yours are pointed toward success.

Three Secret Ingredients for Successful Goals

While harnessing the Babbler is an important step in setting your goals and achieving them, there are other elements you need to make goals work for you. Powerful goals lead to powerful results. Here are three essential tactics used by successful goal setters.

Tactic #1: Be Specific.

To be effective, goals need to be tied to details, such as quantities, dates, or other measurable markers. Setting a goal to "grow my business to success" doesn't do much good—it's too general, and it's difficult to assess. In contrast, setting a goal to "grow my business to $50,000 in gross sales within the next 12 months" is much more targeted. A specific goal enables you to break it down into smaller chunks and tackle it systematically (a technique we'll be talking about in the next chapter).

Being specific also clarifies your thinking. It forces you to determine exactly what you want to achieve and when. Setting detailed goals is often a process of self-discovery, as you reflect on what is valuable to you and why you're working solo.

Goals also need to be challenging. Too often, solo entrepreneurs are timid in their thinking. Someone will be the best in your business—why not decide that it will be you?

Don't be afraid to s-t-r-e-t-c-h your thinking. Let your imagination run free. One popular technique to stretch your mind is to compile a scrapbook filled with colorful pictures linked to goals you want to achieve. You might fill it with pictures of a car or home you'd like to own or photographs of successful business leaders you admire. An image of a paradise island, for example, might signify a tropical vacation that's a reward for your business success or a lifestyle you want to attain.

Your goal picture book doesn't have to include only "thing" goals or materialistic aims. The images might also symbolize spiritual, family, or community goals you have. The goals—and images—express your unique vision.

The impact of the book comes from the visual images that become stored in your brain. They reinforce the mental commitments you've made and help focus your thinking. The images also become powerful visualization aids. You put yourself in the pictures, enjoying success.

Tactic #2: Put It in Writing.

The act of writing down goals transforms them from imagination, the realm of your mind, to reality, the realm of the world, where things happen.

> *If you really want to reach your goals, putting them on paper is the most important step.*

Many solo entrepreneurs shrug off this part, thinking that they have a good mental plan, and that's enough. But studies show that individuals with written goals have a significantly greater chance of success. Putting pen to paper (or fingers to keyboard) is a powerful creative act. It takes your ideas from "this is possible" to "I can—and will—do this."

When you write your goals, make sure you write them in the first person and in positive phrasing. Remember, you are programming your mind to carry out these wishes. Make them personal, by stating them in terms such as "I" or "my business." Writing them in the affirmative ("I am a success") instead of negative ("I don't want to fail") focuses your mind on a productive outcome.

Focusing on positive images also has other effects. Psychologists point out that the subconscious mind doesn't differentiate between what does or does not exist. If one of your goals says, "My business brings abundance to every part of my life," your subconscious accepts that as fact and aligns your thinking to make abundance be a continuous state. In contrast, if you state your goals in the future without tying them to a specific date ("One day I will . . ."), your mind will continually perceive them as yet to happen—one step away, always out of reach.

Similarly, the subconscious mind often doesn't "hear" the negative words in a sentence. If you say, "I don't want delinquent clients," it hears only, "I want delinquent clients." This explains why people who are obsessed with avoiding negative aspects of life—poverty, illness, loneliness, abusive relationships—often end up immersed in these situations, while people who focus on more positive elements experience joy and abundance. Your mind is a mental magnet, and your thoughts decide what will be drawn to it. Remember this when you are charting your goals, and take care to write your goals with clarity and a positive outlook.

Tactic #3: Review Often.

Motivational experts agree that individuals with the highest levels of success and productivity are those who have written goals that they review regularly. As you chart your business plans, you'll be creating goals that cover a wide range of time frames and topics such as sales, marketing, product development, and financial planning. To get the most out of your goal setting, be prepared to set aside time to review your goals and evaluate your progress.

For short-term goals, this review may take place weekly, whereas midrange goals might need monthly assessment. At the very least, set aside two times a year to check in and see if you are on track with your long-term and lifetime goals.

You can see that this approach to goal setting is very different from once-a-year resolutions. We all know what happens to most of those: They get filed away until the next New Year's Eve, when others (or the same ones) get made. It's usually not a very productive or inspiring approach.

To generate the results you want, goals must be actively managed. Your business goals are dynamic tools. They will change as you and your business change. Along the way, they serve as important markers, giving you direction and feedback on what you want your business to become. As your road map, they'll be much more helpful if you post them in a place where you can refer to them often, instead of shoved into a bottom drawer.

Seven Surefire Steps to Keeping Your Goals

Once you've taken the time to create your goals and put them in writing, it's time to shift your focus to follow-through. Many solo entrepreneurs find this a tough challenge, since the motivation must be self-generated. Use these seven steps to fire your inspiration and keep your success on track.

1. Have a written plan that can be broken down into specific smaller actions.

Turn your midrange and long-term goals into a plan of attack, with smaller subgoals. That way it won't seem so overwhelming. Instead of becoming demoralized because there is so much to do, you'll be able to tick off smaller goals you've achieved and find satisfaction in knowing you're moving in the right direction. (In the next chapter you'll discover some fun ways of creating these attack plans and how to personalize them for your own style of time management.)

2. Focus on the benefits you'll receive once you've achieved your goal.

One of the main reasons we're all working solo is the freedom that comes from designing our lives and integrating our work. Focusing on the many positive results our lifestyle choice brings us—instead of on the long hours and hard work—can keep our goals in perspective and remind us that we made a *choice* to be working solo.

Visualization can provide inspiration. Make crystal-clear mental images of how you'll feel once you've achieved your personal definition of success. Feel the sunshine on the beach you'll be walking, hear the thunderous applause, envision the brimming bank account, or imagine the satisfaction and joy from knowing you've turned an idea into a smashing success.

3.   Have a buddy system.

Find someone or a group who can offer moral support along the way. Many solo workers tend to hibernate, and they shy away from sharing their goals with others. "But if I tell them, then I'll have to do it," they say. Precisely the point! We all need outside motivation sometimes.

An approach I've found particularly helpful is to share a year's worth of goals with a fellow independent spirit. We each prepare an annual calendar, with targeted goals and completion dates. Once a month we get on the phone and give each other a progress report. At New Year's, we get together and over champagne we celebrate all that we've accomplished, and chart what the next year's goals will be.

This approach works very well because: (1) It forces you to focus on what needs to be done, both short- and long-term; (2) you have an outside force who holds you accountable, yet understands you as a friend and solo worker; (3) you can get a reality check or bounce new ideas off one another; and (4) it gives you a great sense of satisfaction to move through the year and check off all that you've done.

4.   Find role models.

Even if you think your solo business is unlike any other enterprise, chances are great that there are others who can serve as models of success for you. Hunt for people you admire and find out what makes them tick. Get to know them if they live locally, or read about them in newspapers or magazines if they're major figures. If you're stumped or discouraged when facing your goals, imagine that they're in your shoes and ask yourself what they would do. Oftentimes this clicks your mind into another state of thinking, and new ideas emerge.

It's also important to feed your mind with inspirational and motivational material. Remember, you are what you think. There are hundreds of quality books, tapes, and videos available to keep you on track toward your goals. I've included some of my favorites in Appendix A, "Solo Resources."

5.   Have faith.

No matter what your personal religious preference, you probably accept the notion that there is a higher Creative Power. Trusting in this guidance when striving to reach your goals can bring an inner peace and confidence that spurs you on.

Many solo entrepreneurs tell me that they can vividly imagine where they want to end up, but they can't figure out all the intermediate steps along the way.

I encourage them to think of it as walking down a foggy road. You can't see what's at the very end, but you have faith that the road extends beyond the fog and that it will take you to your destination. You walk as far as you can see, and when you get there, you're able to see a little bit farther.

It's the same with goals. You work as diligently as you can toward an intermediate goal, always keeping the final destination in your mind's eye. Once you're partway there, you can see farther down the road, and you're able to continue your journey to ultimate success.

6. *Reclaim the persistence of a child.*

As adults, we often give up on our dreams too easily. Instead, we need to become children again and regain the ability to focus on our desires.

For example, imagine an adult who dreams of reaching a certain goal. Someone says to him or her, "You can't have (do) that," or an obstacle stands in the way. Chances are, the adult will say, "Oh, okay, you're right," and let the dream slide away.

In contrast, remember the baby learning to walk? No amount of stumbling or falling down will prevent the baby from getting up and trying again. That inner motivation is a key element of childhood—whether it's learning to walk, to climb stairs, or to ride a bike.

The next time you face an obstacle on your path to success, instead of being "adult" and giving in so easily, reclaim that childlike energy, focus, and tenacity. You know what you want, and you deserve to get it. Make the effort to be persistent. The payoffs can be great.

7. *Savor your achievements.*

Once you attain a goal, whether big or small, take time to enjoy your success. Bask in the feelings of satisfaction, knowing you have achieved a personal victory. Your celebration may be something as simple as an ice cream cone or an hour off to read a book. Or it may be an extravagant indulgence. It's up to you to decide what's a luxury and how to acknowledge your success.

Whichever means you choose, don't postpone it. Too often we get so busy in our work that we never stop to tell ourselves, "Well done!" Working solo, there's often no one else to tell us those words, either.

Be good to yourself. Without a chance to reflect on our accomplishments, we can burn out and begin to question why we've chosen this lifestyle. In the long run, the short celebrations help cement our dedication to long-term goals and keep us striving to make our solo dreams come true.

Goals Never End

Every day, dozens of planes leave from west coast airports, bound for Hawaii. As they begin their journeys across the huge expanse of the Pacific Ocean, guess how many of them are on course. None! Yes, that's right. When they leave their main-land airports, none is on an exact course for the islands.

Instead, they will make thousands of minute adjustments along the way. Nav-igational instruments will shift course as wind currents, storms, or other climatic changes occur. Closer to the destination airport, the planes will zero in on an exact landing pattern, and they will successfully complete the long voyage.

So it is with goals. When first we chart them, the destination is in mind, but none of the goals is 100 percent accurate. Along the way, we'll make thousands of decisions and adjustments, until we finally arrive at a successful conclusion to our journey.

Newcomers to goal setting find this fuzziness about the path unsettling. Experienced travelers, however, know that the journey is the reward and the fun. With a shift in focus, the unknown becomes not a threat but an adventure.

Part of becoming a successful solo entrepreneur is knowing how to use goals to inspire, motivate, document, and celebrate your achievements. Once you rec-ognize and exploit the power of goals, you'll find them a treasured part of your everyday life. You'll understand that setting and striving for goals never end—and you wouldn't want it any other way.

Retirement Goals

An important goal for many solo workers is putting away funds for later years, when they don't want to have to work quite so hard. Like other personal and pro-fessional goals, retirement planning begins with a vision of the future that gets translated into weekly, monthly, or annual goals.

You'll want to consult your financial planner for details on the plans that are most appropriate for you and your business. But I've intentionally included this discussion in this section of the book so you won't overlook the impact that finan-cial planning can have in your life.

It's easy to ignore retirement planning as you scurry through the first years of running your business. Often entrepreneurs are scrambling to invest every single cent into their new ventures. It all gets put off for some later day.

Unfortunately, the facts are pretty sobering about financial needs for later years. Financial specialists explain that, as a rule of thumb, each of us should count on needing between 60 percent and 80 percent of our final annual working income *every year* that we're retired. Since Social Security typically provides for only 20 percent of the average retiree's income, it's up to us to have enough sav-ings and investments for our retirement.

Postponing retirement planning robs you of two important benefits: the impact of compound interest and tax savings.

To illustrate the astounding impact that interest can have on your money over time, I've included two charts. Figure 9.1 shows how putting a regular amount of money into savings grows over time. Figure 9.2 demonstrates how a single sum of

CONSTANT AMOUNT SAVINGS

	Rate of Return		
Year	7%	9%	12%
1	1.0000	1.0000	1.0000
2	2.0700	2.0900	2.1200
3	3.2149	3.2781	3.3744
4	4.4399	4.5731	4.7793
5	5.7507	5.9847	6.3528
6	7.1533	7.5233	8.1152
7	8.6540	9.2004	10.0890
8	10.2598	11.0285	12.2997
9	11.9780	13.0210	14.7757
10	13.8164	15.1929	17.5487
11	15.7836	17.5603	20.6546
12	27.8885	20.1407	24.1331
13	20.1406	22.9534	28.0291
14	22.5505	26.0192	32.3926
15	25.1290	29.3609	37.2797
16	27.8881	33.0034	42.7533
17	30.8402	36.9737	48.8837
18	33.9990	41.3013	55.7497
19	37.3790	46.0185	63.4397
20	40.9955	51.1601	75.0524
21	44.8652	56.7645	81.6987
22	49.0057	62.8733	92.5026
23	53.4361	69.5319	104.6029
24	58.1767	76.7898	118.1552
25	63.2490	84.7009	133.3339

Figure 9.1 This chart shows the impact of compound interest on a constant amount you save each year. For example, your goal is to have $50,000 at the end of a certain period. You've decided to save $2,500 a year. Divide your goal ($50,000) by the annual amount saved ($2,500); the result is 20. Referring to the chart, find the place where this figure would be in each of the three columns. You'll see that your investment will reach your $50,000 goal in Year 13 at a 7 percent return, a whole year earlier (Year 12) at a 9 percent return, or in Year 11 at a 12 percent return. Try plugging in other numbers for financial goals, years, or rates of return to stimulate your imagination about financial-planning options.

SINGLE-SUM INVESTMENT OVER TIME

	Rate of Return		
Year	7%	9%	12%
1	1.0700	1.0900	1.1200
2	1.1449	1.1881	1.2544
3	1.2250	1.2950	1.4049
4	1.3108	1.4116	1.5735
5	1.4026	1.5386	1.7623
6	1.5007	1.6770	1.9378
7	1.6058	1.8280	2.2107
8	1.7182	1.9926	2.4760
9	1.8380	2.1719	2.7731
10	1.9672	2.3674	3.1058
11	2.1049	2.5804	3.4785
12	2.2522	2.8127	3.8960
13	2.4098	3.0658	4.3635
14	2.5785	3.3417	4.8871
15	2.7590	3.6425	5.4736
16	2.9522	3.9703	6.1304
17	3.1588	4.3276	6.8660
18	3.3799	4.7171	7.6900
19	3.6165	5.1417	8.6128
20	3.8697	5.6044	9.6463
21	4.1406	6.1088	10.8038
22	4.4304	6.6586	12.1003
23	4.7405	7.2579	13.5523
24	5.0724	7.9111	15.1786
25	5.4274	8.6231	17.0001

Figure 9.2 This chart shows the impact of compound interest on a single sum when the interest is reinvested and accumulates over time. For example, you have $10,000 to invest, and you'd like to find out how long it will take until it grows to $50,000. Divide your goal ($50,000) by your initial investment ($10,000); your result is 5.0. Referring to the chart, find where this figure would be in each of the three columns. You'll see that $10,000 will grow to $50,000 in 24 years at a 7 percent return, in about 18½ years at a 9 percent return, and in slightly more than 14 years at a 12 percent return.

This chart also shows how quickly your money can multiply over time. For example, money invested at 7 percent will double in 11 years or triple in 17 years.

money increases as interest accumulates. I've given examples in the captions beneath each chart. Pull out your pocket calculator and have some fun exploring the "what if" possibilities. I think you'll be as amazed as I was at the financial impact of time and interest.

The key to reaping the financial rewards of compound interest is to start early. If you're no longer young, I'll give you three seconds to feel sorry for yourself. Admit there's nothing you can do about the past. (Yes, I wish I had started earlier, too.) What you can do, however, is take advantage of all the years left. Promise yourself you won't put it off any longer.

The second advantage—tax savings—is one that is often overlooked by solo workers. Facing heavy tax bills, many entrepreneurs wince at the thought of making a retirement contribution. Yet money put aside can *reduce* your tax bill, and it accumulates *tax-free* until you withdraw it in later years.

SEP-IRA, Keogh, or SIMPLE?

The three most popular choices for a solo entrepreneur's retirement plan are a SEP-IRA (Simplified Employee Pension/Individual Retirement Account), a Keogh, or a SIMPLE (Savings Incentive Match Plan for Employees). Each allows solo workers to set aside a percentage of their net income in tax-deferred savings.

THE RULE OF 72

Another quick way of determining how fast your money will grow, after taxes, over a given time frame is to use the "Rule of 72." Divide the number 72 by the rate of growth or return. The answer indicates how many years it will take for the amount saved to double using that rate of growth. For example, an investment returning 8 percent doubles in 9 years (72 divided by 8), while one returning 6 percent takes 12 years to double.

This process can also be used to determine the rate of growth you need to double your money over a set time period. For instance, a 10-year investment will have to return 7.2 percent yearly if you want your money to double in those 10 years, while an investor hoping to double his or her investment in 12 years will require only a 6 percent return.

The lesson is to invest early and often. Then the power of compounding interest can be put to work.

—Reprinted from *The Frugal Entrepreneur* (Portico Press, 1996)

Most financial-planning experts agree that a SEP-IRA is the best choice for solo businesses just starting out because it is easy to set up and maintain. You can contribute flexible amounts each year (from 0 percent to 15 percent of your net earnings from self-employment, up to a current maximum of $24,000). In lean years, you can even skip contributions. SEP-IRAs do not require you to do any annual tax filings.

In contrast, a Keogh is more complex and is designed for those with higher, more stable incomes. Some Keogh plans allow contributions up to 25 percent of your net earnings from self-employment (up to a current maximum of $40,000), but stipulate that you must contribute the same percentage each year—a constraint if your income fluctuates often. In addition, some plans require you to file an IRS Form 5500 each year.

SIMPLE plans are relatively new, and are intended for companies with 100 or fewer employees. Contributions to this plan can be funded in two ways: by both employer and employee, or only by the employer. If you've incorporated your solo business (and now are an employee of the corporation), this may be an appropriate option for you.

As you can see, the options are numerous and the distinctions are subtle with each of these plans. It pays to do your homework and work with a financial planner to find the best plan for you and your business. To get you started, check out the informative booklet, *Retirement Plans for Small Businesses,* published by Fidelity Investments; it is available for free by calling (800) 544-5373.

Another tip: If you can, contribute to your IRA or other retirement program early in the year. For example, retirement contributions for the 1998 tax year can be made until tax filing day on April 15, 1999. Savvy entrepreneurs, however, make at least part of their contribution in January 1998, gaining almost 16 months of interest. Over time, this strategy can have a significant positive impact on your retirement investment as interest accrues. Check with your financial and tax advisors to see how you can maximize your savings.

Even if you can set aside only small amounts toward retirement in the early years of your business, take heart in knowing that the money is growing—and that you've made a commitment to yourself and your future.

Making a Bridge between the Future and Now

Solo entrepreneurs have to stay nimble to maintain the dual focus of future targets and daily operations. Midrange goals play an important role in managing daily progress. Learn to ask yourself questions such as:

✓   Is the business as efficient as it could be? How can I make it better?

✓   Do I need more customers? What's the best way to find them?

✓   Are past customers coming back for repeat business? If not, why not? How can I entice them to do so?

✓ What should I be doing now that will lay the seeds for future business success?

✓ If I continue at my current rate, what will my business be like in a year or two?

Analyzing the answers to these questions can provide valuable insights into your business operations and growth. There are also business tools that can help. One is making graphs and charts to create a pictorial report of your business growth and progress. The other is that trusty document you created in Chapter 3—yes, your business plan. It's not hiding in a drawer, is it? If so, pull it out. It's time to discover how these tools can build a bridge from today's realities to tomorrow's dreams.

Say It with Pictures

If a picture is worth a thousand words, then the graphs and charts you create to demonstrate your business growth speak volumes. The graphs don't have to be slick or fancy to tell the story, either. If you have a computer, your spreadsheet or financial program might generate them with a few keystrokes. If you don't, simple graph paper and colored markers can do the trick.

The aim is to create a visual presentation of your business activity. When most people look at a page of numbers, their eyes glaze over. But show them a jagged line going up or down the page, and they grasp the impact immediately.

Here are some types of graphs and charts you might construct for your business.

✓ *Revenue* This graph can indicate your overall pattern of revenue. For example, you might chart gross revenue or sales for each month. You can see if there are peak seasons or if a certain marketing technique was particularly effective.

✓ *Expenses* This graph shows what it costs you to generate revenue and might include labor, cost of production, and cost of materials. It can also tell you when peak expenses hit your business. You have to fill in the why.

✓ *Sources of revenue* A pie chart indicating sources of revenue can tell you where your greatest amount of business is coming from and might indicate where you should focus your energy (remember the 80/20 rule).

✓ *Break-even* A break-even chart can tell you how much revenue you need to generate in order to make money. It can be extremely helpful in managing revenue growth and expenses. For example, one axis might include expenses related to cost of goods (materials, labor, shipping, and the like) and fixed selling and administrative expenses, while the other axis charts revenue. At a certain point, the two lines will intersect—that's when you start making a profit.

✓ *Profits* Take all your revenue, subtract all your expenses, and you have your operating profits. Remember, out of this you need to pay any taxes and interest expenses if you're borrowing money. Charting this on a monthly, quarterly, or annual basis can give you an overall sense of the financial success of your business.

Posting these charts in a prominent place, along with your goals, can help you stay focused. To derive the fullest power from these images, however, you need to match them with a written strategy. It's time to . . .

Pull Out Your Business Plan!

Chances are, your business has changed (or at least your ideas and goals for it have developed) since we discussed business planning in Chapter 3. You might be a little more focused or have grander ideas. The plan you wrote in Chapter 3 needs to be tweaked to represent the current state of your business goals.

Remember, a business plan is *dynamic*. It's intended to change as you do— and in the early stages of your solo business, that will probably be *a lot*. Don't fret—it's quite common for new businesses to go through refinements. In fact, it's a process that will continue throughout the entire life of your business.

Pull out your business plan and lay it side by side with your new list of goals. How much are they in sync? Probably close in some areas, and not in others.

Now's the time to take all that you've learned about goals and merge it with the original structure you set up in your business plan. Look at your long-range goals. Are they specific? What are the intermediate steps you can take to reach them? How can they be tied directly into action-based steps in your business plan?

Working backward from your newly revised goals, you can plot the multiple intermediate targets needed to get you there. Don't skimp on your planning here—these ancillary goals are important stepping-stones that lie between today's activities and the summit of your success.

"But what if I can't figure out all the steps to get me from here to there?" you ask. That's okay. When engineers construct a bridge, they start from both sides, and somewhere in the middle the junction is made. Similarly, you have a vision of where you'd like to be and the details of where you are now. Work from both sides toward the middle, filling in the intermediate steps with supplemental goals that feed into larger ones.

Don't worry if you can't affix details to every single step. As you approach each part, options will make themselves clear to you. What's important is that you create a viable link between today and your future by maximizing every step along the way. In this way, progress from goal to goal can continue easily and without interruption.

Major success begins with mastery of minor details. In this chapter you've discovered some practical ways to stretch your imagination to create lifetime goals, while keeping an eye on daily business. Successful solo entrepreneurs know that the key is making the most of every single day—and that begins with effective time management. Are you ready to master your days so they add up to long-term success? The secrets await you, beginning in the next chapter.

Chapter 10

Managing Time and Paperwork

Success isn't all of a sudden—success is every day.
—Tom Hopkins

When people ask me what a typical working solo day is like, the image that comes to mind is of the circus plate spinner. With a single flick of the wrist, this performer keeps one, then two, then up to a dozen plates spinning on slender poles at the same time. If one starts to wobble, the plate spinner scurries to give it a slight adjustment to keep it centered and turning.

Plate spinners are masters of timing and balance. They know how to pay attention to each individual plate while never losing sight of the group's performance as a whole. If attention wavers or too much time is spent with a single plate, chances are high that other plates will come crashing to the ground.

As solo entrepreneurs, we're all plate spinners. We have many fragile elements of our businesses spinning at the same time: marketing, sales, relationships with customers, new product development, collections, correspondence, personal responsibilities—you know what they are in *your* life. Each cries out for attention, wobbling and threatening to come crashing down. Some days we feel we've spent most of our time running from crisis to crisis.

If you find yourself pulled in a dozen different directions, you're not alone. A big part of the working solo challenge is managing many business activities simultaneously. If, however, you spend every day hustling from one wobbly plate to another, you're probably not turning any of them well, and you're on a fast downhill path to burnout. One day you'll find yourself exhausted, on the floor with a dozen parts of your business crashed around you.

The secret to the serene smile of the plate spinner is balanced control—understanding the needs of every plate and the degree of action that is needed. For solo entrepreneurs, that control centers on organization and effective time management. In this chapter, you'll discover ways to structure your day and maximize every moment to further your progress on the path to business success.

The Most Precious Commodity

No matter where you live or work or what your solo business may be, you receive the same amount of one important business ingredient as every other independent worker around the world: time. Between the stroke of midnight hailing a new day and a similar one signaling its end, a finite number of minutes pass (1,440, to be exact).

Time does not discriminate. It passes, whether we use it for our benefit or not. We cannot buy more, nor can we stockpile some for later use. After a day, week, or month has passed, it is gone forever. Actions not completed during that time turn into "could have, should have, or would have beens." You can fill them with regret, but not with accomplishment.

What we *can* control, however, is how we use time. The difference between successful independents and their failed counterparts often is not so much a matter of money, talent, or luck. What successful entrepreneurs know is the value of time and how to use it effectively. They know that small actions completed in minutes build into patterns of accomplishment over days, weeks, months, years, and a business lifetime.

As you build your solo business, commit to getting the most out of every day by building on the individual actions in each day. Little things *do* add up.

Effective time management originates with the understanding that each of your day's activities carries a different value or priority. Begin by taking a step back, analyzing your day, and making the distinction between . . .

Activity versus Achievement

All of us have had the experience of finishing an exhausting day, then sitting back and wondering what we *really* accomplished. Sure, we were running around all day, finishing errands or attending to crisis situations. But was the time and energy we spent channeled in a profitable direction?

That's the difference between activity and achievement. Activity fills up your life, but often doesn't lead you forward to your goals. Achievement, in contrast, is a step on the path, a rung up the ladder, an advancement toward success.

> *It is only by focusing our energy on actions that lead to our ultimate goals that we will attain them.*

Think about that sentence for a moment, and reflect on the activities that have filled your recent days. Have you been flitting from one thing to another like a hummingbird? Or have you zeroed in on your target like a hawk and focused all your energies on attaining it, knowing that it is the next important step toward reaching your goal?

Most of us fall somewhere in between—and in reality, the many demands of a solo workstyle cause us to be pulled in multiple directions. Yet to realize the highest levels of success, we must develop that hawklike concentration.

Priorities Set the Stage

Million-dollar salesman and best-selling author Tom Hopkins has devised a simple yet powerful method for maintaining his focus on both short-term and lifetime goals. Hopkins refers to it as his "Golden Dozen," since these 12 words are the central guiding principle in his life.

Hopkins's credo, which he has committed to memory and written on note cards in his office, his car, and his home, is this:

"I must do the most productive thing possible at every given moment."

Sound simple? It is. Easy? Well, not always. Worthwhile? Definitely.

In his book, *The Official Guide to Success,* Hopkins explains the power behind this statement and that it takes only four simple steps to maximize your achievements in any given day:

1. Tell yourself, "I must do the most productive thing possible at every given moment."
2. Decide what the most productive thing is.
3. Do it.
4. When you've pushed that thing as far forward as you can right now, go back to step #1 and start over.

I admit that when I first read this, I thought it was a bit simplistic. But since adopting this approach for my own time management needs, I've changed my mind. Why? Because it has an amazing power to keep you focused on a single track: forward.

This method is even more effective if you have completed your goal-setting session and charted both intermediate and long-term targets for yourself and your business. With a list of them on the wall, you can ask yourself what the most productive action is and be off like a rocket in the right direction. You'll no longer spend your day looking busy or taking part in activities that generate little progress.

The key lies in making the subgoal lists, working your way backward from lifetime goals, to intermediate goals, to yearly, monthly, and, yes, even weekly goals. Remember, these are not etched in stone. But without a detailed plan of how they all build on one another, you won't be able to decipher what genuinely is the most productive thing that you must attack next.

CATHY © Cathy Guisewite. Reprinted with permission of UNIVERSAL PRESS SYNDICATE.
All rights reserved.

To get from point A to point B, you must strive to do the most productive thing *every single moment of every single day.* If you adopt this approach, I think you'll find the same exhilaration I do when you see how efficiently you progress toward your goals. It all centers on changing activity to achievement and putting focus into your daily work.

I encourage you to read Hopkins's book on success and discover his many other practical formulas for achieving your personal and professional goals. Details on this book and other handpicked favorites on effective time management are featured in Appendix A, "Solo Resources," and in the companion *Working Solo Sourcebook.*

Demolishing Procrastination

What happens when "the most productive thing possible" on your list is something you really don't want to do? You know the tasks I mean. They're things you'd rather put off, indefinitely. Things that seem to continually slip to the bottom of that to-do list. Something that seems so painful—until you're in the middle of it, and you think, "Hey, this isn't so bad. I wonder why I thought it was so terrible and put it off so long?"

The trick is to get yourself launched so you'll hit that realization. If you never begin, that task will be staring at you on your to-do list for days, weeks, or months, acting as a pesky rock you keep stumbling against on your path to achievement.

The problem, you see, is inertia. Now, for those of you who never made it to Mr. Harrington's physics class, or for the rest who did but can't remember much about it, let me refresh your memory about this basic rule of our universe.

In his First Law of Motion, Isaac Newton described the two facets of inertia. Newton explained that a body at rest tends to remain at rest, while a body in motion tends to keep on moving. That, to me, sums up procrastination—and how to overcome it—perfectly.

A body at rest—on a couch in front of the TV, in bed under cozy sheets on a chilly morning, at a desk staring at an unappealing To-Do list—has a tendency to stay at rest, or at least in a state of avoidance. This is particularly true for home-based entrepreneurs, whose procrastination can reach epic proportions. Seasoned home-based workers know that when you're facing a sizable To-Do list of business items, even cleaning out the dusty hall closet can seem appealing. Frequent visits to the refrigerator, long phone calls to friends, and errands that eat up an afternoon are other common procrastination traps.

Once a body gets moving in the right direction, however, it has a tendency to keep going. Haven't you noticed how productive you can be when you're "on a roll" and don't want to stop?

The secret lies in making the transition from not moving to moving. In other words, when you are paralyzed with stop-dead inertia and don't know what to do, do *something* on your list, no matter how small. Once you're working, chances are good that you'll keep working, just as Newton described. Just be sure to pick something on your list that's business-related. You want an action that will be productive, one that will lead to achievement at the end of your day.

There are two other ways to organize your day and tackle the temptations of inertia and procrastination. Let's look at them now.

Swiss Cheese Method

This approach to time management is based on that tasty, pale yellow cheese filled with lots of holes. In some varieties, it seems that the cheese is nearly half holes. Increase the holes, and soon you'll have no cheese left at all.

That's the thinking to adopt when you're facing a large project and you don't know where to begin. Take a bite here and a bite there, and soon there's nothing left of the project—or what's left is easy to finish.

Let's say you want to have a new marketing brochure on your business. You've determined that you need it printed within the next two months. Prior to that, you need to hire a graphic designer. Before that, you must *find* a graphic designer. How? By doing some research—maybe calling other solo business owners you know. So the larger task of getting your brochure produced in the next two months begins today by making a simple phone call to a colleague.

If you continue to think of projects only in their larger sense (need a new brochure) they stay vague and out of reach. Once they're broken down into specific actions, they're doable.

All of your business activities work this way. The impact comes when you realize the cumulative effect of daily actions. For example, if you don't call your colleagues for graphic designer referrals today, then the whole project slides to a later date. If you put things off long enough, your business may not be around at all.

The next time you're facing a sizable project, think Swiss cheese. Continue to nibble, and soon you'll find that the project is done—and you've enjoyed the process.

Alphabet Approach

Another popular approach to time management is to assign priority coding to your To-Do list tasks. For example, A items are those that *must* be accomplished; B tasks are *desirable* to complete; C activities are those with the lowest priority. Another method is to assign rankings based on numbers, colors, or other symbols. The alphabetical, numerical, or pictorial approach chosen is not as important as the idea of prioritizing.

The merit of this method is that you give a different value to each task. The hierarchy is a personal one, of course, and it can change anytime you want. A items might become B or C items later, or a C item may suddenly jump to A status, based on changing circumstances.

A priority list is particularly useful for solo entrepreneurs, since we are bombarded with demands on our time from many directions. We must be sure that we're using our time most effectively and that the most important projects receive the greatest amount of our attention.

Basic to the list will be items that you've placed there yourself—actions to help you achieve desired goals. During the day, many other tasks will be competing to make it on your list, too. These are activities generated from individuals other than yourself—phone calls needing to be returned, correspondence to answer, colleagues seeking assistance, family matters requiring attention, and so forth.

The best way I've found to handle this multitude of requests is to put it all down on paper. Everything—from high-level business activities to personal errands—ends up on my list. It keeps me organized, and it lets me see exactly where I've spent my time during a week. You may find that this approach works for you, too. Or adapt it to fit your own time management strategy.

One variation on the A/B/C method I've seen recently is to prioritize the tasks within each letter category. Therefore, you may have some A-1 tasks as well as A-2 and A-3 activities. It's up to you to decide if this approach to detail matches your style.

Problems Can Be Beneficial

When facing unknown territory, many solo entrepreneurs focus only on what they don't know. "How can I ever figure all this out? What if I screw up? I have absolutely no idea where to begin!" These thoughts ricochet around your brain, and paralysis quickly takes over. "Better to do nothing and not make any mistakes," the critical Babbler chimes in.

Remember, nobody knows everything. When you signed on as a solo entrepreneur, the ticket was for adventure—and this is it! Working solo is about creative expression and endless learning. Don't sell yourself short on either part.

The next time you think you know absolutely nothing about solving a problem, think again. You probably know quite a lot—or at least you know what you're trying to achieve. Resist the urge to think of problems as bad. They're an integral part of the solo adventure. If you think of them as stretching you in exciting new ways and teaching you new things, they take on an entirely different hue—and your problem-solving abilities kick into high gear, too.

Accept that there will always be unknowns in your solo business. They bring you grief only if you look at them that way. What they can bring you are opportunities: to gather advice from friends, to network with professional colleagues, to try out new ideas, to stretch your own abilities. Once conquered, they also bring incredible feelings of satisfaction and accomplishment—and the confidence to stretch even further the next time.

On Paper or Computer?

Traditional paper-based calendars and diary systems are the most popular choice among solo entrepreneurs. Systems by Day-Timer, Day Runner, Time Design, and others often include daily, weekly, or monthly calendar pages as well as sheets for planning projects, tracking expenses, scheduling appointments, listing phone calls, and setting goals. Most are modular in format, which allows you to customize the sections and add extra forms to fit your own needs and preferences. Many also include guidebooks on how to use their products, so you can maximize the systems—and your days.

If you want to organize yourself electronically, you can choose from among many popular computer software To-Do list managers and calendar organizers. Many allow you to print out daily lists or weekly, monthly, or yearly calendars. With some programs, if an action is not completed one day, it automatically jumps to the next day's list—a nice feature that eliminates recopying tasks and ensures that carryover items don't get left off a new list inadvertently.

Whichever approach you use, know that it will be as unique as you are. Don't feel compelled to adopt someone else's style if it doesn't feel comfortable to you. On the other hand, keep an eye out for new products and time management methods. It's an area so vitally important to solo entrepreneurs, and we can always improve our own methods.

Once you've discovered a time management system that fits you, use it. Whether it's on your computer, a spiral notebook, a three-ring binder, a Filofax, or some other approach, make it yours. Time is the most precious resource of any solo entrepreneur. Let these systems help you save and spend it wisely.

Seven Surefire Ways to Get the Most out of Your Day

As you develop your own personal time management style, here are seven tips to keep in mind, based on feedback from solo entrepreneurs around the country.

1. *Keep your targets in sight at all times.*

Post your goals in a prominent place where you can refer to them for direction, inspiration, and motivation. This place could be on a wall near your desk, in your personal organizer or calendar, or in a folder you refer to frequently. Remember: out of sight, out of mind. To keep your solo work on track, you want your goals always in sight and on your mind.

2. *Plan your work, work your plan.*

Chart your goals, and work backward in time to create smaller project tasks, so that all aspects of your work build on each other. Define specific annual goals, with monthly and weekly tasks that enable you to reach them. Once your plan is on paper, refer to it regularly to keep your energies focused and as a record of your accomplishments.

When making your daily To-Do list, be realistic and target only six to ten items you'd like to accomplish. If the list is too long, you'll become demoralized and feel that you're never getting ahead.

3. *Know your internal biological clock.*

Be aware of the activities that work better for you at different times of the day. Are you someone who springs out of bed each morning singing? Or do you really start rolling in midafternoon? Whatever your personal bio-clock dictates, try to match important tasks to periods when you're most alert. One of the main attractions to working solo is the liberty to design your day. Use this freedom to optimize your productivity by staying in touch with your physical and mental states.

4. *Bank time for different activities.*

Studies show that individuals can be significantly more productive if they group similar activities into time segments. For example, many solo entrepreneurs avoid telephone interruptions by having a machine, voice mail, or a service pick up their calls during certain hours. They bank return phone calls for a specific time of the day and make all calls then. Others set aside regular periods for mentally intensive tasks or group out-of-office activities to complete at the same time.

5.   End the day with review and planning.

Take a few minutes at the end of each day to review what you've accomplished and what remains to become part of tomorrow's list. You may want to adopt the habit shared by many solo entrepreneurs of planning tomorrow's activities—and creating a detailed To-Do list—at the end of each day. Using this technique, you don't have to think about what needs to be done when you hit the office fresh in the morning—it's there on paper, right in front of you.

An added bonus is that you can walk away from the office at night knowing that you're prepared to make tomorrow a productive day. Some even say that putting plans on paper the night before allows your subconscious mind to do some problem solving while you're sleeping. When you awake, your answer may be waiting for you.

6.   Refine, don't reinvent.

Once you find a time management system that fits you, use it faithfully and continually refine it to suit your changing needs and interests. Resist the temptation to jump on the latest bandwagon or to adopt a new system every year. Ironically, it takes a lot of time to master a time management system, and you don't want to be spending valuable time always trying to get organized. A simple system can serve you well for many years. As your business grows, keep a watchful eye to see if you're spending more time getting organized than you're saving.

7.   Give yourself credit.

No independent entrepreneur can hit peak productivity 100 percent of the time. As seasoned entrepreneurs can attest, some days seem to evaporate and leave little progress to show. Accept this as a natural condition, and don't be hard on yourself. Focus instead on the achievement of the day, and trust that you're working better—and smarter—all the time.

Leisure Can Be Productive

As you're scheduling your daily actions, don't forget to include some leisure time. Many solo entrepreneurs overlook the value of time off and the benefits it can bring. We all hit a point where our effectiveness drops and we need a break. Fortunately, as independent professionals we have the flexibility to do what's needed to refresh. The antidote may be a five-minute coffee break, a half-hour walk around the block, an hour to browse through a few magazines, or even the rest of the day off to play hooky. Once back in the office, we'll feel refreshed and ready to tackle work with renewed energy.

Schedule these appointments with yourself. It may seem silly at first, but if you don't commit to leisure, you'll shrug it off and not take the time. In the long run, the hour off may bring a greater benefit to your overall health and mental attitude than an hour spent working.

One of the biggest challenges of working solo is to achieve a balance among all parts of life and to realize that work is only one aspect. Remember the saying "Work to live, not live to work"? Your solo career is important to you, but the *whole* you is most important of all. Take time to celebrate all aspects of yourself by actively seeking out leisure opportunities. It will enrich you, and it will ultimately improve your business as well.

Getting the Most out of Meetings

If you turned to working solo after spending years in a business environment where meetings were as common as morning cups of coffee, you know what potential time wasters meetings can be. Indeed, many solo careers are born from the frustration of sitting in fruitless meetings and the preference to spend time more productively.

If your independent venture centers on providing services or products to other businesses, it's likely you'll be asked to participate in meetings. The difference, of course, is that as an independent worker, you realize that the time you spend in a meeting usually isn't compensated by a salary, health insurance, vacation time, or other benefits. The financial reality is that a two-hour meeting can be very costly for you.

How can you maximize your time and productivity when someone says, "Let's have a meeting"? Here are five helpful tips, gathered from seasoned solo professionals.

1.   Try to find out if the meeting is truly necessary.
Meetings are often called with no detailed agenda or objective. When the meeting is scheduled, tactfully ask if your presence is needed, or if you can submit your thoughts in writing or through another person.

2.   Suggest alternatives to meeting in person.
A telephone meeting frequently can be just as effective as meeting in person. The bonus? You save travel time, and the meeting may be shorter and more focused. Phone meetings can be one on one, or with a group through the use of a speakerphone.

3.   When you attend a meeting, make the most of it.
Prepare a list of action items you want to accomplish as a result of the meeting. Make it clear that you expect this to be a productive time spent together. A breakfast meeting is an alternative—it gets you back to your office early in the day, and the meeting generally doesn't ramble past that last cup of coffee.

4. Be clear about financial compensation for meeting hours.

Whether you bill clients for meetings is your choice. At the start of negotiations, tactfully ask your clients how they handle financial compensation for meetings. Some seasoned solo entrepreneurs explain, "If a meeting goes over one hour, my rate is $_____."

Meetings seem to be more common in some corporate cultures than in others. Several colleagues who work with Fortune 500 firms observe that one of their first questions when considering a project is, "How many weekly hours of meetings do you anticipate?" The answer, they say, reveals a lot about the nature of the group process running the project and helps them estimate financial compensation for their time.

5. Remind clients that you're working in their best interest.

Your overriding goal is to make the best use of your time and to provide quality work. Particularly in the beginning, meetings are an important way to establish a personal connection and a sense of trust. Reassure your clients that your desire to be productive serves them in the long run, since saving you time also saves them money. Ask for their help in making meetings worthwhile for both of you.

As we come to the close of the time management section of this chapter, let's take a look at how personal habits and routines can transform your daily work.

Personal Rituals Can Empower Your Work

Regardless of whether we're aware of it, we all have a set of rituals we perform each day. From the time we get up to the moment we fall asleep at night, daily habits of thoughts and actions influence our lives.

For example, do you wash your face or brush your teeth first in the morning? Make your bed or not? What do you usually eat first for breakfast—or do you skip breakfast altogether? Do you read the newspaper, listen to the radio, or watch the morning news?

Once aware of their personal routines, solo entrepreneurs can use them to trigger powerful states of mind. These routines can be a potent source of motivation as you face the daily challenges of working solo.

Consider these sample rituals used by solo workers. Walking into your office with your morning cup of coffee means "It's time to start another productive day." Sitting down at your desk is a sign to focus your concentration on the day's planned actions. Standing while you negotiate on the phone might be your personal habit for injecting more authority into your voice. Tilting back in your chair may be all you need to let your mind and body know it's time for a minibreak. Writing out tomorrow's To-Do list, shutting down the computer, and putting on the answering machine may be your ritual to say, "The day's over!"

Whatever your rituals are, become aware of them and infuse them with power. Humans are notorious creatures of habit. In fact, psychologists explain that any action repeated consistently over a 21-day period is well on its way to becoming a habit—for good or bad. With this in mind, commit to creating daily personal habits that will give structure and support to your working solo days. Practiced consistently over time, these rituals can take you to the highest levels of personal development and professional success.

As we've seen up to now, working solo requires individuals to squeak out maximum productivity from every part of their lives. How you set up and use your office also plays an important supporting role in your effectiveness. Let's take a look at how you can get the most out of your office setup.

Making Your Office Work for You

Like the independent workers who occupy them, solo offices must be flexible, efficient, and multipurpose. It's not unusual for a single space to serve as a solo operations hub, customer service center, research and development site, marketing department, planning and financial office, manufacturing site, and shipping facility. With careful planning and design, you can ensure that these diverse functions work together smoothly, maximizing your productivity and profitability.

Think of your office as a partner in your success. The layout, equipment, and supplies you use to assist you in common daily tasks all contribute to your efficiency. To help you in your planning, here are five valuable guidelines.

1. Establish a Space Dedicated Exclusively to Your Business.

In a working-solo lifestyle, where the lines between personal and professional concerns often become blurred, it's critical to set up an office space with distinct boundaries that separate your business and personal lives—particularly if you've chosen to be a home-based professional. A clearly defined space focuses your attention and gives subtle signals to others about your business attitude.

Keep in mind that your office must function not only in the areas of physical productivity, but also on subtler psychological and communication levels. Clients, associates, or suppliers visiting your solo office receive signals about your level of organization, work habits, and general approach to business. If the eyes are the windows to the soul, your solo office is the reflection of your business and all that takes place there.

A separate space is also required if you want to claim the IRS office-in-the-home deduction on your federal income taxes. As explained in Chapter 8, the space must be devoted exclusively to business purposes to qualify for tax savings.

2. Design a Layout with Optimum Functionality.

Before deciding where to locate your desk and other office equipment, take some time to analyze your common work tasks. How much of your time will be spent at your desk? On the phone? At the computer? Meeting with clients? Will you frequently be making photocopies? Creating drawings, designs, or other artwork? Will you need regular access to reference books? If you're making a product, what does your manufacturing site look like? Is it separate from your office space?

The answers to these questions dictate the functional requirements of your space and will help you design your office "on purpose." For many solo entrepreneurs, the ideal design centers around a desk, often in an L-shaped or U-shaped configuration. From a "command center" swivel chair, equipment, tools, and information are all within easy reach, a setup that eliminates wasted time and energy. An example of this can be found in Figure 10.1.

Figure 10.1 A well-designed office space can be an invisible assistant to a solo entrepreneur, providing support and increased productivity. The best arrangements are those in a U- or L-shaped configuration, with everything comfortably in reach from your "cockpit." Experiment to see what works best for you.

Expect to take some time refining your layout when you're first setting up your solo office. What may seem right on paper may not serve you best in the day-to-day reality of office operations. Priorities may shift, or equipment you thought you'd seldom use may be frequently needed.

If you're a seasoned solo entrepreneur, take time to give a fresh look to your office layout and see if it serves you efficiently. Sometimes we become so comfortable with a pattern that we overlook new options. Slight modifications in your office layout often can create a big impact.

Don't overlook the value that windows, lighting, and other environmental elements can contribute to your office environment. For example, a solo colleague gives special emphasis to the fireplace in his office. A crackling fire adds a great sense of ambiance on a chilly winter's day, and clients always enjoy meetings conducted hearthside with a cup of coffee or cocoa.

3. Create Centers of Activity for Common Business Tasks.

You can also increase productivity in your office by grouping equipment or supplies that logically support each other. For example, if you take product orders by telephone, make sure all the necessary tools—forms, pens, calculator, price sheets, and catalogs for reference—are within easy reach. If you frequently make photocopies and then trim them to a smaller size, is your photocopier set up adjacent to your paper cutter? Where do you open your mail? Is it near your files, your recycling bin, and a trash can so you can act on it efficiently?

By thinking through each step of your business operations, you can devise activity centers that can save you time and avoid wasted movements. Of course, sometimes it's great to have an excuse to get up from your desk, stretch, and take a break. I'm not advocating a totally sedentary existence. You just don't want to get up each time the phone rings.

Some of your activity centers may require careful planning due to special equipment requirements such as ventilation or additional electricity. Other tasks may be better performed under certain lighting conditions. By paying attention to these details and grouping similar activities and needs, you can turn your office into a working partner.

4. Customize Equipment to Support Your Tasks.

Personalizing your office equipment with inexpensive add-on features is another way to maximize your office productivity. Some items may increase your mobility, such as an extended telephone cord that lets you walk halfway across the room to hunt for a file without interrupting a phone call. Others, such as adjustable computer keyboards or telephone headsets, increase your comfort level, resulting in less fatigue.

Another category of office items serves you on a more personal level. These articles, such as a music system in your office, artwork on the walls, or fresh flowers, increase your overall enjoyment of being in the office. Since you'll be spending many hours there, it's in your best interest to make it as comfortable and pleasurable as possible. These types of small indulgences often don't cost very much, but they can bring a cheerier outlook to your office environment.

5. Design Your Space So It Can Remain Flexible for Change.

One of the key challenges in designing a solo office space is creating the feeling of a real office yet retaining a level of flexibility for expansion and change. Before you install any permanent office fixture—a wall of bookshelves, a built-in desk—carefully consider future options. Solo businesses are by nature very flexible, and their offices must be, too.

If you're building an office from the ground up or as an addition to your home, be sure to plan ahead. Most solo entrepreneurs agree that the two things most frequently overlooked are adequate electrical outlets and telephone jacks. It seems you can never have enough of either. Installing these in the early stages of construction is much more economical than later. Even if you won't be using multiple phone lines right away, the wiring can be laid with the initial line, and subsequent connections are very easy—and inexpensive—to complete.

When Your Office Isn't Four Walls

If you're a solo entrepreneur whose work frequently takes you traveling, your primary "office" may be a car, truck, bus, train, or airplane. In addition to adapting tips from the five guidelines above, you'll need a well-equipped and organized briefcase that serves as a bridge between your stationary and traveling offices. Many mobile entrepreneurs keep permanent checklists of items they need to carry. Before heading off, they review the contents of their briefcases, car trunks, or trucks and replenish any supplies they need.

Find a system that works for you, and adopt it as your predeparture routine. The security of knowing you're prepared will give you confidence during your business on the road.

Whether your solo office is in a high-rise building, a loft, a home, or on the road, remember that a significant part of your time and energy will be spent there. The environment you create can greatly influence your state of mind, your productivity, your profitability, and, ultimately, your solo success. Design it with care, and personalize it to reflect your individual needs and style. Your solo office is where your future dreams meet current plans—and where you are uniquely, independently you.

Super Office Supplies

Small things can make a big difference in your working solo life, and office supplies certainly fall into this category. (Can any of us imagine life before Post-it® Notes?) Here is a collection of office supplies that solo entrepreneurs have rated as their favorites. Some are tried-and-true standbys; others are noteworthy innovations.

Many of these supplies can be found in your local office-supply store or one of the growing number of superstores such as Office Max, Office Depot, or Staples. These outlets are a great resource for solo entrepreneurs, and if you haven't visited one yet, it's worth the trip for their extensive selection and great prices. Catalogs are another good resource for unusual office supplies. Most offer a toll-free order number and free shipping. For details on the items below and leading mail-order office-supply vendors, see Appendix A, "Solo Resources."

Telephone Headsets

At first you may feel like an astronaut or a rock star, but wearing a telephone headset can be a great investment in your overall health and productivity if you spend more than two hours a day on the phone. Scrunching your shoulder to cradle the phone can give you muscle aches, destroy your posture, and dampen your productivity. New models are light as a feather and have improved clarity and dialing features. Check out models by Plantronics and the catalog from Hello Direct, by calling (800) 444-3556.

Magic Markers

The Magic Marker™ celebrates its 45th birthday this year, and it has become one of those business tools most of us couldn't live without. Try brightly colored fluorescent ones to color-code progress charts, To-Do lists, maps, or product literature. Or use them to create eye-catching marketing pieces, as one solo entrepreneur did. She took inexpensive (and boring) black-and-white business cards and striped them with bright-colored markers. The result: unique, memorable cards that generate a big impact for a tiny investment.

Rubber Stamps

If you have to write the same information more than a few times a week—check deposit endorsements, "First Class Mail," "Paid," or other notations—it's time to invest in a rubber stamp. Preprinted stamps are available in dozens of styles; preinked stamps let you avoid messy ink pads or bottles. Consider date stamps for processing orders or for noting when mail was received.

Scales

Scales for postal use and shipping can save you hours of time waiting in line. Postal scales range from inexpensive spring mechanisms to sophisticated digital devices. Shipping scales for smaller packages come in 5-, 10-, and 25-pound capacities and are useful for calculating UPS weights. A utility scale, rated at 250-pound capacity, can accommodate heavier packages for commercial shipping.

Calculator

Most solo entrepreneurs would agree that life without a trusty calculator would be bleak. Even basic models offer stunning capabilities, and solar-powered options eliminate the need for batteries. Some have built-in business features such as profit calculators—punching in a few digits gives you the anticipated profit and margin figures. When buying one for your business, consider whether you will want or need one that prints on paper tape.

Egg Timer

Yes, that little hourglass device that lets you know when your three-minute egg is cooked can be a handy office tool. One solo entrepreneur uses it to time his long-distance phone calls. As soon as the call starts, the timer gets tipped over. When the sand runs out and if it's not a vitally important call, he knows it's time to say good-bye. Available in the kitchen-gadgets department of your local discount store, they cost less than $2.

Binding and Laminating Machines

If the products of your solo business are finished presentations or reports, consider investing in a binding machine to give them a professional finish. There are two basic models: machines that punch holes for 19-ring plastic comb bindings, and others that punch five holes for plastic strip bindings. The comb bindings allow pages to lie flat and can accommodate documents up to several inches thick. The flat strip bindings create documents more like bound books. Using either approach, you can have a professional-looking bound document for only pennies. GBC makes binding products in many styles and colors, available in most office supply stores.

Laminating machines affix a sheet of transparent plastic to cards or documents, making them waterproof and resistant to damage or wear. Machines vary in price based on size of surface area to laminate; small laminators handle business cards, while larger machines can seal documents up to legal-size.

Accordion Files

These inexpensive paper files resembling a musical squeezebox offer a simple, handy way to keep receipts and other paperwork organized. They're available in a variety of sizes and capacities. Some have a dozen compartments for monthly sorting, while others have 31 daily dividers. Compartments are often doubly labeled, so you can use them for monthly or daily record keeping or for predetermined categories such as credit card receipts and utilities.

Paper Shredder

In an age of dumpster divers and theft from stolen credit card numbers, many solo entrepreneurs have invested in paper shredders. What gets shredded? Anything you want to protect from prying eyes, including receipts with credit card numbers, copies of client invoices, financial data, drafts of proposals, client telephone lists, and direct-mail solicitations that could begin a subscription or credit card. Some soloists use these shredders to create environmentally friendly packing materials—a nice double-duty, ecological arrangement. Smaller, personal models generally come in two styles: one that sits on two edges of a large wastebasket and another that perches on high metal legs and straddles a wastebasket beneath it. When choosing a shredder, check for safety shutoff features and noise level of operation. And if you're a home-based entrepreneur with small children, this is one device you'll want to monitor carefully.

Paper Punches

If your approach to organization includes binders, there is now a variety of paper punches to accommodate many specialty binders. The standard three-ring still reigns as most popular, but punches for seven-ring and six-ring personal organizers now enable you to carry documents of nearly any size with you without fear of their falling loose.

Post-it Notes

Almost everyone knows the story of Art Fry, the 3M corporate scientist who inadvertently invented Post-it Notes on his way to developing a strong adhesive. Fry decided that the semi-sticky adhesive wouldn't work for its original purpose but that it would be a great way to keep track of his Bible passages during his Sunday church readings. His colleagues soon clamored for more, and a multimillion-dollar product category was born.

    If you haven't checked out the recent Post-it line additions, my solo entrepreneur informers agree that you'll soon be addicted to them, too. Post-it Tape Flags, which are half clear and half brightly colored, accept pen or pencil easily and serve as excellent bookmarks or a way to temporarily annotate a document. Post-it fax transmittal forms attach to the top of the first page of your fax and save you money by eliminating the need for an independent cover sheet.

Cassette Recorders

Many solo entrepreneurs report that one of their favorite low-cost office devices is a small microcassette recorder. It's handy to use while traveling to create verbal notes that can be transcribed later. Some people keep them by their beds, so that when brainstorms hit in the middle of the night or just upon rising, they can capture their ideas on tape before they evaporate.

Current models offer voice activation, so the tape advances only when you speak. Most accept microcassettes, which allow you to record for up to three hours. A tape counter is a handy feature, so you can track specific segments of the tape. When choosing a recorder, make sure you feel comfortable with the arrangement and function of the record and playback buttons; some models are better designed than others.

Fasteners and Clips

Clips and fasteners come in all materials, shapes, and sizes these days. Many solo entrepreneurs use them as miniature (and subtle) marketing devices. For example, an independent real estate agent representing high-end homes uses gold paper clips to attach his business card to client correspondence. A graphic artist chooses plastic-coated clips in bright colors to accent her presentation packages and spotlight her cleverly designed letterhead.

The next time you're sending a package to make an important first impression, pass by the mundane silver clips and explore something different. The cost is minimal, and the detail will add an extra dash of professional polish.

Paper

As mentioned in the marketing discussions in Chapter 6, today's selections of paper are remarkable in their diversity of colors, textures, weights, and patterns. Experiment with different papers in your photocopier or computer printer to add greater interest and style to your correspondence, reports, or marketing materials.

Postcards

Prestamped postcards are one of my favorite supplies. I keep a stack of a dozen or so on hand to request information or to send off a quick note to a colleague. They usually cost a penny more than the postage that's on them and are available at your local post office. A bonus: Your message gets through without the reader having to open an envelope.

Electric (or Battery-Operated) Pencil Sharpener

To some, this tool is an indulgence. To those who delight in stiletto-sharp pencils, it's a necessity. Recent models are smaller in size, so they don't eat up valuable desk space.

Bulletin Board

Need a place to tack up those important papers, the week's To-Do list, or monthly goals? Some solo entrepreneurs use a bulletin board; others go right for the tape and adhere things directly to the wall. If a bulletin board is your choice, the options of size, color, thickness, and material keep increasing all the time.

Stacks, Racks, and Trays

Office-supply firms offer a wide variety of bins, racks, trays, and other containers to keep your office organized. Experiment with styles most appealing to you, then find a system that will support you in your efforts. Developing such a system is where we're heading next.

Mastering Information Management

In most solo offices, paper stacks can grow faster than weeds in a summer lawn. Our Information Age is drowning us in a sea of paper, magazines, computer disks, videos, and other materials. As organizing consultant and author Barbara Hemphill observes, "Uncontrolled information is a burden, not a resource."

In her work with individuals and organizations, Hemphill understands well the many facets of information management. "Paper clutter is postponed decisions," she says. "Papers pile up on our desks because there are decisions we need to make about them. Postpone a few of the decisions, and a new pile is born."

To help you manage the flood of paper and other materials in your office, keep the following three principles in mind:

1.   Minimize handling, maximize action.
Try to deal with paper the first time it crosses your desk. Most organizing consultants agree that too many professionals waste hours handling the same piece of paperwork multiple times. Avoid the common scenario of skimming a

piece of mail and putting it back on the pile for later handling if you're uncertain or uninterested in dealing with it now. If you let this cycle continue, you may end up devoting hours to reviewing the same mail.

In her bestselling book, *Taming the Paper Tiger,* Barbara Hemphill advises asking four basic questions about every piece of paper that crosses your desk:

✓   Do I *really* need to keep this?

✓   *Where* should I keep it?

✓   How *long* should I keep it?

✓   How can I *find* it?

Hemphill points out that the last question is very important. "If you don't know you have the material, or you can't find it, it's of absolutely no value to you," she explains. (Setting up a workable filing system is something we'll cover in the next section.)

2.   *Consider mail a potential enemy.*

The daily mail delivery can bring much good news—product orders, correspondence, payments of overdue invoices—but it also includes many unsolicited pieces. Most solo entrepreneurs are far too timid at pitching out marginally useful mail, and as a result their offices become overrun with paper.

In your battle over paperwork, mail is the enemy. If you don't take an aggressive stand, you'll soon lose any control of your workspace. Set up a designated space and time to go through the daily mail. An ideal site is close to your files, your wastebasket, and your recycling bin. Battling paperwork is a continual struggle, but if you don't fight it, the paper will win—because there's sure to be more with the next day's delivery.

3.   *Educate yourself.*

Developing an organizational and filing system is not a talent that evolves naturally, it's a skill that must be learned. Take advantage of the many books, tapes, and other resources on this subject to find a system that works well for you. (I've included my favorites in Appendix A, "Solo Resources," and in the companion *Working Solo Sourcebook.*)

If your struggles with information management are too frustrating, consider calling in some outside help. I've worked with professional organizers for several years, and the systems they've established have enhanced my business greatly. To find a professional organizer in your area, call the National Association of Professional Organizers (NAPO) at (512) 206-0151.

Filing with Finesse

Once you've decided to keep a piece of mail, how do you file it so it doesn't disappear into a Bermuda Triangle filing drawer? Remember, a filed item is useful only if you can locate it again when you need it.

The most important question to ask yourself is not, "Where should I put this?" Instead, ask yourself, "Where would I most look for this the next time I want to find it?" This subtle shift in thinking takes the terror out of making the perfect filing system, and lets you create a system that works for you.

Here are three popular filing methods used by most solo entrepreneurs. Review them all and see which one fits your personal business style—or mix and match to invent your own.

Strictly Alphabetical

This system groups files in alphabetical order. An "Attorneys" file would be at the front of the drawer, "Marketing" in the middle, and "Utilities" near the back. The advantage to this approach is that there is little doubt about where a file should go, since strict alphabetical order is the guiding principle. One challenge—which shows up in other systems, too—is that you must remain clear about the categories you choose. For example, are your law-related materials in an "Attorneys" file or a "Lawyers" file?

Grouped by Categories

Some solo entrepreneurs set up their files according to general categories of materials. For example, you may devote one drawer to pending projects, another to marketing materials, and a third to financial and legal documents.

As with the first system, you must have a clearly organized structure of how you've created the categories. The advantage to this approach is that related materials are gathered in one location and can be quickly accessed.

By the Numbers

Another popular filing method uses a numerical coding system and a directory log. Rather than deciding in which general category an item should be filed, you create a folder and give it a numerical code, which is recorded in a notebook. For example, the contract for the Smith account is filed in folder number 98-321. This means that it was the 321st folder created in 1998. The notebook listing indicates what's in the file, and the file is placed in the drawer immediately behind file 98-320, which may have items of an entirely different topic in them.

The advantage to this system is that you can quickly scan your directory and see everything contained in your files and when you placed it there. If the log is maintained on a computer, you can perform instant searches for filed materials. Also, it's easier to file things in numerical than in alphabetical order.

The downside to this method is the time it takes to create the log. You're also dependent on the log for total access to the system; if it's lost or destroyed, it would require many hours to reconstruct it.

Tracking Bills and Receivables

One of the most compelling reasons to establish and maintain a good filing system is to stay up to date with your outstanding invoices and payments. Many solo entrepreneurs risk poor credit ratings, expensive late fees, or tough cash-flow periods because they don't have a good understanding of when payables or receivables are past due.

When a bill comes in for payment, mark its due date on your calendar, and add it to your To-Do list for the appropriate day or week. One trick is to write the due date on the return payment envelope, where it will be a reminder until it gets covered by a stamp for mailing. Once the bill is on your To-Do list, it's up to you to commit to making the payment on the proper day. Build in a few days' grace time if you know you're the type to let things slide from your To-Do list.

Establish your receivables system so that you know at all times when client payments are due. A business with a limited number of clients annotates its calendar when a check is due and keeps photocopies of outstanding invoices in an easy-to-access file. Many solo professionals call the accounts payable department and check on payment status a week before a check is due. This alerts you to any breakdown in the payment processing, and it gives you enough time to reissue another invoice, if necessary, and get paid on time.

On the very day a payment is overdue, send a second notice and make a phone call asking for payment. Do not delay! Studies show that the longer bills go unpaid, the greater the chances they will not be paid at all. Don't assume that your creditors will pay you soon.

Be professionally persistent on the phone when making collections calls. A direct comment, such as "I'm calling to inquire about the status of an overdue invoice," followed by details such as the invoice number and payment due date, is an effective initial approach. Always try to get some type of commitment from them about payment—even if it is only partial payment at this time—and be sure to keep a log of whom you spoke to and what was discussed. If it becomes necessary to call back again, you'll be prepared to recap what was said in the previous call.

Solo businesses that bill on a monthly basis often set up part of one day each month to send out past due reminders to overdue creditors. Some have computerized their billing and have clients sign an agreement up front indicating that any past due balances will be automatically assessed a 1.5 percent monthly late fee.

The nature of your solo business and your personal style will determine the payables and receivables system that works best for you. Keep in mind that money flowing in and out of your company is the grease that keeps your business machinery moving. Without it, gears wear down quickly and your solo engine will soon screech to a halt. Whichever financial management method you choose, commit to building a strong system that will keep your business running smoothly over the years.

Recycle!

As we end this chapter on managing time and paperwork, I'd like to encourage all independent entrepreneurs to adopt recycling practices in their solo offices. If you're thinking, "I'm only one person, it won't make a difference," remember that there are millions of us working solo worldwide. That's a lot of paper clogging landfills.

Help support global ecology by rethinking how your solo office functions within the larger community. Here are some simple ways each of us can do our part.

- ✓ Use recycled paper and recycled plastic office products whenever you can.
- ✓ As you review your daily mail, sort out junk mail, catalogs, and office paper for recycling.
- ✓ Avoid using Styrofoam peanuts for packing; if you receive some, save them for later reuse.
- ✓ Recycle used batteries instead of dumping them in the trash; better yet, convert to rechargeable batteries.
- ✓ Send in used toner cartridges from your photocopier and/or laser printer for refilling or recycling. (Check your user manual for details.)
- ✓ Turn previously printed paper into handy notepads by using the other side.
- ✓ Recycle cardboard shipping boxes by reusing them or by taking them to your local recycling center.
- ✓ Contribute out-of-date magazines to your local school, hospital, community center, or health club.
- ✓ Support your community's recycling efforts; if appropriate, consider donating some of your business services to assist them.

By now, you've learned how to master the art of plate spinning—keeping all the many parts of your solo business successfully turning at once. You understand how the actions you consistently complete each day contribute to your achievement of intermediate and ultimate goals. You know how to keep your mind focused on accomplishing the most productive thing possible at each moment and ways to set up your office so that it supports you in your efforts.

Now it's time to look beyond working solo—to a period when you want to work with others. There are many ways to reap the benefits of partners and colleagues, without giving up the advantages of your independent status. In the next chapter you'll discover how to incorporate the best of both worlds into your solo adventure.

Chapter 11

Beyond Solo:
Associates and Employees

To reach your goals, you need to become a team player.
—Zig Ziglar

As your solo success builds, there likely will be times when you find your-self facing more than you can do on your own. Perhaps you've set your sights on larger projects, but they require greater resources or different skills. Or you're looking for a collaborator who can be a sounding board and who has a fresh pool of contacts to tap. Maybe you're just overwhelmed with the relentless demands, and you want someone else to handle the bookkeeping or paperwork chores.

If you find yourself facing these situations, it's time to consider outside help. One option is to partner with other solo entrepreneurs, whether they're known as independent contractors, freelancers, subcontractors, or consultants, or have other titles reflecting their independent status. Or you can build a flexible staff with part-time help, temporary services, interns, or seasonal workers. You may even be ready to make the jump to hiring full-time employees.

Another attractive alternative for a growing number of solo entrepreneurs is to band together with other like-minded individuals to form a virtual company. In this structure, independent professionals assemble their talents to provide services as a full-fledged staff, offering corporations the value of high-level expertise with-out requiring a long-term employment commitment. Many teams work together on a regular basis; others gather to complete a specific project, then move on to their next individual opportunity.

Each of these alternatives offers many potential benefits and can lead your business to new levels of success. But there are important managerial, financial, and tax considerations to keep in mind. In this chapter you'll discover ways to get the most from these professional arrangements, while retaining your freedom and flexibility.

Many Tasks, Many Choices

Even the smallest business requires a multitude of daily tasks to survive. In the beginning, it's likely you'll be tackling them all yourself. Later, you may discover that your time is spent more wisely by focusing on work you enjoy or can execute best. For example, if you charge a certain hourly fee for your graphic design work and can find someone to do your bookkeeping for a lower rate, this arrangement might allow you to take on more design projects and generate greater income. See if you face a similar situation in your business.

Value your time for what it is truly worth to you—in emotional and psychological terms as well as financial ones. If you find pleasure in taking a break from intensive mental work by packing boxes of your product for shipment, then do it. But if packing is a bore and you have other opportunities that are income-producing, make the wise choice and find a shipping clerk and delegate the task. In the long run, your business will prosper—and you'll be happier.

Associates or Employees—Which to Choose?

Deciding between working with a fellow independent associate or hiring an employee can be a puzzle, since each option offers benefits and drawbacks. Many solo entrepreneurs grow their businesses with employees, moving beyond the strict definition of "working solo." Others decide to retain an independent focus; they form alliances with professional peers, or hire temporary help or subcontractors to assist them.

Following are some comments from seasoned entrepreneurs about the approaches they used to expand their businesses. See how closely you find yourself aligned with their ideas.

First, those who have found success with employees explain:

> "I always thought of myself as head of a larger business, even when I was just starting out alone. It was a natural outgrowth to hire employees."

> "My business took off so fast that it was quickly beyond my abilities. I knew the only way to survive and prosper was to hire additional workers."

> "I enjoy the sense of family I've been able to establish with my company. Having employees is like having children. It's very rewarding to see them grow and develop."

> "There are so many things I want to do, and I knew I couldn't possibly do them all myself in one lifetime. By hiring employees, I'm able to take one step back and get my ideas done through others."

Those who remain independent and work with associates observe:

"I chose to work solo so that I could determine my own work schedule and commitments. I want to retain that 100 percent independence, without employees depending on me."

"Being responsible for someone else's livelihood is too great an obligation—both psychological and financial—at this point in my business."

"I think I would be swamped by the paperwork and tax burdens of employees."

"I enjoy changing the type of work I do and taking a risk on new ideas. If I had an employee who was counting on me, I don't think I'd be as adventuresome."

Do you find your own voice among these viewpoints? There are thousands of reasons why independent entrepreneurs decide to expand their businesses through hiring employees—and just as many reasons, too, why many remain committed to working on their own. There is no right or wrong answer. Your decision will depend on your unique goals, needs, and attitudes about integrating the work you do into the larger landscape of your life.

The Pluses and Minuses to Consider

Let's take a summary look at the advantages and disadvantages of working with employees or with other independents. To help you further determine what's best for your business, check out the comparison chart found in Figure 11.1.

Working with other independents offers the greatest flexibility and freedom and the least complexity for your business. Each individual runs his or her own business, minimizing any legal or financial entanglements. By pooling talents and resources, each business profits while retaining a separate identity.

There is one key tax requirement to remember when working with associates. If you pay unincorporated independent contractors $600 or more for the year, you must file IRS Form 1099 indicating how much you paid and to whom. You also must furnish copies to those who did work for you, so they can file the form with their own tax returns.

The main disadvantage to relying on other independents is that you are limited in your control. Until you know someone well, it's often difficult to tell if his or her sense of quality, adherence to deadlines, response to pressure, or general set of values corresponds to yours. If peer professionals are in demand, they may not be available to you when you need them. Or they may choose other customers or partners who offer more money or better opportunities. Temporary and part-time workers may have more flexible schedules but may not possess all the skills you need.

WORKING WITH ASSOCIATES AND EMPLOYEES

ASSOCIATES

Advantages

+ Working with another
  independent business
+ Minimal legal, financial,
  or tax complications
+ Access to specialists
+ Flexible time commitment

Disadvantages

– Lack of control over other
  business
– Uncertain availability
– Limited sense of loyalty

EMPLOYEES

Advantages

+ Ability to train
+ Control over workers
+ Long-term relationship
+ Loyalty

Disadvantages

– Legally required benefits
– Complex paperwork
– Financial commitment/
  responsibility
– Training investment

Figure 11.1 As you expand your solo business, there will come a time when you'll turn to outside help. Here's a summary of the advantages and disadvantages of working with associates and employees. Your choice will be based on your business needs and goals as well as your personal workstyle preferences.

With employees, you're assured of much more control. They are trained to perform duties as you wish, and they bring a sense of reliability, stability, and continuity to your business. An assistant can help take your business to the next level, by letting you focus on activities that bring you greater professional compensation and personal satisfaction. As the comments above reveal, employees also bring a sense of family and community to a business, an aspect that many entrepreneurs enjoy developing.

The two major disadvantages to having employees are the expense and the paperwork complexity. In addition to salary, you must withhold federal and state income taxes, contribute to unemployment and workers' compensation systems, and match their Social Security contributions. Many states also stipulate disability insurance. These legally required benefits can add a sizable overhead to a small business, and they don't even begin to address such issues as health insurance and retirement plans.

Having even one employee increases your paperwork substantially. The IRS requires regular payments of withholding, Social Security, and other taxes, accompanied by financial reporting. Some industries also require licenses, registrations, or other forms for new employees. Penalties for late or missed payments or forms can bring additional expense to your business.

In finding others to work with you, the distinction between an independent contractor and an employee holds important consequences for your business, particularly in regard to taxes. Read on to learn more about the difference as the IRS views it.

Independent Contractor or Employee?

For IRS purposes, workers fall into one of two general categories: independent contractors or employees. Central to the distinction is how much control there is over the worker. In theory, if you're working with a fellow independent contractor, you should be concerned only with the results of the work, not the way in which it is performed.

In 1996, the IRS released new guidelines to its agents to help determine worker status. In the past, a list of 20 factors compiled by the IRS had been used in court decisions to determine worker status. The list, sometimes called the 20-Factor Test, will still be used as an analytical tool, although the new guidelines direct agents to focus on the overall situation rather than emphasize one or two of the 20 factors.

Under the new guidelines, the IRS now uses "categories of evidence" to indicate the extent of direction and control present in any work situation. Facts that provide evidence of the degree of control and independence fall into three categories: behavioral control, financial control, and the type of relationship of the two parties.

IRS Categories of Evidence in Determining Worker Status

The following summary of the IRS categories of evidence and the chart featured in Figure 11.2 are reprinted from a booklet published by Paychex, a national payroll service company. This information is provided as a guide; as with any tax matter, it is wise to check with a professional to see how the regulations may affect your solo business.

Behavioral Control

Facts that show whether the business has a right to direct and control how the worker does the task for which the worker is hired include the type and degree of:

IRS CATEGORIES OF EVIDENCE IN DETERMINING WORKER STATUS

Behavioral Control

Facts that illustrate whether there is a right to direct or control how the worker performs the specific task for which he or she is engaged:

- ✓ Instructions
- ✓ Training

Financial Control

Facts that illustrate whether there is a right to direct or control how the business aspects of the worker's activities are conducted:

- ✓ Significant investment
- ✓ Unreimbursed expenses
- ✓ Services available to the relevant market
- ✓ Method of payment
- ✓ Opportunity for profit or loss

Relationship of the Parties

Facts that illustrate how the parties perceive their relationship:

- ✓ Intent of parties/written contracts
- ✓ Employee benefits
- ✓ Discharge/termination
- ✓ Regular business activity

Reprinted with permission from *1099 Employee vs. Independent Contractor,* published by Paychex.

Figure 11.2 The IRS uses the categories of evidence shown in this chart as one of the ways to determine whether a worker is an employee or independent contractor. The determination depends primarily on the extent to which the person receiving the services has the right to direct and control the service provider with regard to what is to be done and how it is to be done. Employers generally have more control over performance; independent contractors determine for themselves how the work is to be performed.

✓ *Instructions the business gives the worker.* An employee is generally subject to the business's instructions about when, where, and how to work. Even if no instructions are given, sufficient behavioral control may exist if the employer has the right to control how the work results are achieved.

✓ *Training the business gives the worker.* An employee may be trained to perform services in a particular manner. Independent contractors ordinarily use their own methods.

Financial Control

Facts that show whether the business has a right to control the business aspects of the worker's job include:

✓ *The extent to which the worker has unreimbursed business expenses.* Independent contractors are more likely to have unreimbursed expenses than employees. Fixed ongoing costs that are incurred regardless of whether work is currently being performed are especially important. However, employees may also incur unreimbursed expenses in conjunction with the services they perform for their business.

✓ *The extent of the worker's investment.* An independent contractor often has a significant investment in the facilities he or she uses in performing services for someone else. However, a significant investment is not required.

✓ *The extent to which the worker makes services available to the relevant market.* Employees don't normally market their services to the public on a regular basis, while independent contractors might. Working for multiple clients usually indicates independent contractor status.

✓ *How the business pays the worker.* An employee is generally paid by the hour, week, or month. An independent contractor is usually paid by the job. However, it is common in some professions, such as law, to pay independent contractors hourly.

✓ *The extent to which the worker can realize a profit or incur a loss.* An independent contractor can make a profit or suffer a loss.

Type of Relationship

Facts that show the parties' type of relationship include:

✓ *Written contracts describing the relationship the parties intended to create.*

✓ *Whether the business provides the worker with employee-type benefits, such as insurance, a pension plan, vacation pay, or sick pay.*

✓ *The permanency of the relationship.* If you engage a worker with the expectation that the relationship will continue indefinitely, rather than for a specific project or period, this is generally considered evidence that your intent was to create an employer-employee relationship.

✓ *The extent to which services performed by the worker are a key aspect of the regular business of the company.* If a worker provides services that are a key aspect of your regular business activity, it is more likely that you will have the right to direct and control his or her activities. For example, if a law firm hires an attorney, it is likely that it will present the attorney's work as its own and would have the right to control or direct that work. This would indicate an employer-employee relationship.

As this overview demonstrates, the distinction between an employee and an independent contractor can often be a fine line. Stiff tax penalties can be imposed on businesses that classify workers as independent contractors when they should be treated (and taxed) as employees. Be aware that the IRS is spending extra effort these days tracking down misclassified workers—primarily because they are losing an estimated $2 billion a year in unpaid income taxes. As more corporations downsize and turn to using nonemployee labor, the number of independent contractors will undoubtedly increase—and IRS scrutiny will, too.

For additional details and case studies, check out IRS Publication 937, *Employment Taxes and Information Returns.* You can get a copy from your local IRS office or by calling (800) TAX-FORM. To obtain a copy of the Paychex booklet, *1099 Employee vs. Independent Contractor,* call (800) 322-7292, or visit the Paychex Web site at http://www.paychex.com.

The Challenge of Managing Others

As seasoned bosses of independent businesses will attest, the biggest shift to make when moving beyond solo is to go from directing yourself to supervising others. Managing people is not a natural-born talent, although some individuals seem to be particularly adept at it. Rather, it is a skill that develops with practice—and like most skills, with trial and error.

Many solo workers have management experience from former work situations and easily apply their abilities to hiring employees or working with other independents. If this isn't your background and you feel that your management experience is lacking, take heart. A natural sense of enthusiasm and mutual respect can go a long way in successfully directing others. You can also get up to speed by using the numerous books, audiotapes and other management training resources on the market. Remember that even the most experienced managers understand that improvement is an ongoing process.

To successfully direct others, here are six key points to remember, contributed by experienced solo managers. Use them in developing your own personal management style.

1. Communicate.

Be clear in your instructions, explanations, and requests with others. Communication is a two-way street—make sure you understand your workers as well. Many solo entrepreneurs know in their own heads the results they want but often can't articulate their needs to others.

Psychologists tell us that each person has one way in which he or she understands and communicates information best—whether it's in written words, visual images, spoken descriptions or sounds, or three-dimensional constructions. If you're a person who has difficulty expressing yourself verbally, don't be afraid to turn to drawings, diagrams, charts, three-dimensional prototypes, or other aids to help you communicate your ideas.

Also keep in mind that *your* best means of communication may not be the same as those of the people with whom you work. Experiment to find an effective communication style. A clear mutual understanding of desired results can help your business progress smoothly.

2. Stay Focused with Goals.

Keep your team on track by committing to goals and proceeding with an organized plan. Workers' energies can become scattered—and morale can plummet—if your business is continually in a reactive crisis mode. With short-term, intermediate, and long-range goals plotted out, workers have confidence that their energies are directed to worthwhile ends. They can chart individual accomplishments related to larger business goals and take pride in their personal contributions.

Goals also ensure that you'll receive full value from the investment you make in your workers. This investment goes beyond wages—you'll be spending valuable time and energy managing them, too. Make it pay off by charting a clear plan of action to take you and your workers to the desired destination.

3. Delegate!

It can be challenging for independent entrepreneurs to adhere to this principle—and it's nearly a cliché to remind you of the positive impact it can have on your business if you follow it. Once you've found and trained an assistant to complete a task, resist the temptation to reclaim the activity and complete it yourself. Your inner voice may be screaming, "I could finish this in half the time if I did it myself!"—but that's *not* why you found an assistant.

Mentally count to ten before you jump in, and remind yourself of the long-term benefit you're trying to achieve: to free up more of your time so you can focus on more productive tasks. Besides, you may find that your assistant brings new ideas and that *your* way of tackling a problem might not be the best solution.

Once you've cleared the hurdle of giving a worker the responsibility and freedom to accomplish a task, you'll discover that the investment in trust and training pays off. You'll begin to think of tasks on your To-Do list in two categories: personal and delegated.

4. Encourage Teamwork.

Building a spirit of cooperation among workers is vitally important for small business owners, since every person must be willing to help out when and where they're needed. As the leader, you will set the tone for group interaction with your energy and enthusiasm. Your challenge is to let each worker know he or she plays an important role—both as an individual contributor and as a member of the team—in achieving the business's goals.

Be aware of the impact of powerful or negative individuals, experienced managers warn. The dynamics of a group can be easily overcome by a single dominant personality. Acknowledge individual contributions, but place primary focus on the achievements resulting from cooperative efforts.

5. Choose—and Use—Workers Wisely.

The best way to ensure management success is to screen potential workers carefully *before* they become part of your business. Do some homework and research past employment references or other avenues that will help you determine their suitability for assisting you. (At the end of the chapter, we'll talk about what to look for in employees and associates and how to find them.)

Once you've found one or more individuals to join you, maximize their particular skills and talents. If you've hired someone for bookkeeping tasks, for example, don't assume he or she will be a dynamo in customer service, too. Understand your assistants' strengths, have faith in their capabilities, and give them latitude to demonstrate their skills. Trusting in their ability to contribute to your business will give them confidence to excel, which in the long run leads to your success.

6. Be Generous with Praise.

One of the most powerful motivational tools is free: recognizing a worker's efforts by saying, "You did a good job." Don't be stingy with your praise. Spoken or written words of encouragement, when properly delivered, can provide a sense of value that often outweighs financial compensation. Recognition of team achievements also keeps your staff inspired and excited about being involved in your business success.

"Free" Help

There is another source of assistance you may want to use in growing your solo business: individuals who won't charge you for their services. This unpaid labor pool may include interns from a nearby college seeking academic credit in exchange for work, or volunteer efforts from friends or family.

Using unpaid labor can bring benefits to your business, particularly if you're facing tight economic times. But don't be lured into thinking it will cost you nothing. Even though you may not be financially compensating your assistants, you will be spending time and energy training and monitoring them—actions that may cost you more in the long run.

Seasoned solo professionals who have successfully utilized unpaid labor observe that the following two principles are crucial in managing volunteers.

Rule #1: Fully Understand the Motives behind Unpaid Labor.

Volunteer workers won't be seeking financial compensation, but they do bring personal reasons for assisting you. For the college intern, it may be to gain academic credit and a line on a resume showing business experience. Friends may find personal satisfaction in giving or in the chance to use talents in new ways. Some individuals may volunteer to get a taste of what it's like to operate a small business. Family members may find helping you out gives them a chance to spend time with you, or their incentive may be a financial necessity, to keep your business going.

The motivations for serving as an unpaid worker can be a complex mix of personal, practical, and psychological needs. Understand that it's a two-way street, and be willing to do your part. That may mean teaching and sharing knowledge or fulfilling these individuals' other needs. Your challenge as a solo entrepreneur is to understand the reasons someone is assisting you, and then . . .

Rule #2: Reward Them Accordingly.

The circle becomes complete when you acknowledge the efforts of volunteer workers. Compensation may be words of encouragement, smiles, a sincere "thank you," a group pizza party, a letter of recommendation on their behalf, or other notices of appreciation. Some workers may find the trust and responsibility you give them to be rich reward; others value the experience of learning a business or working alongside you. These small actions send a signal that you consider your assistants important parts of your business team.

Everyone brings his or her own set of values to the workplace. By understanding what motivates someone to volunteer and rewarding those efforts, you can enrich the life of the volunteer—and your business as well.

A note about finding college interns: The best approach is to contact your local college or university business department and inquire about its work/study programs. Be prepared to explain your business, the duties a student intern would perform, the potential for compensation, and the benefits a student would derive from the situation. Some schools are much more flexible about granting credit than others; you'll have more success if you can document a worker's training and progress. If an internship is not available, the school may offer other work/study programs that could provide a labor pool for you. Once the student graduates, he or she may turn into a great employee for you.

The Benefits of Bartering

Another option for finding services that won't cost you out-of-pocket dollars is bartering. This practice dates back to humankind's earliest days—probably when a skin used for clothing was traded for food or some other commodity. Today bartering has become a way for many individuals to exchange goods and services without using money.

At the most basic level used by many solo professionals, bartering involves an informal trade-off of goods or services. You have experience in X and someone else has abilities in Y. You come to a mutual agreement and swap. The transaction is completed, and you're both satisfied.

The next level takes place when more than two people are involved. For example, individuals A, B, and C all have commodities to trade. Person A wants what person C has, but it's not reciprocal—instead, person C wants what person B has to offer. The result is a three-way swap, in which each party trades with another, and all end up with their desired goals. As you can imagine, when this process gets beyond three people, the complexity increases substantially.

To accommodate multiple trading partners, barter clubs have sprung up. One type publishes an annual directory of members and the services each member provides. Members get in touch with one another directly and bargain for the value of the services or goods to be exchanged.

Another type of barter club involves a central clearinghouse that uses barter units to credit or debit members' accounts for goods or services provided or received. As soon as units are credited to a members' account, the member may use them toward goods or services. Many clubs have annual dues requirements, payable in dollars.

One word of caution about bartering arrangements: Even though no money may have changed hands, the IRS considers goods or services received through bartering as income for tax-reporting purposes. The goods or services must be included as income at their fair market value on the date received.

For more information on the tax regulations regarding bartering, check out IRS Publication 334, *Tax Guide for Small Business,* and Publication 525, *Taxable and Nontaxable Income.* Both are available free by calling the IRS at (800) TAX-FORM.

The Virtual Corporation

On first encounter, the terms *virtual corporation* and *virtual company* may seem like modern buzzwords or another business-school management fad. These entities—whose name expresses the notion of "acting as if they were" real companies—are based on maximizing the power of strategic alliances. They are designed to provide the numerous benefits of a corporate structure with few of the drawbacks. These temporary joint ventures allow partners to contribute specialized expertise, share costs and skills, and take advantage of rapidly changing opportunities. Once the project or goal has been accomplished, the structure disbands.

The concept of the virtual corporation gained prominence in business circles in the early 1990s with the publication of a book by the same name, quickly followed by several articles in leading business magazines. Faced with the downsizing of many corporations, and facing bleak economic news about the traditional workplace, publications such as *Business Week* touted virtual corporations as "the management model of tomorrow."

Does this approach of joint ventures and strategic alliances sound familiar to you? That's because the flexibility and streamlined efficiency heralded as a new virtue by American corporations has been the long-standing hallmark of solo professionals. To independent entrepreneurs, the news that virtual corporations offer a superior solution isn't novel—it's something they've practiced successfully for years.

In a virtual company of solo professionals, individuals retain independent status while banding together to leverage combined expertise. To outsiders, the group may seem to be a large company that offers a spectrum of goods and services; the solo professionals operating within the framework understand that it is really a series of collaborative independent efforts.

Hollywood as a Model

Hollywood has understood the power and benefits of operating this way for years. When it's time to create a film, a producer gathers the best talent available and assembles a top-notch team. Each member contributes his or her expertise, and once the film is completed, the group dissolves and the individuals move on to other projects. Some talents work together on a single project only. Others collaborate often, as demonstrated by the many fine movies that Steven Spielberg and George Lucas have made together.

Increasingly, solo professionals in other fields are embracing this "team of specialized equals" approach. For example, a group of solo professionals who offer marketing services may include three individuals with specific, but related, skills. One may be a writer, another a graphic designer. The third may be a strategist who is also good with financial details. They approach company XYZ and offer their skills as a package, noting that they will be able to provide a full-service solution as a team of independent contractors. The management at XYZ realizes that the team's coordinated effort will cut down on its time directing the project, and since it's using independent contractors instead of employees, it knows it can save some money, too.

The three-person team completes the job, and the team members split the fees according to a predetermined arrangement. They are then free to go on to other individual projects, or they may decide to stay together to target other companies with similar needs. There's also the chance that XYZ will come back to them with other work. If the new projects require additional expertise—say, someone who knows packaging design or special events management—they can easily expand their virtual company to accommodate the need.

Review your business focus and solo skills and consider how participating in a virtual company might impact your business. Even if your situation varies greatly from the example above, chances are that some kind of strategic alliance could benefit your business. Put on your creative thinking cap and imagine the new business opportunities a partnership might bring you.

A cornerstone of operating within these temporary networks is the ability to exchange information quickly, easily, and over great distances. In a virtual company, computers, fax machines, e-mail, and other information technology play a critical role in linking people, data, and ideas. If you've made the connection to the Internet, explore the opportunities for expanding your reach through online relationships with other solo colleagues. If you've yet to maximize your investment in computerization, here's one more example of how technology can connect you to business opportunities—and bring you greater power and profits.

As virtual corporations gain wider visibility and acceptance in the corporate world, opportunities for independent professionals are increasing. Read on to see how your business can benefit from the growing number of professional alliances and temporary work teams.

Forming Your Own Virtual Company

If your solo business is one that could expand by aligning with other independent professionals, consider creating your own version of a virtual corporation. Here are five guidelines to help you in your efforts.

1.   Define areas of expertise.
    The goal of a virtual company is to create a "best of" organization. Before you seek out others, have a clear understanding of your own strengths and weaknesses. That way you'll know what you can offer a group and what you'll be looking for in others.

2.   Find strong partners.
    As in any team effort, strength depends not only on individual abilities but also on partnering skills. You're seeking people who are experts in their field, but who also respect the skills and expertise of others. Don't overlook the importance of members' past experience—in addition to professional skills, you'll be pooling Rolodexes, resources, and lists of potential customers.

3.   Set clear goals.

Define your group's objectives and how you intend to reach them. Is your group together for one specific project, or have you joined forces to comarket yourselves as a team offering ongoing solutions? By clearly charting the group's direction and target, you enable all members to contribute effectively.

4.   Emphasize a win/win philosophy.

Successful teamwork springs from the understanding that the group's efforts bring benefits greater than any individual could gain alone. Each individual should be able to clearly define his or her own gains from group participation. At the same time, no single person should dominate or benefit at the expense of others. In the virtual corporation model, cooperation wins over competition.

5.   Communicate.

Working as a team, you'll need to keep the lines of communication open. This is particularly important when dealing with financial matters—be sure to have a written arrangement of how all fees will be split. You'll also need to set up systems to share information—verbally and in written and electronic form. Commit to keeping everyone involved and up to date on project developments. It may take a bit more effort, but you'll improve your chances of team success.

Just as each solo business is unique, the alliances you make with other independents will take on their own personality and character. Some solo entrepreneurs have built their entire businesses around group efforts. Others form alliances as a project requires, then return to individual work. Your choice will be based on the type of business you operate, as well as on your interests, needs, and enjoyment of working strictly solo or with others.

If you're thinking that you don't want to get entangled in partnerships or alliances, that's okay. Before you rule out the possibility completely, however, carefully consider how the *concept* of virtual corporations might apply to your business. Even if you remain firmly committed to working on your own, chances are good that the ideas behind strategic alliances will start your brain working and bring you valuable insights about improving your solo business.

What to Look for in Others

Whether you choose to hire employees, find volunteers, pay subcontractors, or seek out other professionals for strategic partnerships, you will be looking for individuals who have certain common qualities. Here are the top seven characteristics that solo entrepreneurs say they look for when choosing others to work with them.

Integrity

Above all else, solo entrepreneurs look for assistants and partners who have a sense of integrity. Begin by carefully checking references and speaking with past employers. Your instinct will certainly play a role in this decision, but try to get as much information as you can before you bring someone on board. Remember, your solo business reflects you, and your personal integrity and reputation will be at stake.

Upbeat Personality

A positive, can-do attitude goes a long way in smoothing out the struggles and rough times that are an inevitable part of any small business. Your challenges will be great enough without the extra burden of a whiner or complainer on your hands. In small businesses, every person has a significant impact—particularly in terms of customer interaction. Make sure your business team presents the upbeat image of a successful venture.

Reliability

Your ideal assistant or partner is someone you can depend on to meet deadlines, keep commitments, and understand the importance of completing the work in a professional manner. You're also looking for individuals who can be trusted to put group efforts ahead of personal concerns.

Skills

Solo entrepreneurs ranked skills fourth on this list when referring to finding employees or other types of assistants—primarily because most felt that a certain level of training would be involved with any new hire. In seeking a professional partner for a strategic alliance, you may consider skills and expertise to be a top priority, since they are the backbone of your partnership. Everyone has strengths and weaknesses; try to match your business needs with the strengths of the potential employee or associate.

Complementary Abilities

When you're looking for an assistant or partner, keep in mind that you're seeking someone who fills the holes in your own set of skills. Realize that this situation—even though it may seem uncomfortable at first—actually holds great potential for you and your business. In a virtual company, this distinction is particularly desirable, since your goal is to assemble a team of specialists. Another benefit: Your business or alliance will be able to offer a greater range of goods or services, which will expand the potential opportunities for all involved.

Similar Values

While you don't want to work with someone whose abilities mimic yours precisely, you *do* want to find an individual with values close to your own. Although it's unrealistic to expect anyone to care about your business as much as you do, your goal is to find employees or associates who understand your commitment and are willing to make assisting you part of their own goal.

Communication Style

A large part of the success you'll reap from working with assistants or peer professionals will be due to your abilities to share ideas, feedback, insights, and opposite points of view on both a formal and an informal level. Make sure the person you work with is someone with whom you have rapport and who understands your instructions and overall goals. He or she doesn't have to be a mind reader, but a good communication style between you will benefit your business in ways big and small.

Like so many of the other ingredients that make up solo business success, what you'll be looking for in others will change as your business grows and changes. Along the way, you'll learn from all your coworkers, whether assistants or peers. In the end, your skills and your business will be stronger from the relationships you've developed.

Where to Find Associates and Employees

You know you want them, you know the qualities you're looking for, but *where* do you find associates and employees? Here are five sources suggested by experienced solo entrepreneurs.

Peer Networking

The most popular approach to finding assistants is to turn to your advisory team or other peer-level associates. These referrals often carry the most weight, since they come from individuals who know you and your business the best. If you're seeking to create a virtual company, turn to your business advisors and see if they work with other solo professionals whose talents and abilities complement your own. If you're involved in a team effort, your partners may be able to assist you in finding qualified assistants—or you may end up sharing workers.

Personal References and Referrals

Letting your friends and family know that you are looking for an assistant can be a good way to find suitable applicants. Personal referrals provide an initial level of screening, since the individual is known by someone you know. Don't let this relationship influence your decision too heavily, however. You're still looking for the best individual for the situation—regardless of whether Aunt Marie says he or she is a terrific person.

Professional Organizations and Conferences

Don't overlook the impact that your involvement in professional organizations can have in attracting individuals who want to work with or for you. Your visibility as a member puts your business face forward and can generate interest from other solo professionals seeking strategic alliances. If you're looking for an assistant, the organization may have a member database you can access. Or the group may sponsor a newsletter in which you can run an announcement. Conferences are also a good time to spread the word about your needs, since you can discuss details with a large number of people quickly and easily.

Temporary Services and Employment Agencies

Some solo entrepreneurs avoid the tax and paperwork hassles of employees by hiring their workers through a temporary service, such as Kelly Temporary Services or Manpower Temporary Services. These organizations have pools of qualified individuals who have been prescreened for their skills and are immediately available for short- or long-term positions. You, as the employer, pay the organization directly; the organization pays the worker and takes care of all necessary taxes and paperwork. Some solo entrepreneurs find this option particularly useful when they're faced with immediate short-term staffing needs.

Employment agencies, in contrast, will conduct employee searches for you. They screen the applicants, match them to your stated requirements, and send them to you for an interview. If you hire an individual from among their candidates, you generally pay the agency a fee, often in the range of one month of the new employee's salary.

Newspapers

As a tool for finding qualified associates and employees, newspapers work better for some solo businesses than for others. If you choose this approach, take time to carefully word your listing so that applicants know the specific skills that you're looking for. Even then, be prepared to be inundated with applications from eager job hunters, many of whom will not be qualified for your position. Experienced independent entrepreneurs know that the time and paperwork involved in screening applications can overwhelm a solo office. Instead, they prefer to use some of the other techniques described above.

As you've discovered in this chapter, there are many ways to expand your solo business without giving up the freedom and flexibility you value in working on your own. The path you take will be influenced by your personal goals and style and the needs of your growing business. Perhaps you'll hire part-time or full-time employees and transform your solo efforts into a larger company. Or you may prefer individuals who can complete specific tasks or projects, and you'll work with independent contractors. If you're like an increasing number of solo professionals, you'll consider banding together with peers to expand your business by operating as a virtual company.

At the heart of all of these choices are the individuals with whom you will work. Locating quality employees and other experienced solo professionals can be challenging, but the rewards found in working with others can be many: enhanced opportunities, fresh ideas, additional income, and the ability to share your dreams and success with others.

Building a solo business takes time—and the key to a strong foundation is the relationships you establish with others. It's an ongoing process of strengthening the associations you have and forging new alliances at every opportunity. As your business grows, you'll increasingly value staying connected with other independent professionals and the business world around you. In the next chapter you'll see how connections occur on many levels, and how each can introduce you to new realms of opportunity—and contribute to your overall success.

Chapter 12

Staying Connected—Personally, Professionally, and Electronically

Interdependence is a higher value than independence.
—Stephen Covey

It's remarkable how many cultures in the world remain fascinated by the idea of the loner. The figure of the solo pioneer or solitary adventurer, for example, is an integral part of American history and folklore. Even today, someone who makes it on his own or stands apart from the rest gains admiration and respect.

But when we peel away the layers of idealism surrounding this image, we discover that no major achievement is accomplished alone. Behind the medical genius discovering a remarkable cure is a team of researchers. The astronaut charting new frontiers has a ground crew. The award-winning actor has a producer, director, and agent. The business mogul has a support staff. Even the Lone Ranger had Tonto!

As a contemporary solo entrepreneur charting your business adventure, you realize that your success will result, in large measure, from the ground crew, support staff, or community you create around you. Professional peers, advisors, colleagues, friends, family—all will play a part. Certainly, it will be your vision, determination, and persistence that form the foundation for your achievements. But as we've seen, individual accomplishments are rarely solitary triumphs. The power comes from the support of a wider community.

Creating and extending your personal and professional community is our focus in this chapter. You'll discover how to make connections on local, regional, and national levels, and how to leverage those contacts to improve and expand your business. You'll also see how linking your computer to the Internet can help you find answers to business questions, exchange ideas with fellow entrepreneurs, meet leading figures in your field, locate potential customers, stay up to date on professional developments, or research information from vast electronic libraries.

Staying connected also means being in touch with your personal needs. At the end of the chapter we'll discuss ways that seasoned solo professionals stay mentally and physically fit in spite of unending business demands.

CREATING A MASTERMIND TELEPHONE BRIDGE

Entrepreneurs who have developed strong peer networks under-stand the benefits that come from sharing ideas with like-minded business owners. The power of these business alliances has been known for decades and was one of the central success principles of the noted author and entrepreneur, Napoleon Hill. In his book, *Master Key to Riches* (Fawcett Books, 1991), Hill defines a Master Mind as "an alliance of two or more minds blended in a spirit of perfect harmony and cooperating for the attainment of a definite purpose." He felt that these alliances—often exemplified as regular gatherings of a self-selected group of individuals—were "the basis of all great achievements."

Fast-forward a few decades, and meet the MasterMind Telephone Bridge. No longer do you need to have in-person meetings or be geographically close to achieve the benefits of such an alliance. Using modern telecommunications systems, a MasterMind group can meet by teleconference, and members can be literally anywhere on the planet where there's phone access.

Here's how it works: The ideal group size is four. Members should all share a similar passion, yet be diverse enough to be able to contribute unique abilities and know-how. All members commit to regular meetings, which are held by calling in to a telephone bridge number that links all parties seamlessly without operator assistance. Groups generally speak twice a month, although some groups chat weekly.

During the hour-long call, each individual gets approximately 12 minutes to share news of accomplishments, ask for advice and feedback, and establish one goal to be completed before the next session. One person acts as timer; one as scribe; one as leader. At the close of the session, the scribe recaps each person's self-assigned goal and the group chooses the next meeting time. Within a few days, the scribe e-mails a brief summary of the session to the members.

The power of such a group is remarkable. My own MasterMind Telephone Bridge has been active for several months now, and each of us has experienced breakthroughs on many levels. All four of us agree that the synergy and dynamics of the group provide benefits to our businesses that other relationships can't offer. We all look forward to every phone call—to learn of each other's successes and to

(Continued) ➡

partake of shared wisdom. Best of all, the group meets even when any of us is on the road (instead of our offices in New York, Missouri, and California).

If you think you'd like to create such a group, carefully choose three other colleagues with similar vision and distinct strengths—and make it happen. You'll also find more information on setting up a MasterMind Telephone Bridge at the Working Solo Web site, http://www.workingsolo.com.

Reaching out to others can sometimes seem unnecessary or take too much energy. The effort can bring big payoffs for you and your business, however. Let's begin by hearing from some experienced independents about the value of connections.

The Benefits of Connecting with Others

When asked about the rewards of reaching out and staying in touch with others, these five benefits topped the list for experienced solo entrepreneurs.

Access to a Broader Vision

The interaction that is a part of most work environments doesn't happen as easily when you're working solo. It's easy to become isolated and very subjective about your work and decisions. Seasoned solo professionals know the value of interacting with their peers—to exchange news, share victories, or bounce around ideas. When our vision becomes narrow, we need others to take away the blinders. Your involvement—whether in an informal network or in a more structured organization—can be the catalyst to expand your vision and your opportunities.

Sharing Tasks to Complete Them More Easily

Like barn raisings in rural communities, sharing tasks among others often can allow you to achieve results quicker, cheaper, and more efficiently. For example, if you're tackling a big project, call in some colleagues to help, or barter goods and services for their assistance. On an economic level, banding together to take advantage of bulk-purchasing discounts can help stretch solo budgets. Printers often offer better pricing on larger print jobs; see if you can gang several orders together so each person saves. There is power in numbers; by combining with other solo entrepreneurs, you can leverage the group value while still remaining independent.

Mutual Motivation

It's funny how most of us can offer someone else encouragement and inspiration but cannot give it to ourselves. That's when being connected pays off. Making a pact with a professional "buddy" that you'll each achieve your goals can be a valuable motivational tool. Others create success teams to generate mutual support and inspiration. If you find yourself lagging and feeling overwhelmed by the self-imposed tasks you've undertaken, turn to others for feedback. They'll be able to provide some clarity to your vision. Remember, the reason you set your sights so high was that you sincerely believe you can achieve your goals. Your support team can shore up your confidence and get you started on the path again with renewed energy.

Less Solitude

While most independent entrepreneurs revel in the freedom of working on their own, they also admit that it can be lonely at times. No matter how much of a hermit you may be, humans by nature are social creatures and need to interact with others from time to time. When there's no watercooler down the hall, you have to initiate opportunities for interaction. Phone calls, lunches, mail, electronic messages—a community takes the edge off the harsh isolation that working solo can bring.

Satisfaction of Giving Back to a Community

For many solo entrepreneurs, the chance to contribute their unique talents or abilities to their community brings rich personal rewards. The contribution might be designing the flyer for the local recycling center, serving on a nonprofit board, or donating goods or services for a community campaign. It's a satisfying feeling to recognize that your business operates solo but not in a vacuum. Because of your hard work, determination, and personal vision, you're able to have a positive impact on the lives of those around you.

Making Connections through Professional Associations

One of the best ways to expand your professional network and connect with other independents in your field is through joining an association. People have recognized the benefits of coming together in such groups for centuries. In fact, Benjamin Franklin founded the American Philosophical Society in 1743, even before the United States was officially born. Today, seven out of ten Americans belong to at least one association, and there are more than 100,000 local, state, and national associations serving every interest and industry. There's even an association of association leaders!

Membership in an association can bring you benefits such as educational programs, publications, and group discounts on purchases of insurance, equipment, or supplies. Most of all, associations link you with other professionals and enable you to access the collective experience of each organization's members.

Finding an association that matches your interests and business needs is not difficult. Here are five ways to get connected.

1. Use the Encyclopedia of Associations.

This directory, published by Gale Research, is a comprehensive listing of thousands of associations. You can find a copy in most public or university libraries. The directory gives contact information and a brief description of each organization. Cross-references allow you to track down related interest areas easily.

2. Read publications, including the ads.

Many associations publish journals or magazines for their members (and sometimes for the general public, too). By keeping an eye out for publications that interest you, you might discover an organization that you hadn't heard of before. Reading the ads in publications also can tell you about association activities or programs that can provide valuable contacts for you.

3. Read the fine print of business cards.

If you read the small type on the business cards of colleagues in your interest area, you'll probably discover that many include the names of associations to which these professionals belong. Some associations offer licensing or tiered levels of membership, and members who have achieved this honor often print this information—or an insignia—on their cards. By conducting this research, you'll soon learn the key organizations of your industry.

4. Seek out the leaders in your field.

As you become more involved in your professional arena, you also will become familiar with the names and activities of leaders in your field. When reading articles by or about them, keep an eye out for references to professional organizations in which they participate. Do they write for an association journal or regularly speak at conferences? Do they serve on the board of directors for an organization? The activities of the movers and shakers in your field reveal the sources of power and information.

A good step toward becoming recognized in your field is to get actively involved in organizations other leaders value and participate in. You'll likely be donating your time, expertise, or services, but the connections and friendships you'll make will be invaluable.

5.   *Take part in local or regional events sponsored by national organizations.*
Many national associations sponsor local and regional events, and these gatherings are a good way to sample the personality of the organization and what it can offer you. It's also an excellent opportunity to meet colleagues who can serve as a local resource for you, for sharing ideas or as potential associates.

By participating in a professional organization—whether on a local, regional, or national level—you're linking with others who share your interests and goals. The collective wisdom and power of an association can bring your solo business significant benefits. It's worth the effort to check them out—and join.

Staying Connected through Seminars, Conferences, and Workshops

One of the best parts about working solo is that the adventure of learning never ends. There's always more to know, a new technique to try, a better method to discover.

In addition to expanding your knowledge base and professional network, conferences and seminars provide an opportunity for you to toot your own horn as a speaker or presenter. As you gain experience in your field, stay aware of opportunities to contribute. At first, these will likely be volunteer efforts. But they will give you the chance to see if you enjoy public speaking and will provide you experience and credibility if you decide to pursue future opportunities.

Planning helps you get the most out of a seminar, conference, or workshop. Here are five tips to help you maximize your investment.

1.   *Choose carefully.*
Check out the program content and track record of the sponsors to make sure it will meet your needs. Stay open to topics that may stretch your knowledge, but if you are seeking information about particular issues, make sure the event will be valuable to you.

2.   *Consider the investment of your time.*
Remember, time is the most valuable commodity an independent professional has. In some cases, a high-quality, one-day seminar may be more worthwhile than a less expensive two-day program. Purchasing the audiotapes, videotapes, or written summary of a seminar is another timesaving alternative.

3.   *Come prepared.*
By establishing your own personal and professional goals in advance, you'll be clear about what you want to get out of the event, and you'll have a much better chance of obtaining it. Review the itinerary and decide if there are things you

want to achieve, such as connecting with a particular speaker, learning a specific piece of information, or reviewing the products of a new company.

4.   Don't overlook social and peripheral events.

The value of a conference often comes from networking with peer professionals as much as from attending program sessions. Put your hesitation behind you and reach out to connect with others. Vary your luncheon companions and the colleagues you chat with during breaks. Seek out others who make comments that interest you.

5.   Debrief once you get home.

Studies show that if you don't use new information within 72 hours after learning it, chances are you won't use it at all. On the trip home or upon returning to your office, set aside an hour or so to review the notes and business cards you collected. Put into practice new ideas or procedures, and consider ways to stay in touch with new contacts.

Sending a postcard or a newspaper clipping on a topic of mutual interest is a great way to strengthen the connections you've made. You can turn to your new colleagues for feedback and advice, and you can plan to meet at the next event.

There are literally thousands of seminars, conferences, and workshops given *each day* around the country. As you launch your business and your name gets included on new mailing lists, your mailbox will soon start filling up with invitations to attend. If you join associations, you'll also receive notices of their events.

Increasing Your Business Know-How

Another good way to stay connected professionally is to keep up to date with new developments in your field and small business practices. Reading books and journals allows you to tap into the collected wisdom of others, bypassing time-consuming trial-and-error discoveries on your own. Subscribe to magazines and journals in your field, and set up a system to get the most from them. This may be slating an hour a week to browse, or tearing important articles out and putting them into a file you carry with you. That way, when you have a free moment you can read what is valuable to you, instead of carting a pile of magazines around or having them stack up in a corner of your office.

If you haven't discovered the value of learning through audiotapes, I encourage you to explore the wide array of subjects available in this format. Successful solo entrepreneurs know how to maximize their time, and many have turned to audio learning to expand their business know-how during off-peak moments such as driving, doing chores, or exercising.

When you consider that the average person drives at least 12,000 miles a year, it comes down to the equivalent of a college semester of time annually that could be spent learning. If your solo work takes you on the road—or even if you're just running errands around town—commit to transforming your travel time into opportunities to try out different techniques, explore new ideas, or reinforce your personal and professional goals.

The bonus of audiotapes is that you can listen to them repeatedly and absorb the information during different stages of your professional development. Some psychologists also report that repeated listening to motivational tapes has a stronger positive impact than reading. They explain that the message takes a direct path to your subconscious, bypassing some of the filters that take place when you're reading.

A listing of companies that offer audiotapes on business and motivational topics is included in Appendix A, "Solo Resources," and in the companion *Working Solo Sourcebook.*

Professional Connections through Regional and Community Organizations

In contrast to the connections you can make at national conferences specific to your industry, regional and community organizations offer a different type of professional networking opportunity. In these settings you'll connect with business owners of all different kinds. Their insights can often help you sort out challenges that pertain to your venture, too.

Membership in the local chamber of commerce or other traditional associations can bring you into contact with community business leaders—a connection particularly valuable to solo businesses with local customer bases. Colleagues can help you interpret local regulations, give you tips on available business services, match you up with associates or employees, or do cooperative marketing with you.

Membership also gives you a community presence and credibility. Your business will be listed in organizational business directories or featured in the area newspaper. Instead of a loner, you'll be seen as an active member of the area business community.

Words of Wisdom

On Staying in Touch with Clients and Customers

An essential key to solo success is the ability to establish relationships with both current and potential customers. Here's how one experienced solo entrepreneur maintains his professional connections.

"In my business, it's important to stay in touch with people—to keep my face in front of them. This isn't done in an irritating way. Rather, it comes from the realization that the more people hear or

read about me, or see me in person, the more likely they'll think about me when a project comes along.

"To track my involvement with potential clients, I've created a file in my computer that is indispensable to my business. When I make contact with a potential client, I type in the company's name, address, and phone number and the name and position of the person with whom I've met or spoken. If they say to call back in a few weeks, I'll mark it in the file and on my calendar. When it's time to call again, I can refer to my notes easily. Over time, the file becomes a valuable record of my interaction with an individual and a business.

"I'm surprised at how many independent professionals don't use the telephone to follow up, particularly if they've sent out a promotional mailing. The potential client doesn't have time to call you. And if you don't call, you've wasted your money. Regular informal phone calls are easy to make, and if you track your contacts, you quickly can build a strong network."

—David Tisdale

David Tisdale is president of David Tisdale Design, Inc., a product design and development firm based in New York City.

Staying Connected with Your Suppliers

Another level of connection comes from your network of suppliers and service providers, such as your bookkeeper, lawyer, answering service, photocopy shop, or other firms that support your company's efforts. These businesses can have a significant impact on your effectiveness as an independent entrepreneur, and maintaining strong relationships with them makes smart solo business sense.

One of the most powerful ways of building a strong network of supportive suppliers is easy, inexpensive, and effective: Show your appreciation. For example, once you've received a finished job from your printer, give them a quick phone call to thank them for their work. Small gifts, cards, or referrals for other business are also ways to strengthen this network.

The connection between businesses is a two-way street, and smiles and sincere appreciation make the road a smooth one. Your upbeat attitude turns you into a preferred customer, one who often gets special treatment when it comes time for a rush job or discounts. Referrals you send to other companies create more business for you, as your suppliers pass on the news of your solo venture to their wider circle of contacts.

Informal Networking

Informal networking among your closest colleagues may be the most valuable connection you have. Don't overlook the benefits of sharing a lunch or dinner, sending off a note or an e-mail, or making a phone call to stay in touch. Having kindred spirits who understand you and your business goals is an important part of surviving on your own.

Some colleagues may share your same field of work but live at a distance. Others may be right in the neighborhood, pursuing their own solo ventures. At first there may not seem to be an obvious connection between you, but experienced solo professionals encourage all independents to seek out others working on their own. Common needs or interests may appear later, and if you've laid the groundwork for an informal connection, both parties benefit.

Remember, the majority of solo business customers come from word-of-mouth referrals. The more people who know about your business, the wider your customer base will be. Let your informal network spread the good news about you and what your business has to offer.

The Many Benefits of Staying Connected Electronically

Using your computer, you can connect to a world of information and contacts anywhere in the world—all without leaving your office. Each day, millions of solo workers stay in touch with clients, expand their businesses, learn about new opportunities, and reach out to fellow independent professionals through the power of the Internet.

This new world of electronic communication offers solo entrepreneurs an ever expanding collection of worthwhile services. With full understanding that the Internet is a continually evolving medium (and hence any words in print are easily outdated), here are a dozen benefits the Internet brings that solo workers currently consider the most valuable.

1. Exchanging Mail and Other Files

Electronic mail, or e-mail, is cheaper to send than the paper variety, once you add up the time it takes to print a letter, address the envelope, find a stamp, and cart it to the post office. Electronically, your message is delivered in seconds, waiting for the other person to log on and retrieve it. (Avid users of e-mail are so disdainful of the slow pace of regular mail that they refer to it as "snail mail.")

In addition to letters, you can also send and receive other types of information, ranging from project proposals to book-length manuscripts, sound files, video clips, diagrams, and illustrations—in essence, anything that can be stored on your computer can be sent across the wires. This capability has opened up exciting new markets for solo entrepreneurs who can work with clients in any part of the world.

2. Connecting with Peers

Using the Internet, independents can call on colleagues around the world to exchange ideas, ask questions, or receive feedback. On some commercial online services, you can search membership directories to find people whose businesses, interests, or geographic location matches yours.

If you're seeking a specific piece of information, you can post your request to an Internet newsgroup or online forum where thousands of individuals can read it and respond. Many new entrepreneurs find encouragement and support from people who have started a similar business thousands of miles away—individuals who are willing to share valuable suggestions, since the competition isn't local.

Many commercial online services have created small business forums where members can add their thoughts and experiences to questions posted by the forum leaders; these files then become valuable sources of collective information, accessible to all. For example, both America Online (AOL) and CompuServe have active general-interest small business areas, as well as forums devoted to specific business topics or industries.

3. Connecting with Customers

While millions of people are connected to the Internet, it is estimated that 70 percent use it for e-mail purposes only. Your customers are among them! There are many simple but powerful ways to build a community of loyal customers online.

Autoresponders are prepared text documents that are automatically sent by your computer when certain requests are sent to your e-mail account. They can be very handy in answering routine inquiries or sending standard replies. For example, you may want to set up an autoresponder that explains about your product line, current pricing, or special deals. When a customer sends an e-mail to a specific address, your computer will automatically send your prepared answer within seconds—without you having to do anything. This gives prompt and efficient service, and saves you valuable time. Many e-mail software packages now have autoresponder capabilities built into their programs.

To see how an autoresponder works, send an e-mail to info@workingsolo .com, and our computer will automatically send you back an e-mail with details on Working Solo products, services, and upcoming events.

E-mail newsletters are becoming a popular way of staying in touch with customers on a regular basis. The two main attractions are the simplicity of sending them, and the low-cost approach of having no paper or postage. Begin by gathering the e-mail addresses of your customers, just as you do their phone and fax numbers. Then compile a master e-mail address list and send a short, lively, *useful* e-mail newsletter that gives them helpful tips, news, and notice of your special offers. Write the newsletter in short paragraphs so that it can be read quickly and easily. An important tip: Guard your e-mail names closely. You don't want to alienate your best customers. Don't sell, rent, or barter the names, and make sure any mailing is sent blind, so that no one ever sees who else is getting the mailing.

To see a successful e-mail newsletter in action, you can subscribe to the free monthly Working Solo e-mail newsletter by sending an e-mail to solonews@workingsolo.com. Once a month, you'll automatically receive in your e-mailbox a digest of news, ideas, and insights on self-employment.

Frequently Asked Questions, also known as FAQs, are an easy way to answer common customer questions. They can be sent by autoresponder e-mail, or posted on your Web site. Compose a list of 10 or 12 questions and answers, and don't overlook the obvious—products and services you offer, hours of operation, office location, money-back guarantees, shipping options, how to contact you, and so forth. This is an easy way for customers to find out more about your company, and it frees up your time to focus on more productive activities.

Using technology to maximize your time and serve your customers better is the best of both worlds. Digital capabilities are expanding daily, promising to increase the opportunities for leveraging time and connecting with customers in brand new ways.

4. Worldwide Marketing and Sales Opportunities

Many solo entrepreneurs have turned to the World Wide Web as their global marketplace, setting up digital storefronts to offer their products and services. The best sites are those that feature fresh and valuable content that is updated on a regular basis—and they have a personal connection behind them. Even though the Internet is a worldwide network for millions, it is also a very personal medium. Making Web site visitors feel like they are receiving personalized attention takes a certain style of writing and design. Success comes from trial and error. Fortunately, the Web is one place where you can experiment easily and discover what works in a very short time.

Not every solo business will translate well to the World Wide Web. But even companies with a very localized client base have discovered that a Web site can be a valuable addition to their marketing efforts.

5. Business Information

The Internet also provides access to helpful information from sources such as the Small Business Administration, SCORE, business publications, and other professional organizations. Many have electronic encyclopedias, archives of past publications, and other reference materials. By typing in a few key words, you can conduct an extensive search in a matter of seconds and capture the information on your computer to print out later. Or, if you're looking to do work with a company you know little about and you want to appear more informed, visit the company's Web site. It can often reveal valuable background information and give you a sense of the company's culture.

6. Software and Library Files

One of the big bonuses of online connections is that you have access to tens of thousands of free software programs and files. The software selections are typically small programs designed to solve a specific task, written by computer enthusiasts, and distributed at no charge (known as *freeware*) or for a small donation (*shareware*). By logging on to the Internet, you can *download* the program to your own computer, paying only for the connection time.

You can also download valuable information from software libraries maintained electronically. For example, a small business forum library on a commercial online service might include such files as a sample business plan, employee guidelines, contracts, or marketing tips that have been posted by other business owners. Several software companies have posted business templates designed to work with their programs on their Web sites so you can download them and get a jump-start on using their software effectively.

7. Keeping Up on Specialized News

Most commercial online services and many Web sites are tied into major news wires, so details on late-breaking stories are available to you at the same time as the news media is learning about them. If your business focuses on a specific topic, you can subscribe to search services that will track news on specific topics and have either a summary or full details delivered to your e-mailbox as soon as the news is announced, or once each day. It's a great way to keep informed about recent developments or public opinion, without having to read a dozen newspapers or magazines. Many news organizations also maintain Web sites where you can conduct searches for older news items.

8. Sending Faxes

If you don't have access to a fax machine, you can use a commercial online service or the Internet to send your message by fax. You type in your message, and the service sends the message to the destination fax machine a few minutes later. Charges for this service generally range from $1 to $3, depending on the length of your fax and whether you want to send it to more than one party. The technology to send faxes via the Internet is advancing rapidly, so look for prices to drop and capabilities to increase.

9. Computer Support

Most of the leading computer companies have established extensive Web sites to assist users with questions or problems. If you're having a problem with your computer or software program and you don't want to spend time and money with a long-distance phone call for technical support, you can leave an e-mail message for the company and the company will reply within a day or two. Many Web sites also post FAQs, an easy way to find answers to common questions. Most also post details on future updates they have planned for their hardware or software.

10. Travel Reservations

Going out of town? From your computer keyboard you can check on schedules, find the best rates, and make reservations for airline tickets, hotel accommodations, and car rental. Some solo professionals do the basic research, then turn everything over to their travel agents to work out the details. Others complete the transactions electronically by typing in their credit card numbers and receive the tickets and reservation forms a few days later in the mail.

11. Tracking Stock Market Investments

If keeping an eye on your stock market investments is important to you, online services can give you continuously updated stock quotes. You can type in the profile of your portfolio, and the service will record how much you've gained (or lost!) since you last logged on.

12. Ordering Products

Need to order office supplies, books, or other products? Many companies have set up electronic order systems so you can type or click on items you want, enter your credit card number, and the package is on its way to you pronto. The Internet is also filled with electronic shopping malls, designed to lure you into spending more time online and buying things such as fresh cut flowers, CDs, videos, and a wide variety of other products.

If you haven't yet tried the world of online connections, I encourage you to place it at the very top of your to-do list. For solo entrepreneurs, it is a gold mine of potential—from staying connected with fellow professionals around the world, to expanding your business in ways you haven't even considered yet. There are many valuable books available on the Internet and, on page design, marketing, and commerce, on the World Wide Web. You'll find some of my favorite books—and Web sites—in Appendix A, "Solo Resources," and in the companion *Working Solo Sourcebook.*

By the way, when you do log on, be sure to visit the Working Solo Web site at http://www.workingsolo.com. You'll find a whole collection of valuable information designed specifically for solo entrepreneurs. See you online!

Staying Connected . . . with Yourself!

When solo entrepreneurs think about staying connected, they generally focus on contacts with peer professionals, advisors, and customers. That's understandable, since these links are often the ones that help you maintain and grow your business.

There's another connection, however, that plays a central role in your solo success: staying in touch with your own personal needs.

Now, before you say "Ah, yeah, I know all that stuff about taking care of myself," pause for a moment and consider. What happens to your business when you aren't working at your best? Or you get so frazzled that you snap at customers or overlook important details? Or if you get sick for a week?

As solo workers, we generally give our businesses top priority, and personal concerns often are pushed to the background, to be dealt with later. Unfortunately, "later" usually never arrives—until the stresses or other neglect results in an illness or other condition that can't be ignored.

There's no way around it: When you're working solo, you are your business. Be smart with your business by being attuned to your personal needs. As experienced independent professionals attest, the time you spend caring for yourself is one of the most valuable investments you can make in your business.

Taking care of yourself begins on a physical level. If you're looking for a way to stay stress-free and filled with energy, exercise is the answer. It clears the mind and gets rid of all those tensions your body accumulates from your hard-working days.

The secret is to find an exercise program that matches your personality and needs. This was pointed out to me most clearly in an encounter I had with sports medicine authority and marathon runner Dr. George Sheehan shortly before he passed away. When I asked him about the discipline it takes to exercise, Dr. Sheehan explained, "A successful exercise program hinges on finding an activity you enjoy doing. That way, you can change *will-power* into *want-power,* and it doesn't seem like a chore."

Over the past few years, I've found Dr. Sheehan's advice to be right on target. Once you discover an exercise you enjoy doing, it doesn't seem so unappealing. The trick is to keep searching for something you enjoy, whether it's a sport, running, lifting weights, the treadmill, or any of dozens of other options.

If you find yourself waffling in your commitment, find an exercise buddy. For example, each morning I team up with another solo professional who lives down the street, and we zip around the neighborhood, speed walking for half an hour or so. We both know that there are mornings when neither of us would be out there if it weren't for the other—but when we've finished the circuit, we're always glad we did it. It's a great way to start the morning, and for office-bound independents it's one of the few ways we get to chart the passing of the seasons!

Getting enough sleep also can be pretty tough when you're launching your solo business, because the days can be long and demanding. As all those classic spy movies have shown us, sleep deprivation can cause the mind to do some pretty weird things. Your solo business is going to be challenging enough without your struggling to overcome the depression brought on by lack of sleep. Try to be stingy with your sleep-allotted hours—value them for the impact they can have on your working hours and business success.

If you find you can't sleep at night, or you wake up at 2 A.M. with your mind racing (every entrepreneur's curse), increase your exercise regimen. If your body isn't tired, your mind won't shut down either. Exercise helps keep your sleep patterns closer to normal.

Also, stay in touch with your own internal biological clock. Whether you're a morning person or a night owl, adjust your schedule so that you accomplish your most critical tasks when you're operating at peak performance. If taking catnaps during the day works for you, do it. Often a 15-minute or half-hour break can refresh you for the next several hours.

When it comes time for meals, remember that the food you eat is the fuel that must keep the most valuable part of your business running—you. Choose what you eat carefully, and try to maintain a regular meal schedule. That way, your body will know when to expect its next refueling.

Work Hard, Play Hard

As you put forth the extra energy and long hours to build your solo business, don't overlook the important benefits that leisure can bring. Resist the urge to postpone time off—even if it's only an hour or so break. The time away will refresh you, and it often leads to greater productivity than if you had plowed right on through without stopping.

If you discover you're being consumed by work, here's a tip from experienced solo professionals: Find a hobby. It's one of the best ways to take your mind off the intense concentration of a solo business.

Discover something that will bring you joy and satisfaction from a new source. It may be learning a new language or how to cook gourmet meals, reading the latest popular mystery novel, fixing up your car, puttering in the garden, playing a musical instrument, or something as thrilling as skydiving. Only you know what will bring you pleasure.

The Solo Balancing Act

To outsiders, working solo often seems to be about having enough skills in a particular area to make a living on your own. Those involved in an independent work-

**Workaholic Ned Fulgum takes his
first day off in over 57 years.**

style, however, know that some of the greatest challenges come not from master-ing professional abilities but from trying to cover all the bases of a solo operation while maintaining a balanced life.

The demands of business, personal, and family life will continue to tug on you during the various stages of growing your business. Experienced solo profes-sionals point out that these demands don't go away. But take heart—what changes is your ability to balance them with better grace and control.

Reaching out to others enriches your life in many ways. Each person brings a unique perspective on you and on your solo business. Fellow solo professionals understand the business challenges you face; friends recognize the personal qual-ities you integrate into your work; family members know your deepest motiva-tions and concerns. Each will place demands on you—but the rewards of their interaction, and the support they give, are priceless.

The demands we place on ourselves are often the severest of all. As you strive to find a balance between the personal and professional parts of your life, learn to be "selfish" with your own needs, too. Nourish the mental, physical, and spiritual parts of yourself. Reward yourself for achievements, no matter what their size. Be kind to yourself, and listen to that inner voice that says, "Lighten up!"

Remember, you've chosen to be working solo for the sense of freedom it can bring. Take care that it doesn't end up being a self-imposed slavery.

You've now come to the end of the third section of *Working Solo,* and we've covered "The Details" of keeping your business on a steady course. As your business changes and grows, come back to these pages to review your notes, chart your progress, and discover new ideas you may have overlooked.

We turn now to the last section to celebrate all you've achieved in your independent business and to cast a glance at what the future will bring for individuals who are working solo.

PART IV

THE DELIGHT

One day, the delight of working solo will sneak up on you. It may come after friends comment how lucky you are to be on your own. Or someone may say they sure admire your guts and determination, and someday they'd like to do what you're doing. Then you'll stop, take a breath, and realize, "Hey, I'm doing this! And it feels *great!*" The satisfaction of that moment will erase all struggles and frustrations, and you'll celebrate your arrival as a successful solo professional.

In this, the fourth and final section of *Working Solo,* we review the many steps that have brought you to success and explore how you can go even further. In Chapter 13 you'll see how to tap into the cyclical nature of your business to sustain your prosperity, and you'll discover ways to maintain the momentum you've built. As you manage lean and flush times wisely, your solo business will grow stronger over time.

Changing sometimes means moving on. Some solo business owners enjoy the thrill of launching new enterprises and decide to sell an established business in order to launch a new one. If this approach appeals to you, you'll see what's needed to make the sale a successful one.

In Chapter 14, we take a peek at the future for solo professionals, while contemplating how great a distance we've already covered. The next few years present unparalleled opportunity for independent workers. Those who have the vision, determination, and savvy to create their own personal workstyles will have open horizons for success.

It's an exciting era just ahead. We're on the threshold of countless new discoveries in the outer world of science and technology, and the inner sphere of human understanding. Along the way, an increasing number of individuals will find the freedom, creative expression, and personal satisfaction you've discovered, too—from working solo. These final pages capture the delight of creating a business and the satisfaction that comes from *designing a life* while making a living.

Chapter 13

Celebrating Your Success: Growing, Changing, and Keeping Your Business Fresh

Powerful people know that getting there is all the fun.
—Nancy Anderson

It's time to talk about success—*your* success in this solo adventure. How can you tell when you've achieved it? It's up to you, in every sense. It's your vision, determination, and commitment that have brought you to this stage. It's your dream of things yet to come that keeps you going. And it's your assessment of what you've accomplished that lets you know you've arrived.

In this chapter you'll discover ways to evaluate your achievements and how the natural cycles of business affect success. You'll learn how to navigate the lean times and remain steady when faced with the demands of full-tilt growth.

You'll also hear from seasoned solo professionals about methods of keeping your business fresh and growing. You'll learn how to modify your business as your own needs and interests change, along with techniques to stay in touch with what your customers want.

If you're the type of solo entrepreneur who'd rather *start* a business than manage one, you might consider selling your solo venture once it has become successful and starting another. Later in this chapter you'll find the questions to ask when considering selling and what steps are needed to determine your business's value.

We'll also discuss the importance of staying in touch with your own personal and professional goals for working solo. Creating a solo enterprise is a *choice*—something that's often overlooked in the daily challenges of keeping a business going. Clearly defining your own goals—and what will mark their achievement—is key to celebrating success. By the end of this chapter, you'll have much to celebrate, and you'll know exactly what, why, and how.

Navigating the Cycles of a Solo Business

Every business, no matter what size, has low and high cycles. There will be months when everything seems to be humming along, and all is easy. Then a shift will take place. A key client may leave, or other financial or production snags will occur.

To novice solo professionals, this shift is disconcerting—or terrifying. They wonder if they'll ever have work again, and they spend sleepless nights worrying. Then things turn, and work picks up, and another upward cycle begins.

This ebb and flow is a natural part of business, as common as the tides. But unlike the fisherman who knows without question that the ocean currents will shift, the solo entrepreneur must closely monitor business cycles and take action to make sure the business stays on track.

Nothing can be taken for granted, particularly in the early days of a business. A downward trend may be only a natural ebb cycle—or it could signal a fundamental flaw in your business. To understand the difference, you must stay attuned to the cycles and take positive steps during each phase to ensure the ongoing viability of your venture. Let's take a look at managing each cycle.

Maximize the Prosperity Cycle

When times are flush, it is easy to celebrate—and become complacent. Take time to acknowledge your victories, but always be aware that this is the peak of a cycle. Preparation for leaner times begins in the comfort of prosperity.

Here are five tips from seasoned professionals about making the best use of high cycles.

1. Set aside some money for the future.
When business is going well, set aside a percentage for a rainy-day fund. You'll appreciate your forethought when you next face a cash crunch.

2. Keep your expenses in line.
A new level of prosperity doesn't always continue automatically, so take care when increasing your expenses. Financial trouble can arise if you extend your finances to cover new costs such as vehicles, employees, or equipment, and your business income returns to a lower level.

3. Always keep looking for new business.
It may seem odd, but seasoned solo professionals agree that the best time to be finding new business is when you're at the peak of a cycle. By the time they're ready to become customers, the business tide may have shifted, and your new prospects will be there when you need them.

It's also natural that there will be a certain amount of attrition of customers over time. Customers' needs change as do the interests and abilities of solo entrepreneurs. If you consistently seek new customers, you can build a stable business.

4.   Keep an eye on the future.

Update your goals and see how your new achievements can launch you to the next level. Review your cash flow to make sure that pending receivables will be in hand when you need them. The time to see distant horizons is from the peak you're now on.

5.   Offer support to fellow solo professionals.

If your peers are at the opposite end of the business cycle and are facing tough times, offer them understanding and bolster their spirits. They will appreciate the support, and they'll be valuable colleagues during future rough spots you may encounter on your path to success.

Wise financial management during a peak cycle can prepare you for leaner times, and take the sting out of a temporary downward slide. Your goal is to balance the cycles so there is minimal difference between flush and lean times. The stability you'll achieve will greatly enhance your chances for business success— as well as increase your peace of mind.

Minimize the Lean Times

Experienced solo entrepreneurs know how disheartening the "valleys" can be. But slumps can also be a catalyst to propel you to the next level of growth. Here are four ways to weather the downward cycle and make it productive for you.

1.   Keep things in perspective.

Remember, lean times don't mean you're a failure. Don't be blind to potential problems in your business, but try to give yourself credit for all you've achieved. Battle your discouragement and commit to putting out the extra effort to bring your business to another peak. Seasoned solo professionals know: Persistence pays off.

2.   Get the word out.

This is not the time to hibernate. Let colleagues and former customers know that you're available for work. A few phone calls can often generate new opportunities. Overcome your hesitation and jump in. Also review strategies that have been successful in earning you customers in the past. Analyze why they were effective, and adapt them to current needs.

3.   Take on work to see you through.

When times get tough, even the highest-paid solo professionals know that work at a lower price is better than no work at all. To grow into a thriving solo business, your venture must first survive. If that means taking on work that's not quite your ideal, swallow your pride. Remember, the race can be won only by those who finish.

4. *Expand your skills.*

Don't waste your unexpected free time by sitting around and fretting. Instead, invest in learning new skills and techniques that will empower you to build a stronger business.

Some solo workers view their journey as a spiral: Each time around they get closer to their goal, and the high and low points don't seem so drastically apart. By understanding the natural cycle of solo businesses, you can use the timing wisely and build a stable business with long-term growth.

Words of Wisdom

On Defining Your Revenue Strategy

Business growth is about change. Unfortunately, it can bring some painful moments before the golden insights arrive. Here are some thoughts from an experienced entrepreneur who has seen the peaks and valleys—and pushed on ahead.

"It's taken me nearly a dozen years as an entrepreneur to realize that it takes a big business to offer low prices, and a small business to command high ones. This is a business lesson I started off knowing, forgot, and then relearned again.

"I began my business as a desktop publishing and newsletter writing company, focusing on high-tech and industrial clients. After three years, I built the company to $250,000 in annual sales—and decided that I wanted to create a product-oriented operation instead of a customer service company. I launched the book publishing branch of my operation, and phased out the service side.

"One day I woke to find my business $25,000 in the red. I hadn't paid myself a decent paycheck in three years, and after years as an entrepreneur, I was ready to write a resume, put panty hose back on and re-enter the corporate rat race.

"Today, two years later, I'm $20,000 in the black, I pay myself twice a month, and my resume is back in the dusty file drawer. What's the secret? It's what I call 'building a snow cone.' The snow cone consists of the strategic marketing of ancillary products—something that cost me no additional money in supplies, equipment, or inventory. It's a 'repurposing' and, most important, a 'repricing' of

what I had. I took my $25 book products and spun them off into audio cassettes, disk-based products such as newsletter templates and filler, consulting and writing, training and public speaking, and client services such as one-on-one training and consulting.

"From the broad snow cone top of low-cost books to the pointed tip of specialized, expensive services, I now have products and services at prices from $25 to several thousand dollars—and I can continually funnel clients toward items that generate higher revenue for my company. So if your business is stagnating, what do I suggest? Go build a snow cone!"

—Elaine Floyd

Elaine Floyd is owner of Newsletter Resources, a publisher of books, multimedia products, and customized training on newsletters. To see her "snow cone" in action, visit her Web site at http://www.newsletterinfo.com.

Temporary Strategies

A growing number of solo entrepreneurs have found success by partnering with professional temporary-help companies. These firms match independents on a temporary basis with companies of all sizes.

More than a million people work as temporaries, and the field is expanding beyond the traditional notion of low-skilled tasks or factory work. More than one in four temps are part of the booming elite temps arena that includes experienced computer analysts, architectural engineers, marketing managers, and accountants. In today's economy, a "temporary" situation can often turn into employment for several months, since the hiring companies find the agencies' handling of all screening and paperwork a liberating and financially advantageous arrangement.

As a solo entrepreneur, you may turn to these agencies to take a break from the demands of working on your own or to find prescreened, short-term help for your business. If you choose to take a break or to fill in slack times by becoming a temp, be careful that you don't lose the momentum you've established with your business. If word gets out that you're working somewhere else—even on a temporary basis—customers may think you're not available to serve them.

If success hits your solo business all of a sudden, temporary agencies can help you handle the rush of full-tilt growth and the swings of staffing needs. A call to local agencies can give you information about the skills or specialties of the available pool of workers in your region.

Understanding the Seasons of Your Business

Balancing the inevitable fluctuations of a solo business is easier if you adopt the analogy of the four seasons, an approach Denis Waitley has expressed masterfully in his book, *Timing Is Everything.* As Waitley explains, the timing of every action in our lives can be compared to a season of nature—complete with its own proper sequence and characteristics.

For example, making plans is the task of the *winter* season. Ideas sit in the back of your mind, germinating, and getting ready for the proper time to sprout. *Spring* is when ideas begin to blossom and take shape. You water them with hope and the sunshine of your enthusiasm, and they're off to a good start. *Summer* is the period during which you let your business goals grow strong and mature by feeding them with your energy and continued commitment. When *fall* comes, it's time to harvest what you planted and enjoy the results of your labor. Winter follows, and the seasons begin their cycle again.

What's unusual about the seasons of your solo business is that they don't necessarily correspond in actual time to the seasons of nature. For example, a part of your business may be in the midst of a winter planning season in the month of July or harvesting the rewards of a fall season in February.

The seasons of your success can also vary in length. A winter season of planning may last several years, then make a quick jump through spring into a summer of full activity.

Additionally, different parts of your business will likely be in different seasons at different times. A new product idea may be in a winter strategy stage, while a marketing campaign may be in a full-growth summer season at the same time. The seasons and parts of your business overlap, and each has its own time frame in which to germinate, blossom, mature, and be harvested.

While solo business seasons may have different growing periods, they always come in sequence. To harvest your business rewards, you must first complete the steps of planting and cultivating. Each season is part of the natural progression toward success.

Adopting this analogy for your business brings peace of mind as you realize that everything doesn't need to happen in your business right now. It helps you acquire patience and, as one seasoned solo worker explained, "You begin to realize that waiting can be an active state." If you switch your solo management style to this new seasonal thinking, you'll discover that every business action has its proper time—and that careful planning, tending, nurturing, and harvesting will lead you naturally to success.

If you're intrigued with the notion of managing the seasons of your success, I encourage you to read Waitley's book (details in Appendix A, "Solo Resources"). It can provide a positive shift in your thinking, and can help you gain a new perspective on planning the growth stages of your business. It also reinforces an appreciation of the power and value of patience, a quality generally in short supply in solo entrepreneurs.

Keeping Your Business Fresh

One of the best parts of working solo is the flexibility to make your business into anything you want. Freed of any strict rules, you can create a business that reflects your most creative ideas and deepest passions.

This versatility means there are few excuses for any solo business ever to grow stale. There are, however, several reasons why you may want to change or update your business.

First, since your solo business represents your own dreams and ideas, it's natural that it will change as your thinking and experience develop. You may grow restless with one part of your business, or you might discover a related direction that brings you more enjoyment.

Second, your customer needs and interests may change. Something that was hot for a few years may decrease in popularity, while new developments point out business opportunities for you.

Third, you may need a break from the demands of doing it all yourself. You may decide to shift the focus of your business by narrowing the scope of your offerings or to expand by hiring employees or working with associates.

All solo businesses are organic and ever changing. Like an oak tree that starts out as a tiny acorn, a solo business begins with a kernel of an idea filled with potential. The attentive caretaker knows that if it passes the first few years with a strong main trunk, the sapling is well on its way to becoming a towering, mature tree.

The pruning and caretaking of your oak tree—your solo venture—is the fine-tuning you'll do to keep your business up to date. Here are some insights from seasoned solo entrepreneurs about how they maintain a fresh approach in their businesses.

1.   *Stay in touch with your customers.*

Remember, without customers you don't have a business. Collect feedback from your customers on an ongoing basis—by phone or written surveys, in informal conversations, or at formal events such as trade shows. Listen to what your customers are telling you about their current and future needs and the ways you can serve them better. A new product or service you're thinking about may be one that already has a long list of customers just waiting for someone to offer it.

2.   *Bounce ideas off friends and colleagues.*

Sometimes we get too close to our businesses, and we can't see new ideas that may be obvious to others. That's when peer feedback and networking can really pay off. Brainstorming with colleagues can also lead to ideas you haven't considered before.

3.   Keep your business clearly focused.

It's important to stay aware of current trends, but avoid the temptation to stray too far from the main mission of your business. It takes significant amounts of energy to get a business up and running—remember the analogy of priming the water pump? Don't lose the momentum you've gained by shifting your focus dramatically. Tweaking is fine; changing businesses entirely will cause disruption and potential financial loss.

4.   Continue to set new goals.

As your business vision develops, you'll need new targets to aim for. Continue to set short-term and long-range goals that reflect your current thinking.

5.   Update your business plan.

Once your business shifts, your plans to execute new ideas must also be put into place. Pull out your business plan and fine-tune your thinking and procedures for making your new ideas happen.

6.   Maintain and analyze records.

Written records, charts, and other documents can give you a true picture of your most productive sources of income and whether new ideas are worth pursuing. Seat-of-the-pants instincts are valuable, but when it comes time to commit resources to new ideas, it's good to have a comprehensive picture of the best options.

7.   Give yourself credit.

Sometimes the best way to keep your business fresh is to keep yourself fresh. That may mean a mini-vacation (an afternoon off?) or other small self-indulgences. And don't overlook the value of exercise and good diet for keeping yourself at peak performance level.

Selling Your Business

Some solo entrepreneurs are initiators and creators, individuals who grow restless after getting a business launched. For this reason, many decide to turn over a business to others to manage, or sell the business in order to start another. Other solo professionals sell their businesses when they're ready to retire to a more leisurely lifestyle.

Since solo businesses are closely tied to the individuals who founded them, not all businesses are good candidates for sale. In general, solo businesses with the greatest chance of being sold are those with:

✓ A distinct product or service that can be performed by any individual

✓ Established clients who don't care about the identity of the person supplying the product or service

✓ A product or service created by equipment that can be operated by any individual

Establishing a selling price can be a challenging task for a solo business owner. The market value of a solo enterprise is generally a blend of the *asset* value of the company (based on tangible items such as equipment, buildings, furniture, fixtures, inventory, and accounts receivables and on intangible items such as mailing lists or supplier contracts) and the *perceived* value (based on things such as goodwill, reputation, or brand-name visibility).

What buyers will be most interested in, however, is the *potential earning power* of the business—the ability to provide them with income in the years ahead. This determination is made based on a review of your company's profit and loss statements, cash-flow history, tax returns, and other financial records.

When you sell your business, you must also determine payment arrangements. Are you looking for a cash settlement, or are you willing to finance? If the sale is financed, how much of a down payment do you want? What is the annual financial return you are seeking and over what period? All these details, and others, become important factors in negotiating your sale. As you can see, it's important to have a clear idea of how you want your investment to pay off.

Since the specifics of each solo business vary considerably, it's important to involve professional advisors when you decide to sell. In addition to legal and financial assistance, you may want to engage a professional business appraiser. The American Society of Appraisers, a nonprofit organization of independent appraisers, has more than 6,500 members. You can obtain an international directory of accredited business appraisal experts from them at no charge (details in Appendix A, "Solo Resources"). For additional thoughts on selling your business, see the comments below.

Words of Wisdom

On Selling Your Business

Here's some valuable advice on evaluating and selling your business from a respected small business consultant.

"Solo entrepreneurs should think of their businesses as made up of two valuable parts. Consider your business like an apple orchard. First, there is the crop of apples that is sold each season—call that the annual profit. Then there are the trees that produce the crop— call them the tangible assets. When you sell your business, you sell

both parts. You're selling assets (trees) and earning potential (annual crop).

"The key to getting a fair price for your business is to show its potential earning power. That's really what buyers are buying. It provides the future, both for them and for their families. If you have an established, well-stocked business in a good location but no earning power, getting a good price will be difficult. Not impossible, but difficult. Having all of the above plus earning power provides a very salable business.

"If you cannot show earning potential in your business, then you are faced with the task of finding a potential buyer who is simply interested in buying a job. Then the central issue becomes whether you can get paid for anything over the market value of your tangible assets."

—*James Comiskey*

James Comiskey is the author of *How to Start, Expand & Sell a Business* and a business consultant in Santa Barbara, California.

Celebrating Your Success

Everyone's journey along the path to solo success is unique. It's up to you to chart the way, decide the route, and determine the milestones that will show when you've achieved success.

For some, it may mean generating a part-time income that allows you to take a special vacation or send a child to college. Others may celebrate the thrill of successfully turning a lifetime interest or hobby into an income-producing business. Those pursuing full-time solo work may target the day when their solo venture matches—or exceeds!—the income they received from a former "regular" job.

These markers of success are uniquely yours. Each solo entrepreneur has personal reasons for launching a business, and no one else can understand or rank these dreams or desires.

What's important is that *you* know what your standards for success are—and that you clearly define them and put them on paper. That way, when you've achieved them, you can celebrate with a full heart, instead of worrying about other goals you have yet to accomplish further down the road.

As we close this chapter on success, take time to consider what success means to you. When we're caught up in the daily operations of our solo efforts, it's often easy to lose touch with the things that bring us the most joy and satisfaction. What are the things that prompt you to celebrate success?

In considering success, seasoned solo entrepreneurs know that there is no *ultimate* success. Rather, it springs from a series of individual accomplishments.

Like business itself, success is a process. There is no single moment when you say, "I've made it"—for you know that tomorrow holds additional goals to attain.

Yet if you ignore the intermediate steps, you'll rob yourself of the deep satisfaction of personal triumphs. Realize that there are many stages along the pathway of growing a solo business, and many opportunities to acknowledge how far you've already traveled. As you're climbing to the top, catch your breath and celebrate the little things. You deserve it!

Sharing Completes the Cycle

Many solo entrepreneurs multiply the enjoyment of their success by reaching out and sharing their success with others less fortunate. "It's one thing to achieve a goal," explains one solo entrepreneur. "But it doubles the satisfaction when you know your efforts can help so many others."

As your solo business blossoms, consider the many ways your accomplishments can help others. In addition to the obvious option of making a financial contribution to a local, regional, or national charity, there might be other donations that also would be valuable. Does your company have a product or service that could help the group or be offered for a raffle prize? Could you offer discounts on a certain day as a fund-raising effort? Or donate a certain percentage of a day's sales?

Perhaps your contribution will take the form of your time—sitting on a board of directors or advising others in your field of specialization. Maybe you'll serve as a mentor to young people thinking of entering your field by participating in a high school career day or involving interns in your business operations. If you're a master of organization, you might assist in coordinating a benefit event or make valuable connections for an organization.

While many solo entrepreneurs point out the potential networking and PR benefits that can be gained from becoming involved in philanthropic efforts, most agree the primary motivation is a personal one. Being able to expand the impact of a solo business beyond your individual needs brings rewards that can't be measured in monetary terms. In the giving, you'll receive so much more. To many independent entrepreneurs, that's one of the real delights of working solo.

Chapter 14

The Future Is Here

The future belongs to those who believe in the beauty of their dreams.

—Eleanor Roosevelt

A s we approach the year 2000, more than two million individuals each year are choosing to launch solo businesses in the United States alone— and this entrepreneurial enthusiasm is spreading worldwide. What has caused this remarkable phenomenon, and what lies ahead? Can the momentum established by millions of independent entrepreneurs be maintained? What role will traditional business and technology play in the years ahead? And what will this mean for you as a solo entrepreneur? Answers to these questions form the core of the final chapter of *Working Solo*, as we cast a glance to the future.

A Moment in Time

As we consider the impact of the independent entrepreneurial movement and con- template its future, several distinct patterns emerge. Three independent factors are propelling this phenomenon forward at an incredible pace, worldwide: technolog- ical developments, the global business climate, and a resurgence of individualism.

Each of these factors has contributed its unique spin on the movement, and each will continue to affect the world of solo entrepreneurs in the years ahead. Here in the late 1990s, their joint impact has created a burst of entrepreneurial energy that has not been seen for nearly a century.

Let's take a look at each of these factors now and at the impact they'll have on your future as a solo entrepreneur.

Technology, and Where It's Leading Us

In the early days of my solo business in 1978, if someone had told me I would be working independently with Fortune 100 clients whose offices were 3,000 miles from mine, I would have laughed and thought they were creating a science fiction tale. These were the days when a "pocket" calculator was the size of a paperback book and cost at least $100.

Now, 20 years later, calculators the size of credit cards are powered by the sun and are given away free as marketing premiums. My clients are scattered throughout the United States, and my "office" can be wherever I happen to be (and if traveling, wherever I find a phone jack for my laptop). None of this even raises an eyebrow. What would have been unimaginable two decades ago has now come to be commonplace.

Technological advances have had a remarkable impact on nearly every aspect of our lives in the last 25 years. For many of us, it's difficult to imagine life without answering machines, pagers, fax machines, cellular phones, voice mail, bank automatic teller machines, microwave ovens, video cameras, VCRs, Walkmans, CD players, or personal photocopiers—not to mention computers and instant global communication via the Internet.

The microprocessor technology represented in these types of machines has played a key role in the flourishing of independent entrepreneurs. Computers, fax machines, and other communication devices have dissolved distances between a solo business and its customers. Office walls have disappeared as individuals connect electronically with clients and partners to offer services worldwide.

Computers have leveled the playing field by bringing the power of many into the hands of an individual. Armed with a computer, fax machine, modem, and telephone, independent entrepreneurs are successfully matching the capabilities and services provided by much larger firms. Their secret: They can compete because of flexibility and low overhead, since they are working solo.

Small Wonders

While the pace of technological advances has been dizzying in the last 20 years, I firmly believe that the next decade will hold even more opportunities for individuals working solo. As this book goes to press, leading computer and communication companies are forming exciting strategic alliances to create future generations of technology.

A quick look in the crystal ball reveals a proliferation of advanced hand held personal communicators. Intelligent enough to turn your handwritten notes or voice dictation into text, these palm-size devices will allow you to send messages to colleagues and retrieve information from your desktop computer miles away, all via radio signals (meaning no cords). In a few years, these communicators—which combine a pager, computer, fax machine, Internet service, and cellular telephone all in one—will be as common as a Walkman.

Doing Business Electronically

To help you better understand the power and flexibility these devices will bring to solo professionals, take this short, imaginary trip with me.

You're on a business trip in a city you've never visited before. Along with your rental car, you pick up an electronic guidebook to the city that comes on a credit-card-size disk. Slipping this disk into your personal communicator, you quickly review details of the city—maps, points of interest, activity calendars, restaurant listings, and other tourist information.

Checking your electronic calendar, you see that you're right on time for your meeting. As you're driving along the highway, your personal communicator beeps, indicating an incoming fax. You receive word that some late-breaking news will change the strategy of your meeting. Parking the car, you send back a quick acknowledgment and head off to meet with your clients.

The meeting goes well, and when they ask for information on a similar project you didn't bring with you, you're able to retrieve the details quickly and easily from your office computer thousands of miles away, without leaving the room. They're impressed with your offer and sign you up for the project. Tapping in a few changes to your standard contract stored on your communicator, you electronically send the file to one of their printers and leave them with a customized printed agreement.

Afterward you are ready to celebrate a successful new account and are in the mood to taste the city's best Italian food. Pulling out your communicator, you search the database of Italian restaurants and ask to see their menus, which pop up on the screen. It looks like one is just around the corner, so you head there. In the five minutes you're waiting for your table, you check your communicator to see if there are any important messages waiting for you. All of them can wait. You settle into a comfortable booth, check your electronic calendar, and plan the next day's tasks. It's been a good day.

Sound far-fetched? It's not. In fact, devices with these capabilities exist now—and the technology holds exciting opportunities for solo entrepreneurs in the years ahead. Imagine having access to specialists you can call on, any time of day or night, to help you with your business. Your clients can be anywhere in the world, since meetings happen via two-way teleconferencing. Business associates for team projects can live next door or a thousand miles away.

New Methods, New Businesses

In addition to new ways of doing business in this coming era, there will also be new businesses to create. With the growth of the Internet, whole industries of instant information and communication are evolving. The term *digital convergence* sums up the blurring lines between media such as television, cable, video,

music, the Internet, and other information and entertainment sources. Anything that can be converted into digital data can be repackaged and customized for another target audience, in another medium.

These new media outlets will need content material and other programming to fill their expanded offerings. As a result, many thriving businesses will be spawned by innovative solo entrepreneurs just like you.

What can you do to take advantage of these coming advances in technology and communications? If you haven't computerized your business yet, make a point to do so. If you have, set aside some time each month to stretch your abilities. You don't need to become a full-blown techno-wizard, but it's good to steadily increase your understanding and abilities.

Also, stay up to date on new technological developments in the press, on the Internet, and in other media. As you hear about new inventions, let your mind wander and speculate how you might put these devices to use in your business. This imaginative thinking can give you a jump start on the technology once it enters the marketplace and becomes more widely available.

Technology is a key tool for the solo entrepreneur. It provides you the power of an army of assistants, yet allows you to retain your freedom and flexibility. Independents who learn to leverage it wisely will be those who prosper, particularly in the years ahead.

Words of Wisdom

On Technology's New Tools and Rules

Advances in technology bring new ways of doing business and new rules governing how to use it most effectively. Here are some insights from one of America's leading technology forecasters about future technology directions and their impact on solo entrepreneurs.

"Today most organizations apply technology such as computers and fax machines in the same way as their competition. In contrast, successful solo entrepreneurs must apply technology in more creative ways. By innovating rather than imitating, they go beyond the technology's original intended use and gain a competitive advantage.

"Successful independent professionals also will exploit technology to leverage time. They'll maximize their flexibility by using technology to do two, three, or four things at the same time—or to allow them not to be there at all. Some of these tools are already in place, such as multimedia computers that can optimize your self-directed education, and interactive fax machines that can fax back information unattended.

"The successful solo entrepreneur of the future will need to do more than focus on a customer's needs—he or she will create the customer's needs. Most customers are too busy scrambling to keep up with the present. If you can think ahead clearly with new technology in mind and start defining what your customer will really need based on this new world, then you'll have something that will be very valuable—and for which people will be willing to pay a great deal."

—*Daniel Burrus*

Daniel Burrus is president of Burrus Research Associates, Inc., a research and consulting firm in Milwaukee, Wisconsin. He is the author of *Technotrends: How to Use Technology to Go Beyond Your Competition* (details in Appendix A, "Solo Resources") and can be reached on the Internet at http://www.burrus.com.

Business Shifts Gears

The second factor affecting the rise of solo entrepreneurial activity is the current state of business worldwide. On a global scale, we're seeing the results of crumbling corporate structures. Old managerial styles and multitiered hierarchies can't respond to the fast-paced changes of the modern business world and the shift to flexible, global business models. Unwilling or unable to change, these organizations have let their stodginess lead them to ruin.

The result is that we are seeing record numbers of individuals being forced into change, as companies downsize or right-size. After facing the fact that the security of lifetime employment no longer exists, millions of these hardworking individuals have joined the ranks of the self-employed. Others, seeing the writing on the wall, have taken early retirement in order to launch businesses and build their dreams.

All signs point to this downsizing trend continuing, as businesses in many countries struggle to regain their competitive flexibility in a global environment. Additional layoffs will mean that solo forces will continue to grow.

What of the future for the growing number of independent businesses? First, the good news is that the companies who have laid off the employees will still need individuals to get the work done. Opportunities are plentiful for skilled workers who can convince companies that hiring an independent can be an efficient and cost-effective solution to their needs.

A second positive element is the increasing number of solo entrepreneurial teams who are working with companies as virtual corporations. The Internet dissolves geographic limitations, enabling far-flung specialists to combine their individual efforts to create quality products and services. As more businesses gain exposure and confidence working with groups of independents, opportunities will grow for all.

Third, as the pool of independent talent expands in both size and quality, the number of solo entrepreneurs working in partnership with others also will increase. These new partnerships will bring innovation and creative solutions to business. All of us will benefit from the new businesses they spawn.

Today's news from the front lines of traditional business is somewhat gloomy. Tomorrow, however, looks bright. The tumultuous changes in business throughout the world are bringing exciting new opportunities. Success in companies both large and small will be achieved by those who can stay nimble and responsive to their market and their customers. In this, solo entrepreneurs have a decided edge.

The New Revolution of Independence

The third key ingredient in the booming growth of solo professionals is a renewed interest in the spirit of independence and personal responsibility.

All around the world, people are talking about getting back to basics. People are searching for a less complicated way of life and one filled with more meaning. We can see this in the growth of personalized services and the value placed on customer service. Savvy businesses know that in this atmosphere, a company grows one customer at a time.

This individualism is the heart of working solo. Two hundred years ago, the majority of the world's businesses were independent enterprises. Each person contributed a singular skill to his or her community, whether it was the butcher, baker, candlestick maker, or newspaper publisher. Today's communities often include these businesses, as well as contemporary additions such as the computer programmer, pet sitter, answering service, or personal trainer.

What hasn't changed over the centuries is the business owner's sense of individualism, resourcefulness, and a can-do attitude. All these qualities come together in the solo entrepreneur.

Yesterday's Renegades, Today's Innovators

A quantum leap in public perception and acceptance has taken place in the last 20 years I've been working solo. Independent entrepreneurs in the late 1970s were seen as renegades, unable to survive within the corporate culture. Now, as corporations are dissolving around us, solo professionals are viewed as the leaders of a new revolution—one in which the whole person is involved in creating a quality life that blends personal and professional ambitions.

As businesses worldwide continue their shift from impersonal, oversized organizations to smaller, responsive entities, the value placed on individual contributions will continue to rise. The solo entrepreneurs of today will be viewed as the pioneers who have helped businesses regain their vitality within the expanded global marketplace.

You will be among those pioneers. Your success as an independent professional will serve as an example of the numerous benefits this workstyle can bring. You'll also lend a hand, provide encouragement, and offer inspiration to the countless others who will soon be joining our revolution.

Future Possibilities

As we look to the future, the possibilities for working solo are bright. Technological advances will bring us greater power and mobility, giving us the freedom to reach customers and work with associates in all parts of the world. Major corporations, while continuing their downsizing, will turn to independent professionals to complete the work formerly done by employees. The rising number of people working solo will lead to new partnerships and to exciting opportunities for individuals interested in working in these new relationships.

Above all, a spirit of independence will lead many into the new frontiers of the global marketplace. Millions of people will discover a way to integrate making a living with creating a life. Along the way, they'll start innovative businesses that will inspire and encourage others to do the same.

Is this all too idealistic? If asked 20 years ago, many people would have agreed. But times have changed, and the way we value our contributions in work and life has changed, too. Today millions of individuals have found deep personal and professional satisfaction working solo.

The best part is—you're among them.

Conclusion

Congratulations! You've arrived at the end of this course in working solo, and you're ready to embark on the most exciting adventure of your life—a journey to turn your dreams and goals into a successful independent business. As your solo business coach, I'm here to pat you on the back and say, "Great job!"

You've followed the plans outlined in these pages, and you now know how to:

✓ Choose the solo business that's perfectly matched to your interests and abilities

✓ Chart your way by using a business plan as your road map

✓ Put together a team of advisors to guide you to success

✓ Find the financing to launch a business—without necessarily going to a bank

✓ Select the best legal structure for your new venture

✓ Find those important first clients and start the growth process

✓ Use creativity instead of cash to market your business

✓ Maximize your office operations by using computers and other technology

✓ Set goals and manage your time to get you to the top

✓ Painlessly manage bookkeeping, taxes, insurance, and financial planning

✓ Hire employees and work with associates on your own terms

✓ Stay connected through personal, professional, and electronic networks

✓ Evaluate your business if you decide to sell

✓ Design your business so it stays fresh and exciting over time

and much, much more.

Perhaps most important, you've learned how to define your success, so you can fully celebrate your achievements. If you commit yourself to following the information in these pages, I know the accomplishments will be many and the celebrations frequent.

When you reach your goal, do let me know. My own adventure to assist people in building successful independent businesses continues, and I'm sure your experiences will be valuable and inspiring to others.

Remember, as a reader of this book, you're entitled to a subscription to my free monthly e-mail newsletter, *Working Solo eNews*. It's easy to join the list; just send an e-mail to solonews@workingsolo.com. Each month, you'll automatically receive news, tips, advice, and insights about self-employment and issues of importance to the solo community—all delivered free to your e-mail in-box. If you'd like to contact me directly, send an e-mail to terri@workingsolo.com. And don't forget the valuable information that's waiting for you at the Working Solo Web site at http://www.workingsolo.com.

I hope you'll stay in touch. The exploration along this journey never ends, and there is always more to learn. The number of solo professionals is growing every day, and we each have unique experiences and insights to share. Even though we're scattered around the world, we're all part of the same community.

This match is over and, as the coach, I'm off to prepare for our next meeting. Until then, I salute your vision and determination in joining our community of entrepreneurial pioneers—working solo.

Appendix A

Solo Resources

W hile *Working Solo* is chock full of practical details and cost-effective tips to help you succeed as an independent entrepreneur, no single book can answer every question. The following pages serve as a guide to additional information for your solo adventure. In it, you'll find details on books, videos, audiocassettes, magazines, newsletters, associations, government agencies, Internet Web sites, and other valuable resources to help your business.

The sections below are arranged according to the topics covered in each chapter. This makes it easy to flip back to details within the chapter for review or to find other resources in areas of interest to you.

These pages are only the tip of the iceberg in terms of the vast resources available to you. In fact, so many readers asked for *more* resources that I created a whole book of them! That publication, the *Working Solo Sourcebook,* is the companion volume to *Working Solo.*

The *Working Solo Sourcebook* contains full descriptions and details on how to find more than 1,200 resources specifically for solo entrepreneurs and small business owners. Think of the listings below as the highlights; in contrast, the *Working Solo Sourcebook* is your complete Yellow Pages of small business contacts and information.

To get your own copy of the *Working Solo Sourcebook,* contact your favorite bookseller, or call us toll-free at (800) 222-7656. To purchase one of the books listed below, check your local bookstore, or log on to one of the major Internet bookselling sites (for example, http://www.amazon.com).

Chapter 1: The World of Working Solo—and What It Can Offer You

General resources for the solo business

Books
Country Bound: Trade Your Business Suit Blues for Blue Jean Dreams, by Tom and Marilyn Ross. Chicago: Upstart Publishing, 1997. (800) 621-9621. $19.95.

Homemade Money, by Barbara Brabec. Cincinnati, OH: Betterway Publications, 1997. $21.99.

The Joy of Working From Home, by Jeff Berner. San Francisco, CA: Berrett-Koehler Publishers, 1994. (800) 929-2929. $12.95.

Kiplinger's Working For Yourself: Full-Time, Part-Time, Anytime, by Joseph Anthony. Washington, DC: Kiplinger Books & Tapes, 1995. (800) 280-7165. $15.00.

Making a Living Without a Job, by Barbara J. Winter. New York: Bantam Double-day Dell, 1993. (800) 323-9872. $12.95.

The Perfect Business, by Michael LeBoeuf. New York: Fireside/Simon & Schuster, 1996. (800) 223-2336. $11.00.

Secrets of Self-Employment, by Paul and Sarah Edwards. New York: Putnam Publishing Group, 1996. (800) 788-6262. $13.95.

The SOHO Desk Reference, by Peter H. Engel. New York: HarperCollins, 1997. (800) 242-7737. $35.00.

201 Great Ideas for Your Small Business, by Jane Applegate. Princeton, NJ: Bloomberg Press, 1998. (800) 233-4830. $19.95.

The Virtual Office Survival Handbook, by Alice Bredin. New York: John Wiley & Sons, 1996. (800) 225-5945. $16.95

Visionary Business: An Entrepreneur's Guide to Success, by Marc Allen. Novato, CA: New World Library, 1997. (800) 972-6657. $12.95.

Internet Resources
The following Web sites have valuable information to offer solo entrepreneurs, and the list is growing daily. Other Web sites are included within individual listings in this resource section as well.

American Express Small Business Exchange at
  http://www.americanexpress.com/smallbusiness/

Apple Computer Small Business Web Site at
  http://www.smallbusiness.apple.com

Claris Small Business Web Site at http://www.claris.com/smallbiz

Costco Small Business Zone at http://www.pricecostco.com

The Edward Lowe Foundation at http://www.lowe.org

First American GPA's Top Ten Web Sites for Small Business at
  http://www.firstgpa.com

The Fran Tarkenton Small Business Network at http://www.ftsbn.com

Idea Cafe at http://www.ideacafe.com

Microsoft Small Business Web Site at http://www.microsoft.com/smallbiz

SCORE Web Site at http://www.score.org

Small Business Administration Web Site at http://www.sba.gov

Working Solo Online at http://www.workingsolo.com

Magazines and Newspapers

Business Week, Forbes, Fortune, Kiplinger's, and *Money* are good for keeping up with general business news. While they include many articles of interest to solo entrepreneurs, they are targeted to businesses of all sizes. The following publications focus primarily on small businesses and their owners. Many also have extensive Internet Web sites that include archives of past issues, which makes searching on specific topics quick and easy.

Entrepreneur Magazine, 2392 Morse Ave., Irvine, CA 92714. (800) 274-6229, phone; http://www.entrepreneurmag.com, Internet. $19.97/year for 12 issues.

Fast Company, 77 N. Washington, Boston, MA 02114. (800) 688-1545, phone; http://www.fastcompany.com, Internet. $14.95/year for 6 issues.

Inc., 38 Commercial Wharf, Boston, MA 02110. (800) 234-0999, phone; http://www.inc.com, Internet. $19/year for 18 issues.

Self-Employed Professional, 425 Boston St., Topsfield, MA 01983. (800) 874-4113. $18.00/year for 6 issues.

Success: The Magazine for Today's Entrepreneurial Mind, 733 Third Ave., New York, NY 10017. (800) 234-7324, phone; http://www.successmagazine.com, Internet. $16.97/year for 12 issues.

The Wall Street Journal, 200 Liberty St., New York, NY 10281. (800) 841-8000, phone; http://www.wsj.com, Internet. $175/year for subscription (weekdays).

Working at Home, 33 Third Ave., New York, NY 10017. (800) 352-8202. $11.97/year for 4 issues.

Newsletters

The Accidental Entrepreneur, editor/publisher Dixie Darr. 3421 Alcott St., Denver, CO 80211; (303) 433-0345, phone; sknkwrks@ix.netcom.com, e-mail. $24/year for 6 issues.

Bottom Line Business, editor Peter Goldmann. 55 Railroad Ave., Greenwich, CT 06830. (800) 234-3834, phone; blbiz@boardroom.com, e-mail. $49/year for 12 issues.

The Small Business Advisor®, editor/publisher Joseph Gelb. P.O. Box 436, Woodmere, NY 11598; (800) 295-1325. $45.00/year for 12 issues.

Winning Ways, editor/publisher Barbara J. Winter. P.O. Box 39412, Minneapolis, MN 55439; (612) 835-5647, phone; babswin@aol.com, e-mail. $36/year for 6 issues.

Working Solo eNews, free monthly e-mail newsletter on self-employment topics; editor/publisher Terri Lonier. To subscribe, send an e-mail to solonews@workingsolo.com.

Chapter 2: How to Choose a Solo Business That's Perfect for You

Resources to help you choose the right business, stay abreast of trends and discover your personal abilities

Audio Program

Working Solo: Getting Started, by Terri Lonier. New Paltz, NY: Portico Press, 1996. (800) 222-7656. $17.95.

Books

Clicking: 16 Trends That Drive America, by Faith Popcorn and Lys Marigold. New York: HarperBusiness, 1998. (800) 242-7737. $14.00.

Finding Your Perfect Work, by Paul and Sarah Edwards. New York: Putnam Publishing Group, 1997. (800) 788-6262. $16.95.

I Could Do Anything If I Only Knew What it Was, by Barbara Sher and Barbara Smith. New York: Bantam Doubleday Dell, 1995. (800) 323-9872. $12.95.

Joy Is My Compass: Taking the Risk to Follow Your Bliss, by Alan Cohen. Carson, CA: Hay House, Inc., 1996. (800) 654-5126. $11.95.

Megatrends 2000, by John Naisbitt and Patricia Aburdene. New York: Avon Books, 1996. (800) 223-0690. $6.99.

The Popcorn Report, by Faith Popcorn. New York: HarperBusiness, 1992. (800) 247-7737. $13.00.

The Third Wave, by Alvin Toffler. New York: Bantam Doubleday Dell, 1991. (800) 323-9872. $7.99.

Work with Passion: How to Do What You Love for a Living, by Nancy Anderson. Novato, CA: New World Library, 1995. $12.95.

Other Resources

Johnson O'Connor Research Foundation, Inc., 11 E. 62nd St., New York, NY 10021. (212) 838-0550. This foundation provides aptitude testing and career counseling. It has testing offices in most major cities across the United States.

TTI Performance Systems, Ltd., 16020 North 77th St., Scottsdale, AZ 85260. (800) 869-6908, phone; http://www.ttidisc.com, Internet. Working in conjunction with Terri Lonier, TTI has developed an Entrepreneurial Assessment Profile to help you determine your strengths and success potential as an entrepreneur.

Chapter 3: Charting Your Road Map to Success with a Business Plan

Resources to help you plan an effective success strategy for your solo business

Books and Pamphlets

The U.S. Small Business Administration (SBA) publishes many books and videotapes that can help you with your business planning. Request the SBA's free catalog from the Small Business Answer Desk by calling (800) 827-5722, or visit the
SBA Web site on the Internet at http://www.sba.gov. Some of the more popular
SBA booklet titles include:

#MP4, *Business Plan for Small Manufacturers*. $3.00.

#MP5, *Business Plan for Small Construction Firms*. $3.00

#MP6, *Planning and Goal Setting for Small Business*. $3.00.

#MP9, *Business Plan for Retailers*. $3.00.

#MP11, *Business Plan for Small Service Firms*. $4.00.

#MP15, *Business Plan for Home-Based Business*. $3.00.

#MP21, *Developing a Strategic Business Plan*. $3.00.

Anatomy of a Business Plan, by Linda Pinson and Jerry Jinnett. Chicago: Dear-
born Financial Publications, 1996. (800) 245-2665. $19.95.

The Business Planning Guide: Creating a Plan for Success in Your Own Business,
by David H. Bangs, Jr. Chicago: Upstart Publishing, 1995. (800) 621-9621.
$22.95. Disk-based computer templates (PC and Macintosh formats) relating
to the book are available separately for $12.95.

The Successful Business Plan: Secrets & Strategies, by Rhonda M. Abrams.
Grants Pass, OR: Oasis Press, 1993. (800) 228-2275. $27.95.

Your First Business Plan by Joseph Covelo and Brian Hazelgren. Naperville, IL:
Sourcebooks, 1997. (800) 727-8866. $12.95.

Software

Biz Plan Builder: Strategic Business & Marketing Plan Template, published by
JIAN, available for Windows and Macintosh computers. (800) 346-5426,
phone; http://www.jianusa.com, Internet.

Business Plan Toolkit, published by Palo Alto Software, available for DOS,
Windows, or Macintosh computers. (800) 229-7526, phone; http://www.
palo-alto.com, Internet.

Chapter 4: Finding Support: Money, Advisors, Friends

Resources on networking and issues related to launching your business

Books

Borrowing to Build Your Business: Getting Your Banker to Say Yes, by George M.
Dawson. Chicago: Upstart Publishing, 1997. (800) 621-9621. $16.95.

Free Money from the Federal Government for Small Businesses and Entrepreneurs, by Laurie Blum. New York: John Wiley & Sons, 1996. (800) 225-5945. $16.95.

The Frugal Entrepreneur: Creative Ways to Save Time, Energy and Money in Your Business, by Terri Lonier. New Paltz, NY: Portico Press, 1996. (800) 222-7656. $12.95.

Great Idea, Now What?, by Howard Bronson and Peter Lange. Naperville, IL: Sourcebooks, 1997. (800) 727-8866. $12.95.

Honey, I Want to Start My Own Business: A Planning Guide for Couples, by Azriela Jaffe. New York: HarperCollins, 1997. (800) 242-7737. $13.00.

How to Raise a Family and a Career Under One Roof, by Lisa M. Roberts. Moon Township, PA: Bookhaven Press, 1997. (800) 782-7424. $15.95.

The Money Connection: Where & How to Apply for Business Loans, by Lawrence Flanagan. Grants Pass, OR: Oasis Press, 1995. (800) 228-2275. $24.95.

Start Up Financing, by William J. Stoltze. Franklin Lakes, NJ: Career Press, 1997. (800) 227-3371. $16.99.

Wishcraft: How To Get What You Really Want, by Barbara Sher and Annie Gottlieb. New York: Ballantine Books, 1986. (800) 733-3000. $12.00.

Service

The SCORE Association (Service Corps of Retired Executives) is a nonprofit organization dedicated to entrepreneurial education and the success of small business nationwide. SCORE has nearly 13,000 volunteer members who provide individual counseling for aspiring entrepreneurs and small business owners. There are 389 SCORE chapters throughout the United States and its territories. Call (800) 634-0245 for the location of the SCORE chapter in your community, or visit the SCORE Web site at http://www.score.org.

Chapter 5: Choosing Your Business Structure: Legal Matters and Physical Setup

Resources to help you decide the best legal and physical structure for your business

Books

The first eight books listed below are published by Nolo Press, 950 Parker St., Berkeley, CA 94710. (800) 992-6656, phone; http://www.nolo.com, Internet.

The Copyright Handbook: How to Protect and Use Written Works, by Stephen Fishman. 1997. $29.95.

The Inventor's Notebook, by Fred Grissom and David Pressman. 1996. $19.95.

The Legal Guide for Starting and Running a Small Business, by Fred S. Steingold. 1997. $24.95.

The Partnership Book: How to Write a Partnership Agreement, by Dennis Clifford and Ralph Warner. 1997. $34.95.

Patent, Copyright & Trademark: A Desk Reference to Intellectual Property Law, by Stephen Elias and Kate McGrath. 1996. $24.95.

Patent It Yourself, by David Pressman. 1997. $44.95.

Trademark: How to Name Your Business and Product, by Kate McGrath and Stephen Elias, with Sharon Shena. 1997. $29.95.

Wage Slave No More: The Independent Contractor's Legal Guide, by Stephen Fishman. 1997. $29.95.

The Complete Book of Small Business Legal Forms, by Daniel Sitarz. Carebondale, IL: Nova Publishing, 1997. (800) 748-1175. $19.95, book only; $29.95 book/disk set.

Home Office Design, by Neal Zimmerman. New York: John Wiley & Sons, 1996. (800) 225-5945. $19.95.

Inc. Yourself, by Judith McQuown. New York: HarperBusiness, 1995. (800) 242-7737. $25.00.

Service
Colby Attorneys Service works with attorneys and other professionals to expedite document filing and information retrieval. This can save you both time and money if you decide to incorporate or want to do a trademark search. Service is available in all 50 states. Colby Attorneys Service Co., Inc., (800) 832-1220.

Chapter 6: Getting (and Keeping!) Clients and Customers
Marketing resources for your solo business

Audio Program
Working Solo: Getting Customers, by Terri Lonier. New Paltz, NY: Portico Press, 1997. (800) 222-7656. $12.95.

Books
Jay Conrad Levinson has written several books of interest to solo entrepreneurs (four are listed immediately below). They can be found in your local bookstore or by contacting Guerrilla Marketing International, P.O. Box 1336, Mill Valley, CA 94942. (800) 748-6444.

Guerrilla Marketing: Secrets for Making Big Profits from Your Small Business, by Jay Conrad Levinson. Boston: Houghton Mifflin, 1993. (800) 225-3362. $12.95.

Guerrilla Marketing for the Home-Based Business, by Jay Conrad Levinson and Seth Godin. Boston: Houghton Mifflin, 1995. (800) 225-3362. $12.95.

Guerrilla Trade Show Selling, by Jay Conrad Levinson, Mark S. A. Smith, and Orvel Ray Wilson. New York: John Wiley & Sons, 1997. (800) 225-5945. $19.95.

The Way of the Guerrilla: Achieving Success and Balance As an Entrepreneur in the 21st Century, by Jay Conrad Levinson. Boston: Houghton Mifflin, 1997. (800) 225-3362. $19.95.

Bulletproof News Releases, by Kay Borden. Marietta, GA: Franklin-Sarrett Publishers, 1994. (770) 578-9410. $18.95.

How to Drive Your Competition Crazy, by Guy Kawasaki. New York: Hyperion. (800) 759-0190, 1995. $12.95.

Marketing with Newsletters, by Elaine Floyd. St. Louis, MO: Newsletter Resources, 1997. (800) 264-6305. $29.95.

Marketing Without Advertising, by Michael Phillips and Salli Rasberry. Berkeley, CA: Nolo Press, 1997. (800) 992-6656. $19.00.

101 Ways to Promote Yourself, by Raleigh Pinskey. New York: Avon Books, 1997. (800) 223-0690. $5.99.

The One to One Future: Building Relationships One Customer at a Time, by Don Peppers and Martha Rogers. New York: Currency/Doubleday, 1997. (800) 323-9872. $15.95.

Six Steps to Free Publicity, by Marcia Yudkin. New York: Plume, 1994. (800) 526-0275. $9.95.

The Unabashed Self-Promoter's Guide: What Every Man, Woman, Child and Organization in America Needs to Know About Getting Ahead by Exploiting the Media, by Dr. Jeffrey Lant, 1992. JLA Publications, 50 Follen St. #507, Cambridge, MA 02138. (617) 547-6372. $43.50.

Other Resource
Experienced actor, speech coach, and broadcaster Batt Johnson offers The Visual and Verbal-Personal Training Program™ in New York City. He also coaches individuals by phone, and offers video and audio critiques and coaching. (212) 501-1957.

Chapter 7: Solo Office Power: Computers and Technology

Resources to help you get the most from your technology investment

Books
Growing Your Business Online, by Phaedra Hise. New York: Owl/Henry Holt, 1996. (800) 488-5233. $14.95.

The Little Web Book, by Alfred and Emily Glossbrenner. Berkeley, CA: Peach Pit Press, 1996. (800) 283-9444. $14.95.

New Income: Cut Costs, Boost Profits and Enhance Operations Online, by Wally Bock and Jeff Senne. New York: Van Nostrand Reinhold, 1997. (800) 842-3636. $29.95.

Online Marketing Handbook, by Daniel S. Janal. New York: Van Nostrand Reinhold, 1997. (800) 842-3636. $29.95.

Telecom Made Easy, by June Langhoff. Newport, RI: Aegis Publishing Group, 1997. (800) 828-6961. $19.95.

Web Wealth, by Jeffrey Lant. Cambridge, MA: JLA Publications, 1997. (617) 547-6372. $27.95.

Magazines

Home Office Computing, 411 Lafayette St., 4th floor, New York, NY 10003. (800) 288-7812, phone; http://www.smalloffice.com, Internet. $16.97/year for 12 issues.

Wired, 520 Third St., San Francisco, CA 94107. (800) 769-4733, phone; http://www.wired.com, Internet. $39.95/year for 12 issues.

There are dozens of other computer magazines targeted to specific machines or industries. Check a local, well-stocked newsstand for other titles that will keep you informed.

Online Services

America Online (AOL), available for Windows and Macintosh computers. Free software includes several hours of initial connection time. (800) 827-6364.

CompuServe (CSI), available for Windows and Macintosh computers. Introductory kits often include several free hours of online time. (800) 848-8990.

Microsoft Network (MSN) is a hybrid service that is similar to an Internet service provider, while offering proprietary content. Available only for Windows 95 and later. (800) 373-3676.

Prodigy Information Service, available for Windows and Macintosh computers. (800) 776-3449.

Other Resources

Mac Warehouse/Micro Warehouse, mail-order software outlet for Macintosh and Windows software. (800) 255-6227 for Macintosh; (800) 367-7080 for PC products.

Safeware, The Insurance Agency, Inc., 5760 North High Street, Worthington, OH 43085. (800) 848-3469. Safeware offers a variety of computer insurance packages, including repair coverage for mechanical breakdowns and policies for data loss.

Chapter 8: Money Matters: Bookkeeping, Taxes, and Insurance

Resources to guide you in financial and insurance matters

Books

Business Finance for the Numerically Challenged, by the editors of Career Press. Franklin Lakes, NJ: Career Press, 1997. (800) 227-3371. $11.99.

J.K. Lasser's Tax Deductions for Small Business, by Barbara Weltman. New York: Macmillan/Simon & Schuster, 1997. (800) 223-2336. $15.95.

Keeping the Books: Basic Recordkeeping and Accounting for the Small Business, by Linda Pinson and Jerry Jinnett. Chicago: Upstart Publishing, 1996. (800) 621-9621. $22.95.

Minding Her Own Business, by Jan Zobel. Oakland, CA: East Hill Press, 1997. (800) 490-4829. $16.95.

Money Smart Secrets for the Self-Employed, by Linda Stern. New York: Random House, 1997. (800) 726-0600. $20.00.

Small Time Operator: How to Start Your Own Small Business, Keep Your Books, Pay Your Taxes and Stay Out of Trouble, by Bernard Kamoroff. Laytonville, CA: Bell Springs Publishing, 1998. (800) 515-8050. $16.95.

Tax Accounting for Small Business: How to Prepare a 1040C, by Joseph Gelb. Woodmere, NY: The Small Business Advisors, Inc., 1997. (800) 295-1325. $14.95.

Tax Savvy for Small Business, by Frederick W. Daily. Berkeley, CA: Nolo Press, 1997. (800) 992-6656. $26.95.

Insurance Information

Aon Enterprise Insurance Services represents a consortium of leading insurance companies that offer insurance policies designed specifically for small business entrepreneurs. The toll-free Technical Center hotline for small business customers is (888) 781-3272.

The Insurance Information Network has access to rates of over 100 different insurance companies across the country. For a cost of $49.95, it will send you an easy-to-read report of the top five companies and their rates. It offers a money-back guarantee if the report does not save you at least $50 over your current insurance rates. (800) 808-7791.

Quotesmith Corporation, 8205 South Cass Ave., Suite 102, Darien, IL 60561. (800) 556-9393; fax: (630) 515-0270. This company will generate a free price-comparison report reviewing approximately 400 leading insurance companies on several types of insurance policies, including term life, tax-deferred annuities, Medicare supplement, and individual and family health insurance; call (800) 431-1147, 24 hours per day. Instant quotes are available from the company's Web site at http://www.quotesmith.com.

Tax Pamphlets

The IRS has a series of free tax publications that are available by calling (800) TAX-FORM (800-829-3676). Several guides that may be of particular interest to solo entrepreneurs are listed below.

#334, *Tax Guide for Small Business*

#463, *Travel, Entertainment, Gift, and Car Expenses*

#505, *Tax Withholding and Estimated Tax*

#508, *Educational Expenses*

#529, *Miscellaneous Deductions*

#533, *Self-Employment Tax*

#535, *Business Expenses*

#538, *Accounting Periods and Methods*

#541, *Partnerships*

#542, *Corporations*

#544, *Sales and Other Dispositions of Assets*

#551, *Basis of Assets*

#552, *Recordkeeping for Individuals*

#560, *Retirement Plans for the Self-Employed*

#583, *Starting a Business and Keeping Records*

#587, *Business Use of Your Home*

#590, *Individual Retirement Arrangements (IRAs)*

#911, *Direct Sellers*

#946, *How to Begin Depreciating Property*

Tax Forms by Fax, Phone, and Internet

The IRS has also set up a Tax Fax Service to provide easy access to frequently requested tax forms and information. To use this service, dial (703) 487-4160 from the handset of your fax machine. Follow the voice prompts, and select up to three items from the index. Activate your fax receive setting (often by hanging up and pushing "Start"), and your forms and information will be sent to you. (To be acceptable for filing, forms must be on plain paper, not thermal fax paper.)

Forms are also available by calling (800) TAX-FORM, or on the Internet via the following three access options:

FTP at ftp.fedworld.gov/pub/

Telnet at iris.irs.ustreas.gov

World Wide Web at http://www.irs.ustreas.gov

Software

M.Y.O.B. (Mind Your Own Business) integrated accounting software, published by BestWare, Inc., available for Windows and Macintosh computers. (800) 216-9722, phone; http://www.bestware.com, Internet. $79.95–139.95.

Quicken and QuickBooks financial software, published by Intuit, available for Windows and Macintosh computers. (800) 446-8848, phone; http://www. intuit.com, Internet. $39.95–99.95.

Chapter 9: Using Goals to Maximize Your Success

Resources on setting and reaching your goals

Audio and Video Programs

Nightingale Conant Corp., 7300 N. Lehigh Avenue, Niles, IL 60714. (800) 525-9000. Nightingale Conant is one of the country's premier producers of video and audio materials geared toward personal achievement, wellness, and motivation.

Books

Awaken the Giant Within: How to Take Immediate Control of Your Mental, Emotional, Physical and Financial Destiny, by Anthony Robbins. New York: Fireside/Simon & Schuster, 1993. (800) 223-2336. $12.00.

Feel the Fear and Do It Anyway, by Susan Jeffers, Ph.D. New York: Fawcett Books, 1992. $12.00.

The Magic of Thinking Big, by David J. Schwartz. New York: Fireside/Simon & Schuster, 1987. (800) 223-2336. $11.00.

Maximum Achievement, by Brian Tracy. New York: Fireside/Simon & Schuster, 1995. (800) 223-2336. $12.00.

See You at the Top, by Zig Ziglar. Gretna, LA: Pelican Publishing Co., 1982. (800) 527-0306. $20.95.

Chapter 10: Managing Time and Paperwork

Resources to assist you in controlling time and paperwork

Books

Everything's Organized, by Lisa Kanarek. Franklin Lakes, NJ: Career Press, 1997. (800) 227-3371. $16.99.

Life Beyond Time Management, by Kim Norup and Willy Norup. Sonoma, CA: Geodex International, 1997. (800) 833-3030. $21.95.

The Official Guide to Success, by Tom Hopkins. Scottsdale, AZ: Tom Hopkins International, 1997. (800) 528-0446. $19.95.

The 7 Habits of Highly Effective People: Powerful Lessons in Personal Change, by Stephen R. Covey. New York: Fireside/Simon & Schuster, 1990. (800) 223-2336. $14.00.

Taming the Paper Tiger: Organizing the Paper in Your Life, by Barbara Hemphill. Washington, DC: Kiplinger Books, 1997. $13.00.

Timing Is Everything: Turning Your Seasons of Success Into Maximum Opportunities, by Denis Waitley. New York: Pocket Books, 1996. (800) 223-2336. $6.50.

Calendar Systems

Day-Timers, Inc., 794 Roble Rd., Allentown, PA 18103. (800) 225-5005, phone; http://www.daytimer.com, Internet. Preprinted personal organizers and planners.

Geodex International, Inc. P.O. Box 219, 35 Maple St., Sonoma, CA 95476. Strategic paper-based planning tool for balancing work, self, home and goals, based on first establishing a vision of your future. (800) 833-3030, phone; http://www.geodex.com, Internet.

Planner Pads, Inc., P.O. Box 27187, Omaha, NE 68127. Integrated calendar and To-Do list/project manager. (402) 592-0676.

Office Supplies

There are a growing number of office-supply superstores across the United States, such as Staples, Office Max, and Office Depot. Business service centers such as Kinko's and Mailboxes, Etc. also carry office supplies. Check your local phone directory for stores and locations nearest you.

Global Computer Supplies, 11 Harbor Park Dr., Port Washington, NY 11050. (800) 845-6225, phone; http://www.globalcomputer.com, Internet. Computers, computer supplies, and office furniture.

Hello Direct, 5893 Rue Ferrari, San Jose, CA 95138. (800) 444-3556, phone; http://www.hello-direct.com, Internet. Telephone productivity tools such as headsets and other telephone/fax equipment.

NEBS Computer Forms and Software, 500 Main St., Groton, MA 01471. (800) 234-4324, phone; http://www.nebs.com, Internet. Custom-order computer forms, stationery, and labels.

Paper Access, 23 W. 18th St., New York, NY 10011. (800) 727-3701. Papers for personal, professional, and promotional use also art papers. Call for free catalog.

Paper Direct, Inc., 100 Plaza Dr., Secaucus, NJ 07094. (800) 272-7377, phone; http://www.paperdirect.com. Designer laser printer and photocopy papers; software design templates also available. Call for free catalog.

Queblo, P.O. Box 8465, Mankato, MN 56001. (800) 523-9080, phone; http://www.catalog.orders.com, Internet. Full line of assorted papers, note cards, preprinted papers, labels, and other desktop publishing supplies.

Quill Corporation, 100 Schelter Rd., Lincolnshire, IL 60069. (717) 272-6100, phone; http://www.quillcorp.com. Mail-order office supply.

Reliable Home Office, P.O. Box 1501, Ottawa, IL 61350. (800) 869-6000, phone; http://www.reliable.com, Internet. Furniture, electronics, storage, and accessories for home offices.

Software
Taming the Paper Tiger software, published by Monticello in conjunction with organizing consultant Barbara Hemphill, 1997. (800) 430-0794. Available for Windows computers. $79.95.

Chapter 11: Beyond Solo: Associates and Employees
Resources to help you expand your business through employees and other solo professionals

Audio and Video Programs
CareerTrack, 3085 Center Green Dr., Boulder, CO 80308-1778. (800) 334-1018. CareerTrack offers a wide selection of audio and video training materials as well as a series of national seminars designed for both managers and employees. Call for a free catalog.

Booklet and Books
Hire, Manage and Retain Employees for Your Small Business, by Joel Handelsman (editor). Riverwoods, IL: CCH Inc., 1997. (800) 248-3248. $24.95.

Hiring Independent Contractors: The Employers Legal Guide, by Stephen Fishman. Berkeley, CA: Nolo Press, 1997. (800) 992-6656. $29.95.

96 Great Interview Questions to Ask Before You Hire, by Paul Falcone. Saranac Lake, NY: AMACOM Books, 1996. (800) 262-9669. $17.95.

Teaming Up, by Paul and Sarah Edwards and Rick Benzel. New York: Putnam Publishing Group, 1997. (800) 788-6262. $13.95.

1099 Employee vs. Independent Contractor, free booklet published by Paychex, (800) 322-7292. To learn more about Paychex payroll services, visit its Web site at http://www.paychex.com.

Chapter 12: Staying Connected—
Personally, Professionally, and Electronically
Resources to help you create a dynamic success network

Associations and Organizations

American Association of Home-Based Businesses (AAHBB), P.O. Box 10023, Rockville, MD 20849-0023. (301) 963-9153, phone; http://www.aahbb.net, Internet. This nonprofit organization, run by home-based business professionals, offers group discounts and acts as a voice on your behalf in Washington, DC. Dues are $30/year for home-based businesses.

The American Woman's Economic Development Corporation (AWED), 71 Vanderbilt Ave., 3rd floor, New York, NY. 10169. (800) 222-AWED. This nonprofit corporation assists women in business. Services include training and counseling programs and a telephone hot line.

Center for Entrepreneurial Management (CEM), 180 Varick St., New York, NY 10014. (212) 633-0060, phone; http://www.ceo-clubs.org; Internet. CEM has a network of more than 3,000 entrepreneurs and publishes a monthly newsletter entitled *Entrepreneurial Management.* Annual dues are $96 and include a subscription to *Inc.* and *Success* magazines as well as the CEM newsletter.

National Association for the Self-Employed (NASE), P.O. Box 612067, Dallas, TX 75261. (800) 232-6273, phone; http://www.nase.org, Internet. NASE has over 300,000 members, provides membership services, and acts as a watchdog for the self-employed community. It publishes a bimonthly newsletter entitled *Self-Employed America,* and offers a toll-free hot-line service. Membership is $72/year.

National Association of Women Business Owners (NAWBO), 1100 Wayne Ave., Silver Spring, MD 20910 (301) 495-4975, phone; http://www.nawbo.org, Internet. NAWBO promotes business ownership by women and serves as a forum for education and professional development. More than 50 active local chapters throughout the country provide networking and business development opportunities. The organization publishes a monthly magazine and hosts an annual meeting in the summer. Membership is $75/year, plus local chapter dues.

National Federation of Independent Business (NFIB), 53 Century Blvd., Nashville, TN 37214. (800) 634-2669, phone; http://www.nfib.com, Internet. NFIB represents more than 600,000 small and independent business owners as an advocacy organization that lobbies to protect the interests of small business. It publishes a bimonthly magazine, *Independent Business,* and reports on legislative issues in its quarterly *Capitol Coverage.*

National Small Business United (NSBU), 1156 15th St. NW, Suite 100, Washington, DC 20005-1711. (800) 345-6728, phone; http://www.nsbu.org, Internet. This lobbying organization strives to represent in Washington the interests of more than 22 million small businesses. Members receive a weekly fax update of small business legislation.

For other organizations, be sure to check out *The Encyclopedia of Associations,* by Gale Research. It is available in most libraries.

Books

Dig Your Well Before You're Thirsty, by Harvey Mackay. New York: Currency/ Doubleday. (800) 323-9872. $24.95.

How to Master the Art of Selling, by Tom Hopkins. New York: Warner Books, 1994. (212) 522-7200. $14.99.

Secrets of Savvy Networking, by Susan RoAne. New York: Warner Books, 1993. (212) 522-7200. $12.99.

What Do I Say Next?: Talking Your Way to Business and Social Success, by Susan RoAne. New York: Warner Books, 1997. (212) 522-7200. $20.00.

Chapter 13: Celebrating Your Success: Growing, Changing, and Keeping Your Business Fresh

Resources to assist you in sustaining, updating, or selling your business

Books

Focus Your Business, by Steven C. Brandt. Friday Harbor, WA: Archipelago Publishing, 1997. (800) 360-6166. $14.95.

Selling Your Business, by Holmes F. Crouch. Saratoga, CA: Allyear Tax Guides, 1997. (408) 867-2628. $18.95.

Succeeding in Small Business, by Jane Applegate. New York: Plume, 1994. (800) 526-0275. $13.95.

Success Is the Quality of Your Journey, by Jennifer James. New York: Newmarket Press, 1986. $10.00.

The Upstart Guide to Buying, Valuing and Selling Your Business, by Scott Gabehart. Chicago: Upstart Publishing, 1997. (800) 245-2665. $29.95.

Service

American Society of Appraisers, P.O. Box 17265, Washington, DC 20041. (703) 478-2228. This organization publishes the *Directory of Professional Appraisal Experts* that contains more than 4,000 accredited appraisers, including approximately 1,700 business appraisers. Publication price: $12.00.

Chapter 14: The Future Is Here

Resources to help you take advantage of approaching technological developments and entrepreneurial opportunities

Association

World Future Society, 7910 Woodmont Ave., Suite 450, Bethesda, MD 20814. (301) 656-8274. Annual $35.00 dues includes magazine.

Books

Future in Sight: 100 Trends, Implications and Predictions That Will Most Impact Business and the World, by Barry Howard Minkin. New York: MacMillan General Reference, 1995. (800) 223-2336. $22.95.

Net Gain: Expanding Markets Through Virtual Communities, by John Hagel III and Arthur G. Armstrong. Boston: Harvard Business School Press, 1997, $24.95.

Release 2.0: A Design for Living in the Digital Age, Esther Dyson. New York: Broadway Books, 1997. $25.00.

Technotrends: How to Use Technology to Go Beyond Your Competition, by Daniel Burrus. New York: HarperBusiness, 1994. (800) 242-7737. $15.00.

What Will Be: How the New World of Information Will Change Our Lives, by Michael Dertouzos. New York: HarperCollins, 1997. $25.00.

Newsletter

John Naisbitt's Trend Letter, published by the Global Network. (800) 368-0115. $195/year.

Appendix B

Solo Business Directory

The Solo Business Directory is your guide to finding the solo business that's a perfect match for you. More than 1,000 solo businesses are listed under 20 different interest areas. Businesses that seem to straddle two interest areas appear in both categories.

Take time to browse the listings and brainstorm solo possibilities. Depending on your goals and the market in which you plan to establish your business, some businesses may offer full-time potential, while others may be better matched for part-time or seasonal solo work. Or you may decide to combine several solo business ideas listed here to create a new company uniquely yours.

If you create a solo business that is not on this list, please let me know by sending an e-mail to me at terri@workingsolo.com. That way I can let others know of your creativity and include your business idea in future editions of *Working Solo*.

Animals

Animal Remover
Animal Show Judge
Animal Trainer
Aquarium Cleaning Service
Beekeeper
Blacksmith
Cattle Breeder
Chicken Hatchery and Egg Farmer
Dog Breeder
Doghouse Manufacturer
Dog Obedience Trainer
Earthworm Propagator
Exotic Bird Breeder
Fish Bait Supplier
Guard Dog Trainer
Horseback Riding Instructor

Horse Boarding Service
Horse Breeder
Horseshoeing Service
Insect Cultivator
Jockey
Llama Raiser
Mobile Veterinarian
Ornithologist
Pet and Kennel Fencing Service
Pet Cemetery Owner
Pet Groomer
Pet Motel Operator
Pet Sitter
Pet Taxi Service
Petting Zoo Keeper
Pet Toys Creator

Animals (Cont.)
Pet Walker
Rare Butterfly Dealer
Sheep Farmer
Tropical Fish Breeder

Veterinarian
Veterinary Livestock Inspector
Zoologist

Automobiles/Transportation
Aircraft Body Repairer
Airplane Chartering Service
Airport Limousine Service
Antique Car Show Organizer
Auto Body Painter
Auto Body Restorer
Auto Detailer
Auto Driving Instructor
Auto Glass Installer
Auto Glass Tinter
Auto Mechanic
Automobile Test Driver
Auto Purchasing Consultant
Auto Security Installer
Auto Upholstery Cleaner
Battery Reconditioning Service
Bicycle Repairer
Boat Fleet Maintenance Service
Bus Chartering Service
Bus Driver
Car Stereo Installer
Carriage Driver
Chauffeur
Coffee Route Service
Courier Service
Delivery Route Driver
Driving School Instructor
Flight Instructor

Freight Broker
Grocery Delivery Service
Handicapped Person Transportation
    Service
Hauling Service
Independent Trucker
Lunch Delivery Service
Mobile Auto Mechanic
Mobile Car Wash
Mobile Lunch Wagon
Mobile Tune-Up Service
Motorcycle Broker
Oil Change Service
Pet Taxi Service
Pilot
Recreational Vehicle Rental Service
Sail Repair Service
Sunroof Installer
Taxicab Dispatch Service
Taxi Driver
Trailer Rental Service
Truck Driver
Tugboat Operator
Used-Car Broker
Used-Car Rental Service
Van and RV Customizing Service
Vintage-Auto Broker
Vintage-Auto Restoration Service

Business
Accident Investigator
Accountant/CPA
Advertising Agency
Aptitude Testing Service

Arbitrator
Art Show Promoter
Audiotape Duplication Service
Bill Collector

Business (Cont.)

Bookkeeper
Bouncer
Braille Typist
Budget Analyst
Bulk Mailing Service
Business Mediator
Business Plan Writer
Certificate and Award Creator
Collating Service
Collection Agency
Color Consultant
Computer Data Recovery Service
Computer Disk Duplicating Service
Computer Network Consultant
Conference Planner
Convention Widows Events Organizer
Corporate Art Consultant
Corporate Benefits Consultant
Corporate Trainer
Courier Service
Courtroom Transcription Service
Custom Bumper Stickers Creator
Customized Business Card Maker
Customs Broker
Dental Practice Consultant
Dental Referral Service
Disabled Training Service
Dispute Resolution Service
Editorial Assistant
Employee Benefits Consultant
Employment Agency
Energy Conservation Consultant
Envelope Stuffing Service
Errand Service
Executive Search Service
Expert Witness Legal Service
Fax-on-Demand Service
Film or Tape Librarian
Find-Anything Service
Flyer Distribution Service
Freelance Legal Secretary
Freelance Paralegal

Freelance Trade Show Assistant
Freight Broker
Fund-raiser
Handbill Distributor
Handwriting Analyst
Hauling Service
Hazardous Waste Removal Service
Image Consultant
Import/Export Broker
Insurance Agent
Insurance Investigator
Inventory Service
Investment Banker
Investment Consultant
Laminating Service
Lawyer
Legal Typing Service
Lobbyist
Logo Designer
Mail Automation Consultant
Mailing List Broker
Mail-Order Fulfillment Service
Marketing Consultant
Market Research Service
Matchbook Imprinting Service
Messenger Service
Migrant Worker Coordinator
Mobile Document Shredding Service
Moving Consultant
News-Clipping Service
Newsletter Writer
Odd-Lot Merchandise Consolidator
Office Cleaning and Maintenance
   Service
Office Plant Service
Office Records Storage Service
Pack and Ship Service
Paging Service
Parking Lot Resurfacer
Payroll Service
Pest Control Service
Photocopy Service

Business (Cont.)

Physician Referral Service
Polling Service
Polygraph Technician
Printer/Toner Cartridge
    Remanufacturer
Product Demonstrator
Real Estate Abstract Searcher
Recycling Broker
Refuse Container Maintenance
    Service
Retail Credit Researcher
Retail Delivery Service
Sandwich/Snack Route Service
Security Consultant
Security Guard
Sign Painter
Singing Telegram Service
Slide Duplicating Service
Speaking Coach
Speech Writer
Staff Development Consultant
Storage Space Rental Service

Survey Interviewer
Telephone Answering Service
Telephone Repair Service
Temporary Help Agency
Trade-Show Exhibit Builder
Trailer Rental Service
Transcription Service
Translator
Utility Auditing Service
Video Producer
Videotaping Service for Insurance
    Industry
Videotaping Service for Special
    Events
Waste-Management Consultant
Web Site Designer
Web Site Maintenance Service
Weekly Flower Service
Window Cleaning Service
Window Display Designer
Word Processing/Typing Service

Children

Adoption Agency
Adoption Representative
After-School Shuttle Service
Au-Pair Coordinator Service
Baby Knitwear Creator
Baby Stroller and Wheelchair Rental
    Agency
Bookmobile Operator
Camping Trip Escort
Child Care Provider
Child Care Referral Service
Children's Book Illustrator
Children's Book Writer
Children's Clothing Designer
Children's Cooking Class Instructor
Children's Costume Creator
Children's Craft Workshop Organizer

Children's Furniture Manufacturer
Children's Party Entertainer
Children's Party Organizer
Children's Portrait Artist
Children's Psychotherapist
Children's Stories on Tape Service
Children's Television Producer
Children's Theater Director
Day Care Provider
Diaper Service
Dollhouse Maker
Hospital Playroom Entertainer
Missing Child Search Service
Parent Guidance Counselor
Pediatrician
Petting Zoo Keeper
Play Equipment Builder

Children (Cont.)
Playground Designer
Psychological Testing Specialist
Puppeteer
Social Worker

Storyteller
Stuffed-Toys Creator
Summer Camp Director
Tutor

Computers
CAD/CAM Consultant
CD-ROM Mastering Service
Computer Animator
Computer Artist
Computer Backup Service
Computer Bulletin Board Service
Computer Cables Manufacturer
Computer Database Consultant
Computer Data Recovery Service
Computer Data Storage Service
Computer Disk Duplicating Service
Computer Disk Formatting Service
Computer Hardware Consultant
Computer Installation Consultant
Computer Instructor
Computerized Accounting Service
Computerized Accounting Software
   Consultant
Computerized Presentations Creator
Computerized Slide Output Service
Computer Network Consultant
Computer Programmer
Computer Rental Service
Computer Repair Technician

Computer Software Buying
   Consultant
Computer Software Tester
Computer Special Effects Creator
Computer Technical Writer
Computer Upgrade Service
Customized Computer Accessories
   Manufacturer
Desktop Publisher
Desktop Publishing Service Bureau
Desktop Video Consultant
Digital Typeface Designer
Electronic Publicity Consultant
Fax-on-Demand Service
Image-Scanning Services
Internet Service Provider
Multimedia Story Editing Service
Software Marketing Service
Software Packaging and Fulfillment
   Service
Technical Support Provider
Used-Computer Dealer
Web Site Designer
Web Site Maintenance Service

Construction/Home Improvement
Air-Conditioning Installer
Apartment and Home Locator
Apartment Maintenance Service
Appliance Repairer
Architectural Scavenger
Balcony Landscaper
Basement Cleaning Service

Basement Finishing and
   Waterproofing Service
Blueprint Service
Boiler/Furnace Repair Service
Bricklayer
Building Inspector
Building Restorer

Construction/Home Improvement (Cont.)

Cabinetmaker
Cane Chair Repairer
Carpenter
Carpet Cleaning Service
Carpet Layer
Carpet Recoloring Service
Chimney Cleaner
Concrete Repairer
Construction Job Estimator
Crane Operator
Curb Address Painter
Custom Closet Builder
Custom Draperies Service
Custom Mirror Creator
Custom Slipcover Service
Demolition Consultant
Doghouse Manufacturer
Driveway Resurfacer
Drywall Installer
Electrician
Electronics Broker
Energy Conservation Consultant
Fence Construction Service
Fireplace Cleaner
Fire Protection Specialist
Firewood Delivery Service
Flooring Installer
Floor Refinishing Service
Furniture Maker
Furniture Refinisher
Furniture Stripping Service
Garage Door Installer
Glass Installer
Greenhouse Construction Service
Gutter Cleaner
Handyperson
Home Contractor Referral Service
Home Security Installation Service
Housecleaning Service
Household Hints Hotline Operator
Household Machine Rental Service

Housepainter
Housewatching Service
Housing Inspector
Housing Renovation Service
Installation Contractor
Interior Designer
Kitchen Designer
Kitchen Remodeler
Lamp Shade Repairer
Lawn Mower Maintenance Service
Lighting Designer
Locksmith
Mailbox Installer
Mailbox Repair Service
Mason
Mobile Barbecue Cleaning Service
Parking Lot Resurfacer
Patio and Deck Constructor
Pest Control Service
Pet and Kennel Fencing Service
Plasterer
Plumber
Radon Detection Service
Real Estate Appraiser
Real Estate Broker
Rent-a-Husband (-Wife) Service
Roofer
Rug Repairer
Set Designer
Skylight Installer
Solar Power Consultant
Stained Glass Window Repairer
Stencil Artist
Stucco Mason
Swimming Pool Painter
Telephone Installer
Tile Installer
Tile Maker
Trade-Show Exhibit Builder
Upholsterer
Urban Planner

Construction/Home Improvement (Cont.)

Wallpaper Hanger
Water Purification Service
Water Softener Service
Welder

Well Drilling Service
Window Cleaning Service
Window Glass Repair Service
Woodworker

Education

Art Historian
Astronomer
Auto Driving Instructor
Bilingual Programs Organizer
Bookmobile Operator
Chemist
College Admissions Consultant
College Matching Service
College Scholarship Search Service
Community Service Program
   Coordinator
Computer Instructor
Consumer Information Consultant
Cooking Instructor
Corporate Trainer
Dance Instructor
Dog Obedience Trainer
Driving School Instructor
Educational Game Designer
English as a Foreign Language
   Instructor
Exchange Student Coordinator
Flight Instructor
Foreign Language Tutor
Golf Coach
Ham Radio Instructor
Home Schooling Consultant

Interviewing Coach
Kayak Instructor
Knitting Instructor
Librarian
Linguist
Mathematician
Musicologist
Navigation Instructor
Parent Guidance Counselor
Piano Teacher
Psychological Testing Specialist
Public Speaking Coach
Reunion Planner
Sailing Instructor
Sales Trainer
Sewing Instructor
Sign-Language Instructor
Sign-Language Interpreter
Slide Librarian
Speech Therapist
Substitute Teacher
Test Tutor
Textbook Author
Tutor
Videotaped Yearbooks Service
Voice Instructor
Yoga Instructor

Fashion and Beauty

Athletic-Clothing Manufacturer
Barber
Beauty Products Representative
Body-Makeup Artist

Bridal Consultant
Bridal Veil Maker
Catalog Clearinghouse Service
Clothing Alterations Service

Fashion and Beauty (Cont.)

Cosmetologist
Costume Maker
Costume Rental Service
Custom Fabric Sew-On Patches
   Creator
Custom Shoemaker
Doll-Clothing Creator
Dressmaker
Fashion Coordinator
Fashion Illustrator
Fashion Merchandising Consultant
Formalwear Rental Service
Freelance Fashion Editor
Hair Care Products Manufacturer
Hair Jewelry Creator
Hairstylist
Hatmaker
Hospital-Patient Beauty Services
Lingerie Party Sales Service

Makeover Specialist
Makeup Artist
Makeup Consultant
Manicurist
Mobile Hairstylist
Mobile Manicurist
Model
Modeling Agency
Mortuary Beautician
Outlet Shopping Tour Operator
Personal Shopper
Plastic Surgeon
Reweaving Service
Sewing Instructor
Tanning Salon
Vintage-Clothing Broker
Wardrobe Consultant
Wig Dresser
Wig Maker

Financial

Accountant
Art Appraiser
Auctioneer
Bail Bond Broker
Bill Collector
Bookkeeper
Budget Analyst
Business Plan Writer
Casino Dealer
Collection Agency
College Scholarship Search Service
Computerized Accounting Service
Construction Job Estimator
Corporate Benefits Consultant
Customs Broker
Financial Planner
Fund-raiser
Grant-Writing Consultant
Import/Export Broker
Income Tax Preparer
Investment Banker

Investment Consultant
Jewelry Appraiser
Mail-Order Fulfillment Service
Marketing Consultant
Medical Claims Billing Service
Medical Insurance Advisor
Mortgage Accountant
Payroll Service
Political Campaign Manager
Publishing Rights Negotiator
Real Estate Appraiser
Real Estate Developer
Recycling Broker
Repossessor
Retirement Advisor
Securities Trader
Stock Analyst
Stockbroker
Tax Preparation Consultant
Utility Auditing Service

Food

Baker
Bartender
Beekeeper
Bottled-Water Delivery Service
Box Lunches Creator
Breakfast Delivery Service
Bulk-Food Broker
Butcher
Cake Decorator
Caterer
Chef
Coffee Route Service
Cookbook Recipe Tester
Cooking Instructor
Custom Wedding Cake Maker
Doughnut Baker
Farmer
Film Location Catering Service
Fish Farmer
Food Stylist
Fruit Tree Farmer
Gourmet Cookware Salesperson
Gourmet Popcorn Seller
Grocery Delivery Service
Herb Grower

Ice Carver
Ice Cream Maker
International Food Broker
Lunch Delivery Service
Meal Delivery Service
Menu Designer
Microbrewery Operator
Mobile Lunch Wagon Service
Muffin Maker
Mushroom Grower
Nutrition Counselor
Pastry Chef
Recipe Developer
Restaurant Food Broker
Roadside Fruit Stand Operator
Sandwich/Snack Route Service
Soup Kitchen Organizer
Specialty Jam and Preserve Maker
Street Vendor
Vending Machine Repair Service
Vending Machine Route Service
Vitamin Distributor
Waitress
Wine Maker

Leisure and Entertainment

Antique Car Show Organizer
Autograph Collection Dealer
Ballroom Dancing Instructor
Bandleader
Bartender
Barware Rental Service
Baseball Card Dealer
Beach Umbrella/Chair Rental Service
Bed-and-Breakfast Clearinghouse
Bed-and-Breakfast Innkeeper
Boat Broker
Boat Cleaning Service
Boat Repair Service
Casino Dealer
Chair and Table Rental Service

Charter Fishing Tour Guide
Children's Party Organizer
Children's Stories on Tape Service
Coat-Check Service
Comedy Writer
Comic Book Dealer
Concierge
Convention Widows Events Organizer
Cruise Ship Entertainer
Custom Party Favors Service
Disc Jockey
Fish Bait Supplier
Fishing Guide
Golf Course Designer
Golf Tour Organizer

Leisure and Entertainment (Cont.)

Guidebook Publisher
Horseback Riding Lessons
Hot-Air Balloon Rides Service
Hotel Management Consultant
Hotel Marketing Consultant
Housing Swap Clearinghouse
Ice Carver
Independent Film Distributor
Magician
Mountain Climbing Guide
Napkin Imprinting Service
Nature Tour Operator
Outlet Shopping Tour Operator
Parade Consultant
Party Entertainer

Party Tent Rental Service
Rare Recording Search Service
Rare Stamp Dealer
Rent-a-Husband (-Wife) Service
Reunion Planner
River Rafting Guide
Rollerblade Rental Service
Square-Dance Caller
Summer Camp Director
Television Rental Service
Tour Guide
Travel Agent
Travelogue Creator
Vacation Home Broker
VCR Rental Service

Medical and Health

Acupuncturist
Adult Day Care Provider
AIDS Counselor
AIDS Researcher
Anesthesiologist
Art Therapist
Biochemist
Birthing Method Instructor
Cardiac Rehabilitation Service
Children's Psychotherapist
Chiropractor
Clinical Sociologist
Dental Hygienist
Dental Practice Consultant
Dental Referral Service
Dentist
Dermatologist
EKG Technician
Elder Care Companion
Elder Care Service
Emergency Medical Services
    Coordinator
Epidemiologist
Euthanasia Consultant

Folk Healer
Forensic Presentation Service
Forensic Reconstruction Specialist
Home Health Aid Service
Homeopathic Pharmacist
Hospital Patient Beauty Service
Human-Reproduction Consultant
Injury Rehabilitation Advisor
Laboratory Researcher
Medical Claims Billing Service
Medical Examiner
Medical Forms Processing Service
Medical Illustrator
Medical Insurance Advisor
Medical Testing Volunteer
Medical Transcription Service
Midwife
MRI Technician
Music Therapist
Neurologist
Nurse
Nutrition Counselor
Occupational Therapist
Ophthalmologist

Medical and Health (Cont.)

Organ Transplant Coordinator
Orthopedic Physician
Pediatrician
Personal Fitness Trainer
Physical Therapist
Physician Referral Service
Physician's Assistant
Plastic Surgeon
Private-Duty Nurse
Psychotherapist
Public Health Physician

Radiologist
Recreational Therapist
Respiratory Therapist
Smoking-Cessation Clinic
Speech Therapist
Toxicologist
Ultrasonographer
Vitamin Distributor
Wellness Center Service
X-ray Technician

Outdoors

Aerial Photographer
Agronomist
Aquaculturist
Arborist
Archaeologist
Archery Range Manager
Balcony Landscaper
Bonsai Cultivator
Botanist
Camping Equipment Rental Service
Camping Trip Escort
Canoe Rental Service
Chain Saw Operator
Chicken Hatchery and Egg Farmer
Christmas Tree Grower
Citrus Grower
Cowboy/girl
Crop Duster
Dairy Goat Farmer
Deckhand
Environmental Consultant
Environmental Planner
Farm Equipment Repair Service
Farmer
Firewood Splitter
Fishing Guide
Fishing Lure Maker
Fleet Fisherman/woman

Flower Stand Operator
Forest Service Trail Contractor
Fruit Tree Farmer
Game Bird Propagator
Gardener
Geologist
Geophysicist
Greenhouse Construction Service
Gutter Cleaner
Hay Cutting and Baling Service
Herb Grower
Herbicide Service
Home Portraitist
Horticulturist
Hunting and Fishing Guide
Independent Logger
Irrigation Equipment Technician
Irrigation System Consultant
Landscape Architect
Landscaping Service
Land Surveyor
Lawn Mower Sharpening Service
Leaf Raking and Mulching Service
Lifeguard
Llama Raiser
Migrant Worker Coordinator
Mushroom Grower
Nature Tour Operator

Outdoors (Cont.)

Navigation Instructor
Oceanographer
Office Plant Service
Orchid Grower
Ornithologist
Ranch Hand
Real Estate Developer
Rototilling Service
Scuba Diving Equipment Rental
  Service
Scuba Diving Instructor
Seed Warehouse Operator
Sheep Farmer

Sheep Shearing Service
Snow Removal Service
Soil Conservationist
Soil Testing Service
Stable Attendant
Swimming Pool Painter
Swimming Pool Service
Taxidermist
Tree Planting Service
Tree Pruning Service
Tree Removal Service
Well Drilling Service
Wood Stacking Service

Performing Arts/Theater/Music/
TV/Film/Radio

Acoustics Engineer
Actor
Auctioneer
Audiotape Duplication Service
Ballroom Dancing Instructor
Bandleader
Body-Makeup Artist
Booking Agent
Casting Director
Children's Costume Creator
Children's Television Producer
Children's Theater Director
Choreographer
Clown for Hire
Commercial Scriptwriter
Communications Engineer
Composer
Costume Rental Service
Dance Instructor
Dancer
Disc Jockey
Documentary Filmmaker
Film Producer
Fireworks Display Producer
Freelance Foreign Correspondent

Fretted-Instrument Repairer
Hospital Playroom Entertainer
Impersonator
Instructional Video Maker
Laser Light Show Producer
Lighting Designer
Magician
Makeup Artist
Meteorologist
Movie Director
Movie Location Scout
Musical Accompanist
Musical Instrument Builder
Musical Instrument Repair Service
Music Conductor
Music Copyist
Musician
Musicologist
Music Samples Clearing Service
Music Therapist
Music Tour Coordinator
Party Entertainer
Photojournalist
Pianist
Piano Teacher

Performing Arts/Theater/Music/ TV/Film/Radio (Cont.)

Piano Tuner
Playwright
Professional Speaker
Projectionist
Puppeteer
Radio Announcer
Radio News Analyst
Radio Scriptwriter
Radio Time Sales Representative
Recording Engineer
Rodeo Performer
Satellite Communications Consultant
Screenwriter
Set Designer
Singer
Singing Telegram Service
Songwriter
Sound Effects Creator
Sound Mixer
Speaking Coach

Square-Dance Caller
Stage Manager
Stand-up Comedian
Storyteller
Stuntperson
Talent Booking Agent
Television Camera Operator
Television Director
Television Producer
Television Repair Service
Television Scriptwriter
Travelogue Creator
Ventriloquist
Video-Clipping Service
Video Editor
Video Producer
Voice Actor
Voice Instructor
Wind Instrument Repairer

Personal Services

Accident Investigator
Addiction Counselor
Adoption Facilitator
Adult Day Care Provider
AIDS Counselor
Aptitude Testing Service
Arbitrator
Astrologer
Bail Bond Broker
Balloon Bouquet Service
Barber
Bed-and-Breakfast Clearinghouse
Birth-Parent Matching Service
Birthing Method Instructor
Boat Cleaning Service
Boat Repair Service
Bottled-Water Delivery Service
Bottle Redemption Service

Bouncer
Braille Typist
Breakfast Delivery Service
Bridal Registry Service
Bronzing Service
Career Counselor
Ceiling Cleaner
Child Care Referral Service
Christmas Tree Decorator
Closet Organizing Service
Clothing Alterations Service
Coin-op Laundry Operator
Color Consultant
Corporate Art Consultant
Curb Address Painter
Custom Poster Printer
Dating Service
Deckhand

Personal Services (Cont.)

Dietitian
Disabled Training Service
Divorce Mediator
Driveway Resurfacer
Elder Care Companion
Elder Care Service
Engraving Service
Errand Service
Estate-Planning Service
Estate Sale Coordinator
Etiquette Consultant
Euthanasia Consultant
Expert Witness Legal Service
Find-Anything Service
Fine Fur Storage Service
Firewood Delivery Service
Firewood Splitter
Flower Delivery Service
Gift Wrapping Service
Golf Ball Recovery Service
Golf Caddie
Hairstylist
Handicapped Person Transportation
    Service
Handwritten Addressing Service
Home Health Aid
House Sitter
House-watching Service
Human-Reproduction Consultant
Image Consultant
Immigration Advisor
Income Tax Preparer
Insurance Agent
Insurance Investigator
Interviewing Coach
Ironing Service
Jewelry Appraiser
Laminating Service
Laundry Service
Lawyer
Luggage Rental
Mailbox Installer

Mailbox Repair Service
Manicurist
Marriage Counselor
Massage Therapist
Meal Delivery Service
Medical Forms Processor
Messenger Service
Mobile Barbecue Cleaning Service
Mortuary Beautician
Moving Consultant
Pack and Ship Service
Paging Service
Party Planner
Pen Pal Matching Service
Personal Bodyguard
Personal Fitness Trainer
Personal Shopper
Pet Motel Operator
Physical Therapist
Plant Sitter
Private Investigator
Professional Organizer
Psychotherapist
Rent-a-Husband (-Wife) Service
Resume Service
Retirement Advisor
Roommate Finder
Scissors and Knife Sharpener
Security Escort Service
Self-Defense Instructor
Shoe Repairer
Silver Polishing Service
Smoking Cessation Advisor
Snow Removal Service
Speaking Coach
Storage Space Rental Service
Stress Management Consultant
Substance Abuse Counselor
Swimming Pool Service
Tattoo Artist
Television Rental Service
Trailer Rental Service

Personal Services (Cont.)

Tree Removal Service
Union Grievance Handler
VCR Rental Service
Videotaping Service for Insurance
    Industry
Videotaping Service for Special
    Events

Vocational Testing Service
Wake-up Service
Wardrobe Consultant
Wedding Planner
Weekly Flower Service
Wellness Center Service
Zipper Repair Service

Sales/Retail

Advertising Sales Representative
Architectural Scavenger
Art Rental Service
Autograph Collection Dealer
Baseball Card Dealer
Boat Broker
Bonsai Cultivator
Braille and Talking Books Distributor
Bulk-Food Broker
Button Maker
Catalog Clearinghouse Service
Christmas Tree Grower
Coin-op Laundry Operator
Comic Book Dealer
Computer Rental Service
Coupon Books Creator
Delivery Route Driver
Electronics Broker
Estate Sale Coordinator
Exotic-Bead Broker
Eyewear Specialist
Fashion Merchandising Consultant
Flower Stand Operator
Freelance Trade Show Assistant
Gemstone Dealer
Gift Basket Service
Gourmet Cookware Salesperson
Gourmet Popcorn Seller
Government Surplus Broker
Hair Care Products Manufacturer
Hotel Marketing Consultant
Lingerie Party Sales Service

Literary Agent
Livestock Broker
Mailing List Broker
Mail-Order Consultant
Modeling Agency
Motorcycle Broker
Motorcycle Parts Dealer
Odd-Lot Merchandise Consolidator
Photographer's Representative
Printing Broker
Product Demonstrator
Publishing Agent
Publishing Rights Negotiator
Radio Time Sales Representative
Rare Book Dealer
Rare Coin Dealer
Real Estate Broker
Real Estate Photographer
Restaurant Food Broker
Retail Clothing Buyer
Retail Delivery Service
Roadside Fruit Stand Operator
Sales Representative
Sales Trainer
Scrap and Salvage Broker
Secondhand Clothing Broker
Solar Equipment Broker
Sports Marketing Specialist
Stockbroker
Street Vendor
Talent Booking Agent
Telemarketer

Sales/Retail (Cont.)

Travel Agent
Used-Car Broker
Used-Computer Dealer
Vending Machine Route Service

Vintage-Auto Broker
Vintage-Clothing Broker
Waterfront Concession Stand

Sports

Aerobics Instructor
Archery Range Manager
Athletic-Clothing Manufacturer
Bicycle Custom Construction Service
Boatbuilder
Camping Equipment Rental Service
Canoe Rental Service
Charter Fishing Tour Guide
Equestrian Trainer
Fishing Lure Maker
Golf Ball Recovery Service
Golf Caddie
Golf Coach
Golf Tour Organizer
Gun Repair Service
Gymnastics Instructor
Home Exercise Equipment Dealer
Hunting and Fishing Guide
Ice-Skate Sharpening Service
Ice-Skating Coach
Jockey
Kayak Builder

Kayak Instructor
Martial Arts Instructor
Orthopedic Physician
Personal Trainer
Race Car Driver
River Rafting Guide
Rollerblade Rental Service
Saddle and Tack Repair Service
Sailing Instructor
Scuba Diving Equipment Rental
    Service
Scuba Diving Instructor
Self-Defense Instructor
Sports Equipment Repairer
Sports Events Organizer
Sports Marketing Specialist
Surfboard Rental Service
Tennis Coach
Tennis Racket Restringing Service
Umpire
Yoga Instructor

Technical/Mechanical

Acoustics Engineer
Aerodynamicist
Air-Conditioning Installer
Antiques Restorer
Appliance Repairer
Architectural Model Maker
Art Conservationist
Auto Body Painter
Auto Body Restorer
Auto Glass Installer

Auto Glass Tinter
Auto Mechanic
Auto Security Installer
Battery Reconditioning Service
Bicycle Repairer
Blacksmith
Blueprint Service
Boat Motor Tune-up/Repair Service
Boiler/Furnace Repair Service
Bookbinder

Technical/Mechanical (Cont.)

Bronzing Service
Cable Splicing Technician
Camera Repair Service
Car Stereo Installer
Cartographer
Ceramic Design Engineer
Chain Saw Operator
Chemical Research Engineer
Church Maintenance Service
Clockmaker
Coin-op Machine Maintenance
   Service
Communications Engineer
Computer Programmer
Computer Repair Technician
Crop Duster
Custom Bicycle Construction
Demolition Consultant
Die Designer
Dollhouse Maker
Doll Repairer
Electric Fan Installation Service
Electroplating Service
Experimental Aircraft Mechanic
Farm Equipment Repair Service
Fiber-Optics Technician
Fine China Repairer
Fire Protection Specialist
Floor Refinishing Service
Fretted-Instrument Repairer
Furniture Refinisher
Furniture Stripping Service
Garage Door Installer
Gun Repair Service
Hazardous-Waste Removal Service
Hot Tub/Jacuzzi Cleaning Service
Ice-Skate Sharpening Service
Industrial Engineer
Inventor
Irrigation System Consultant
Jewelry Repair Service
Kiln Builder

Lamp Repair Service
Laser Technician
Lawn Mower Maintenance Service
Lawn Mower Sharpening Service
Locksmith
Metallurgical Technician
Mechanical Draftsperson
Meteorologist
Microfilm Service
Microwave Repair Service
Mobile Auto Mechanic
Motorcycle Mechanic
Musical Instrument Repair Service
Music Tour Coordinator
Nuclear Engineering Consultant
Nuclear Imaging Technologist
Oil-Well Fire Fighter
Patternmaker
Photocopy Machine Repair Service
Photo Restorer
Photo Services Provider
Physicist
Piano Tuner
Picture Framing Service
Potter
Power and Manual Tool Repair
   Service
Printer
Printer/Toner Cartridge
   Remanufacturer
Recording Engineer
Refuse Container Maintenance
   Service
Reweaving Service
Sail Repair Service
Satellite Communications Consultant
Satellite Dish Installer
Scissors and Knife Sharpener
Scrap and Salvage Broker
Seamstress
Seismologist
Semiconductor Designer

Technical/Mechanical (Cont.)

Sewing Machine Repair Service
Shoe Repairer
Small Engine Repairer
Soil Conservationist
Sound Mixer
Space Analyst
Sports Equipment Repairer
Statue Repairer
Stereo Repair Service
Stress Testing Engineer
Taxidermist
Technical Illustrator
Telephone Installer
Telephone Repair Service
Television Repair Service
Test Engineer

Typesetter
Typewriter Repair Service
Vacuum Cleaner Repair Service
Van and RV Customizing Service
VCR Repair Service
Vending Machine Repair Service
Video Editor
Vintage-Auto Restoration Service
Vintage-Book Repairer
Vinyl Repair Service
Watch Repairer
Wedding Photographer
Wind Instrument Repairer
Window Screen Repairer
Woodstove Installation Service
X-ray Technician

Visual Arts/Design/Crafts

Aerial Photographer
Airbrush Artist
Antiques Dealer
Antiques Restorer
Architect
Architectural Draftsperson
Architectural Model Maker
Art Appraiser
Art Conservationist
Art Critic
Art Gallery Owner
Art Historian
Art Rental Service
Art Show Promoter
Art Therapist
Baby Knitwear Creator
Billboard Painter
Birdhouse Creator
Boatbuilder
Bookbinder
Bridal Veil Maker
Button Maker
Cabinetmaker

CAD/CAM Consultant
Cake Decorator
Calligrapher
Candle Maker
Caricature Artist
Carpet Weaver
Cartographer
Cartoonist
Ceramic Design Engineer
Certificate and Award Creator
Children's Book Illustrator
Children's Clothing Designer
Children's Portrait Artist
Christmas Tree Decorator
Christmas Tree Ornaments Creator
Clockmaker
Color Consultant
Computer Animator
Computer Artist
Corporate Art Consultant
Costume Maker
Courtroom Artist
Craft Supplies Dealer

Visual Arts/Design/Crafts (Cont.)

Curator
Custom Bumper Stickers Creator
Custom Draperies Service
Custom Fabric Sew-On Patches
   Creator
Customized Business Card Maker
Custom Lamps Creator
Custom Mirror Creator
Custom Poster Printer
Custom Shoemaker
Custom Slipcover Service
Custom T-Shirt Manufacturer
Desktop Publisher
Die Designer
Digital Typeface Designer
Doll-Clothing Creator
Doll Maker
Doll Repairer
Dried-Flower Arrangements Creator
Educational Game Designer
Exotic-Bead Broker
Fabric Designer
Fashion Illustrator
Fiber Artist
Film Negative Cutter
Fine China Repairer
Floral Arranger
Food Stylist
Freelance Photographer
Furniture Maker
Gemologist
Glassblower
Glass Etcher
Goldsmith
Golf Course Designer
Graphic Designer
Greeting Card Designer
Hair Jewelry Creator
Hatmaker
Home Portraitist
Illustrator
Industrial Engineer

Interior Designer
Jeweler
Jewelry Repair Service
Kayak Builder
Kiln Builder
Kitchen Designer
Kite Maker
Landscape Architect
Leatherworker
Logo Designer
Mechanical Draftsperson
Medical Illustrator
Menu Designer
Mold Maker
Monogramming Service
Movie Location Scout
Museum Exhibit Designer
Musical Instrument Builder
Necklace Restringing Service
Needlework Artist
Neon Artist
Painter
Papermaker
Patternmaker
Photographer's Representative
Photojournalist
Photo Researcher
Photo Restorer
Photo Services Provider
Photo Stylist
Picture Framing Service
Play Equipment Builder
Playground Designer
Potter
Printer
Printmaker
Quilt Maker
Radon Detection Service
Real Estate Photographer
Rubber-Stamp Artist
Rug Maker
Saddle Maker

Visual Arts/Design/Crafts (Cont.)

Sculptor
Seamstress
Sign Maker
Sign Painter
Silversmith
Slide Duplicating Service
Stained-Glass Artist
Statue Repairer
Stencil Artist
Stone Carver
Stuffed-Toys Creator
Tattoo Artist
Technical Illustrator

Textile Designer
Tile Maker
Tool Designer
Typesetter
Upholsterer
Videotaped Yearbooks Service
Weaver
Wedding Photographer
Wildlife Artist
Window Display Designer
Woodworker
Wool Spinning and Dyeing Service

Writing/Research

Agronomist
Anthropologist
Apartment and Home Locator
Archaeologist
Art Critic
Astrologer
Astronomer
Behavioral Researcher
Biochemist
Biologist
Book Editor
Book Indexer
Botanist
Chemist
Children's Book Writer
Clinical Sociologist
College Matching Service
College Scholarship Search Service
Comedy Writer
Commercial Scriptwriter
Computer Technical Writer
Consumer Information Consultant
Cookbook Recipe Tester
Copy Editor
Copywriter
Coupon Books Creator

Courtroom Reporter
Curator
Dating Service
Desktop Publishing Service Bureau
Documentary Filmmaker
Editorial Assistant
Environmental Consultant
Environmental Planner
Expert Witness Legal Service
Fiber-Optics Researcher
Film or Tape Librarian
Foreign Language Proofreader
Freelance Fashion Editor
Freelance Foreign Correspondent
Freelance Journalist
Freelance Paralegal
Freelance Writer
Genealogist
Geologist
Geophysicist
Ghostwriting Service
Government-Surplus Broker
Grant-Writing Consultant
Greeting Card Writer
Guidebook Publisher
Handwriting Analyst

Writing/Research (Cont.)

Independent Archivist
Indexer
Inventor
Laboratory Researcher
Librarian
Linguist
Literary Agent
Magazine Editor
Market Research Service
Mathematician
Medical Transcription Service
Memoir Writer
Music Samples Clearing Service
News-Clipping Service
Newsletter Writer
Oceanographer
Online Research Service
Pen Pal Matching Service
Photo Researcher
Poet
Polling Service
Postcard Publisher
Printing Broker
Private Investigator
Proofreader
Publisher
Publishing Agent

Publishing Rights Negotiator
Radio Scriptwriter
Rare Book Dealer
Rare Coin Dealer
Rare Stamp Dealer
Real Estate Abstract Searcher
Resume Service
Retail Credit Researcher
Romance Novelist
Roommate Finder
Safety Clothing and Equipment
   Developer
Screenwriter
Seismologist
Slide Librarian
Songwriter
Speechwriter
Stock Analyst
Technical Manual Writer
Television Scriptwriter
Textbook Author
Transcription Service
Translator
Urban Planner
Vintage Book Repairer
Web Site Content Creator
Word Processing/Typing Service

Index

About the Author

TERRI LONIER is the nation's leading expert on solo entrepreneurs. As president of Working Solo, Inc., she advises clients including Microsoft, Hewlett-Packard, Apple Computer, Bank of America, Claris, and Seagram's on how best to access and communicate with the rapidly growing small business and SOHO (small office/home office) market.

Her award-winning Working Solo resources—including books, audiotapes, Web site (www.workingsolo.com), monthly e-mail newsletter, and seminars—offer information and inspiration to thousands of solo entrepreneurs worldwide. (For details, send an e-mail to info@workingsolo.com, or call (800) 222-7656.)

A successful entrepreneur since 1978, Lonier is an in-demand business speaker on entrepreneurial topics and a frequent media guest. Her work has been featured in *The New York Times, Wall Street Journal, Inc., Fast Company, Business Week,* and other leading business publications, as well as on CNBC, CNN/fn, and radio programs nationwide. She was honored as the keynote speaker at the First International Conference of Women in Business in Tokyo.

Lonier lives in New Paltz, New York, with her husband, Robert Sedestrom.